T0369873

THE I TATTI
RENAISSANCE LIBRARY

James Hankins, General Editor

MARULLUS

POEMS

ITRL 54

MICHAEL MARULLUS
✦ ✦ ✦
POEMS

TRANSLATED BY

CHARLES FANTAZZI

THE I TATTI RENAISSANCE LIBRARY
HARVARD UNIVERSITY PRESS
CAMBRIDGE, MASSACHUSETTS
LONDON, ENGLAND
2012

Series design by Dean Bornstein

Library of Congress Cataloging-in-Publication Data

Marullo Tarcaniota, Michele, d. 1500.
Poems / Michael Marullus ; translated by Charles Fantazzi.
pages. cm. — (The I Tatti Renaissance library ; 54)
English and Latin on facing pages.
Includes bibliographical references and index.
ISBN 978-0-674-05506-3 (alk. paper)
1. Marullo Tarcaniota, Michele, d. 1500 — Translations into English.
I. Fantazzi, Charles. II. Marullo Tarcaniota, Michele, d. 1500. Works.
Latin. 2012. III. Marullo Tarcaniota, Michele, d. 1500. Works. English. 2012.
IV. Title. V. Series: I Tatti Renaissance library ; 54.
PA8547.M554A2 2012
871'.04 — dc23   2012007928

Contents

༄༅༅

Introduction   vii

Epigrams

Book I   2

Book II   52

Book III   100

Book IV   146

Hymns to Nature

Book I   194

Book II   218

Book III   254

Book IV   278

Poems of Lament   314

Miscellaneous Epigrams   340

The Education of a Prince   350

Appendix: Two Letters of Marullus   394

Note on the Text   401

Notes to the Translation   403

Bibliography   446

Index of First Lines   448

General Index   453

Introduction

ॐ

Little is known with certainty about the early life of Marullus, beginning with his birth. According to his own account in *Epigrams* 2.32 he was still an unformed fetus in his mother's womb when Constantinople fell on May 29, 1453. Giving credence to those words we may conjecture that the day of his birth may have been in late 1453 or early 1454. He refers to himself consistently as *Constantinopolitanus* on the title pages of his published works, but as with other exiled Byzantine Greeks at this time, this may simply have been a nostalgic desire to regard Constantinople as his native city. In that same brief autobiography he boasts of the noble lineage of his father, Manilius Marullus, a soldier of fortune like himself, who was banished from his ancestral kingdom of Dyme in Achaia. In another poem, *Epigrams* 1.52, he speaks of the outstanding virtues of his mother, Euphrosyne Tarchaniotes, who also is said to have belonged to a noble Greek family. After the fall of Constantinople it seems that the family moved to Ragusa (modern-day Dubrovnik) on the Dalmatian coast, if we are to believe Marullus's words in a poem in honor of that city (*Epigrams* 4.17), where, he says, as a boy he poured out the first lamentations of an unhappy exile. From there they may have crossed over to Ancona on the coast of Italy, as is attested in a series of epitaphs that once existed there in the church of San Domenico.[1]

By the age of seventeen, according to the autobiographical narration, he began his career as a *stratiota* (mercenary soldier) in the remote regions of Scythia and the desolate wastes of Thrace. He describes the peoples and regions he visited in vague, poetic terms taken from classical literature: the Getae, mentioned by Ovid in his poems of exile, and the Bessi, an ancient people of Thrace; he employs obscure toponyms like the Mesta River in Thrace, the cities of Budua and Brazza, and Byces, which may be a lake near the Sea of Azov. It is certainly possible that Marullus participated in various military campaigns during these years, but it is difficult to ascertain his exact whereabouts at any given time. We do know that he was in Naples in the latter part of the 1470s, where he was a familiar figure in the Academy of Giovanni Pontano. This is clearly manifested in a Catullan hendecasyllable entitled "Ad sodales" (*Epigrams* 1.54) addressed to his literary companions in the Neapolitan circle. He names many of them in the opening lines: Lorenzo (Bonincontri), Compatre (Pietro Golino), Giovanni Pardo, and others, but especially Iacopo Sannazaro and Pontano. In his *Baiae* 1.10 Pontano mentions inviting these same poets and scholars together with Marullus to celebrate the return of Francesco Elia Marchese, another of their company. Some of the same personages, including Marullus, were present at Sannazaro's birthday, which was also the feast day of his patron saint, San Nazario. In this convivial poem, *Elegies* 2.2, Sannazaro makes reference to Marullus's predilection for Lucretius. There can be little doubt that during his Neapolitan sojourn Marullus drew inspiration from Pontano's *Urania* for his own hymns. He must also have discussed his conjectures in the text of Lucretius with Pontano, with whom he shared an interest in the Epicurean poet. Pietro Candido, who published an edition of the *De rerum natura* (1512), mentions Pontano and Marullus as collaborators in the editing of the text, but expresses his preference for the emendations of the latter.[2]

It was during this period that he attracted the favor of certain important political figures in Naples, Antonello Petrucci, a royal secretary, and Antonello Sanseverino, prince of Salerno and grand admiral of the kingdom. Both of these men were prominently involved in the Second Revolt of the Barons in 1485 against the Aragonese dynasty. Petrucci and his two sons were put to death ignominiously, but Sanseverino escaped to France in 1487 and enrolled in the army of the newly crowned Charles VIII. Marullus accompanied him later on an expedition to Naples, as we learn in *Poems of Lament* 1, where he describes his shipwreck off the coast of Corsica. It seems certain that Marullus was on the side of the rebellious barons, but he did not take an active part in the conspiracy. It is supposed that he participated in the struggle for the liberation of the city of Otranto from the Turks in 1480–81, but there is no recorded proof of this.

Two letters from Cardinal Marco Barbo to his secretary, Giovanni Lorenzi, attest to Marullus's presence in Rome in the summer of 1487. During his brief stay there he published the first two books of epigrams with the printer Eucharius Silber. The poet was definitely in Florence by August 3, 1489, as we know from a letter of that date sent by Alessandro Farnese to Stefano D'Aquila with greetings to Marullus. Here he found favor with the Francophile branch of the Medici, descended from a brother of Cosimo, Pierfrancesco. It was the younger son of Pierfrancesco, Lorenzo di Pierfrancesco de' Medici, who provided him with hospitality and patronage. He shared Marullus's interest in Lucretius and Epicureanism, which had become a sort of counterculture in the circle of scholars that had formed around him.[3] In the spring of 1494 Marullus hearkened to the call of Prince Sanseverino and other Neapolitan exiles in Lyons to join in Charles VIII's invasion of Italy to conquer the kingdom of Naples, which he claimed by virtue of his Angevin inheritance. Marullus's hopes were that the French king would then set out to liberate Constantinople from the Turks. As it happened, Charles victoriously entered Naples on February 22, 1495, but the threat of the League of Venice forced him to depart a few months later. In *Poems of Lament* 4 Marullus reproves the king for deserting friends, the gods, fame, honor and glory, and even himself. It was during this time that Marullus began his *Education of a Prince*, intended for the king's son, Charles Roland, who died in 1495 at the age of three. The piece remained unfinished.

Returning to Florence sometime in 1496 or shortly thereafter, he married the beautiful and talented Alessandra Scala, daughter of the secretary of the Signoria, the poet and humanist, Bartolomeo Scala. In the epigrams dedicated to her he called her the tenth Muse in Rome, as Sappho had been in Greece, save that she was superior to Sappho because of her chastity. In 1497 he published the four books of epigrams, dedicating them to Lorenzo di Pierfrancesco de' Medici, and the four books of *Hymns to Nature*, dedicated to Sanseverino. In 1498, Giovanni di Pierfrancesco, the younger brother of Lorenzo, died, whom Marullus mourned with great emotion in *Poems of Lament* 3, despairing of his own fate. Giovanni had married Caterina Sforza, countess of Forlì, the year before. Marullus then became a *uomo d'arme* of the widowed Caterina and defended the fortress of Forlì against Cesare Borgia and the French, but they succeeded in capturing it on January 12, 1500. Marullus probably remained with Caterina for a while and may also have been imprisoned by the conquering army. The next notice we have of him is as the guest of his learned friend Raffaello Maffei, in Volterra. Against his friend's advice, on Palm Sunday, April 11, 1500, he tried to cross the floodwaters of the Cecina River on horseback and was drowned. According to Pietro Candido, editor of Lucretius, a copy of Lucretius was found in his saddle bag. Maffei saw to his burial in the church of San Giovanni Battista in Pomerance, where he is remembered in an epitaph. Many poems were written to mourn his death, the most beautiful and heart-felt being that of Ariosto.

The first edition of the *Epigrams*, dated by Perosa to some time between June 1488 and July 1489,[4] was published in Rome by Eucharius Silber. It contains only the first two books of the four found in the final edition and is dedicated to Lorenzo di Pierfrancesco. From July 1489 to the spring of 1494 Marullus was in Florence, where he completed the book of epigrams and the greater part of the hymns, which were published together in Florence, November 26, 1497, by the Stamperia del Drago. The epigrams retain the dedication to Lorenzo di Pierfrancesco, to whom a dedicatory poem is addressed at the beginning of each book. The epigrams number 199 in all and vary greatly from one another in length, meter, theme, and content. Metrically, elegiac distichs predominate, as is fitting in this genre, but there are also epodes, with alternating iambic trimeters and dimeters, numerous examples of the Phalaecean hendecasyllable, Asclepiadean meters, glyconics, and Alcaic and Sapphic stanzas. In the medley of themes we find playful love poems in the style of Catullus, longer love elegiacs, invectives, epitaphs and funeral laments (1.22 on the death of his brother bears a great resemblance to Catullus's famous poem to his brother, buried in the Troad), *ekphraseis*, a long autobiographical poem on his own exile, clever (albeit heavy-handed) two-liners in the style of Martial, and much else. Among the invectives are a series of venomous epigrams directed against Poliziano, for whom Marullus nourished a fierce hatred, which seems to have arisen from the publication of the *Miscellanea*, in which Poliziano makes some derogatory remarks about Greeks (*Graeculi*). Among these are several examples of a genre that might be called the "philological epigram," in which Marullus challenges readings in various classical texts discussed in Poliziano's *Miscellanea*, but was invariably wrong.[5]

The work to which he must have devoted most of his attention during his Florentine sojourn was the *Hymns to Nature* in four books. A first version of them exists in two manuscripts first brought to light by Perosa: Florence, Biblioteca Nazionale Centrale MS Magl. VII 1146 and Florence, Biblioteca Riccardiana MS Ricc. 971. The latter is very important in determining the composition of the hymns since it exhibits what Perosa in his brilliant analysis of the textual tradition proved to be authorial variants.[6] The definitive edition, delayed somewhat by Marullus's return to arms in the expedition of Charles VIII, was published in 1497. The four books of hymns are dedicated en bloc to Antonello Sanseverino, Prince of Salerno and fellow warrior. It is generally agreed that the title *Hymns to Nature* (*Hymni naturales*) harks back to the designation Ὕμνοι Φυσικοί, by which the poems of Parmenides and Empedocles were known. The rhetorician Menander defined them as poems in which the natural world is allegorized under the name of the gods. The adjective *naturalis* has the same sense as in *philosophia naturalis*, as opposed to *philosophia moralis* and *philosophia rationalis*, explained in Macrobius (*Saturnalia* 2.17.15), where its meaning is "that which treats of divine bodies." The hymn belongs to a tradition of theogonic poetry beginning with Hesiod and the Homeric hymns and continuing through Cleanthes, Callimachus, and Proclus. Marullus draws on this rich tradition, using mythological narratives from Homer and Callimachus and even inventing myths of his own. At the same time there is a clear sense of the Lucretian universe, at odds with the Platonic or Neoplatonic tradition. Certainly the stamp of Lucretian vocabulary is very evident in expressions like *alma Venus, semina rerum, magnum per inane, lucida templa, daedala tellus*, and in various syntactic configurations.

The four books of hymns are carefully organized. The first book is concerned with the hyperuranian or extracelestial realm, beginning with Jupiter (writing in Latin, Marullus was constrained to use the Roman names of the deities). The poem begins *Ab Iove principium*, a phrase taken from Vergil, *Eclogues* 3.60, which in turn echoes the famous opening of Aratus's *Phainomena* (Ἐκ Διὸς ἀρχώμεσθα). The description of the creation of the world is an interesting mixture of Ovid and the Vulgate Genesis, reflecting the latter more in the order of creation, but the matrix is clearly pagan. There is no trace of the Christian God who creates ex nihilo, but rather a demiurge who shapes the primeval matter, although the description of the spirit of god hovering over the waters seems to evoke Genesis. While Genesis emphasizes man's creation in the image of God, Marullus recalls the Pythagorean-Platonic doctrine of the preexistence of the soul of man and Plato's image of the body as a prison in which the soul is confined. The next two hymns, to Pallas Athena as divine intelligence, and to Love in her twin guises of celestial and terrestrial Venus, are so filled with multiple allusions to Orphic religion, Zoroaster, the *Platonic Theology* (both of Proclus and Ficino), Julian's *Hymn to the Sun*, Hermes Trismegistus, and various mythological elements, as to become quite bewildering. The fourth hymn is dedicated to the heavenly beings who contemplate the godhead for all eternity. The fifth hymn, to Eternity, is rooted in the Platonic tradition and breathes an atmosphere of mysticism and sublimity. It is a particularly beautiful composition, which inspired Ronsard's *Hymne à l'Éternité*. The last hymn, addressed to Bacchus, is an extraordinary mixture of various exotic elements, written in rushing galliambics, the meter used by Catullus in his poem describing the frenzy of the devotees of Cybele, who unmanned themselves in an orgiastic rite. It is as if the poet himself were carried away in an ecstatic, Orphic rapture. Here Bacchus hypostatically takes on many of the qualities of the supreme divinity. He is given the exalted title of "father of gods and men," and the epithet proper to Jupiter, *Optimus Maximus*, is assigned to him as well.

In the second book there is a descent to the lower heavenly bodies. It begins with a hymn to Pan, depicted here through a false etymology of his name ($\tau\grave{o}$ $\pi\hat{a}\nu$) as father of all things, recalling the Platonic concept of *anima mundi*. Like Zeus in Plato's *Phaedrus* myth (246d–247a), he traverses the heavens in a winged chariot, followed by the eleven principal gods, who celebrate him in song as "the father of the earth and of the windy sea and the fecund ether" (vv. 59–60). He also sustains the sluggish mass of the inert world machine and sets it in motion, and consolidates the dissonant seeds (this last concept is derived from Lucretius). After addressing hymns to heaven and to the stars, which are seen as the inexorable arbiters of our fate, Marullus turns to the planets, presented in the so-called Egyptian order used by Plato in the *Timaeus*. These heavenly bodies, according to the Platonic chain of being, have direct influence on the life of humans. The first of them is Saturn, god of the Golden Age, patron of agriculture and fruitful activity, god of silence and quietude. Only in the concluding prayer does Marullus allude to his gloomy hatred, which he prays may be turned on others rather than on himself. The hymn to the planet Jupiter differs from the initial hymn and from a later hymn to Jupiter, wielder of the thunderbolt. In places it shows distinct similarities to Pontano's *Urania*. For Mars he reserves an Alexandrian epyllion in two parts: first, Mars's participation in the war against the Giants in imitation of Claudian's *Gigantomachia*, followed by an original erotic postlude in which Venus appears and restrains Mars from further warfare. This surprise ending leads to a more developed scene of seduction in the next hymn to Venus, which begins appropriately with an invocation to the Muse Erato arriving in her chariot to render homage to the goddess. Venus is depicted at first with features taken from Lucretius's proemium, instilling life and beauty into all creation, populating the earth and the seas. Coppini justly evokes the Botticellian qualities of the lines that describe Venus, her holy head garlanded with fresh flowers, nimbly leading the dance, accompanied by lusty Youth and the Graces, as in the famous strophe of Horace, *Odes* 1.30.5–8.[7] Marullus adds his own touch, influenced perhaps by the sensual mannerisms of Pontano, by including Mars in the episode, who observes the scene with burning desire from a concealed rose garden. In the final hymn to Mercury, the poet vaunts his renewal of Orphic rhythms, long absent from the silent tripods of Delphi. He exalts the usual functions of the messenger god as bringer of

civilization and patron of commerce, magic, soothsaying, and ath-
letics, as well as *psychopompos*, companion in our last journey to the
next world. Horace's simple but lovely poem (*Odes* 1.10), in the
same Sapphic meter, lies at the heart of Marullus's musings. He
seems in this poem to express a sincere devotion to the god, source
of the poetic gift through his discovery of the lyre and the sweet
solace of his exile.

The *Hymn to the Sun*, by far the longest of the collection, occu-
pies an important position as the initial poem in the third book,
thus forming the central piece of the *Hymns to Nature*. It is an im-
pressive poetic fusion of various physical, philosophical, and theo-
logical theories, chiefly Julian's *Hymn to the Sun*, which had recently
been discovered and had drawn the avid attention of Ficino, Pico,
and others. There are also reminiscences of Plato's *Timaeus, Repub-
lic* and *Laws*, the hymn of Proclus to the sun, and perhaps Ficino's
De sole and *De lumine*. In an important article Eugenio Garin pro-
vided a transcription of Ficino's copious annotations to Julian's
hymn, which are contained in Florence, Biblioteca Riccardiana,
MS Ricc. 76.[8] It is relevant, I believe, that several works of Gemi-
stus Pletho, who had advocated a return to the Olympian gods,
are found in that same manuscript. In one theoretical matter Ma-
rullus is at variance with Julian and the Neoplatonists. He deliber-
ately departs from the concept of the immateriality of the sun,
adhering to the more naturalistic views of Lucretius. For Marullus
the sun must be material in order to interact with nature, as the
poet proceeds to demonstrate in verses impregnated with vocabu-
lary and phraseology of the *De rerum natura*. Marullus places the
sun between Mercury and the moon according to the Egyptian
ordering of the planets, affirming that it is the sun, and no other
heavenly body, that penetrates all things and is their sole unifying
force, without, however, becoming contaminated with them. The
second part of the hymn, beginning at line 127, is more concerned
with astrology than cosmology. Here the Neapolitan experience of

Marullus manifests itself as well as an underlying Lucretian fatalism. He recounts how the sun measures out the apportioned time for each individual and as he glides past the signs of the zodiac determines what kind of life each will lead. In this passage he owes much to the proemium of the third book of Lucretius. Concerning the fate of future princes he adheres to the Hellenistic notion of their being favored by the sun from birth. The poem ends with a sad lament for the fall of Constantinople, a sight from which the sun averted his eyes, enveloping himself in a dark night of mourning. In closing he prays that the sun will protect the members of the Medici family, who helped to preserve Greek language and culture. The friendship of the Medici, in the person of his patron, Lorenzo di Pierfrancesco, is acknowledged in the opening to the hymn to the moon and at the end announces his own departure, referring no doubt to his joining Charles VIII in Lyons in 1494. The poem then takes the form of an amoebean exchange in epodic verse between Marullus and an attendant getting ready for the voyage. It has more resemblance to Marullus's epigrammatic style than to the usual hymn structure and is more lighthearted in spirit. It celebrates Diana, goddess of the moon, who will guide them in their nocturnal journey. There is no final prayer, only an exhortation to set out on their mission.

The five hymns of Book 4 are dedicated to the realm of the sublunar world, the four divinized elements and Aether, which is considered the soul of the universe. This concept is indebted to Aristotle's *De caelo* as well as to the world soul of the *Timaeus* and is also the subject of an Orphic hymn. Once more he credits himself with treading new ground never before explored, perhaps referring to the rather esoteric character of the subject matter, which goes back to Empedocles. The next hymn celebrates the element of fire in the guise of Jupiter Fulgerator. In this book Marullus delights in ferreting out, in Alexandrian fashion, little-known myths about the gods. The epithet "Fulgerator" (hurler of the thunderbolt) is a translation of the Greek ἀστράπαιος or κεραύνειος, the latter commonly used of Zeus. The Latin word is very rare, occurring only in a single inscription and in the late writer Apuleius. The novelty of the epithet prepares us for the unconventional nature of the myth that occupies an important place in the poem. In a daring demystification Marullus dismisses the story that related how the infant Jupiter was protected by the Curetes, who muffled his wailing by the clangor of their armor, thus saving him from being devoured by his father, Saturn (here identified with Hyperion). According to Marullus this story was merely servants' gossip. The truth, according to Marullus's version, is that his father introduced him as an infant into the council of the gods without his wife's knowledge. Following Callimachus's *Hymn to Zeus* and Pausanias's account, Marullus locates Jupiter's birth in Arcadia, in a cave called Cretea, rather than in Crete. Yet he keeps the Curetes though they were born on Mount Ida in Crete. This is quite a different treatment of myths pertaining to the gods, which he will continue throughout the book.

The hymn to Jupiter's consort is written, purposely it would seem, in the same meter as the previous one, to link the two gods. The first part recounts Juno's reluctance to leave her parents and her nurse and to venture out into the world. Her brother spied her naked one day, immediately desired her, and fulfilled his desires. She was beside herself with sorrow for a long time, but then she concealed the light of day in a dark cloud and encircled herself in completely motionless air, the element celebrated in this hymn. (Her Greek name, Hera, was associated with the word for air, ἀήρ). She was resolved to die, but Apollo took her up into the ether and consoled her with words of reason. She is reconciled to her brother but she does not cease from her tears, which the father of the gods turns into light breezes and distributes them to various places. The poem ends with a prayer to her in her role of protectress of fields and flocks. For Ocean, Marullus devises an etiological myth of his own to describe the limitless and inexhaustible extent of the ocean. He tells the story of how Charybdis swallowed up the seas twice, but was prevented by Neptune, who threw his trident into her gullet. This part of the story and what follows is the invention of Marullus, but the basic story is from Aesop, quoted by Aristotle in his *Meteorology* (356b10–16).

The last poem of the collection sings of Earth, specifically identified as Magna Parens, the great Phrygian goddess. In placing it at the end Marullus purposely sets her against the sky god of the opening hymn. Though a powerful goddess, she preserves the pious affections of a mother. Unlike nature, who often acts as a stepmother, she is our natural mother. Marullus imitates very closely, in homage to his beloved Lucretius, a passage from Book 5 (lines 222–227) that describes how the newborn child, terrified by the sudden intake of air, sends its wailing into the light of day, naked, needy, helpless, fortunate only in one respect, that it does not understand its plight and all the trials it has yet to suffer. The poet then elucidates the symbolism of the ceremonies connected with the worship of the great mother goddess. Yet, he says, we have dishonored our common mother with war and pillage and driven by a fatal fury of avidity, we forget that we all will lie in the same earth, which does not distinguish between prince and pauper. The last prayer of the book is that we be delivered from present ills and be added to those who are buried, a sober ending to these extravagant meditations.

In the end it is difficult to determine the true significance of these poems. There are so many elements at work in this syncretic vision: the Homeric and Orphic hymns, the *Corpus Hermeticum*, the hymns of Proclus, Cleanthes, and Callimachus, Julian's *Hymn to the Sun*. In addition to these some perceive Christian allegory as well, but I must confess that I see no trace of Christianity in them. Rather I see a resemblance to the attempted revival of paganism by Gemistus Pletho, prophet and high priest of a new religion at Mistra in the Peloponnese in the middle of the fifteenth century, with whose works Marullus must have been familiar. In this appraisal I am in agreement with Erasmus's simple comment: "I always think he sounds just like a pagan."[9] This was his judgment also in the *Ciceronianus*. It was echoed by many others. Concerning his poetic talent, both in the *Hymns* and the *Epigrams*, there can be no doubt, despite the syntax, which is often redolent of Greek and contributes to his obscurity. Julius Caesar Scaliger's strictures in the fourth chapter of Book 6 of his *Poetices libri septem*[10] were certainly a little too harsh. He ends by saying that Marullus was totally without charm (*omnino invenustus*), referring to his style, but this description might also suit Botticelli's well-known portrait of him, in which he peers at us with an arrogant and disdainful glance. Later poets imitated Marullus in vernacular love poetry, especially Ronsard, who in his *Second livre des amours*, models nineteen of his *chansons* after him. We meet him again much later, a shadowy figure in the pages of George Eliot's *Romola*, where he is depicted as a confirmed pagan.

I owe an immense debt of gratitude to Luke Roman, who read the whole manuscript with great care and made many improvements to the translation and commentary. Similarly, I gratefully acknowledge the expert critical judgment of Luc Deitz in the rendering of difficult passages and convey my thanks to John Grant for ingenious solutions of several enigmatic epigrams. Like all authors of the series, I am indebted to the ever vigilant attention and kind encouragement of the General Editor, James Hankins.

I wish humbly to dedicate this edition to the undying memory of that incomparable master of humanistic philology, Alessandro Perosa.

NOTES

1. These were published by R. Shrader in *Monumenta Italiae libri IV* (Helmstaedii, 1592), 275v–277r. Michael McGann proved quite conclusively that one of the epitaphs was of Marullus's father, Manilius. The imperial connection is documented in the *Historia Augusta*, Gordian 1.2.2, who is said there to be the son of a certain Maecius Marullus. See Michael McGann, "The Ancona Epitaphs of Manilius Marullus," *Bibliothèque d'humanisme et de la Renaissance* 42 (1980): 401–404. Ronald Syme, however, considers it a forged genealogy; see his *Ammianus and the Historia Augusta* (Oxford, 1968), 163 and 215.

2. See Mayotte Bollack, "Marulle, ou la correction latine," in *Penser entre les lignes*, ed. Fosca Mariani Zini (Villeneuve d'Ascq, 2001), 53–76.

3. See the fascinating account of this movement in Brown, *Return of Lucretius*.

4. Perosa, "Studi sulla formazione," 3:209.

5. Another group of virulent epigrams directed against Poliziano were once attributed to Marullus (already by Benedetto Varchi in the sixteenth century), but now it has been shown persuasively that they were written by Sannazaro. See Carlo Vecce, "Multiplex hic anguis. Gli epigrammi di Sannazaro contro Poliziano," *Rinascimento*, ser. 2, 30 (1990): 235–255.

6. Perosa, "Studi sulla formazione," 3:214–20.

7. Michele Marullo Tarcaniota, *Inni naturali*, 218.

8. Eugenio Garin, "Per la storia della cultura filosofica del Rinascimento. I. Letteratura solare," *Rivista critica di storia della filosofia* 12 (1957): 3–21.

9. *Correspondence of Erasmus*, tr. R. A. B. Mynors and D. F. S. Thompson, 14 vols. (Toronto, 1992), 10:344 [Ep. 1479].

10. Julius Caesar Scaliger, *Poetices libri septem*, vol. 5, Book 6, ed. Gregor Vogt-Spira, and Book 7, ed. Luc Deitz (Stuttgart, 2003), 58.

POEMS

EPIGRAMMATON

Liber Primus

I.

Inter mille neces durique incommoda Martis
    Quis putet Aonias posse iuvare deas?
Hic quoque, Laure, iuvant perque arma ensesque sequuntur,
    Militiae comites nec pudet esse meae,
5 Quaeque manus ferrum, posito fert ense libellos.
    Et placet et Musis est sine dulce nihil,
Sed tamen his studiis debetur lassa senectus;
    Interea certe sudor uterque decet.
Tu modo, diverso gladios dum stringimus orbe,
10   Hoc tibi sinceri pignus amoris habe.

II. *Ad Neaeram*

Salve, nequitiae meae, Neaera,
Mi passercule, mi albe turturille,
Meum mel, mea suavitas, meum cor,
Meum suaviolum, mei lepores,
5 Te ne vivere ego queam relicta?
Te ne ego sine regna, te sine aurum
Aut messes Arabum velim beatas?
O prius peream ipse, regna et aurum!

III. *De Neaera*

Inventa nuper, nervum cum tenderet acrem,
    Obstupuit visa victus Amor domina.
Sensit laeta suas vires oculosque retorsit,

EPIGRAMS

Book I

I.

Amid a thousand deaths and the hardships of cruel Mars, who would think that the Aonian goddesses[1] could be of help? Here too, Lorenzo,[2] they are of help and follow me into armed warfare, and are not ashamed to accompany me into the fray, and the hand 5 that wields the sword bears books once the sword has been laid down. Nothing is pleasing or delightful without the Muses. Yet these pursuits are the province of weary old age; in the meantime, at least, an effort in both activities is appropriate for me. But you, while we unsheathe the sword in sundry parts of the world, receive 10 this pledge of sincere affection.

II. To Neaera

Greetings Neaera, my wicked temptress, my little sparrow, my little white turtledove, my honey, my sweetness, my darling, my kisses, my delight. If I were to leave you, could I go on living? Without 5 you could I desire kingdoms, gold or the rich harvests of the Arabs? Oh! may I perish first, kingdoms and gold along with me.

III. About Neaera

Coming upon my mistress of late, as he was drawing his fierce bow, Love was struck dumb, vanquished at her sight. She was thrilled to sense his powers and shot back a glance to put him to

3

Dum fugiat : ventis ocior ille fugit.
5 Sed dum forte fugit, plenae cecidere pharetrae,
    Devicti spolium quas tulit illa dei,
    Induiturque humerum pariterque hominesque deosque
      Una ferit: victus errat inermis Amor.

IV. Ad falconem

Ingrate falco et crimen alitum omnium,
Quascunque mollis aura sublevat solo,
Coelumque pennis nubila et tranant suis
Ac regna solae coelitum et vident domos,
5 Quis te repente tantus invasit furor,
Tam mite regis perpeti ut nolles iugum,
Qui te tam amabat virgo quam puppas solet,
Nondum mariti virgo quae sedit sinu,
Nec ad iugales deiicit lumen faces?
10 An nesciebas regias longas manus?
Insulse, inepte, perfide, ignave, impie,
Cuius opera huc rex toto et huc vagus die,
Vix nocte multa lassulus redit domum.

V. Ad Paulum Tarchanioten

Quid me, Paule, tuis vocibus enecas?
    Non dis, non Veneri placet,
Quae curis lacrimas mitibus ingerit,
    Nec fas est posito iugo
5 Oblitum dominae vivere et ignium,
    Quem tactum semel improbus
Miris versat Amor saevitia modis.
    Tu, cui maior inest vigor
Et mens desidiae non patiens malae,
10   Artes et patrium decus

4

flight. He fled away swifter than the wind. But by chance, as he 5
was fleeing, his loaded quiver fell and she picked it up as the spoils
of her victory over the god, put it on her shoulder and alone of all
women strikes men and gods alike. Love wanders aimlessly, van-
quished and unarmed.

IV. To a falcon

Ungrateful falcon, a disgrace to all winged creatures whom the soft
breeze lifts from the earth and who soar through the sky and the
clouds and are privileged to see the dwellings and kingdoms of the
gods, what great madness suddenly entered into you that you re- 5
fused to endure the mild yoke of the emperor,[3] who loved you as a
young girl loves her dolls, a young girl who has not yet enjoyed the
embraces of a husband nor lowered her gaze at the nuptial torches?
Did you not recognize the long hands of the king? Stupid, foolish, 10
faithless, cowardly, impious bird, because of whom the emperor
wanders hither and thither and reluctantly returns home, ex-
hausted, late at night.

V. To Paul Tarchaniotes[4]

Paul, why do you weary me with your complaints? It is not pleas-
ing to the gods nor to Venus, who supplies tears for slight anxi-
eties, and it is not right that one whom implacable Love has touched
and cruelly tosses about in all directions should live forgetful of his 5
mistress and love's passion. You, who are possessed of greater vigor
and whose mind does not suffer harmful idleness, protect the arts 10

Tutanda et titulos suscipe Achaicos.
    Nos contra tenues sine
Assueto dominae servitio premi,
    Contentos placito sinu
15 Inter nequitias mutuaque oscula
    Turpem canitiem pati.

VI. *Mortui pro patria*

Tu, quicunque virum vacuo tot milia in arvo
    Cernis ab hirsutis dilaceranda feris,
Desine mirari. Patrii est hoc moris, honestam
    Pugnando mortem quaerere, non tumulum.

VII. *Ad Antonium principem Salernitanum*

Quaerite Maeoniden, Musae, redit alter Achilles;
    Quaerite Peliden, Maeonides remeat.
Hic erit, et magnum referat qui solus Homerum
    Et renovet Phthii fortia facta ducis.
5 Vos modo felices annos et candida vitae
    Tempora tam raris dotibus apta date.

VIII. *Epitaphium Theodori Gazae*

Hic Gazes iacet et Gazae Sophia addita mater,
    Alterutrum quoniam mors rapere haud potuit.

IX. *Ad Franciscum Scalam*

Scala, delitium tui Marulli
Et veri columen decusque amoris,
Quis te, quis deus huc venire iussit
Solatum ad veterem tuum sodalem,
5 Qui solus Calabris misellus oris

and ancestral honor and Greek glory. But as for me, on the other
hand, allow me, weak as I am, to be crushed by the customary
servitude imposed by a mistress, happy to suffer a shameful old   15
age in wanton erotic embraces and shared kisses.

VI. Those who have died for their country

You, whoever you are, who behold so many thousands of men left
in an empty field to be torn to pieces by shaggy wild beasts, cease
from your wondering. This is the custom of our ancestors: to seek
an honorable death in battle, not a tomb.

VII. To Antonio, Prince of Salerno[5]

Seek out the Maeonian,[6] O Muses, another Achilles returns; seek
out Pelides,[7] the Maeonian returns. He will be here, the only one
who can both bring back great Homer and revive the brave deeds
of the Phthian warrior.[8] It is up to you to offer prosperous years   5
and joyous moments suitable to such rare talents.

VIII. Epitaph of Theodore Gaza[9]

Here lies Gaza and to Gaza is joined his mother, Wisdom, since
death could not take one without the other.

IX. To Francesco Scales[10]

Scales, delight of your friend Marullus, pillar and glory of true
friendship, what god directed you to come here to give solace to
your old comrade who, alone and forlorn on the shores of Calabria,   5

Eiectus patria sodalibusque,
Uni qui mala patriae levabant,
Flendo tempora conterit maligna?
O diem nitidum! quis huc, quis unquam
10   Venturum mihi, Scala, te putaret?
Venisti tamen, o amice, nec te
Tam longae labor est viae moratus.
En, cape oscula tam diu cupita,
Amplexus cape tam diu negatos.
15   Fruamur pariter die beato!
Qui scis crastina quid minetur hora?

X. Ad Maximilianum Caesarem

Siquis opum largus, siquis virtutis alumnus,
   Siquis sincerae cultor amicitiae,
Si quisquam dubia fati sublimior aura,
   Siquis fortunam qui facit ipse sibi,
5   Siquis Marte ferox, siquis post arma benignus,
   Siquis qui, quod habet, hoc habet ille bonis,
Siquis possessor fidei, probitatis, honesti,
   Ne vivam, si non tu mihi, Caesar, hic es.

XI. Dido in anulo

Tu, qui me casusque meos in imagine parva
   Aspicis et digito tristia fata refers,
Vera haec effigies, nex vera est, hospes, Elissae,
   Sed non vera necis causa pudendus amor.
5   Nec mihi Phryx nocuit — nec enim Phryga novimus ullum —
   Cura sed antiqui casta tenaxque tori,
Quam ne coniugio Lybici violare tyranni
   Cogerer, hac cecidi fortiter usa manu.

8

exiled from his native land and friends, who were the only ones
who assuaged his nostalgia for his country, consumes his gloomy
days in tears? O bright day! Who would ever have thought that   10
you would come here to see me? Yet you came, good friend, and
were not deterred by the fatigue of so long a journey. Come, re-
ceive kisses so long desired and the embraces we have so long been
denied. Let us enjoy this happy day together! How do you know   15
what threats tomorrow will bring?

X. To Emperor Maximilian[11]

If there is anyone lavish of his resources, a paragon of virtue, a cul-
tivator of true friendship, one who is above the uncertain breezes
of fortune, one who forges his own destiny; if there is anyone who   5
is fierce in war but merciful when war is over, one who, whatever
he has, awards it to the good; if there is anyone who is endowed
with good faith, uprightness and honor, may I cease to live if you
are not that person in my eyes, O Caesar.

XI. Dido on a ring

You who look upon me and my woes in a tiny image and carry my
tragic fate on your finger, this is a true image, the true death of
Elissa,[12] O stranger, but the true cause of death was not a shame-
ful love. A Phrygian[13] did not do me harm — for I knew no Phry-   5
gian — but it was the chaste and tenacious fidelity to a previous
marriage.[14] In order not to be forced to defile it through marriage
to a Carthaginian tyrant I took my life,[15] making courageous use

9

At vos, o vates, si sunt haec praemia laudi,
10   Quae feret incesti foemina adulterii?

XII. Ad Antonium principem Salernitanum

Das gemmas aurumque, ego do tibi carmina tantum:
    Sed bona si fuerint carmina, plus ego do.

XIII. Ad Neaeram

Sic me, blanda, tui, Neaera, ocelli,
Sic candentia colla, sic patens frons,
Sic pares minio genae perurunt,
Ex quo visa mihi et simul cupita es,
5 Ut, ni me lacrimae rigent perennes,
Totus in tenues eam favillas.
Sic rursum lacrimae rigant perennes,
Ex quo visa mihi et simul cupita es,
Ut, ni, blanda, tui, Neaera, ocelli,
10 Ni candentia colla, ni patens frons,
Ni pares minio genae perurant,
Totus in riguos eam liquores.
O vitam miseram et cito caducam!

XIV. Epitaphium Germanici Caesaris

Parce, hospes, tumulo: Caesar Germanicus hic sum.
    Saepe etiam ignotis ipse dedi requiem.
Quod siquem tituli nihil huius gratia tangit,
    At moveat patria fraude quod hic iaceo.
5 Sed iaceo, quamvis non vitae, at plenus honorum,
    Hoc uno ingratus, quod genui, patriae.

of this hand. But you, O poets, if these are the rewards of good renown, what will a woman suffer for an impious adultery?   10

XII. To Antonio, Prince of Salerno

You give me jewels and gold, I give you only poems: but if they are good poems, mine is the greater gift.

XIII. To Neaera

Your gentle eyes, sweet Neaera, your dazzling white neck, your ample brow, your rosy cheeks so inflame me since I first saw you and instantly desired you, that if I were not bathed in ever-flowing tears, I would be completely turned into insubstantial ash. Then,   5 inversely, I am so bathed in ever-flowing tears from the day I first saw you and instantly desired you that if your gentle eyes, sweet Neaera, your dazzling white neck, your ample brow, your rosy   10 cheeks did not inflame me, I would be completely dissolved into liquid water. O unhappy life, quick to flee away!

XIV. Epitaph of Caesar Germanicus[16]

Show respect, O stranger, to this tomb: Caesar Germanicus lies here. I myself often granted peace even to those whom I did not know. But if no one is moved to sympathy by this inscription, may the fact that I lie here, victim of my country's guile, move you to pity. I lie here, devoid of life, yet laden with honors, regarded with   5 disfavor by my country for one sole reason, that I fathered a child.[17] Both the common people and the senators testified to my

Testata est mores lacrimis plebesque patresque.
  Haec sunt sinceri iudicia ingenii.

XV. Epitaphium vituli et asellae

Moerenda Vitulus atque Asella coniuges,
Qui morte praeventi mala, nec ille bos
Nec illa quivit emori asina. Hoc ex suis
Sibi bonis sumpsere, quod vides soli.

XVI. De poetis Latinis

Amor Tibullo, Mars tibi, Maro, debet,
  Terentio soccus levis,
Cothurnus olim nemini satis multum,
  Horatio satyra et chelys,
5 Natura magni versibus Lucretii
  Lepore Musaeo illitis,
Epigramma cultum, teste Rhallo, adhuc nulli,
  Docto Catullo syllabae:
Hos siquis inter caeteros locat vates,
10 Onerat quam honorat verius.

XVII. In Mancinum

Effigiem quaeris, nec vis, Mancine, poetam:
  Quid, nisi quod comedit nil statua, hic comedit?

XVIII. Ad Neaeram

Sic istos oculos tuos, Neaera,
Avertis, quotiens perire me vis,
Tanquam perdere non queas tuendo:
Sed tu ne peream times beatus.
5 Ne time. Ah miser, ah miser peribo!

good morals with their tears. This is the judgment of a sincere heart.

XV. Epitaph of a calf and a she-ass

We must mourn the calf and the she-ass, yoke-partners who died a bad death before their time. He could not die as an ox nor she as an adult she-ass. Of their possessions they took with themselves this plot of land that you see.

XVI. Of Latin poets

Love is indebted to Tibullus; Mars to you, Vergil; the loose-fitting shoe to Terence. The buskin for some time now does not owe very much to anyone; to Horace the satire and the lyre are indebted; Nature is indebted to the verses, daubed by the charm of the 5 Muses, of great Lucretius. The polished epigram still owes nothing to anyone, according to Rhallus;[18] the hendecasyllable is beholden to Catullus. If anyone wishes to place these poets among the others, it would be more of an onus than an honor. 10

XVII. Against Mancinus

You want a likeness, not a poet, Mancinus: why so, save that a statue doesn't eat anything, a poet does?

XVIII. To Neaera

You turn those eyes of yours away from me, Neaera, in such a way, whenever you want me to die, as if you couldn't kill me with just a look, but you are afraid that I may be happy to die. Fear not! Ah! 5

Sed hoc tam miserum — ut putas — perire,
Tuo servitio magis beatum est.

XIX. De Nape

Quod Sappho Aoniis decima est soror addita Musis,
    Inter Pieridas negligit esse Nape
Miraturque pati scelus hoc coelestia corda
    Et sanctum impuro carmine nectar emi.
5 Usque adeo ne intacta Nape? nil spurcius immo est!
    Sed certe vati filiola obiicitur.

XX. Epitaphium Francisci Sfortiae

Si genus audieris, spernes; mirabere gesta:
    Illud fortunae est, hoc opus ingenii.

XXI. Ad Neaeram

Has violas atque haec tibi candida lilia mitto;
    Legi hodie violas, candida lilia heri.
Lilia, ut instantis monearis virgo senectae,
    Tam cito quae lapsis marcida sunt foliis;
5 Illae, ut vere suo doceant ver carpere vitae,
    Invida quod miseris tam breve Parca dedit.
Quod si tarda venis, non ver breve, non violas, sed —
    Proh facinus! — sentes cana rubosque metes.

XXII. De morte Iani fratris

Per Scythiam Bessosque feros, per tela, per hostes
    Rhiphaeo venio tristis ab usque gelu,
Scilicet exequias tibi producturus inanes,

I shall die unhappy, unhappy, but this unhappy death — as you think — is happier than a life spent as your slave.

XIX. Concerning Nape

Because Sappho was added to the Aonian Muses as a tenth sister, Nape makes no effort to be numbered among the Pierians, and she is astonished that celestial hearts suffer this crime and that holy nectar is bought with impure poetry. Is Nape so undefiled? On the contrary, no one is more besmirched! But no doubt the poetess is charged with the crime of having a little daughter.[19]

XX. Epitaph of Francesco Sforza[20]

If you learn about his ancestry, you will despise him, but you will marvel at his deeds: the first is the result of chance, the other of native ability.

XXI. To Neaera

I send you these violets and these white lilies;[21] I picked the violets today, the white lilies yesterday. The lilies are to remind you of fast-approaching old age, though you are but a young girl, since they soon wither and their petals fall; the violets so that by their springlike freshness they will persuade you to pluck the spring of life, this brief period that the envious Fates have given to us wretched mortals. But if you come to me too late, you will not reap the brief spring, nor violets but — horrible thought! — old and gray, you will reap briars and brambles.

XXII. On the death of his brother Janos[22]

Through Scythia and the land of the savage Bessi,[23] through enemy weapons I come, sadly, all the way from the icy Riphaean mountains,[24] to bring to you the vain obsequies owed to the dead,

Fraternis unus ne careas lacrimis,
5 Teque peregrina, frater, tellure iacentem
Et tua sparsurus fletibus ossa meis.
Quandoquidem post tot casus patriaeque domusque—
Tanquam hoc exempto nil nocuisset adhuc—
Te quoque sors invisa mihi, dulcissime frater,
10   Abstulit, Elysium misit et ante diem,
Ne foret aut fletus qui solaretur acerbos
Iungeret aut lacrimis fratris et ipse suas.
Heu, miserande puer, quae te mihi fata tulerunt,
Cui miseram linquis, frater adempte, domum?
15 Tu mea post patriam turbasti pectora solus,
Omnia sunt tecum vota sepulta mea,
Omnia tecum una tumulo conduntur in isto:
Frater abest, fratrem quaeso venire iube!
Cur sine me Elysia felix spatiare sub umbra
20   Inter honoratos nobilis umbra patres?
Occurrunt Graiique atavi proavique Latini:
Frater abest, fratrem quaeso venire iube!
Hic tibi pallentes violas legit, alter amomum,
Narcissum hic, vernas porrigit ille rosas,
25 Attolluntque solo carisque amplexibus haerent:
Frater abest, fratrem quaeso venire iube!
Interea, quoniam sic fata inimica tulerunt,
Nec mihi te licuit posse cadente mori,
Accipe, quos habeo lugubria munera, fletus,
30   Aeternumque, meae, frater, ave, lacrimae!

XXIII. Ad Laurentium Petri Francisci

Quod solus, bone Laure, adamas ornasque poetas,
Nil mirum est: solus carmine digna facis.

so that you will not be the only one deprived of a brother's tears, and to shed my tears upon you, my brother, lying in a foreign land, and upon your bones. After so many misfortunes that befell our country and our family—as if without this loss I had not already suffered enough harm—cruel fate has taken you from me as well, dearest brother, and has sent you to the Elysian Fields before your time, leaving no one to console my bitter grief or add his tears to those of a brother. Alas! pitiful young man, what destiny has taken you from me? To whom, dear brother, taken from us, do you leave our wretched home? You alone, after my native land, gave me distress; all my hopes are buried with you, all my hopes are with you in this tomb. Your brother is not there; bid him come to you, I implore you! Why do you, noble shade, wander happily among your honored ancestors in the Elysian shade without me? Your Greek and Latin forefathers run to meet you. Your brother is not there; bid him come to you, I implore you! One picks pale violets for you, another amomum; one offers you a narcissus, another spring roses, and they lift you from the ground and hold you tenderly in their affectionate embrace. Your brother is not there; bid him come to you, I implore you! In the meantime, since the hostile fates have taken you away, and it was not allowed me to die with you, accept these doleful gifts, my lamentations, and accept my greetings forever, my brother, source of my tears.

XXIII. To Lorenzo de' Medici, son of Pierfrancesco[25]

Good Lorenzo, that you alone love and reward poets is no surprise: you alone do things worthy of poetry.

XXIV. Epitaphium Deipyles

Deipyle iacet hic prima intercepta iuventa,
  Et saecli et sexus gloria rara sui:
Quae, dum vita fuit, superos ipsumque Tonantem
  Torserat, inferno nunc movet arma Iovi.

XXV. Ad Accium Sincerum

Acci, non ego tela, non ego enses,
Non incendia pestilentiasve,
Non minas vereor ferociorum,
Non hymbres, mare, turbines, procellas,
5   Non quaecunque aliis solent nocere,
Quae cuncta unius aestimamus assis:
Verum tristius his malum puella est,
Quae me, cum libuit, potest necare.

XXVI. De Leucothoe

Odit Leucothoe, sed quo plus odit, ego illam
  Plus pereo. Quid? Si non ita acerba foret,
Blanda minus poterat. Hoc in me callida vidit,
  Et fugit, invitam quo magis ipse velim.

XXVII. Epitaphium Michaelis Tarchaniotae
avi materni

Parce, hospes, cineresque pios ne laede profanus:
  Si nescis, castis haec loca sola patent.
Nec te privata moveat quod claudor in urna.
  Haec quoque fortunae, non mea cura fuit.
5   Longe, hospes, longe tamen erras, si mea credis
  Nomina in exiguo tota reposta solo,

XXIV. Epitaph of Deiphyle

Deiphyle lies here, carried off in her early youth, a rare glory of her age and of her sex, who when she was alive tormented the gods and the Thunderer himself; now she takes up arms against the infernal Jove.[26]

XXV. To Actius Sincerus[27]

Actius, I have no fear of spears, nor of swords, nor of fires or pestilence, nor of the threats of violent men, nor of rain, sea, whirlwinds, storms, nor all those things that usually bring harm to   5
others, all of which I esteem of no account. But a more fearsome evil than all of these is a young girl who, when she pleases, can kill me.

XXVI. About Leucothoe

Leucothoe dislikes me, but the more she dislikes me the more I die for her. Why is that so? If she were not so hostile, she would be less attractive. Shrewd as she is, she saw this in me and runs away, so that I will desire her all the more when she is unwilling.

XXVII. Epitaph of Michael Tarchaniota,
maternal grandfather[28]

Be merciful, passerby, and do not profane these pious ashes. If you do not know it, these places are reserved only for the chaste. Do not be alarmed that I am enclosed in an urn of an ordinary citizen; this too was fortune's doing, not mine. But you are very much   5

Quaeque tot ob patriam pugnando vulnera passus,
    In cineres mecum versa abiisse leves.
Atque utinam ob patriam tantum, nec dicerer, hospes,
10   Cum patria et natis oppetiisse tribus:
Quos ego suprema comites hortatus in hora,
    Vincere dum nequeo, cum patria perii.

XXVIII. *Ad Neaeram*

Rogas quae mea vita sit, Neaera.
Qualem scilicet ipsa das amanti, est.
Infelix, misera, inquies, molesta
Aut si triste magis potest quid esse.
5 Haec est, quam mihi das, Neaera, vitam.
Qui — dicis — comites? Dolor, Querelae,
Lamentatio, Lacrimae perennes,
Langor, Anxietas, Amaritudo,
Aut si triste magis potest quid esse.
10 Hos tu das comites, Neaera, vitae.

XXIX. *De Antonio principe Salernitano*

Olim rogatus quid sibi relinqueret
    Tam multa qui cuivis daret,
'Hoc' inquit 'ipsum' Antonius, 'siquid dedi:
    Nam caetera haud puto mea.'

XXX. *De Xysto*

Senserat Ausoniam vix dum bene foedere iungi,
    Cum 'Perii!' Xystus dixit, et interiit.

in error, stranger, if you think my entire fame has been laid to rest
in a tiny plot of earth, and that the many wounds I suffered for the
sake of my country have turned into light ashes and died with me.
And let people not say, O stranger, that I met death together with   10
my country and three children only for the sake of my country: in
my last hour, urging them on, when I could not win the victory, I
perished together with my country.

XXVIII. To Neaera

You ask me, Neaera, what kind of life I lead; none other than the
kind you give to one who loves you: unhappy, miserable, restless,
troubled, or whatever more dismal fate you could imagine. This   5
is the life you give me, Neaera. "Who are your companions?"
you ask. Sorrow, Complaints, Lamentation, everlasting Tears,
Languor, Anxiety, Bitter Anguish, or whatever more depressing
state you could imagine. These are the life-companions you give   10
me, Neaera.

XXIX. On Antonio, Prince of Salerno

Asked once what he would leave to himself after giving so much to
anyone at all, Antonio replied, "Whatever I gave to others: for all
else I do not consider to be mine."

XXX. On Sixtus IV[29]

He had scarcely heard that Italy was united by a good treaty when
Sixtus exclaimed, "That's the end of me," and died.

XXXI. De Thrasybulo

Cum fugeret civem civis devictus ut hostem,
    In patriam sceleris conscius ipse sui,
'State viri!' Thrasybulus ait. 'Victoria vestra est,
    Nec mihi sed vobis vicimus et patriae.'
5 Dixit, per mediosque ruens ensesque virosque,
    Parcendum passim civibus ingeminat.

XXXII. Ad Antonium Petrutium

Qui fit, Petruti, ut siquis est mihi visus,
Siquem saluto, si cui manum porxi
Caputve movi, protinus mare et montes
Aut siquid usquam est impudentius iactent
5 Et se patronos offerant vel invito?
Idem rogati, certa postulat cum res,
Mirantur unde tam audiant novum nomen,
Nec iam Marullum verba nec sua agnoscunt,
Homines crepitui quam simillimi ventris,
10 Pontanus illos ut meus bene appellat.
Tu solus a me cultus unice quicquam
Nec polliceris, vana nec mihi iactas,
At, cum videtur postulare res, ultro
Imples parentis munus atque agis mecum,
15 Non ut patronum, sed pium ut decet patrem:
Nimirum amasque solus et tibi constas.

XXXIII. Epitaphium Albinae

Hic Albina iacet, sed non tamen hic iacet una
    Albina — hoc Veneris non tulit ipse puer —
Sed tela atque arcus pharetraeque, Cupidinis arma,

XXXI. On Thrasybulus[30]

When, as a defeated citizen, he fled his fellow citizens, as though
they were his enemies, conscious of his crime against his country,
Thrasybulus said: "Stand firm, men! Victory is yours, we have
conquered not for me but for you and our country." Thus he   5
spoke, and rushing headlong through the midst of men and
swords, he shouted repeatedly that citizens should be spared indis-
criminately.

XXXII. To Antonello Petrucci[31]

How is it, dear Petrucci, that if I see someone, or greet anyone, or
if I shake hands with anyone or make a motion with my head,
they immediately promise me the moon, or make some other ex-
travagant offer, and volunteer to be my protector without my ask-   5
ing? But if I ask a favor of these same persons when there is a real
need, they express their wonder at the sound of this new name
and no longer recognize either Marullus or their own words.
These men are like farts, as my friend Pontano[32] well calls them.   10
You are the only one whom I respect above all others, since you
never promise me anything or make vain boasts, but when you see
that the situation demands it, without being asked, you fulfill the
role of a parent and deal with me, not as behooves a patron, but as   15
a loyal father. Obviously, you are the only one who loves me and
you remain true to yourself.

XXXIII. Epitaph of Albina

Here lies Albina, yet it is not only Albina who lies here — Venus's
child did not allow it — but the weapons and the bow and the
quivers, Cupid's arsenal, and the gentle beauty that always distin-

Quique fuit mollis semper in ore decor.
5   Spargite humum foliis, verno nec parcite flori:
        Haec quoque, quae cinis est, flos modo vernus erat.

XXXIV. *In superbientem*

Cum felix regnoque potens videare paterno
    Inque dies crescat gloria honorque magis,
Nec tua maiorum titulis concedat imago
    Et facile ex animo sit tibi cuncta fore,
5   Fastidire tamen victos miserosque caveto
    Et tua Fortunae regna minora puta.

XXXV. *Ad Alexandrum Cortesium*

Commendo tibi, Cortesi, Soavum,
Ipsum non secus ac tuum Marullum,
Nanque est nobilis atque litteratus
Et, nisi manifesta pernegamus,
5   Urbanus, facilis venustulusque.
Si me diligis — ut facis — Soavum
Ipsum dilige, ama, fove adiuvaque.
Dignus est — mihi credito — Soavus
Et sodalitio tuo et favore.

XXXVI. *Epitaphium Simonettae Vesputiae*

Si lacrimis decoranda novis generosa puella est,
    Haec una est lacrimis condecoranda novis.
Sin deflere nefas tam rarae funera vitae,
    Haec eadem siccis una adeunda genis.

guished her. Spread leaves upon the earth, do not spare the spring   5
flowers: she too, who is ash, was once a flower of spring.

XXXIV. *Against a disdainful person*

Though you seem fortunate and powerful as heir to your father's
kingdom, and your glory and honor increase day by day, and your
image be not inferior to the distinctions of your ancestors, and
though everything go smoothly according to your wishes, be care-   5
ful not to treat the vanquished and the unfortunate with dis-
dain, and bear in mind that your kingdoms are less than those of
Fortune.

XXXV. *To Alessandro Cortesi*[33]

I commend Soavus[34] to you, Cortesi, a man no different from your
Marullus, for he is of noble family and cultured and, unless we
wish obstinately to deny what is plainly evident, he is urbane, af-   5
fable and quite charming. If you love me — as you do — hold Soa-
vus dear, love, cherish and help him. Soavus is worthy, believe me,
of your companionship and favor.

XXXVI. *Epitaph of Simonetta Vespucci*[35]

If a young woman of noble birth should be honored by fresh tears,
this woman alone should be honored by fresh tears; but if it is
forbidden to mourn the end of such an exceptional life, we must
approach the tomb of this one woman alone with dry cheeks.

XXXVII. *De suo amore*

Iactor, dispereo, crucior, trahor huc miser atque huc,
    Ipse ego iam quis sim nescio aut ubi sim,
Tot simul insidiis premor undique. Proh dolor! in me
    Saevitiae Cypris dat documenta suae.
5   Saevitiae documenta suae dat, ego hanc tamen unam
    Depereo, utque nocet, sic libet usque sequi.
Qua siquis miserum solam me liberet horam,
    Hic mihi sit Phoebo doctior et melior.

XXXVIII. *De Amore et Mercurio*

Forte Iovi dum iactat Amor sua tela, deorum
    Nuntius ex humero surripuit pharetram.
Sensit Amor fraudes, et 'Me ne, ignave, lacessis,
    Cuius' ait 'mentem surripui totiens?'

XXXIX. *Epitaphium Philippi Marulli avi paterni*

Siste, hospes, atque haec verba, si placet, lege,
Neque enim rogamus nisi lubentem quempiam:
Ego Philippus hic Marullus contegor.
Posuit superstes filius Manilius
5   Uxorque Thomae. Hoc satis. Caetera alii,
De se Marullo proloqui ulterius nefas.

XL. *In Posthumum*

Scribis, agis, recitas semper nova, Posthume: quid ni?
    Posthume, crede mihi, quicquid agis, novus es.

XXXVII. *About his love*

I am tossed about, I perish, I am tormented, I am dragged hither
and yon in my misery; I no longer know who I am or where I am,
harassed by countless snares on every side. O agony! The Cyprian
goddess gives proof of her savagery toward me. She gives proof of 5
her savagery, but I perish because of this one love, and the more
she hurts me the more I desire to follow after her. If someone can
free hapless me from her for but an hour, he will be to me wiser
and better than Apollo.

XXXVIII. *On Love and Mercury*

As it happened, once when Love was hurling his weapons at Jupi-
ter, the messenger of the gods stole the quiver from his shoulders.
Love sensed the theft and said, "Coward, do you challenge me af-
ter I have stolen your mind so often?"

XXXIX. *Epitaph of Philippus Marullus, paternal grandfather*

Stay, stranger, and read these words, if you please — for we ask it
only of one who is willing. I, Philippus Marullus, am buried here.
My surviving son, Manilius, and the wife of Thomas laid me in
the tomb. That is enough. Others will add the rest: it is wrong for 5
Marullus to say anything further of himself.

XL. *Against Postumus*[36]

You write, you act, you recite new verse always, Postumus: why
not? Postumus, believe me, whatever you do, you are a novice.

XLI. *Ad Martiam Bocontiam*

Cum sit Acidaliae facies artesque Minervae
    Et Latonigenae pectora casta deae,
Cur tibi Mars tribuit speciosum, Martia, nomen?
    An contra quod me tam fera bella facis?
5   Bella facis faciasque licet, tibi dedita servit
    Mens tamen et duros serviet ad cineres.
Quod siquis misero post funera sensus amori est,
    Tunc quoque amet vultus ossea forma tuos.

XLII. *Epitaphium Pholoes*

Hic choreae cantusque iacent Veneresque iocique:
    Unius neque enim est hic tumulus Pholoes.
Nam, simulac decimum, necdum bene, venit ad annum,
    Protinus et raris annumerata fuit.
5   Mille illam petiere proci, sed mille repulsis
    Maluit in viduo casta iacere toro
Taedarumque expers sine coniuge degere vitam,
    Libera perpetuo nec dare colla iugo.
Atque ita reste brevi veloque ornata sacerdos
10   Virgineos intrat non diuturna focos.
Risit Amor Claralem habitum mentemque puellae,
    Et leviter 'Nostra est haec quoque miles!' ait.
Nec longum: ardet inops mentis vittasque perosa
    Sedit sub Maenni conspicienda cavis.
15   Et tamen antiquusque rigor et nescia amorum
    Rusticitas animo pristina, ut ante, fuit.
Non illam rixae, non lenia murmura amantum
    Iuverunt, medio non vaga lingua ioco,
Non partes egitve suas lassataque saepe
20   Immoto miserum corpore cepit onus,

XLI. To Marzia Bocontia[37]

While Venus is famous for her beauty and Minerva for her art,
and the daughter of Latona[38] for her chastity, why did Mars give
you such a beautiful name, Marzia? Is it because you wage such
fierce wars against me? You wage wars, and though you do this, 5
my devoted heart serves you and will continue to serve you until
it is reduced to unfeeling ashes. But if there is any feeling left to
a hapless love after death, then may a skeletal form love your
visage.

XLII. Epitaph of Pholoe[39]

Here lie dances and songs and amours and gaiety: for this is not
just the tomb of Pholoe. As soon as she reached her tenth year,
even a little earlier, she was immediately recognized as a woman of
rare qualities. A thousand suitors sought her hand, but a thousand 5
she rejected, preferring to lie chaste in an empty bed and, free of
the marriage torch, to spend her life without a spouse and not
submit her free neck to a lifelong yoke. And so, putting on the
short cincture and the veil, she entered as a nun into the virginal 10
ménage,[40] but not for long. Love laughed at the habit of the Poor
Clares[41] and the young woman's intention, and said mockingly,
"She too is one of our warriors." It was not long before she burned
with love, driven out of her mind, and loathing her religious garb,
sat under the porticoes of Menius[42] to attract attention. But her 15
previous austerity and rustic inexperience in love affairs still re-
mained with her as before. She took no delight in the quarrels
or soft whisperings of lovers, and was not adept in using her
tongue in the midst of her amorous games, and did not play her
part, but wearily accepted the unwelcome burden of the man on 20

Donec, rugosa vultus mutante senecta,
    Vilis amatori visa gravisque suo est.
Tum demum faciem et formae mala damna caducae
    Conqueri et auxilium quaerere ab arte novum:
25 Et modo compositum blanda latus arte movere,
    Saepe iocis tardos sollicitare viros.
Nunc pariter digitisque loqui nutuque fideli
    Verbaque de tacitis mutua ferre notis;
Interdum insano Veneris cogente furore,
30   Cum iam flamma tegi non satis apta foret,
Dulcia concentu modulari carmina blando
    Et placida captos ducere ab arte animos.
  Aut matronalem verbis mollire rigorem
    Et precibus castas sollicitare nurus
35 Aut iam mutatos animis coniungere amantes
    Duraque mellita flectere corda prece.
Quae dum dulcis anus curat, proh tristia fata!
    Ante diem nigrum per Styga fecit iter,
Flens tamen, ut flentes se circumspexit amicos,
40   Tot defecturo iam dedit ore sonos:
'Eripior, sed vos, dum lux brevis ista, cavete
    Nequis iners vitae tempus abire sinat.'
Dixit, et in tenues mens aegra evanuit auras.
    Fleverunt Charites funera, flevit Amor.
45 Vade, anus egregia, tibi ver, tibi cinnama surgant
    Et crescat tumulo spica Cilissa tuo!

XLIII. De Venere et Vulcano

Moesta Venus rapti casum plorabat Adonis
    Factaque fulminei vulnera dente suis.
Sensit, et indignans 'Quid fles, dea?' Mulciber inquit.
    'Non habet in Martem ius violentus aper.'

her motionless body until, when the wrinkles of old age altered her features, she became contemptible and repugnant to her lover. Then, in the end, she lamented her appearance and the ravages done to her former beauty and sought new help from art, and learned to move her hips seductively and to tempt slow-witted men with her games. She learned the art of expressing herself through gestures and a telling nod of the head and to communicate through silent signals; sometimes, when the insane frenzy of Venus took hold of her and the flame could no longer be concealed, she sang sweet songs in pleasant harmonies and beguiled and enamored hearts by her captivating art. Or she would temper the sternness of older married women with her words and encourage young married women with her entreaties and join lovers together who had become estranged and softened hard hearts with her honeyed prayers. While the sweet old woman was occupied with these tasks, O sad fate! she made the journey across the dark Styx before her time. Weeping, as she saw her weeping friends around her, she uttered these words as her voice was fading: "I am taken away, but you, while this brief light lasts, take care that you do not pass your lives in apathy." Thus she spoke, and her weary soul vanished into thin air. The Graces mourned her death, Love mourned her. Go, admirable old woman. May spring and cinnamon rise up around you, and may Cilician saffron[43] sprout up upon your tomb.

XLIII. On Venus and Vulcan

Sadly, Venus mourned the fate of Adonis and the wounds inflicted by the tusk of the lightning-swift boar. Vulcan sensed it, and filled with righteous anger, exclaimed, "Why do you weep, O goddess? A violent boar has no rights against Mars."

XLIV. *Ad Accium Sincerum*

Miraris, Acci, cur tacet Linus patrem:
    Mater Nape non prodidit.

XLV. *Ad Avitam*

Quid frustra totiens necas rogando
Nec firmum tibi, Avita, nec fidelem,
Contentum solito perire amore?
Non sum cui placeant simul trecentae,
5 Non ego cupio hanc et hanc et illam:
Primus ardor et ultimus Neaera est.
Tu, siquid tibi, Avita, cordis usquam est,
Si me audis, eadem roga volentem
Optantemque, libet rogare quando
10 Nos uri sine mutuis favillis:
Nam miserrimum amare non amantem est.

XLVI. *Ad Antonium principem Salernitanum*

Quod regni, quod opum, largi quod nominis heres,
    Fortunae, Antoni, non leve munus habes:
At quod perpetui cultor generosus honesti es,
    Ingenuo debes, quicquid id, ingenio.

XLVII. *De Iacobo quarto Appiano*

Quartum rogabam leucophaeam mutuam:
    Donavit ille coccina.
'Non' inquam 'adeo beatus est vates tuus!'
    'Nec tam ipse' respondit 'miser.'
5 At cur rogavi, quam daret, non crederet,
    'Quod nec dii' ait 'credant mihi.'

XLIV. To Actius Sincerus

You wonder, Actius, why Linus says nothing about his father: his mother, Nape, didn't tell him who he was.

XLV. To Avita

Why do you weary me, Avita, endlessly pursuing me in vain, when I remain faithless and inconstant, content to pine away for my customary love? I am not one who has hundreds of lovers at the same time. I don't love this one and that one and that other one. 5
Neaera is my first and last passion. Avita, if you have any feelings at all, if you will listen to me, make overtures to someone who wants and desires the same things as you do, whenever you feel like it. I too am scorched with desire without any return of affec- 10
tion: for it is the height of misery to love someone who does not love you.

XLVI. To Antonio, Prince of Salerno[44]

That you are the heir of dominion, of great wealth and of a noble line, Antonio, is no small gift of Fortune, but that you are a paragon of unending generosity and moral rectitude is owed totally to your own inherent qualities.

XLVII. Concerning Jacopo Appiano IV [45]

I asked Quartus to lend me an ash-colored cloak.[46] Instead he made me the gift of a scarlet one. I said, "Your poet is not so wealthy." "And I am not so cheap," he replied. But I asked why he 5

O digna, Quarte, vox tuis virtutibus,
    Notanda cunctis saeculis,
Qui vim deorum principes sequi mones,
10   Quorum vicem inter nos gerunt!

XLVIII. *Consolatio ad Andream Matthaeum Aquavivium*
de morte Iulii patris

Nuntia fama patris ad nos pervenit adempti,
    Protinus et lacrimas visa novare meas:
Nec tua tam, fateor, quam me mala publica tangunt
    Et subit Hesperii flenda ruina soli.
5 Occidit Ausonidum vir nulli laude secundus,
    Sive velis belli seu magis arte togae.
Ille dies primum metuendos reddidit hostes,
    Et cecidit Latiae gloria militiae.
Vidi ego confusas peditumque equitumque catervas
10   Rorantes oculos vix bene tollere humo,
Et modo militiam, modo deplorare Latinum
    Nomen et erepti iura fidemque ducis,
Et voluisse mori, nec te, fortissime Iuli,
    Amisso vilem continuisse animam.
15 Quid tibi nunc tot pulsi hostes, tot moenia prosunt
    Diruta, quid titulis fulcta superba domus,
Quid Ligurum devictae acies, quid Gallica signa
    Partaque pugnaci gloria rara manu?
Non minus, infestos medius deprensus in hostes,
20   Dum tibi turpe putas cedere mille viris,
Occidis, heu, titulis saevi accessurus Achumi.
    Me miserum, quantum nex dedit una mali!
At pia pro patria, pro dis arisque tuendis,
    Indueras Latium, dux, caput arma tibi

did not lend it to me rather than give it to me as a gift. He said, "Because the gods do not lend things to me either." Quartus, these words are worthy of your virtues, to be acclaimed by all ages, since you warn princes to emulate the authority of the gods, whose role 10 they play among us.

XLVIII. Consolation for Andrea Matteo Acquaviva on the death of his father, Giulio [47]

News has reached us that you have lost your father,[48] and immediately my tears were renewed. I must confess that it is not so much the evil that befell you as the general disaster that touches me, and the tragic desolation of the Hesperian land rises up in my mind. An Italian second to none in the art of war as in the art of peace 5 has died. That day for the first time made us stand in fear of the enemy, and the glory of Italian armed forces perished. I saw the confused ranks of foot soldiers and cavalry barely able to lift their 10 tear-filled eyes from the ground, and I saw them mourning the loss of military might, the Latin name and the authority and honor of their leader who was taken from them, and they wished to die, and with you lost, courageous Giulio, they did not wish to go on living a life of little value. Of what use to you now are the 15 defeat of so many enemies, the demolishing of so many walls? Of what use is a proud household, bolstered by so many honors? Of what use the defeated army of the Ligurians, the French banners and the exceptional glory won with a band of fierce-fighting troops? Nonetheless, caught in the midst of the menacing enemy forces, and deeming it disgraceful to yield to a thousand men, you 20 perished, alas! adding to the triumphs of cruel Achmed.[49] Woe is me! How much evil a single death procured for me! But you, great Italian general, had taken up righteous arms to defend the country,

25 Ultoresque deos iurata in bella trahebas,
　　Si modo sunt curae iusque piumque deis.
　Sed neque fas neque iura deos mortalia tangunt,
　　Et rapit arbitrio sors fera cuncta suo.
　Nam quid prisca fides iuvit pietasque Pelasgos?
30　　Nempe iacent nullo damna levante deo.
　Aspice Byzanti quondam gratissima divis
　　Moenia, Romanae nobile gentis opus.
　Haec quoque iam pridem hostili data praeda furori est,
　　Solaque de tanta gloria gente manet.
35 Vivit honos, vivunt benefacta virumque labores,
　　Et fugit hostiles fama decusque rogos.
　Sic tua longinquum late diffusa per aevum
　　Nomina per gentes fama loquetur anus,
　Certatimque canent docti tua gesta poetae
40　　Factaque erunt populis dictaque nota tua.
　Hic verus virtutis honos, haec digna laborum
　　Praemia magnanimis iure petenda viris.
　Parcite praeclarum funus violare querendo:
　　Hostibus eveniant funera lenta meis,
45 Hostibus eveniat molli tabescere lecto,
　　Amplexus inter foemineosque mori!
　Arma viros caedesque decent; quid tempora vitae
　　Natalesque viri connumerare iuvat?
　Sat vixit, siquem vitae non poenitet actae;
50　　Laudibus et fama longa petenda dies.
　Nil magis est certum summa mortalibus hora,
　　Serius aut citius una terenda via est.
　Quid fraudare iuvat momento temporis aevum?
　　Sera licet, nunquam est sera futura dies.
55 Optima pars vitae supremo ex funere pendet;
　　Felix cuicunque est fas bene posse mori.
　Quod siquis casusque hominum seriemque laborum

the gods and the altars, and you led vengeful gods into a legitimate   25
war, if only justice and piety were a matter of concern to the gods.
But neither divine law nor human rights touch the gods, and fierce
fate carries off all things at will. Of what benefit to the Pelasgians[50]
were their ancient faith and piety? They lie prostrate with no god   30
to alleviate their losses. Look at the walls of Byzantium, at one
time most dear to the gods, a noble work of the Roman people.
They too have long since fallen prey to the enemy's violence, and
of such a great people only their glory remains. Honor lives on,   35
and good deeds, and men's labors, and fame and glory escape the
enemy's conflagrations. So fame in future years will tell of your
name widely diffused among nations for ages to come, and poets
will rival one another to sing of your exploits and your deeds and   40
words will be known to all people. This is the true honor accruing
to virtue, these are the worthy awards of great struggles, justly
sought by men of noble spirit. Refrain from profaning a glorious
death with lamentations; let a long drawn-out death be the fate of
my enemies, let it be the lot of my enemies to waste away in a soft   45
bed and die in the embraces of women. Arms and death by the
sword befit real men. What good is it to count the years of a life-
time or successions of birthdays? He has lived long enough who
does not regret the life he has led; a lifetime rich in fame and   50
praise is to be desired. Nothing is more certain than man's last
hour; sooner or later one path must be trod. What use is it to
defraud life of a moment of time? Late as it may be, the day that
is to come is never too late. The best part of life depends on the   55
last day; happy is he who has the good fortune of dying well. If
one considers life's experiences and the sequence of toils and the

Cogitet et vitae tot mala damna brevis,
Iam primos mecum ille ortus, non ultima flenda
60   Tempora mortali sentiet esse viro.
Debita naturae mors est: quid pectora planctu
Concutis? invidiam parce movere deis.
Parce, precor, Matthaee, modumque impone dolori;
Ingenium luctus dedecet iste tuum.
65 At non sic Tynichusque senex Spartanaque natum
Flevit. Eris molli mollior ipse nuru?
Si tibi consultum non is, at consule fratri,
Consule amicitiis coniugioque tuo.
Aspice qui populi, quis te circumspicit ordo,
70   Imposita est humeris sarcina quanta tuis.
Sume animos, nec te vaesano trade dolori,
Et populis tandem da sua iura tuis.
Da populis sua iura tuis terrisque beatus
Vive diu: meruit quae pater astra tenet.

XLIX. Ad Neaeram

Non tot Attica mella, littus algas,
Montes robora, ver habet colores,
Non tot tristis hyems riget pruinis,
Autumnus gravidis tumet racemis,
5 Non tot spicula Medicis pharetris,
Non tot signa micant tacente nocte,
Non tot aequora piscibus natantur,
Non aer tot aves habet serenus,
Non tot Oceano moventur undae,
10 Non tantus numerus Lybissae arena,
Quot suspiria, quot, Neaera, pro te
Vaesanos patior die dolores.

multitude of evils of our brief life, he will agree with me that it
is mortal man's first beginnings, not his last day that must be   60
mourned. Death is owed to nature. Why do you beat your breast
in lamentation? Avoid provoking the ill will of the gods. Desist, I
pray you, Matteo, and put a limit to your sorrow; mourning does
not become your nature. Old Tynichus[51] and the Spartan woman[52]   65
did not mourn their son in this way: will you be softer than a soft
woman? If you do not wish to take thought for yourself, be mind-
ful of your brother, think of your friends and your wife. Observe
what peoples and what social classes are looking at you, how great   70
a burden has been placed on your shoulders. Take heart, and do
not abandon yourself to frenzied sorrow and, I beg of you, give
your people their just rights and live long and happily upon the
earth: your father has the place he merited among the stars.

XLIX. To Neaera

Attica has less honey, the seashore less algae, the mountains fewer
oaks, the spring colors, gloomy winter is not so stiff with hoar-
frost, nor does autumn burst forth with as many heavy clusters of
grapes; there are not as many arrows in Median[53] quivers or con-   5
stellations shining in the silent night, not as many fish swimming
in the seas, nor as many birds in the cloudless sky, nor waves stir-
ring Ocean's depths, nor are the sands of Libya as numerous as the   10
sighs, O Neaera, and the frenzied sorrows that I suffer for you in
a single day.

L. De Euphrosynea

Quicquid agit, Veneres agit Euphrosynea; sed hae me
    Dispeream si non disperimunt Veneres.
Nam quotiens video, totiens et pectus et ipsum
    Cor silet et totus deficio ac pereo.

LI. Ad Gemmam

Qui dedit Aiaci, Thesidae, Protesilao,
    Ille dedit nomen, lucida Gemma, tibi.
Nam neque fulgidior neque te formosior ulla est,
    Quaeque hominum possit corda movere magis.
5 Iure igitur Gemma es, quod si tibi displicet illud,
    Dum dea, vel Pallas vel magis esto Venus.

LII. Epitaphium Euphrosynes Tarchaniotae matris

'Quaenam hoc in tumulo tegitur matrona?' 'Venustas.'
    Ille Pudicitiam dixerat; haec eadem est.
'Quod genus?' 'Inachidi.' 'Generis fortuna?' 'Beata,
    Sed cecidit patria deficiente sua.'
5 'Quis torus?' 'Unus, et hic felix sine lite Marulli.'
    'An mater?' 'Seno pignore fecit avum.'
'Quae vita?' 'In tenebris.' 'Quae causa indigna doloris?'
    'Occasus patriae servitiumque grave.'
'Ecquem cum patria luxit?' 'Fratresque patremque,
10   Sed quas felices diceret esse animas.'
Felices nimirum animae, sed enim haec quoque felix,
    Foemina tam rari pectoris in patriam.

L. *Concerning Euphrosynea*

Whatever she does, Euphrosynea stirs up sexual desires; but I'll be damned, I swear, if these desires are not the death of me. Every time I see her, my mind and my heart itself grow silent and I faint away and die utterly.

LI. *To Gemma*

He who gave a name to Ajax, Hippolytus and Protesilaus[54] gave a name to you, radiant Gemma. For there is no one more radiant or beautiful than you, and who can more touch the hearts of men. Rightly therefore are you Gemma, but if that does not please you,   5 as a goddess, be either Pallas Athena or, preferably, Venus.

LII. *Epitaph of his mother, Euphrosyne Tarchaniota*[55]

"What woman is buried in this tomb?" "Loveliness." He had said Chastity, which is the same thing. "What race?" "Greek." "What was the Fortune of her race?" "Happy, but she died when her country was dying." "What was her married state?" "She had one   5 husband, Marullus, without discord." "Was she a mother?" "She had six children." "What kind of a life did she lead?" "A life of obscurity." "What was the cause of her undeserved sorrow?" "The fall and heavy servitude of her country." "Did she mourn anyone together with her country?" "Brothers and sisters and a father, but   10 she said their souls were blessed." Undoubtedly they were blessed souls, but her soul is also blessed, a woman who loved her country dearly.

LIII. De Neaera

Viderat intactam nuper Venus alma Neaeram,
    Et puero 'Cessant quid tua spicula?' ait.
Cui deus humentes lacrimis deiectus ocellos,
    'Spicula' ait, 'mater, quae tenet illa, refers.'

LIV. Ad sodales

Laure, Compater, Altili, Elisi, Aeli,
Parde, Phosphore, Rhalle, Zenobi, Acci,
Pontane, unanimi mei sodales,
Quam bene est mihi cum mea Thalia,
5 Quam mecum bene rursus est Thaliae!
Ambo dulciculi, venustuli ambo,
Ambo lusibus erudituli isdem,
Isdem moribus educatuli ambo,
Fortunae pariter malignae uterque,
10 Quam neuter tamen aestimat caballi,
Ut qui me videt, hanc putet videre.

LV. Ad Manilium Rhallum

Foenerat, et levis Endymion tibi, Rhalle, videtur:
    Crede mihi, nimis est hic homo, Rhalle, gravis.

LVI. De Mnestheo

Matrem rogatus faceret an patrem pluris
    Iphicrate satus nobili,
'Matrem' inquit: 'haec enim Atticum edidit, Graecus
    Quem voluerat Thracem pater.'

LIII. *Concerning Neaera*

Kindly Venus recently saw Neaera unharmed and said to her son, "Why are your arrows idle?" To which the god, casting his tearful eyes on the ground, answered, "Mother, the arrows you refer to are in her possession."

LIV. *To my companions*

Lorenzo,[56] Compatre,[57] Altilio,[58] Elisio,[59] Elia,[60] Pardo,[61] Lucido,[62] Rhallus,[63] Zanobi,[64] Actius,[65] Pontano,[66] my fellow comrades, how well things are going for me with my Thalia, and likewise 5 how well things are going for Thalia with me! We are a delightful and lovable pair, both of us reasonably adept at the same amorous sports, both possessed of the same morals, each of us equally the victims of spiteful Fortune, whom neither of us considers of 10 any importance. So alike are we that whoever sees me thinks he sees her.

LV. *To Manlius Rhallus*

Endymion is a moneylender and he seems to you to be a man of little importance: believe me, Rhallus, this man is not to be treated lightly.

LVI. *Concerning Mnestheus*[67]

Born of noble Iphicrates,[68] Mnestheus was asked whether he valued his mother or his father more. He answered, "My mother, for she gave birth to an Athenian, whom my Greek father had wished to be a Thracian."

LVII. *Epitaphium L. Crassi Neapolitani*

Lustrabas, dum vita fuit, vagus advena terras,
    Scilicet antiquae, Crasse, memor patriae.
Nunc functus vitaque hominumque laboribus aegris,
    Protinus in veram rursus abis patriam.

LVIII. *Ad Neaeram*

Iuravi fore me tuum perenne,
Per me, per caput hoc, per hos ocellos,
Qui te disperiere contuendo,
Per quod plurima cor tulit dolenda.
5 'Haec' inquis 'mea sunt.' 'Tua ista sunto!'
At certe lacrimae meae, Neaera,
Quas iuro fore me tuum perenne.

LIX. *De Amore*

'Quis puer hic?' 'Veneris.' 'Plenae quae causa pharetrae est?'
    'Non bene provisus certa quod arma movet.'
'Cur sine veste deus?' 'Simplex puer odit opertum.'
    'Unde puer?' 'Pueros quod facit ipse senes.'
5 'Quis pennas humeris dedit?' 'Inconstantia.' 'Quare
    Nulla deo frons est?' 'Signa inimica fugit.'
'Quae sors eripuit lucem?' 'Immoderata libido.'
    'Cur macies?' 'Vigilis cura dolorque facit.'
'Quis caecum praeit?' 'Ebrietas, Sopor, Otia, Luxus.'
10 'Qui comites?' 'Rixae, Bella, Odia, Obprobrium.'
'Qui coelo dignati?' 'Homines.' 'Quae causa coegit?'
    'Mitior auctore est credita culpa deo.'

LVII. Epitaph of Lucius Crassus Neapolitanus[69]

You traversed the world as a wandering stranger while you had life, mindful, of course, Crassus, of your ancient native land. Now having completed your life and the troublesome labors of mortals, you return again directly to your true native land.

LVIII. To Neaera

I swore that I would be yours forever, by my life, by this head, by these eyes, which have perished in contemplating you, by my heart, which has suffered so many sorrows. But you say, "These 5 things are mine." "They may be yours, but surely these tears are mine, Neaera, by which I swear that I shall be yours forever."

LIX. On Love

"Who is this child?" — "The son of Venus." — "Why is his quiver full?" — "So that he can draw out his unerring arrows on the spur of the moment." — "Why does the god have no clothing?" — "As a simple child he hates being covered up." — "Why is he a child?" — "Because he makes old men into children." — "Who put wings on 5 his shoulders?" — "Inconstancy." — "Why does the god not have a godly mien?" — "He avoids giving unfriendly signals." — "What fate took away his sight?" — "Immoderate passion." — "Why is he so emaciated?" — "The anxiety and distress of sleepless nights causes it." — "Who guides the blind child?" — "Drunkenness, Sleep, Leisure, Soft Living." — "Who are his companions?" — 10 "Quarrels, Wars, Hatred, Opprobrium." — "Who made him worthy of heaven?" — "Mankind." — "What made them do this?" — "Guilt was believed to be lighter when a god was responsible."

Heu, curvum genus et veri corda inscia: quo ius
    Fasque, scelus miseri si scelere abluimus?

LX. De Neaera

Mutatum, visa Phorcinide, credite Phineum:
    Res antiqua, tamen teste probata suo est.
Nec iam vana putet veterum miracula quisquam.
    Ipse ego cum visa dirigeam domina,
5   Mens tamen et veteris remanent incendia mentis:
    Sic etiam Niobe flet lapis in Sipylo.

LXI. Ad Neaeram

Puella mure delicatior Scytha
    Foliive serici comis
Vel educata rure Pestano rosa
    Vel anseris pluma levi,
5   Eademque duris dura cautibus magis,
    Quas tundit hibernum mare,
Cum nubilosis Africus pennis gravis,
    Saevit Ligustico sinu,
Remitte cor, siquis pudor, mihi meum,
10 Quod mille cepisti dolis —
Dum nunc ocello dulce subrides nigro,
    Nunc fronte spem certa facis —
Quod nunc habes in vinculis quasi Syrum
    Aut comparatum Sarmatam.
15 Verum remitte, dura, non ultra tuum:
    Iam enim rogat melior sibi,
Quae nos ocellis diligit suis magis,
    Neque hoc neque illud imputat.
An tu putabas scilicet firmum tibi

Alas! perverse race and hearts ignorant of the truth, what is the use of natural and divine law if we miserable creatures wash away crime with crime?

LX. *Concerning Neaera*

Believe that Phineus[70] was changed after he saw Medusa. It is an ancient tale, but it was proved by a witness. Let no one think that ancient miracles are false, since I myself at the sight of my mistress become rigid as stone; but memory and the fires of the old feelings 5 remain: so also Niobe weeps, a stone in Sipylus.[71]

LXI. *To Neaera*

Young maiden, more delicate than a Scythian mouse or the bloom the Chinese gather from the trees[72] or a rose cultivated in the Paestum countryside or the light feather of a goose, and yet harder 5 than the hard crags buffeted by the wintry sea, when the southwest wind, heavy with its cloudy wings, rages in the Ligurian gulf, give me back my heart, if you have any sense of shame, which you 10 stole from me with a thousand stratagems—at one time sweetly smiling with your dark eyes, at another time giving me hope with an assuring glance—the heart you now hold in chains like a Syrian or Sarmatian[73] slave. Give it back to me, hard-hearted girl, for 15 it is no longer yours. Someone better than you asks for it, who loves me more than her very eyes and does not accuse me of this or that fault. Or did you think perhaps that I would always remain

20   Tot barbare affectum modis?
      Quanquam beati centies et amplius,
        Siquos tenaci compede
      Quae prima vix dum puberes iunxit fides,
        Eadem extulit pios senes!

LXII. Ad Quintilianum

    Quod nimium castus liber est nimiumque pudicus,
      Displicet; ingenium, Quintiliane, probas.
    Gratulor ingenio quantum sinis, heus age, sed dic:
      Cur tibi non adeo carmina casta placent?
5   Casta placent Phoebo, castissima turba sororum est,
      Casta pios vates Pieriosque decent.
    Nos quoque casta movent, quamvis distamus ab illis,
      Et vetat ingenuus verba inhonesta pudor.
    Tu licet huc Marsumque feras doctumque Catullum
10   Et quoscunque alios Martia Roma legit,
    Non tamen efficies, ut Phrynae scribere malim,
      Quam tibi vel turbae, Laodamia, tuae,
    Et tamen haec possunt Phrynae quoque grata videri,
      Illa nisi Phrynae displicitura palam est.
15   Sit procul a nobis obscoena licentia scripti;
      Ludimus innocuae carmina mentis opus,
    Utque nec arma virum nec magni orientia coeli
      Signa nec immensum mundi aperimus opus —
    Quid pluat, unde homines, quae vis maria inficit alta,
20   An Deus, an Manes, an Flegethontis aquae —
    Sic iuvat in tenui legem servare pudori
      Et quae non facimus dicere facta pudet.
    Sit satis auratos crines laudare Neaerae,
      Sit satis in duram multa queri dominam

faithful to you after such barbarous treatment? And yet, happy a   20
hundredfold and more are those whom the same loyal bond joined
at first, with tenacious shackle, in their youth, and carried off to
the grave in their pious old age.

LXII. *To Quintilian*

You are displeased, Quintilian, that my book is too chaste and too
modest, but you commend my poetic talent. I am glad that you
approve of the poetic talent, but come now, tell me, why do you
not like chaste poems? Chaste things are pleasing to Apollo, and   5
the Muses Nine are most chaste; chaste things are becoming to
true poets and those devoted to the Muses. Chaste things move us
also although we are distant from them, and an inborn modesty
prohibits unseemly words. If you reply by mentioning Marsus[74]
or the learned Catullus and whatever other poets martial Rome   10
reads, you will not persuade me to write for Phryne[75] rather than
for Laodamia[76] and those many others like her. And yet these
things can also appeal to Phryne, whereas those other poems will
displease everyone except Phryne, that is certain. Let obscene li-   15
cense in writing be far from us; we write love poetry that is the
product of an innocent mind. We do not sing of arms and the
man nor of the constellations that arise in the great heavens or the
immense fabric of the firmament, what causes rain, what is man's
origin, what force dyes the deep sea, whether there is a god, or the   20
spirits of the dead or the waters of Phlegethon,[77] but find pleasure
in preserving the rules of simple modesty, and we are ashamed to
say that we have done things that we do not do. Let it be enough
to praise the golden tresses of Neaera, to make much complaint

25　Et facere iratum saevo convitia Amori,
　　　Nec nisi de Scythica credere rupe satum.
　　Caetera Thespiadum prohibet chorus. Haec ego. Phoebus
　　　Annuit et sanctis ora rigavit aquis.

LXIII. Ad Manilium Rhallum

Non vides verno variata flore
Tecta, non postes viola revinctos?
Stat coronatis viridis iuventus
　　Mixta puellis.

5　Concinunt Maias pueri Kalendas,
Concinunt senes bene feriati,
Omnis exultat locus, omnis aetas
　　Laeta renidet.

Ipse, reiectis humero capillis,
10 Candet in palla crocea Cupido,
Acer et plena iaculis pharetra,
　　Acer et arcu.

Et modo huc circumvolitans et illuc,
Nectit optatas iuvenum choreas,
15 Artibus notis alimenta primo
　　Dum parat igni.

Nunc puellaris medius catervae
Illius flavum caput illiusque
Comit et vultus oculisque laetum
20　Addit honorem.

Mitte vaesanos, bone Rhalle, questus;
Iam sat indultum patriae ruinae est.
Nunc vocat lusus positisque curis
　　Blanda voluptas.

against my harsh mistress and utter angry rebuke against cruel   25
Love and believe that he was born of Scythian rock. Other things
the chorus of Muses prohibits. Such were my words. Apollo nod-
ded assent and bathed my countenance with sacred waters.[78]

LXIII. To Manilius Rhallus

Don't you see the houses adorned with colorful spring flowers, and
the doors wreathed with violets? Lusty youths stand next to gar-
landed young girls. The children sing May Day songs, and the old   5
men in festive mood join in the singing, everywhere there is exul-
tation, every age of life beams with joy. Cupid himself, his hair
streaming over his shoulders, is resplendent in a saffron-colored   10
mantle, a vibrant figure with his quiver full of arrows and his bow
ready. And flying about hither and yon, he links the young couples
in the longed-for dances, while with his well-known arts he pre-   15
pares fuel for the first flames of love. Then, entering into the midst
of the maiden throng, he arranges the blond locks of one girl and
adorns the visage of another and adds a joyous grace to their eyes.   20
Cease from your mad laments, my good Rhallus; we have wept
enough over the ruin of our country. Now amorous sport and

25   Quid dies omnis miseri querendo
      Perdimus dati breve tempus aevi?
      Sat mala laeti quoque sorte, coelum hoc
         Hausimus olim.

      Profer huc cadum, puer Hylle, trimum,
30   Cedat et moeror procul et dolores.
      Tota nimirum Genio mihique
         Fulserit haec lux!

Liber Secundus

I.

Cum tot vasa, aurum, vestes Fortuna ministret,
      Haec dare, Laure, tibi, maxima stultitia est.
Cur igitur vati — dices — mea carmina mitto?
      Nempe dare est aliud et celebrare aliud.

II. Ad Neaeram

Ignitos quotiens tuos ocellos
In me, vita, moves, repente qualis
Cera defluit impotente flamma
Aut nix vere novo calente sole,
5 Totis artubus effluo, nec ulla
Pars nostri subitis vacat favillis.
Tum qualis tenerum caput reflectens
Succumbit rosa verna liliumve,
Quod dono cupidae datum puellae
10 Furtivis latuit diu papillis,

sweet pleasures invite us to lay aside our cares. Why do we con- 25
sume every day in misery, complaining and wasting this brief time
that has been given us? We have been happy enough even in our
ill fortune once we breathed in the air of these climes. Bring here
the cask of three-year-old wine, Hyllus, and may grief and sadness 30
depart far from us. This whole day will undoubtedly shine on me
and my Genius.

Book II

I.

Although Fortune hands out vases, gold and clothes, to give these
things to you, Lorenzo, would be the greatest stupidity. "Why,
then," you ask, "do I send my poems to a poet?" Obviously it is
one thing to give and another to celebrate.

II. To Neaera

Whenever you turn your flaming eyes toward me, my life, sud-
denly like wax that melts on contact with a raging flame or snow
under the rays of the warm spring sun, I feel my limbs melting 5
away, and no part of me remains, suddenly turned into ashes.
Then as a spring rose, reclining its tender corolla, sinks to the
earth, or like the lily that I gave as a present to a passionate young
girl, which remained for a long time hidden in her bosom, so my 10

Ad terram genibus feror remissis,
Nec mens est mihi nec color superstes
Et iam nox oculis oberrat atra,
Donec vix gelida refectus unda,
15 Ut quod vulturio iecur resurgit,
Assuetis redeam ignibus cremandus.

III. De Pasiphae

Cum male formosum sequeretur in avia taurum,
    Sic Venerem contra Gnosia questa feram est:
'Si mihi bos fuerat, dea, vir te dante futurus,
    Cur non insanae Proetidos ora dabas?'

IV. Ad Neaeram

Suaviolum invitae rapio dum, casta Neaera,
    Imprudens vestris liqui animam in labiis,
Exanimusque diu, cum nec per se ipsa rediret
    Et mora lethalis quantulacunque foret,
5 Misi cor quaesitum animam; sed cor quoque blandis
    Captum oculis nunquam deinde mihi rediit.
Quod nisi suaviolo flammam quoque, casta Neaera,
    Hausissem, quae me sustinet exanimum,
Ille dies misero, mihi crede, supremus amanti
10   Luxisset, rapui cum tibi suaviolum.

V. De Maximiliano Caesare

Rex, legum iurisque dator placidaeque quietis,
    Ceperat hostili percitus arma dolo,
Iamque truces bello Morinos concusserat acri
    Et dederat famulas Tabula victus aquas,

knees are slackened, and I fall to the ground and lose consciousness and there is no color left in me, and dark night hovers before my eyes, until barely revived by a dash of cold water, like Prometheus's liver, which grew back to be devoured by the vulture, I return to be burned by the usual flames. 15

III. Concerning Pasiphaë[1]

When she was following the fatally beautiful bull into the wilderness, the woman from Knossos complained about the wild beast to Venus: "If the bull was to play the role of a man by your gift, O goddess, why didn't you give me the face of a mad daughter of Proteus?"[2]

IV. To Neaera

As I was snatching a kiss from you against your will, O chaste Neaera, unwittingly I left my soul upon your lips and I remained unconscious for a long time. When it did not return on its own and even the slightest delay might prove fatal, I sent my heart in 5 search of my soul; but my heart too, captured by your sweet glances, has never returned to me since. If I had not also absorbed with that kiss the flame that sustains my lifeless body, chaste Neaera, that day, believe me, when I snatched that kiss from you, 10 would have been the last to shine upon this hapless lover.[3]

V. Concerning Emperor Maximilian

The king,[4] giver of laws and rights and quiet peace, stirred to action by a hostile plot, had taken up arms, and had already struck down the fierce Morini[5] in a bitter war and the conquered Scheldt[6]

5   Cum subito fractosque animi veniamque precantes
     Non tulit ulterius mens generosa viri
   Inque fidem et veteris accepit foedera pacis,
     Nil ultra victus quod dare posset erat!
   Quaerenti hostilem gentem cur perdere nollet,
10   Rettulit: 'Ut victis parcere saepe queam.'

VI. De fortitudine Lacaenae

Mater Lacaena conspicata filium
   Relicta inermem parmula,
Progressa contra traiicit ferro latus,
   Super necatum his increpans:
5 'Abi hinc, morere, non digna me proles, abi,
   Mentite patriam et genus!'

VII. Epitaphium Aurae

'Quaenam haec pompa?' 'Aurae.' 'Quis circum planctus?'
   'Amorum.'
   'Quae tam lugubri veste adoperta?' 'Charis.'
'Unde rogus?' 'Fracti struxere Cupidinis arcus.'
   'Quis simul indigno qui iacet igne?' 'Decor.'
5 Heu, sortem miserandam hominum, quo fastus inanis?
   Delitias aevi tam brevis hora tulit.

VIII. Ad Neaeram

Quo te depereo magis magisque,
Odisti magis et magis, Neaera,
Nec te noster amor movet precesque
Nec vides fieri tuo periclo,

had offered its waters to serve him, when suddenly the generous 5
soul of the man could no longer bear the broken spirit of the van-
quished, who begged for mercy, and he took them into his confi-
dence and accepted the terms of a previous peace.[7] He only admit-
ted defeat when there was nothing else he could give! To someone
who asked him why he was unwilling to destroy a hostile people
he replied, "So that I may often be able to spare the conquered." 10

VI. On the fortitude of a Spartan woman[8]

A Spartan mother, seeing her son return unharmed, after having
abandoned his shield on the battlefield, advancing toward him
thrust a sword into his side, uttering these reproaches over his
dead body: "Away from here, die, offspring unworthy of me; away, 5
you have betrayed your country and your race!"

VII. Epitaph of Aura

"Whose funeral procession is this?" — "Aura's." — "Whose lamen-
tations are these?" — "Of the Cupids." — "Who is that covered in
mourning garments?" — "One of the Graces." — "Whence came
the funeral pyre?" — "It was built with Cupid's broken bows." —
"Who is that who lies together with her in the unmerited fire?" —
"Beauty."
    Alas, O pitiful fate of mankind, what good is empty pride? 5
Such a brief hour has taken away the favorite of our age.

VIII. To Neaera

The more I die for you, the more you hate me, Neaera, and
my love and my prayers do not move you, and you do not see

5 Quam necem mihi scilicet minaris.
Non, non sum meus amplius, Neaera:
Ut iam dispeream, tuus peribo!

IX. Ad Antonium principem Salernitanum

Tanta tua est probitas, cor, virtus, gratia formae,
    Ut credam Curium, Nestora, Achillea, Hylam;
Nec tamen aut Curius quod tu nec Nestor Hylasve est,
    Quique suis victor Hectora traxit equis.
5 Sic modo par unus cunctis, ex omnibus unum
    Non potes, ut cupias, deligere ipse parem.

X. Ad Posthumum

Et sapiens et amans vis idem, Posthume, haberi:
    Posthume, vis idem desipere et sapere.

XI. Epitaphium Roberti Sanctoseverini principis Salernitani

Tu ne hic, Roberte, es? te ne haec tegit urna sepultum?
    An tantum fatis de te etiam licuit?
Tecum arma et paces, tecum splendorque decusque
    Spesque iacent regni praesidiumque tui.
5 At non et tecum fama est, quae plurima ubique
    Vivit et ex ipso funere maior adest:
Scilicet haec una est laudum mensura tuarum,
    Par tibi, par meritis sola reperta tuis.

XII. Ad Neaeram

Donec liber eram, Neaera, nec sic
Tota mollibus haeseras medullis,
Et centum simul hinc et hinc petebant,

that the death you are threatening me with involves your own risk. 5
No, I no longer belong to myself, Neaera; if I were to die at this
moment, I will die as yours.

IX. To Antonio, Prince of Salerno[9]

Such is your honesty, understanding, virtue, and graceful beauty
that I think of you as Curius,[10] Nestor,[11] Achilles and Hylas;[12] not,
however, that Curius or Nestor or Hylas is like you, or he who
victoriously dragged Hector with his horses. You alone are equal 5
to them only in the sense that you cannot choose any one or all of
them as your equal, no matter how much you would wish to do so.

X. To Postumus

You want to be considered both a wise man and a lover at the
same time, Postumus: Postumus, you want to be foolish and wise
at the same time.

XI. Epitaph of Roberto Sanseverino, Prince of Salerno[13]

Are you here, Roberto? Does this urn contain your mortal re-
mains? Did the fates have such power even over you? With you
war and peace, with you splendor and honor and hope and the
protection of your reign lie prostrate. But your fame is not with 5
you, but lives on abundantly everywhere and is even greater be-
cause of your death: evidently this is the only true measure of your
grandeur, the only thing found to be equal to you and to your
merits.

XII. To Neaera

As long as I was free, Neaera, and you were not so completely
stuck fast in my soft marrow, and a hundred women who could

Ipsum quae poterant Iovem movere,
5   Vixi carior omnibus medullis —
Nisi iam hoc quoque denegas — tuisque,
Qui nunc sic miserum necant, ocellis.
Heheu, tunc ubi fastus iste, ubi irae
Et vultus oculique saevientes,
10   Ubi cor prece nescium moveri?
Nunc captum semel artibus, Neaera,
Cum nulla amplius est fugae potestas,
Cogis, ah, decies perire in hora,
Nec quicquam miseret mei doloris.
15   Nam quo me referam? quis ah, quis, heheu,
Eiectum alterius sinu petisset?
Quis, o, adiuvet? unde opem rogabo?
Quis praesto mihi erit, Neaera, si tu
Quaeris perdere, quae beare debes?

XIII. *Epitaphium Luciae Phoebes*

Lucebas superis, mea Lucia, lucida Phoebe:
At nunc Persephone tertia regna tenes.

XIV. *Ad Aeglen*

Sollicitus siquis visus, tibi displicet, Aegle,
Segnior, indigni nomen amantis habet;
Hic, quia non queritur, ficti simulator amoris,
Ille dolet, famae causa maligna tuae est;
5   Qui non magna dedit formosae munera, avarus,
Displicet hic donis muneribusque suis.
Non tot, crede mihi, Proteus mutatur in ora:
Hei mihi, quam placeam ne prius emoriar!

move Jupiter himself pursued me on every side, I was more en- 5
deared to all hearts and—unless you deny this too—dearer in
your own eyes, which now annihilate me in my misery. Alas!
Where was that haughtiness then, and that wrath, those savage
looks, where was your heart that refuses to be moved by any 10
prayer? Now that I have been captured by your wiles, Neaera,
when I no longer have the power to escape, you force me, ah! to
perish ten times in an hour, and take no pity on my suffering.
Where shall I seek refuge? Alas! who would ever seek out some- 15
one who has been repudiated by another woman? Who will help
me? From whom shall I seek aid? Who will be at my side, Neaera,
if you seek to undo me, you who ought to give me happiness?

XIII. Epitaph of Lucia Phoebe

You gave light to the gods above, my Lucia, shining Phoebe: but
now, as Persephone, you rule the third kingdom.[14]

XIV. To Aegle

If anyone seems agitated, you don't like him, Aegle; if he is too
lethargic, he is labeled an unworthy lover; one who makes no com-
plaints is a false lover, another who suffers pain is responsible for
giving you a bad reputation; he who has not given valuable gifts to 5
a beautiful woman is miserly; another is disliked because he gives
gifts and presents. By my faith, not even Proteus changes into so
many forms! Woe is me! May I find favor with you before I die!

XV. De Caecubo

Dum vota supplex suscipit Iovi optimo
Vultuque recto fundit ad coelum preces,
Deos quiete nec sinit frui sua
Oculum reposcens Caecubus nepotulo,
5 Volantis ipse stercore e summo alitis
Utroque capitur. Nunc suo demum malo
Edoctus, optimum Iovem atque omnis deos
Coelo reliquit et sibi non amplius
Ipsi precatur quos prius nepotulo.

XVI. Ad Franciscum Ninum Senensem

Quid mirare unos non uno tempore vultus,
    Nec mea tam multis pectora victa malis?
Turpe est arbitrio rerum, Francisce, moveri
    Atque animum dominae supposuisse rotae
5 Exiliique malis rationem perdere vitae
    Et sinere incertis certa perire bona.
Non ego vel primus patior vel talia solus;
    Saepe premit magnos ista ruina viros,
Utque parum felix, certe sine crimine dicor.
10   Turpior est damno culpa pudenda suo.
Sic pius Aeneas, sic Teucer fugerat olim
    Et tamen in media vixit uterque fuga,
Nec puduit nimio linguam movisse Lyaeo
    Et madidam sertis implicuisse comam.
15 O quotiens moestos verbis solatus amicos,
    Miscuit haec dictis ille vel ille suis:
'Dum licet et fas est, vigilaces pellite curas,
    O mihi non vana cognita corda fide,
Nec vos aut moveant pelagique viaeque labores

XV. About Caecubus[15]

While in supplication Caecubus was offering vows to highest Jupiter and pouring forth prayers to heaven, his face upraised, and allowing the gods no peace, demanding back his grandson's eye, he is   5
struck in both eyes by the dung dropping down from a bird in flight. Having finally learned his lesson from the misfortune that befell him, he left highest Jupiter and all the gods to heaven and no longer offers prayers for himself to the gods to whom he had previously prayed for his grandson.

XVI. To Francesco Nino of Siena[16]

Why do you wonder that I preserve one unchanging attitude in times that are not unchanged, and that my courage does not falter in the face of many adversities? It is a shameful thing, Francesco, to be affected by the caprices of fortune and to subject one's soul to the mercy of the mistress of the wheel of fortune, and in the   5
midst of the evils of exile to lose one's purpose in life and allow blessings that are certain to perish because of life's uncertainties. I am neither the first nor the only one to suffer such things; often such disasters befall great men, and though I may have little good fortune, at least I can be declared to be without blame. Shameful   10
guilt is more dishonorable than personal loss. So pious Aeneas, so Teucer[17] once had to flee their native land and yet each of them lived in the midst of exile, and was not ashamed to loosen his tongue with deep drafts of wine and entwine his perfumed hair with garlands. How often both of them consoled their dejected   15
friends with words like these: "While it is lawful and permissible, drive away obsessive cares, O hearts known to me through your unfailing fidelity. Do not be disturbed by tribulations on sea and

20   Aut tangat patrii rustica cura soli.
    Quicquid ubique viris patria est, nec gloria vobis
        Tempora desidia perdere cara gravi.
    Iam quota pars rerum superat? Piget ante laborum
        Ultima perpessos, si leviora premunt.
25   His quoque finis erit, nec vos sperate perennem,
        Tam levis in toto quae volat orbe dea.'
    Dixit, et ingenti largus se proluit auro.
        Insequitur plausu caetera turba frequens
    Dulciaque apposito celebrant convivia Baccho
30   Corque deo curas dissoluuntque graves.
    Quamvis victus erat, quamvis miserandus et hosti,
        Squallidus impexis hirta per ora comis
    Carnifices Mariusque manus et terruit hostem.
        Victus et est victi victor ab ore ducis,
35   Nec, mendicato domita Carthagine pane,
        Magnanimi cecidit spiritus ille viri.
    Nos quoque, si magnis fas est componere parva,
        Omnia quis placida mente tulisse vetat?
    Si lacrimis redimi posset, si patria questu,
40   Arguerer, si non illa redempta foret.
    Nunc ea conditio gemitu est, ea lex data nostro,
        Utilis ut nulli sit noceatque mihi.
    Sparge, puer, violas et candida lilia . . . cessas?
        Lenia foecunda funde Falerna manu.
45   Ite procul, curae insomnes, procul ite, labores:
        Quantumcunque mali, si patiare, leve est.

XVII. Mortui pro patria

Inachii spes una soli, bis dena, viator,
    Milia in hoc tumulo cum patria tegimur,
Dum natosque patresque, larem patriamque tuemur,

land or be touched by a nostalgic solicitude for your native land. 20
Any place whatever is a native land for men of valor, and it is not
to your credit to waste precious time through oppressive idleness.
At this point how much time is left to us? We regret having suf-
fered perilous trials if matters of little consequence beset us. These 25
things will also have an end, but do not think the end will last
forever. The goddess who flies throughout the world is so incon-
stant."[18] His speech was followed by the applause of the crowded
assembly and he drank profusely from a huge gold goblet. And
they celebrated a joyful banquet with abundance of wine and dis- 30
solved their worries and cares in drink. Though he had been de-
feated and roused pity even among his enemies, reduced to squa-
lor, his matted hair scattered over his rough beard, Marius[19] stayed
the hand of his executioner and terrified the enemy, and the victor
was vanquished by the bearing of the vanquished general. And 35
when he was forced to beg his bread in defeated Carthage, the
spirit of that great-souled hero did not waver. And for us also, if
we can compare great with small, who forbids us to bear up with
everything with untroubled mind? If one could redeem his coun-
try by tears and lamentation, I would be proven guilty, if it were 40
not redeemed. But this condition and this law has been given to
our weeping, that it is not useful to anyone and is harmful to me.
Boy, scatter the violets and white lilies . . . do you hesitate? Pour
out the mild Falernian[20] with generous hand. Retreat far from me, 45
sleepless cares, away all travail! No matter how great the evil, if
you bear it patiently, it is light.

XVII. Those who died for their country

O passerby, we, the one hope of the land of Greece, twenty thou-
sand of us, are buried in this tomb with our native land. While we
were defending our children and our parents, our home and native

Imperioque ducis Tarchanii obsequimur.
5 Nam rex, indignus patriam qui protegat armis,
    Turpiter et regnum fugerat et patriam.

XVIII. De Iove et Amore

Lascivum iratus pater obiurgabat Amorem.
    Huic Amor: 'Europen quis, pater, orbis habet?'

XIX. Ad Amorem

'Cum tot tela die proterve spargas,
Tot figas sine fine et hic et illic
Infensus pariter viris deisque,
Nec unquam manus impotens quiescat,
5 Quis tot spicula, tot, puer, furenti
Lethales tibi sufficit sagittas?
Cum tot aethera questibus fatiges,
Tot spargas lacrimas et hic et illic
Infensus pariter viris deisque,
10 Nec unquam madidae genae serescant,
Quis suspiria crebra, quis dolenti
Tam longas tibi sufficit querelas?'
'At tu nec mihi tela, dum Neaera est,
Nec curas tibi crede defuturas.'

XX. Ad Iacobum quartum Appianum

Miraris quid moesta dies, quid turbidus aether,
    Cur tegat obscuris nubibus ora dies
Incubuitque freto subitis nox atra procellis
    Et querulum toto murmur in orbe sonat.
5 Digressu dant signa tuo — procul omen abesto! —
    Teque dolent patria tam procul ire tua.

land, we obeyed the commands of our leader, Tarchaniotes.[21] For   5
our king,[22] who was unworthy to protect his country by arms,
shamefully had fled both his kingdom and his native land.

XVIII. On Jupiter and Cupid

Enraged, Jupiter reprimanded lascivious Cupid. Cupid answered:
"Father, in what part of the world does Europa[23] dwell?"

XIX. To Love

"Since you impudently let fly so many arrows daily and unceas-
ingly transfix so many victims far and wide, a menace to men and
gods alike, and your uncontrolled hand never rests, who supplies   5
you, young child, with so many barbs and lethal arrows for your
frenzied forays? As you weary the airs with cries of complaint
and scatter tears far and wide, a menace to men and gods alike,
and cheeks drenched with tears never become dry, who supplies   10
you with constant sighs and prolonged complaints for the doleful
lover?" "You may be sure that while Neaera is around, I will not be
lacking in arrows nor you in cares."

XX. To Jacopo Appiano IV[24]

You wonder why it is a gloomy day, why the sky is stormy, why the
shore is covered with dark clouds and black night has descended
on the sea with sudden storms and a querulous murmuring re-
sounds through the whole world. They signal your departure —   5
depart, all evil omens! — and they are grieved that you are going

Hinc liquet et fratri et populo mens quae sit et urbi,
    Ipsa abitu cum sint mota elementa tuo.

XXI. In Censorium

Censorius, quod ipse nil agit prorsus
Quod optimo non iure debeat carpi,
Reprendit unumquenque. Sive quis mutit,
Seu quis tacet, seu ridet, ore seu moesto est,
5 Reprendit ille; sive quis dedit quicquam,
Sive accipit quis, seu timetve speratve,
Seu quis sedet, seu quis deambulat, seu quis
Quodcunque qualecunque qualitercunque
Ubicunque agit, reprendit: id homini est moris,
10 Si mos vocari tam evidens furor possit.
Atqui, si is esset hic novus Cato noster
Quem continentis optimus tenor vitae
Sanctique pigra tollerent humo mores,
Tamen reprendentem usquequaque quis ferret?
15 Nunc impudicus, helluo, vorax, mango,
Insulsus, aleo, improbus, salax, leno,
Cinaedulorum pessimum omnium fulcrum,
Bonos malosque iudicat sui oblitus.
O ante nullis cognitum nefas saeclis!

XXII. Epitaphium Iulii Aquavivi

Quam bene pro patria, Iuli, cadis, inclyte, si non
    Tecum etiam infelix concideret patria!

far away from your native land. From this it is clear what feelings your brother and the people and the city have for you, when the elements themselves are moved by your departure.

XXI. *Against Censorius*

Since Censorius does nothing at all not fully deserving of blame, he censures everyone. Whether someone murmurs, or is silent, or laughs, or is sad, he censures him; whether someone has given   5
something or received something, or fears, or hopes; whether one sits down, or walks around, or does anything at all of whatever kind or in whatever manner, he censures him. This is a habit with him, if one can call such mad behavior a habit. And yet, even if   10
this man were our new Cato,[25] whom an exceptional tenor of life marked by self-restraint and blameless morals set apart from this sluggish earth, who would put up with his faultfinding in every conceivable situation? But the fact is that he is shameless, a squan-   15
derer, voracious, a slave dealer, insipid, a gambler, presumptuous, lecherous, a pimp, a champion of all perverts, and completely blind to his own failings, judges both the good and the bad. O abomination never heard of in any former age!

XXII. *Epitaph of Giulio Acquaviva*[26]

What a fine thing that you fell for your native country, illustrious Giulio, if your unlucky country did not also fall with you!

XXIII. De Phyllide

Dixerat immitem Venerem, modo Phyllide rapta,
    Accius, invidiam quaesieratque deae.
Huic Amor: 'Immitem, quam fles, temerarie, dicis;
    Nanque eadem Phyllis, quae mea mater, erat.'

XXIV. In Linum

Cum possis, Line, conticere, scribis,
Et tibi veniam petis subinde
Tanquam durior infacetiorque
Et scriptor modo factus ex colono:
5   Scriptorem, Line, te novum sciebam,
Nunc primum scio teste te colonum.

XXV. Ad Petram

Et petra es, mea lux, et vere Petra vocaris,
    Et peream si quo nomine digna alio es.
Non tam quod Parium certas evincere marmor
    Et facies caeli rara videtur opus
5   Attritisque nitet corpus magis aequore saxis,
    Littore quae primo casta puella legit,
Quam quia Caucaseas vincunt tua pectora cautes
    Et quoscunque vides saxea signa facis.
Et tamen hic etiam vaesana incendia durant:
10   Me miserum, cinerem hoc, non facere est lapidem!

XXIII. On Phyllis

Actius[27] said that Venus was merciless when Phyllis was taken away from him, and he had earned the ill will of the goddess. Love answered him: "Thoughtless man, you try to say that the one for whom you weep is merciless; Phyllis was no different from my mother."

XXIV. Against Linus

Although you could keep silence, Linus, you write and often beg indulgence for yourself, pleading that you are rather slow-witted and boorish and recently became a writer after being a farmer. I   5
knew, Linus, that you were a new writer, now for the first time I know by your own admission that you are a farmer.

XXV. To Pietra[28]

You are a rock, my light, and are rightly called Pietra; and may I perish if any other name is worthy of you. Not so much because you strive to surpass Parian marble, or that your exquisite features seem to be the work of the chisel, or that your body is more re-   5
splendent than the stones smoothed and polished by the sea's waves that a chaste young girl gathers by the seaside, as because your heart is harder than the peaks of the Caucasus, and whomever you see you turn into a stone statue. And yet these mad fires continue to burn: that is turning poor me into ashes, not stone!   10

XXVI. Ad Accium Sincerum

Acci, quid piperi negas cucullos?
Quid scombri meruere, quid siluri?
Quare non sinis hunc et hunc et illum
Quidvis evomere improbum, infacetum,
5   Et thuri dare olivulisque vestem?
Rara, rara avis est bonus poeta,
Nec omnes tibi possumus placere.
An nescis Baviosque Meviosque?
Omni tempore Caesios habemus.
10   Haec licentia pessimis poetis
Iam pridem, vetus hoc genus veneni est.
An tu scilicet hos pati recusas,
Quos Maro tulit et tulit Catullus?

XXVII. De iubilaeo Antonii Petrutii

Quae modo per terras et longa per aequora vecti
    Quaerebant lasso foemina virque pede,
Ante fores sceleris quicunque piacula sumant.
    Nec labor: admissi poenituisse sat est.
5   Hoc quoque divini praestat tibi cura Petruti,
    O felix tanto Parthenopea viro!

XXVIII. Alexander Magnus in sacrilegum

Dure, quid angusto tumulatum subtrahis auro?
    Hoc unum domino terra subacta dedit.

XXVI. To Actius Sincerus

Why do you deny wrapping for pepper, Actius? What have mack-
erel or catfish deserved? Why don't you let anybody at all vomit
forth any old mediocre or unsophisticated ditty and provide wrap- 5
pings for incense and olives? A good poet is truly a rare bird. We
cannot all please you. Don't you know about poetasters like Bavius
and Mevius?[29] People like Caesius[30] are always around. This li- 10
cense has been granted to the worst poets for a long time now, this
kind of poison is chronic. Do you refuse to put up with those
whom Vergil and Catullus endured?

XXVII. On Antonello Petrucci's[31] fiftieth birthday

What until recently men and women sought to obtain traveling
over land and sea in a wearisome journey to make reparation for
their crimes anyone can do on his doorstep, and it is very easy: all
you have to do is repent of your crime. The attentive care of the 5
divine Petrucci provides this for you as well. Naples is fortunate to
have such a man!

XXVIII. Alexander the Great against a sacrilegious person

Heartless man, why do you rob the one buried here of a tiny bit of
gold? This is the only thing the subdued earth gave to its master.

XXIX. De Laurentio Medice Petri Francisci filio

De puero quondam Lauro certasse feruntur
    Mercurius, Mavors, Iuno, Minerva, Venus.
Iuno dat imperium, Pallas cor, Cypria formam,
    Mars animos, Maiae filius ingenium.
5 Stant Phoebi arbitrio, Dictynnae Thespiadumque.
    Hic vero maior lis alia exoritur.
Delius hunc sibi vult, artes largitur honoras;
    Plectra deae, castum casta Diana animum.
Iuppiter his aderat; communem censet habendum.
10   Hoc uno avertit iurgia consilio.
Nequa tamen solidi puero pars deesset honesti,
    Ipse Pater divum ius dedit, ipse pium.

XXX. De fortitudine Byzantiae

Senserat exanimum mater Byzantia natum,
    Forte facit patriis dum sua sacra deis;
Uniusque dolor totam concusserat urbem
    Atque erat in luctu vir mulierque novo.
5 Illa immota diu, postquam stata sacra peregit,
    Respicit adverso pectore vulnus hians
Impositumque suis iuvenem, quae gesserat, armis
    Et madida hostili tela manusque nece.
Mox nec scissa comam mater nec territa casu
10   Foemina, fortuna celsior ipsa sua
'Nate,' ait 'egregium patriae per saecula nomen,
    Quam non degeneri funere, nate, iaces!
Agnosco quae saepe mihi promittere suetus,
    Oraque adhuc hosti pene tremenda tuo.
15 Nunc demum peperisse iuvat; dolor omnis abesto!
    Nunquam ego, te nato, non bene mater ero.'

XXIX. On Lorenzo de' Medici, son of Pierfrancesco[32]

It is said that Mercury, Mars, Juno, Minerva and Venus once contended for the favor of the boy Lorenzo. Juno offers power, Pallas Athena intelligence, the Cyprian goddess beauty, Mars courage, the son of Maia cleverness. They abide by the judgment of Phoebus Apollo, Diana[33] and the Muses.[34] Hereupon, however, another greater dispute arises. Apollo wants him for himself and generously donates honorific arts; the goddesses offer the lyre, chaste Diana a chaste mind. Jupiter was present at these proceedings; he rules that Lorenzo must be held in common. Through this one decision he avoids a quarrel. But lest any portion of complete integrity be lacking to the boy, the father of the gods gave him responsible authority.

XXX. On Byzantia's courage

Byzantia sensed that her son was dead as she happened to be making sacrifice to her country's gods. The grief of a single person shook the whole city, and men and women were plunged into unexpected mourning. She remained motionless for a long time after she completed the appointed rites, and looked directly upon the gaping wound and the young man placed upon the arms which he had borne and the weapons and hands drenched in the enemy's blood. Then as a mother she neither rent her hair in grief nor as a woman was she terrified by the fateful occurrence, but rising above her fortune, she said: "My son, whose outstanding renown will endure through the centuries in your native land, in how glorious a death you have fallen, my son! I remember what you used to predict to me, and I recognize the features that are still almost awe-inspiring to your enemies. Now at last I am glad to have given birth; let all sorrow be banished! With you as my son I shall never not be a good mother."

XXXI. Ad Musas

Casta, Pieriae, cohors, puellae,
Quae Pindi iuga, quae tenetis Haemi
Et quae dulcibus Aonum viretis
Permesso premitis comam madentem;
5 Tuque, o, quae Cnidon incolis Paphumque,
Piscoso dea procreata ponto,
Quam circumsiliunt Iocusque Amorque
Et passis Charites comis decentes,
Cum per Idalium Cytheraque alta
10 Aut Colchos Amathuntave Eriosve
Exerces faciles levis choreas:
Vos, o, vos totiens deae vocatae,
Quarum muneris est honor canendi,
Fronde cingite myrtea capillum
15 Et chelym date Lesbiumque plectrum,
Ac me dente nigro rapacis Orci
Ereptum media locate Cirrha,
Unde Seribus audiarque Hiberis.

XXXII. Ad Neaeram

Haec mandata tibi mitto, formosa Neaera,
    Quae cuperem praesens aptius ipse loqui.
Sed tamen interea dum mens assuescit amanti
    Et fiunt iusta mollia corda prece,
5 Candida signatis peraratur littera verbis
    Et peragit nostras conscia charta vices.
Tu modo deposita rugae gravitate molestae,
    Quicquid id, ingenua perlege fronte, precor.
Perlege, sic faveat castis Venus aurea votis,

XXXI. *To the Muses*

Chaste band of the Muses who dwell on the ridges of Pindus and
Haemus[35] and tread on the green swards of Boeotia watered by
the Permessus;[36] and you who dwell in Cnidus and Paphos,[37] god- 5
dess begotten in the sea, teeming with fish, about whom Love and
Frolic and the comely Graces with their flowing locks leap with
joy, when through Idalium[38] and lofty Cythera[39] or through Golgi 10
or Amathus or Mt. Eryx[40] you nimbly exercise your agile dancers:
O you goddesses, so oft invoked, whose function is the honor of
singing, encircle my hair with the myrtle leaf and give me the lyre 15
and the Lesbian plectrum, and delivering me from the black jaws
of voracious Orcus,[41] place me on Mount Parnassus where I shall
be heard by the Chinese and the Iberians.

XXXII. *To Neaera*

I send you this message, O beautiful Neaera, which I would rather
deliver more appropriately in person. Nevertheless, in the mean-
time, while your mind becomes accustomed to a lover and your
heart is softened by just prayers, one can only inscribe words on 5
the blank page and allow the paper, which is privy to our love, to
plead our cause. But putting aside the severity of your knitted
brow, read it through, whatever its worth, I pray you. Read it
through with an open mind, so may golden Venus show her favor

10 Sic precibus referas uberiora tuis.
  Non ego virgineum venio temerare cubile,
   Nec formosa magis quam mihi casta places.
  Dum potuit tantum Lucretia bella videri,
   Quem caperet formae munere nemo fuit.
15 Quid Danaen fecit, nisi turris aenea, caram?
   Nempe quod hic magno visa pudica Iovi est.
  Nec bene eras formosa, tamen pia cura mariti
   Scis tibi quot dederit, Penelopea, procos.
  O quotiens aliquis faciem culpavit, at illi
20 Haesit in attonito pectore casta fides;
  O quotiens dixit felicem coniuge Ulyxem,
   Cum foret in toto non bonus ore color!
  Tu licet hinc oculis facias, hinc vulnera vultu,
   Crede mihi, sola es quod proba, sola capis.
25 Rustica dos nimium est simplex in virgine forma,
   Digna vel aeternis sit licet illa deis.
  Sed tamen et castis sunt quae censura remittit,
   Ulla nec ingenuas lex vetat esse nurus,
  Utque procax male grata animis, sic rustica laedit.
30 Sit procul, o, procul hinc altera et illa mihi!
  Forsitan incultas decuit rigor iste Sabinas,
   Cum pavit patrias consul et uxor oves
  Deque paludigenis surgebat curia cannis,
   Ilice praetori dante sedile novo.
35 Nos melius sequimur nostri bona commoda saecli
   Et facilem populum non nisi laeta iuvant.
  Nupta tamen siqua est duro male iuncta marito,
   Arbitrio vivat coniugis illa sui;
  Illa domi lateat fusis addicta severis,
40 Iussa, verecundis abstineatque iocis.
  Quis ferat occursu sperati coniugis aegram?
   Discidio facies convenit ista gravi.

to your chaste desires, and so may you have more abundant fulfill-   10
ment of your prayers. I do not come to violate your virginal bed,
and you do not please me more by your beauty than by your chas-
tity. For as long as Lucretia was conspicuous only for her beauty,
there was no one whom she could conquer by the gift of beauty
alone. What made Danae[42] desirable if not the bronze tower? Ob-   15
viously, since she was enclosed in it, great Jupiter was convinced of
her chastity. And you, Penelope, were not very beautiful, but you
know how many suitors your loyal affection to your husband at-
tracted. O how often someone found fault with your appearance,
but in his heart he admired your chaste fidelity; how often was   20
Ulysses called fortunate for having such a wife, although she did
not have a perfect complexion! Although you wound me now with
your eyes, now with your countenance, it is only because of your
virtue, believe me, that you enthrall me. Simple beauty in a young   25
woman is too rustic an endowment, even if it be worthy of the
eternal gods.

Yet even for chaste women certain concessions are made, and
no law prohibits young married women from acting naturally. As a
flirtatious girl does not find acceptance, so one who is rustic gives
offense. May both one and the other stay far away, oh, far away   30
from me! Perhaps this sternness was suitable for the primitive Sa-
bine women,[43] when the consul and his wife pastured the family
sheep and the senate house took rise from swamp reeds and the
trunk of an ilex tree provided a seat for the newly elected praetor.
We do better to adapt ourselves to the advantages of our own time   35
while the complaisant populace seeks only things that give plea-
sure. If, however, a woman has the misfortune of being married to
a harsh husband, she must live in conformity with her husband's
wishes. She must confine herself to the house and dedicate her-
self to the severe spindle, and if so ordered, must abstain from in-   40
nocent entertainment. Who would put up with a disagreeable
woman when he returns home? Such an attitude leads to grave

Tyndariden Phrygius violentam viderit hospes,
    In patriam vidua linthea puppe dabit.
45 Ah nimium simplex, ne dicam stulta puella,
    Siqua supercilii dote placere studet!
    Quid, quod Amor laetus pharetramque arcumque resumit,
    Et queritur, questu quae modo laeta fuit?
    Parcite tormentis iuvenum gaudere, puellae,
50   Parcite: habet magnos iusta querela deos.
    Neu blandas ridete preces, neu spernite fletus,
    Neu pigeat nostris ingemuisse malis,
    Et, quotiens aliquis flendus succurrit amator,
    'Parcere Anaxarete' dicite 'acerba monet.'
55 Atque utinam moneat sic ut persuadeat illa,
    Nec meus ex omni parte laboret Amor!
    Sed furit interea fax intima ad ossa medullis,
    Qualis in Aetnaeo vix solet esse iugo.
    Nunc ego Rhiphaeas vellem calcare pruinas,
60   Nunc gelidum Tanaim pectore habere meo,
    Nunc succos ferrumque pati sensuque minutus
    Stare procelloso littore truncus iners.
    An gravis hic etiam Fortunae iniuria saevit,
    Nequando misero non sit acerba mihi?
65 Vix bene adhuc fueram matris rude semen in alvo,
    Cum grave servitium patria victa subit.
    Ipse pater, Dymae regnis eiectus avitis,
    Cogitur Iliadae quaerere tecta Remi.
    Hic, ubi Pierio quamvis nutritus in antro,
70   Mille tuli raram damna habitura fidem.
    Iamque nigrescebant prima lanugine malae
    Iunctaque erat lustris altera bruma tribus,
    Cum fato rapiente vagus Scythiamque per altam
    Auferor et gelidi per loca vasta Getae.

discord. If the Phrygian guest[44] saw the daughter of Tyndareus[45] in an angry mood, he would have set sail for home on an empty ship. Ah! too simpleminded, not to say stupid, is the girl who strives to be attractive by adopting a haughty demeanor! What if joyful Love takes up his quiver and bow again, and she who was previously happy at another's grief now complains herself? Cease, young maidens, cease to rejoice in the torments of young men: just complaints have the support of the great gods. Do not laugh at seductive pleas, and do not spurn tears, and do not be reluctant to be moved by our sufferings, and when you happen to meet a lover worthy of compassion, say: "Cruel Anaxarete[46] warns us to be compassionate." And would that her admonition were persuasive and that my love would not suffer in every way. But in the meantime a torch is raging in the marrow of my bones, such as cannot easily be found on the slopes of Mount Etna. I would like to tread on the frozen snows of the Riphaean mountains or have the frigid Don in my breast or suffer lethal potions or the sword and lie senseless like an inert tree trunk on a stormy shore.

Or will the injustice of Fortune unleash her fury against me even now and never cease her hostilities against this wretched creature? I was still a formless seed in my mother's womb when my country was conquered and had to endure a cruel servitude. My father, banished from the ancestral kingdoms of Dyme,[47] was forced to seek a home in the land of Remus, son of Ilia.[48] Here, though brought up in the cave of the Pierides, I suffered a thousand deprivations, which one would hardly believe. My cheeks were already growing dark with soft down and I had reached the age of sixteen when in the grip of fate I was carried off to wander through the depths of Scythia and the desolate wastes of frozen

45

50

55

60

65

70

75   Quid referam interea pelagique viaeque labores
      Et totiens strictas in mea fata manus
    Maternosque rogos miserandaque funera fratris,
      Funera non illo tempore agenda mihi?
    Omnia quae tulimus constanti corde, nec inter
80   Tot mala mens animis concidit ipsa suis.
    At cadit, ut semel est arcu male saucia Amoris.
      Fallimur, an facies est Amor ista mihi?
    Ista mihi certe est facies Amor, inque pudicis
      Vultibus et tenero qui stat in ore decor;
85   Nec Colchos regit atque Cypron, sed conditus imis
      Sensibus in vacuo pectore regna tenet.
    Ista arcus cilia, ex istis sunt spicula ocellis,
      Fervida purpureae quid nisi flamma genae?
    O decus, o nostri rarissima gloria saecli,
90   O desideriis unica cura meis!
    His ego quid mirum si sum tibi victus ab armis?
      Pars quota de numero vincere digna fuit?
    Sed tamen arbitrium vitaeque habuisse necisque
      Est satis, ulterior convenit ira feris.
95   Non ego dedignor dominae servire potenti.
      O ubi libertas nunc prior illa iacet?
    Et vitare fui certus grave nomen amantis,
      Siqua homini res est certa, vetante deo!
    Victus opem precor extremam, miserere precantis:
100   Non sum qui peream dignus amore tui.
    Quod nisi Graiugenae sordet tibi taeda mariti,
      Non equidem coniunx dissimulandus ero.
    Prima olim sine more fuit, sine legibus aetas,
      Quam rudis antiqui, tam male gnara sui,
105 Inque feris sylvis populus vivebat agrestis,
      Glande cibum, molles cespite dante toros.

Thrace. Why should I recount my struggles over land and sea and   75
the violence that threatened my life so many times and my moth-
er's funeral and the tragic death of my brother, to whom I had to
render premature obsequies? All of these calamities I bore with
courageous heart, and my spirit never faltered amidst all these   80
evils. But it fell as soon as it was wounded by the shafts of Love.
Am I mistaken, or is this face Love for me? This certainly is the
face of Love, and the grace that stands out in her modest expres-
sion and delicate features. Love does not rule over Golgi or Cy-   85
prus, but has established his kingdom in my inmost senses and in
my heart, free of all other affection. Those eyebrows are his bow,
and his arrows come from those eyes, and what is his flaming
torch but your ruddy cheeks? O splendor, O most exquisite glory
of our time! O single object of my desires! What wonder is it if I   90
am vanquished by these weapons? How small a part of your arse-
nal was able to vanquish me? But to have control over my life and
death should be enough, to add anger belongs more to wild beasts.
I do not disdain to be the slave of a powerful mistress. O what has   95
become of my former liberty? And yet I had made up my mind to
avoid the solemn name of lover, if one can decide anything when a
god forbids it. Defeated, I make a last supplication, have mercy on
one who prays for help. I do not deserve to die for your love. If   100
marriage to a Greek husband is not repugnant to you, I will cer-
tainly not be a husband whose identity must be concealed.

Primitive ages were without customs, without laws, as ignorant
of past ages as they were of their own, and this rustic population
lived in the virgin forests, acorns were their food and the soft turf   105
their bed. They counted their flock with nuts, and with nuts they

In nucibus pecudes, nucibus armenta notabant:
    Rarus adhuc digitos qui numeraret erat.
Prima rudes hominum formavit Graecia mentes
110   Eloquii blandis viribus usa sui,
Prima cava circumvallavit moenia fossa,
    Prima vagis patriam certaque tecta dedit,
Prima artes commenta bonas. Hac vita magistra
    Edidicit leges, hac data iura pati,
115 Hac duce coelestes divum conscendimus arces,
    Hac duce naturae sancta adaperta via est.
Quid, quod priscorum repetas si facta parentum,
    Haec quoque, qua nata es, Inachis ora fuit?
Nam quid ego Etruscos memorem pubemque Sabinam
120   Et quae pars olim Graecia maior erat?
Ipsa caput rerum quondam pulcherrima Roma —
    Certa fides — Graiis condita gaudet avis.
Nec te terruerit peregrini nomen inane;
    Crede mihi, nulla est terra aliena viro.
125 Et, quanquam mihi regna et opes Fortuna paternas
    Abstulit, est proprio sanguine partus honos,
Divitiaeque animo frugi et satis ampla domi res,
    Si qua velit parto mens moderata frui.
Quid, quod sive animi petitur constantia certi,
130   Sive magis simplex et sine fraude fides,
Seu bello manus apta, bonae seu pectora paci,
    Tempus ad hoc nullos degeneramus avos?
Nam genus et veterum praeconia nota parentum
    Vix ausim nostris annumerare bonis,
135 Et tamen est aliquid proavos habuisse Marullos,
    Quos totiens tulerit Martia Roma duces.
Scilicet est olim vis rerum in semine certa
    Et referunt animos singula quaeque patrum,
Nec leporem canis Aemathius timidamve columbam

counted their herds. The person who could count on his fingers
was still a rarity. Greece was the first to form the untrained minds
of men, making use of the persuasive power of its language, it was   110
the first to surround the walls with a ditch, the first to give no-
mads a country and permanent dwelling, the first to devise the
liberal arts. From this teacher life learned laws and learned to obey
them, under her leadership we ascended to the celestial citadels of   115
the gods, with her as guide the path to understand the holy secrets
of nature was opened up. What is more, if you were to retrace the
history of your ancient ancestors, this land in which you were
born is the land of Inachus, king of Argos.[49] Why should I men-
tion the Etruscans and Sabine youth and that part of Italy that   120
was once Magna Graecia? Beautiful Rome itself, once ruler of the
world, by sure testimony, rejoices in having been founded by
Greek ancestors. And do not be alarmed by the mere name of
foreigner; believe me, no land is foreign to a man of courage. And   125
although Fortune has bereft me of ancestral realms and posses-
sions, the honor that I have acquired by my own blood remains,
and sufficiently ample family possessions are riches for a frugal
person and for one who knows how to enjoy his acquisitions with
moderation. If what you seek is constancy of spirit and sincere fi-   130
delity without deceit, or ability in war, or a mind predisposed to
peace, we have not fallen below the standards set by any of our
forebears up to this day. I would be hesitant to enumerate the no-
bility and commendations of my ancient lineage among my bless-
ings, and yet it means something to have the Marulli as one's   135
ancestors, whom martial Rome hired many times as *condottieri*.
Obviously there is a certain power in the seeds of things and each
thing reproduces the characteristics of its begetters. A Macedo-

140   Notus Hyperboreo falco sub axe creat.
      Nam tua quod supplexque petam connubia et ultro,
        Non ideo nostrum sperne superba torum:
      Me quoque nobilium natae petiere virorum,
        Dignae opibus, facie dignae atavisque peti.
145 Et nunc cum dicar sine te non vivere posse,
        Invenies cupiat quae tamen esse mea.
      Sed vetat hoc decor iste tuus mellitaque verba
        Et magis Alpina pectora cana nive,
      Quaeque micant passos subter bona colla capillos,
150   Quale sub aurata candet ebur statua.
      Hoc vetat Idaliusque puer materque Dione,
        Et qui iam pridem me tibi donat Hymen.
      Tu modo tot contra divos pugnare puella
        Desine — non tutum est cedere nolle deis! —
155 Totque meis olim tandem exorata querelis,
        Coniugis in caros labere, nympha, sinus.
      'Sed nimium properas' dices 'cum messis in herba est.'
        Me miserum! properat nemo in amore satis.
      Crede mihi, non est meus hic qui torpeat ignis.
160   Nam potes ex vultu tu quoque nosse meo,
      Cum nunc ora rubor subitus notat et modo rursum
        Pallet purpureo sanguine cassa cutis
      Et nunc desinimus mediis sermonibus et nunc
        Moesta repentinas aggravat unda genas.
165 Quod nisi quam primum misero succurris amori,
        Auxilio frustra postmodo lenta venis.
      Si tamen est mora cur placeat, dum civicus ensis
        Saevit et ultrices excitat ira manus,
      Nec fas in tanto rerum patriaeque periclo est
170   Coniugiis civi posse vacare novis,
      At potes interea verbis lenire dolorem
        Multaque colloquio demere damna tuo

nian dog does not generate a hare nor does a prized Hyperborean 140
falcon from the polar skies generate a timid dove. As for the fact
that I ask your hand as a suppliant and without being invited, do
not for that reason proudly spurn my offer of marriage: the daugh-
ters of noblemen sought me as their spouse, though they were
worthy to be sought themselves because of their wealth, their
beauty and their lineage. And even now, when people say I cannot 145
live without you, you will find some woman who wishes to be
mine. But your beauty and your honey-sweet words forbid this
and your breast whiter than Alpine snows, and the beautiful neck
that gleams beneath your free-flowing tresses like ivory in a gold 150
statue; the Idalian youth[50] and his mother Dione[51] forbid this,
and Hymen,[52] who long ago consecrated me to you. But you, a
young girl, cease fighting against the gods — it is not safe to re-
fuse to yield to the gods! — and at last, won over by my many la- 155
ments, surrender yourself, my maiden, into the loving arms of
your spouse.

"But you are in too much of a hurry," you will say, "when the
harvest is still in blade." Alas! No one can hurry too much in mat-
ters of love. Believe me, this fire of mine is not the kind that grows
languid. You can see it in my face, for at times I suddenly turn red 160
and then my skin, deprived of blood, grows pale and at times I
stop talking in the middle of a conversation, and at other times a
sad wave of tears suddenly bathes my cheeks. If you do not come 165
to the aid of my desperate love, your succor will arrive in vain,
when it is too late. If, however, you prefer to wait, while civil war
rages and anger excites men to vengeance, and you think it is not
right in the midst of great civil turmoil that a citizen should be 170
occupied with new marriages, you can at least soothe my sorrows
with your words and dispel much distress by your conversation

Solarique animum et praesens relevare iacentem:
  Si nescis, pietas coniugis ista probae est.
175 Tunc ego iurabo sanctissima numina divum —
  Numina non ullo tempore laesa mihi —
Meque meis dictis astringam in foedera quaevis,
  Parte sit ut nulla non rata nostra fides.
Tunc tibi dictatis faciam sponsalia verbis
180   Et te consulta vir tibi iuris ero.
Tu modo, siquis amor, nostri si pectore cura est,
  Parce mora, coniunx, perdere velle virum.

XXXIII. In libellum infacetum

Salve, nec lepido libelle versu
Nec lingua facili nec ore docto
Nec sana satis eruditione,
Missa longior eloquente Magni,
5 Nec rudi melior poeta et ipso
Infacetior infaceto agello:
Ten putat, rogo, quispiam disertum?
Tu te infers numero peritiorum?
Et cessas, miser, emori, Marulle?

XXXIV. Ad Marcum Barbum cardinalem Sancti Marci

Creta, Asia, Illyricum, Lybie, Germania, Parthus,
  Multorum ut nomen, sic quoque praeda virum est:
At Spes atque Metus incertaque Gaudia rerum
  Concedunt animis non nisi, Marce, tuis.
5 Haec est, haec virtute tua victoria digna,
  Quae te fortunae, Marce, facit dominum.

and console my spirit and by your presence raise me up from my
state of prostration: you may not know this, but pity is a quality
of a virtuous spouse. Then I will swear by the most holy power of   175
the gods — whom I have never offended — and I shall bind myself
to you with my words by whatever pact you wish, so that our
union will be sanctioned by every formality. Then I will recite the
words of the marriage ceremony, and when you have given your   180
consent, I will be your legal husband. For your part if you nurture
any love for me, do not, my spouse, wish to annihilate your hus-
band by your demurral.

XXXIII. *In condemnation of an insipid little book*

Greetings, little book, not remarkable for your witty verse or spon-
taneous style, or learned eloquence or sound learning, more prolix
than an eloquent message of Pompey, no better than an untaught   5
poet, and more rustic than a rustic plot of land. I ask you, does
anyone think you are learned? Do you include yourself among the
number of the cognoscenti? And do you hesitate to die, unhappy
Marullus?

XXXIV. *To Marco Barbo,*[53] *Cardinal of San Marco*

Crete, Asia Minor, Illyricum,[54] Libya, Germany, the Parthians:
many are the names of nations, many the men to whom the booty
belongs. But Hope and Fear and uncertain Joys surrender only to
you, Marco. This is a victory worthy of your virtue, which makes   5
you, Marco, the master of fortune.

XXXV. *Ad Barabam*

Et Venus est uxor et tu claudusque faberque:
    Si dederis Martem, Mulciber es, Baraba.

XXXVI. *Epitaphium Manilii Marulli patris*

Flens primum has auras hausi puer omine diro,
    Flebilis erepta vita fuit patria,
Nunc quoque flens morior nequid non flebile restet:
    Haec est humani conditio generis.

XXXVII. *De Venere et Maximiliano Caesare*

Dum neque Gradivum neque vult dimittere Adonin
    Diversique unam Marsque puerque trahunt,
Incidit in mentem Caesar. Tunc prosilit amens
    Cypris, et 'Hic nobis' dixit 'utrunque dabit!'
5 Dixit, et iniectis hederae de more lacertis,
    Mille dat amplexus, oscula mille viro.
At Mars 'Vincor' ait, 'sed certe vincor ab illo,
    Armatum vinci qui prius edocuit.'

XXXVIII. *Epitaphium Alcini infantis*

Alcinus hic iaceo, moesti posuere parentes:
    Hoc precium vitae est atque puerperii.

XXXIX. *Ad Neaeram*

Moris erat sceptris teneras arcere puellas
    Et mollem curis exonerare animum,
Nec vel consilio rebusve admittere agendis,
    Sed tantum lanis esse putare satas.
5 Multarumque — nefas! — vitium sceleraverat omnis,

XXXV. To Barabbas

Venus is your wife and you are the lame blacksmith. If you produce a Mars, then you are Vulcan, Barabbas.

XXXVI. Epitaph of his father, Manilius Marullus[55]

Weeping, I first breathed in this air as a child with dire omen; my life was full of tears when my country was taken from me. Now too I die weeping so that nothing not worthy of tears remains: this is the condition of the human race.

XXXVII. On Venus and Emperor Maximilian

While she was unwilling to send either Mars or Adonis away, and both Mars and the young boy were pulling her toward themselves from different directions, Caesar came to mind. Then the Cyprian goddess jumped up in wild excitement and said: "He will serve for both of them." Thus she spoke and throwing her arms around him   5
like ivy, as she was wont to do, she gave him a thousand embraces and a thousand kisses. Thereupon Mars said: "At least I am defeated by one who previously taught defeat to an armed man."

XXXVIII. Epitaph of the child Alcinus

Here I lie, Alcinus, my grieving parents laid me here: this is the price of life and of childbirth.

XXXIX. To Neaera

It was once customary to keep tender young girls away from politics and exempt their delicate spirits from responsibilities, and not to admit them to decision-making and business affairs, but to think that they were born only to spin wool. The defects of many   5
women — oh, horror! — had been unjustly imputed to all women,

Nec nisi naturae foemina crimen erat.
At nunc tantus honos nuribus, reverentia tanta est,
   Tanta pudicitiae consiliique fides,
Ut iam nemo sibi, mulieri speret ademptum,
10   Et cedat victus pene virilis honos,
Blanda nec incertos suspendant vota parentes,
   Cum sat iam matri sit peperisse hominem:
Sic quas tot vitia et tam longum infecerat aevum,
   Unius laus et gloria condecorat.

XL. Ad Neaeram

Vaesanos quotiens tibi furores
Atque ignes paro, quos moves, referre
Et quantus deus ossibus pererret,
Qui me nocte die necat, Neaera,
5 Et vox et sonus et parata verba
Desunt tum mihi linguaque ipsa torpet
Et vix sustineor genu labante.
Moerent pectora perque membra passim
Perque artus fluor it repente salsus
10 Et diem subitae occupant tenebrae,
Nec quicquam nisi lacrimae supersunt,
Quae mutae quoque opem precantur unae.

XLI. De Venere

Aurea Mulciberum nato Venus arma rogabat,
   Immemor huic nato facta sit unde parens.
Ingemuit deus inviso sub nomine, et illi:
   'Cur non Anchisae, diva, rogas potius?'

and a woman was nothing but a reproach to nature. But now how much honor and respect is given to women, how much trust is given to their virtue and advice, so that no one thinks anymore that they should be deprived of their rights, and manly virtue, al- 10 most in defeat, gives way to them. Parents should no longer remain uncertain about the fulfillment of their wishes since it is satisfaction enough for a woman to have borne a child. So those women who were tainted by so many defects and a long tradition of distrust are now adorned by the praise and glory of one woman.

XL. To Neaera

Whenever I prepare to relate the mad frenzies and fires you inspire and how great a god wanders freely through my body, who annihilates me night and day, Neaera, voice and sound and pre- 5 pared words fail me and my tongue itself is paralyzed and I can hardly stay on my feet, my knees tottering. My heart grieves and through my limbs a salty stream suddenly flows and a sudden 10 darkness blots out the day, and nothing remains but tears, which, though mute, cry alone for help.

XLI. On Venus

Golden Venus entreated Vulcan for arms for her son, forgetting who was the father of this son. The god groaned at the thought of the hated name and said: "Why don't you rather ask Anchises,[56] O goddess?"

XLII. De Saladino

Littore dum Phario prima Saladinus in alga
    Barbara devicto castra Oriente locat,
Venit adulatrix — regum comes unica — turba,
    E quibus ut lingua promptior unus erat,
5 Nunc domitam Aegyptum iactat, nunc littora rubra
    Fractaque pugnaci Gallica sceptra manu,
Ostentatque virum duris tot milia in armis
    Et iubet hinc vires aestimet ipse suas.
'Scilicet hinc,' ille 'atque adeo ex hac' infit 'arena,
10   Quae te semiustum littore, Magne, tenet.'

XLIII. Epitaphium Federici Urbinatis

Invictus potui, nisi mors vicisset, haberi:
    Haec quoque non vicit, sed potius soluit.

XLIV. Ad Neaeram

Cum tu candida sis magis ligustro,
Quis genas minio, Neaera, tinxit?
Quis labella tibi notavit ostro?
Unde sunt capiti aurei capilli?
5 Quis supercilii nigravit arcum?
Quis faces oculis dedit potentes?
O quies animi laboriosa!
O labor nimium mihi quiete!
O amarities petita votis,
10 Qua mori sine amem volens lubensque!

XLII. On Saladin[57]

When Saladin was stationing his barbarian camp on Pharos's shore, strewn with seaweed, after conquering the East, an obsequious crowd — the sole companion of kings — gathered, among whom there was one with a ready tongue who boasted that Egypt 5 was now subdued, and the shoreline was now red with blood and French rule was broken by a band of doughty fighters, and he pointed with pride to the many thousands of well-armed men and asked Saladin to assess his strength from this display. "Of course" he said, "I derive strength from them and even from this sand, which holds your scorched remains on its shore, O Pompey."[58] 10

XLIII. Epitaph of Federico, Duke of Urbino[59]

I could have been regarded as invincible if death had not conquered me: this too did not defeat me, but rather set me free.

XLIV. To Neaera

Since you are whiter than the white-flowered privet, Neaera, who colored your cheeks bright red? Who branded your lips purple? Where did this golden hair come from? Who blackened your 5 arched eyebrows? Who put that fiery gleam in your eyes? O laborious peace of mind! O labor too peaceful for me! O bitterness sought in prayers, deprived of her I would love to die, freely and 10 willingly.

XLV. In Caesarianum

Quod tibi tam multus Caesar dictator in ore est,
    Ignosco. Laudas, vir bone, quem sequeris.
At Cato non hastam, non dictatoria regna,
    Non probat infamem consulem adulteriis,
5   Non tot opes ventre aut patrimonia pene vorata,
    Non edicta foro lata, nocente manu,
Non fas unius versum ambitione nefasque,
    Non casus tantarum urbium avaritia,
Non Bibulo toto factum nil consule in anno,
10   Non pro divitiis tot patriae aera data.
Miramur tamen arma viri, miramur acumen:
    Rex quoque miratus tabuit haec eadem.

XLVI. De morte Orphei

Orphea dum miseranda parens tumularet ademptum
    Tactaque melliflui cerneret ora viri,
'At tu, nate, facis' dixit 'praeconia divis:
    Quid nisi damnatus fulmine et Enceladus?'

XLVII. De Amore

Spreverat Idalium rerum plebs indiga numen
    Iamque puer Veneris cesserat urbe fame:
Ergo boves iungit curvoque innixus aratro
    Pinguia ruricolae suscitat arva modo.
5   Semina restabat terrae dare; semina dantem
    Non expectatis obruit Auster aquis.
Ille irae impatiens, 'Agedum omnia, Iuppiter,' inquit
    'Sterne, neca: enecto tu bove taurus eris.'

XLV. Against a follower of Caesar

I pardon you for always having the name of Caesar the dictator on your lips. You praise the one you follow, my good man. But Cato does not approve the spear, nor the powers of a dictator, nor a consul notorious for his adulteries, nor so much wealth and fortune practically devoured by the belly, nor edicts passed in the forum by a guilty hand, nor right and wrong overturned by the ambition of one man, nor the fall of such great cities because of avarice, nor the fact that nothing was accomplished during the entire year when Bibulus[60] was consul, nor that so much of the country's money was given to create his wealth. Nevertheless we admire the military exploits of the man, we admire his acumen: as king he also admired these things, and wasted away. 5 10

XLVI. On the death of Orpheus[61]

When the pitiful mother was burying her lifeless son Orpheus and caressing him, she gazed at the face of the mellifluous man and said, "But you, my son, give praise to the gods: wasn't Enceladus[62] also stricken by the thunderbolt?"[63]

XLVII. On Love

The needy masses had scorned the Idalian deity and Venus's son, suffering from hunger, had already left the city. Therefore he took a team of oxen and leaning on the curved plow, he stirred up the rich fields like a farmer. It remained only to sow the seeds, but as he was sowing them the South Wind flooded the fields with an unexpected rainfall. Unable to control his anger, he said, "Go ahead, level and annihilate everything, Jupiter; when you have killed the ox you will be the bull." 5

XLVIII. *Ad Neaeram*

Quod levis ima pedum verrit vestigia crinis,
   Quod sedet in niveo discolor ore rubor,
Quod colla et Parium vincentia pectora marmor,
   Quod dens Gaetuli nobile dentis opus,
5   Quod digni imperio vultus, quod tantus honorae
       Frontis honos, Paphiae quod labra verna rosae,
Quod micat urbanus generoso risus ocello,
   Quod, quicquid dicis seu facis, omne decet —
Adde genus regesque atavos fratresque patremque
10   Et congesta deum regnaque opesque manu —
Non tamen ista tuae fuerint praeconia laudis.
   Sunt maiora quibus, lux mea, rara venis:
Ingenium sollersque animi prudentia rerum
   Pectoraque in tenera virgine digna viro,
15   Et decor et probitas contra tua saecula et artes
       Fessaque virgineis Calliopea choris.
Fortunata animi tot dotibus: haec bona vera,
   Haec tua sunt, fati caetera dona brevis.

XLIX. *Ad patriam*

Terrarum ocelle, patria, ocelle gentium,
   Quascunque curru eburneo
Laboriosae metiens iter rotae,
   Lucis creator Sol videt,
5   Quam te cadaver flebile aspicio miser,
       Vix ipse adhuc credens mihi
Oculis videre coelitum tantum nefas!
   O miserum et infelix genus,
Quo decidit fortuna gentis pristina?
10   Tu ne illa domina gentium,

XLVIII. *To Neaera*

That your tresses sweep lightly over the ground as you walk, that
a contrasting rosy color resides in your snow-white countenance,
that your neck and breasts are whiter than Parian marble, that
your teeth surpass the noble workmanship of Gaetulian[64] ivory,
that you possess a majestic bearing, that the dignity of your glance 5
confers honor upon you, that your lips have the vernal bloom of a
Paphian rose, that a sophisticated smile flashes in your aristocratic
eyes, that, whatever you do or say, all becomes you — add to this
your race and ancestral kings, your brothers and your father, and 10
the kingdoms and riches accumulated by the gift of the gods — not
all of this would be sufficient praise. There are greater things than
these, light of my eyes, that make you stand out: your intelligence
and astute practical wisdom and courage in a tender young woman,
worthy of a man, and propriety and uprightness opposed to the 15
morals of your day, and your artistic achievements and poetic gift
acknowledged by virgin choruses. You are fortunate to possess all
these gifts of the mind: these are true blessings, these are yours;
other gifts are of brief duration.

XLIX. *To his native country*

O darling of the earth, my native land, favorite of all peoples that
the Sun, creator of light, sees while tracing his strenuous journey
in his ivory chariot. In my misery I look upon you, a pitiful corpse, 5
still scarcely believing when I see with my own eyes such a wicked
act of the gods! O wretched and unhappy race, to what depth has
your former good fortune fallen? Are you that mistress of nations 10

Quam tot tyranni, tot duces, tot oppida,
    Tot nationes efferae
Ab usque Bactris ultimisque Gadibus
    Flexo precabantur genu?
15 Iam iam nihil non fragile sub coelo, nihil
    Non percaducum gentibus.
Sors cuncta versat aeque et impotens hera
    Nullo beata termino,
Nec fas piumque sontibus fatis moram
20   Affert et instabili rotae.
Felix tamen, quae morte sensu perdito
    Semel deos passa es graves,
Infanda casus damna nec sentis tui.
    O surda Mors precantibus,
25 An tu quoque irae quos premunt deum fugis,
    Nequis refugio ultra locus?
I, dura, vade, fuge: tamen lacrimae et dolor
    Quos tu recusas finient.

Liber Tertius

I.

Quod tua longinquum diffundo nomina in aevum
    Et sine te crescit pagina nulla mihi,
Non hoc tu nobis debes, bone Laure, sed aetas
    Postera et exemplis saecla renata tuis.
5 Macte vir ingenio, quem nil nisi vivida virtus
    Tangit et ex vero gloria vera bono.

to whom so many tyrants, so many rulers, so many towns, so many fierce nations from Bactria[65] to farthest Cadiz made entreaty on bended knee? There is nothing under the heavens that is not 15 fragile, nothing among all peoples that is not doomed to die. Fortune turns all things equally and she is an arrogant mistress, not satisfied with any limit, and neither divine law nor piety can obstruct the guilty fates and the ever-changing wheel. Yet you are 20 fortunate, since bereft of your senses in death, you have suffered the harsh gods once and for all, and no longer feel the unspeakable losses of your downfall. O Death, deaf to those who pray to you, do you also flee those whom the anger of the gods oppresses so 25 that they have no place of refuge? So, run away, hard-hearted one: the tears and sorrow which you refuse will end.

Book III

I.

That I publicize your name for ages to come and that no page of mine comes into existence without you is not something you owe to me, good Lorenzo, but future ages and centuries reborn after your example. Be honored for your inspired mind, O man touched 5 only by vigorous virtue and true glory born of true goodness.

II. De Livore et Neaera

Dum nuper nitidos Neaerae ocellos
Spectat semianimis dolore Livor—
Et nunc purpureas genas puellae
Miratur, modo tortulos capillos,
5 Modo colla, manus modo nitentes,
Modo brachiolum lacertulosque,
Modo compositum latus decenter,
Modo artus Scythicis pares pruinis,
Modo os nectare dulcius, modo illa,
10 Quae me disperimunt, perita verba—
Ad me versus—ut aeger assidebam—
'Quem' dixit 'laqueum mihi parasset,
Si tibi magis haec foret benigna!'

III. Ad Maximilianum Caesarem

Qualiter in medio tuta rate navita portu,
    Hesternae adhuc hyemis memor,
Nunc intexta cavae vestigat pinea puppis,
    Modo carinam examinat,
5 Nunc ligat antemnas, nunc collocat ordine remos,
    Oculisque lustrat singula,
Non aliter quam si rapientibus aequora ventis
    Iam nunc minax hiet fretum;
Et quamvis positum placidus mare spondeat aer,
10   Hic se procellae praeparat,
Sic, ubi Fortunae vindex gravis aspra per arma
    Tutatus es patrium decus
Totque dolos contra sola virtute renixus
    Regnare docuisti deos.
15 Post patriam larga donatam ubicunque quiete

II. On Envy and Neaera

When recently Envy, half-dead with anguish, was looking at the radiant eyes of Neaera, now admiring the young girl's rosy cheeks, now her curly hair, now her neck, now her lovely white hands, 5 now her delicate forearms and upper arms, now her elegantly proportioned figure, now her limbs as white as Scythian hoarfrost, now her mouth, sweeter than nectar, and now her cultured speech, 10 which drive me to despair, turning to me as I sat there, sick at heart, he said: "What a noose she would have prepared for me if she were more kind to you."

III. To Emperor Maximilian

As a sailor on his safe ship in port, still remembering yesterday's storm, now checks the pine frames of the hollow ship, now examines the keel, now makes fast the yardarms, now places the oars in 5 proper order and scans each detail, just as if the winds were whipping up the surface of the sea and the menacing storm was about to break; and though the placid air gives promise of a calm sea, prepares himself for a gale, just so, as the liberator from oppressive 10 Fortune, you have defended the country's honor by means of fierce warfare and through valor alone have struggled against countless wiles and have shown that the gods rule supreme. After establish- 15

   Hunnosque tandem non graves
Atque hinc exutos atque illinc finibus hostes,
   Dotale qua regnum patet,
Ipse tamen duris aptas accomoda bellis
20   Civesque, Caesar, excitas,
Et nunc per ludum exploras aptissima quondam
   Robora duellis fortibus,
Nunc pulchrae accendis patriam virtutis amore,
   Positis merenti praemiis,
25 Civilesque manus longa assuetudine firmas,
   Qua maius in terris nihil,
Providus et sapiens vitare instantia bella
   Bellis parato robore.
Macte, pater, merito, patriae, virtutibus istis,
30   Quo sospite omnibus est bene.

IV. De Alexandra Scala Bartholomaei Scalae filia

Auxerat Aonias Sappho, dea facta, sorores,
   Et poteras numero cedere, Roma, novo,
Dulcia cum Scalae miratus carmina Apollo,
   Dixit: 'Habes numerum tu quoque, Roma, tuum.'

V. De Demetrio Chalcondylo

Dum ver Hymetium diu
Nequicquam apis quaerit vaga,
In os sacrum Chalcondyli
Et labra suaviflua incidens,
5 'Heus' inquit, 'aequales bonae,
Huc, huc adeste sedulae:
Matrem videtis Attida.'

ing widespread peace in the country and after the Huns were no
longer a serious menace and after driving off the enemy from our
borders on this side and on that, through the entire extent of the
kingdom you acquired through marriage,[1] nonetheless you make
preparations for bitter wars and stir up the citizen body, O Caesar.   20
At one moment you explore through public games the potential
source of strength for future wars, at another moment you enflame
the people with love of glorious bravery, offering prizes for the
meritorious, and strengthen civic forces through prolonged drills,   25
than which there is nothing more effective on earth. Wise and
provident, you avoid sudden wars by preparing for war through
military might. Be honored for your virtues, you who deserve to
be Father of your Country. As long as you are alive, there is gen-   30
eral prosperity.

IV. *Concerning Alessandra Scala,[2] daughter of Bartolomeo Scala*

Sappho, becoming a goddess, increased the number of the Aonian
sisters,[3] and you could have accepted a new number, Rome, when
Apollo, amazed by the poems of Scala, said: "Rome, you have your
own number too."

V. *On Demetrius Chalcondylas[4]*

While the wandering bee had been seeking Hymettian spring for
a long time in vain, happening upon the sacred mouth and mellif-
luous lips of Chalcondylas, he said: "Hey, good comrades, come   5
here quickly. Here is our Attic mother."

VI. Homerus

Vane, quid affectas patriam mihi dicere terram
    Metirisque hominum conditione deos?
Non me Smyrna creat, non me Colophonia tellus,
    Non Pylos, aequoreis non Chios icta minis,
5 Non Ithace, praenobile equis non Argos alendis,
    Non quae de dominae nomine dicta deae est,
Non Salamis, non clara suo Rhodos aurea Phoebo,
    Aut Ios aut Pharii fertilis ora soli.
Mortalis sunt ista viri: me lucidus aether
10   Parturit, enatum terra fretumque colunt.

VII. Ad Ioannem Picum

Pice, delitiae novem sororum,
Qui secreta patrum recludis antra
Et novissima comparando primis
Cogis tam varios idem sonare,
5 Quid me versiculis tuis lacessis,
Nunc vultus nitidae meae puellae,
Nunc mirantibus aureos capillos
Et quae non tua sunt, sceleste, colla?
An quod divitiis tumes paternis
10 Atque ista tetrica tua Minerva,
In nostros tibi ius putas amores?
Atqui non ita, nam feros per enses
Et meum latus haec tibi petenda est.
Quod ni desinis esse iam molestus
15 Et tandem sceleris piget cupiti,
Non cum nescio quo Platone faxo
Et tectis hominum solo favillis,

VI. Homer[5]

Fool, why do you try to tell me what is my native land and measure gods in human terms? Smyrna[6] did not give me birth, nor the land of Colophon,[7] nor Pylos,[8] nor Chios,[9] battered by the threatening waves of the sea, nor Ithaca,[10] nor Argos,[11] celebrated for 5 the raising of horses, nor the city that takes its name from a goddess, nor Salamis,[12] nor golden Rhodes, famous for its Phoebus Apollo,[13] nor Ios,[14] nor the fertile shore of Pharos.[15] All of these pertain to mortal men: the bright ether bore me, the earth and the sea looked after me when I was born.

VII. To Giovanni Pico[16]

Pico, delight of the nine sisters, you who open up the secret caverns of our forefathers and by comparing ancient with new bring diverse authors into harmony,[17] why do you provoke me with your 5 little ditties that magnify, now the features of my radiant girl, now her golden locks, and the neck which does not belong to you, you villain![18] Is it because your rich patrimony makes you swollen with pride, and because by virtue of your austere wisdom you 10 think you have the right to my beloved? But that is not the case, for you will have to seek her with the sharp sword and over my dead body. And if you do not stop being such a nuisance and do 15 not tire of your wicked desires, I will show you that you are not dealing with some Plato or other and the ashes of men buried

Sed mecum tibi senties agi rem,
Qui verbis nequeam tribus moveri.

VIII. De Laodamia et Protesilao

Dum fugit amplexus evanida coniugis umbra
    Osculaque ab Stygiis usque petita vadis,
'Quo sine me' inquit, 'amans? non est ratis ima puellis
    Clausa: satis, satis, o, sola relicta semel!'
5 Dixit, et in mediis subito collapsa querelis,
    Magnanimo comes it Laodamia viro.

IX. Ad Gemmam

Quod facias nil, Gemma, tuus mihi questus Haletes.
    En, iubet et coniux: quid, rogo, Gemma, negas?

X. De laudibus Senae

Mater nobilium nurum,
    Antiqui soboles Remi,
    Sena, delitiae Italae,
Seu libet positum loci
5   Convallesque beatas

Tot circumriguis aquis,
    Seu ver conspicere annuum
    Nativisque rosariis
Semper purpureum solum
10   Et colles viridantes.

Nam quid dicam operum manus
    Aut tot ditia marmora?
    Quid spirantia signa tot

under the earth, but with me, whom you cannot get rid of with two or three words.

VIII. *On Laodamia and Protesilaus*[19]

As the shade of her spouse, disappearing from sight, summoned by the Stygian wave, fled her embraces and kisses, she said: "Where are you going without me, my love? The skiff in the nether world is not denied to young girls. Enough, enough to have been aban- doned once." Thus she spoke, and suddenly collapsing in the midst   5 of her laments, Laodamia went to accompany her greathearted husband.

IX. *To Gemma*

Your friend Haletes complained to me that you do nothing. Look, your husband asks it too. Why, I ask, do you say no, Gemma?

X. *On the praises of Siena*

Mother of noble young women, offspring of Remus of old,[20] Siena, the delight of Italy, whether we wish to behold your physi- cal situation and the pleasant well-watered valleys that surround   5 you, or the yearlong spring and the soil always radiant with native rose beds and your verdant hills. What shall I say of the works of   10 human hands or the many rich marbles? What of the many life-

Passim? quid fora? quid vias?
15   Quid deum sacra templa?

Adde publica civium
    Iura parque iugum et pares
    Cunctis imperii vices,
Adde tot populorum opes,
20   Tot parentia late

Oppida, adde virum ingenia,
    Adde artes, nec inhospita
    Corda Pieridum choris.
O vere soboles Remi,
25   Digna nomine, digna

Urbs tantis titulis patrum,
    Te concordia, te bona
    Pax alat, famis et minarum
Immunem, tibi defluat
30   Flavis Brandus arenis!

XI. In Ecnomum

Oarionem pro Erigone citat Ecnomus: unde?
    Non facit ad mores virgo, sed Oarion.

XII. De Maximiliano Caesare

Cum modo pacatis devicta per oppida ripis
    Laetus in aequoreas curreret Ister aquas,
Et modo surgentes operoso ex marmore villas
    Arvaque non una passim habitata domo,
5   Nunc impressa solo tot miraretur aratra,
    Nuper ubi saevis lustra fuere lupis,
Cunctaque laetitia et blanda resonantia pace,

like statues everywhere? or the piazzas, the streets, the sacred 15
temples of the gods? Add to this the communal laws of the citi-
zens and equal burdens and equal opportunities for all to govern,
and also the resources of the people, the numerous towns subject 20
to you, spreading far and wide. Take into account as well the arts,
and hearts not alien to the Muses. O true offspring of Remus,
worthy of the name, a city worthy of the many distinctions of 25
your forefathers, may concord and good peace preserve you free of
famine and threats, and may the Fonte Branda[21] flow along on its 30
yellow sands.

XI. Against Ecnomus[22]

Ecnomus reads Oarion[23] instead of Erigone.[24] For what reason?
The young maiden does not suit his morals, but Oarion does.

XII. On Emperor Maximilian

While but recently the Danube flowed joyfully by its peaceful
banks through conquered towns into the waters of the sea, and
past newly built villas of highly wrought marble and a countryside
dotted with many landed estates, now it would look with won- 5
der upon the great number of plows marking off the new territo-
ries, where just a short time ago there were the lairs of savage
wolves, and all resounds with joy and quiet peace, and here and

Hic illic chorea luxuriante levi:
Postquam operis causam didicit te, maxime Caesar,
10   'His' ait 'his manibus sceptra regenda mea.'

XIII. De Dante Aligero

'Quis sacer hic, Erato, vates, dic, aurea.' 'Dantes
      Aliger.' 'At vocis quod genus et numeri?'
'Vox patria illa; viro numeros sine nomine nuper
      Miserat auctoris Sicilis Aetna sui.'
5   'Materiam nunc ede.' 'Animarum horrenda piacla,
      Quodque iter ad superos, ad Styga quodque ferat.'
'Unde domo?' 'Veterem agnoscit Florentia alumnum.'
      'Ecquae tot merces dotibus?' 'Exilium.'
Heu sortem indignam et virtutibus invida saecla,
10   Quamvis, cui virtus contigit, et patria est!

XIV. De Cydone Eliensi

Sero deorum iam tenentem altaria,
      Rebus tyrannum perditis
Cydo assecutus, 'Quam' inquit 'ex voto hoc quoque,
      Dis patriis iuvantibus,
5 Ut liberatae patriae potissimum
      Hac vota solvam victima!'
Dixit, sacrisque maximum invocans Iovem,
      Transverberat pectus nocens.

XV. Ad Bartholomaeum Scalam

Cum Musae tibi debeant Latinae
Tot iuncto pede scripta, tot soluto,
Tot sales Latio lepore tinctos,

there with reveling, fleet-footed dancers. After the river was told
that all this was owed to you, greatest Caesar, he said: "With   10
these, these hands my kingdom is to be ruled."

XIII. On Dante Alighieri

"Tell me, golden Erato[25] who is this sacred bard?" — "Dante
Alighieri." — "And what is his language and meter?" — "The lan-
guage is that of his native land, and Sicilian Etna previously sent
him the meter[26] of one of its authors, whose name is unknown."
— "Tell me now his subject." — "The horrible atonement for sin   5
that souls suffer, and which path leads to heaven and which to the
Styx." — "Where did he come from?" — "Florence acknowledges
him as its former son." — "And what reward was given for his
talents?" — "Exile."[27]

O! What an unworthy fate! O age hostile to virtue! — although   10
to one whom Virtue has favored, she is also his native land!

XIV. Concerning Cylon[28] of Elis

In pursuit of the tyrant who clung, too late, to the altar of the
gods when all his fortunes were lost, Cylon said: "In accordance
with my vow I shall accomplish this also, with the help of my
country's gods, with this victim above all I shall fulfill my vow in   5
thanksgiving for the liberation of the country." So he spoke, and
calling upon mighty Jupiter, he transfixed his guilt-stained breast.

XV. To Bartolomeo Scala[29]

Although the Latin Muses owe you so many writings both in verse
and in prose, so many witticisms imbued with Latin charm, so

Tot cultis documenta sub figuris,
5   Tot volumina patriae dicata,
Quae nulli taceant diu minores,
Tot praetoria iura, tot curules,
Tot fasces proprio labore partos,
Plus multo tamen, o beate amice, est,
10   Quod Scalam Latio pater dedisti
Aucturam numerum novem sororum
Casto carmine, castiore vita.

XVI. Epitaphium Laurae Comitae

Has lacrimas tibi, Laura, damus tristissima dona,
    Sed tamen, heu, moestis debita funeribus,
Funeribusque tuis et nostro, Laura, dolori,
    Nulla licet mutae gratia sit cineri.
5 Heu, ubi flos ille oris? ubi decor? abstulit, heheu,
    Abstulit, in cineres et dedit hora nocens.
At non et nostras lacrimas dedit. Accipe amantis
    Quod superest, lacrimas accipe, acerba cinis!
Hic animum sensusque meos tibi, Laura, sacramus,
10   Qua licet extinctam nunc quoque parte sequar.

XVII. De victoria Ferdinandi regis Hispaniarum

Quis mihi annosum propere Falernum
Ingerit? multa quis humum colorat
Splendidus rosa? procul omnis esto
    Cura dolorque!

5 Hic dies nota meliore dignus
Leniet longas patriae querelas,
Dum iuvat gravem merita catena
    Dicere Malcen,

many teachings couched in an elegant style, so many volumes 5
dedicated to the country, of such quality that future generations
will speak of them for years to come, so many praetorian laws,
curule magistrates, so many offices won by your own efforts, nev-
ertheless, blessed friend, you did much more as a father in giving 10
to Latium a Scala who would increase the number of the nine
Muses by her chaste poetry and even more chaste life.

XVI. Epitaph of Countess Laura[30]

We offer you these tears, Laura, saddest of gifts but alas! owed to
your mournful funeral rites, to your final rites, Laura, and to my
sorrow, though the mute ashes cannot return thanks. Alas! where
is the flower of that face? Where the beauty? Alas! the baleful pas- 5
sage of time has taken it away and reduced it to ashes. But our
tears it has not reduced to ashes. Accept what a lover has left to
him, accept my tears, cruel ashes! We consecrate our soul and our
feelings to you, Laura, and in this way I shall follow you now also, 10
though you are dead.

XVII. On the victory of Ferdinand, King of Spain

Who will pour me quickly the aged Falernian? Who will color the
ground brilliantly with a profusion of roses? Away all care and
sorrows! This day, worthy of a superior wine, will alleviate the 5
prolonged laments of the country, as we celebrate the deserved
subjection of Málaga[31] and tell of you raised aloft on your snow-

Teque sublimem niveis quadrigis
10 Ferre votivis pia thura templis,
Sancte rex, claudente latus beata
    Coniuge sacrum.

Macti avis, macti ditione, macti
Tot feris late populis subactis,
15 Digne vir sponsa mulierque tanto
    Digna marito!

XVIII. Ad elenchum

Felix elenche — sive tu Rubri venis
Civis profundi sive qua ditis freti
Extrema fessum Circium Tethys videt —
Qui tam remotis hospes ex oris vagus
5 Pendes puellae candido e collo meae,
Unde et volucris patriae dites rogos
Spernis, potentis desidens herae sinu,
Et multodoras Indiae messes tuae.
Sed, sive fatis hoc tibi stabat deum
10 Sive huc secunda sorte movisti pedem,
Dic, o beate, effare, dic, felix, age,
Ecquid pudico mane cum levat toro
Vultus nitentis, patrium agnoscis iubar
Indosque solos iam negas diem dare?

XIX. In Ecnomum

Foedus es aspectu — quid ni? — tam dispare ocello,
    Verum idem lingua foedior et gravior.
Si tamen ingenium spectas, foedissima mens est:
    O tot inauditis obrute flagitiis!

white chariot, bearing pious incense to the churches built in fulfill- 10
ment of your vows, holy king, with your happy spouse by your
revered side. Be ye honored for your ancestry, honored for your
sovereignty, honored for your subjugation of so many fierce peo-
ples far and wide, a man worthy of his spouse and a woman wor- 15
thy of so great a man.

XVIII. To a pearl

O fortunate pearl — whether you come as a citizen from the deep
Red Sea or some other rich sea where the far-off ocean sees the
weary northwest wind — who, as a wandering guest displaced from
such remote shores, now hang from the white neck of my beloved, 5
spurning the rich pyres of your volatile native land, leaving the
breast of your powerful mistress and the many-scented harvests of
your land of India. But whether this was the will of the gods or 10
whether you moved here through some stroke of good fortune, tell
me, O blessed one, say it, declare it, whether when she raises her
radiant countenance from her chaste bed in the morning, you rec-
ognize the first light of day and are now ready to say that India is
not the only source of daylight?

XIX. Against Ecnomus

You are ugly in appearance — how could it not be so? — with one
eye so different than the other, but you are more repulsive and
obnoxious because of your tongue. If, however, one looks at your
mental abilities, your mind is utterly repellent, O man debased by
so many unparalleled shameful acts.

XX. Ad Amorem

Quo me, saeve, rapis, puer,
    Intermissa diu bella iterum movens,
Et truces renovas minas
    Nec gnarae precibus nec lacrimis virum
5 Ullis cedere Martiae?
    Atqui tempus erat servitio gravi
Lassum solvere iam latus
    Et finem miseris ponere questibus,
Nec rursum facibus novis
10   Vexare immeritos post Glycerae rogos
Donandum rude debita.
    Quod si nec subitum discidium Cloes
Nec durus Glycerae cinis,
    Quae tandem lacrimis finis erit meis?

XXI. De se et Cosmo Pactio

Pulchre convenit optimis amicis,
Marullo profugoque Pactioque.
Nec mirum: pariles ruinae utrisque,
Urbana altera et illa Fesulana,
5 Confectae resident, nec elevantur.
Insontes pariter, miselli utrique
Uno in exilio, educatuli ambo,
Non hic quam ille minus vorax amari,
Concordes comites novem sororum.
10 Pulchre convenit optimis amicis.

XXII. De Aenea

Cum ferret medios proles Cytherea per hostes
    Impositi collo languida membra patris,

XX. To Love

Where are you carrying me off, savage child, stirring up wars that had long been discontinued, and renewing the cruel threats of Marzia, who is incapable of surrendering to men's prayers and 5 tears. And yet the time was long overdue to free my weary breast from its oppressive servitude and to put an end to my tearful plaints, and not to torment it with new flames of love after the 10 undeserved death of Glycera. The time is long overdue to be given the wooden sword[32] of discharge from service. But if the sudden separation from Chloe and the cruel death of Glycera was not enough, what end will there be to my tears?

XXI. Of himself and Cosimo Pazzi[33]

It turned out very conveniently for two very good friends, Marullus and Pazzi, to be exiles together. It is no wonder: both suffered similar disasters, one in Rome, the other in Fiesole; both cities lie 5 prostrate with no hope of being raised up again. Both of us are equally innocent, both disconsolate in their exile, both reasonably well educated, neither one nor the other less eager to be loved, both at one in the cultivation of the nine sisters. It turned out very 10 conveniently for two very good friends.

XXII. On Aeneas

When the offspring of Venus was carrying the languid limbs of his father on his shoulders through enemy lines, he said: "Be merciful,

'Parcite,' ait 'Danai! levis est sene gloria rapto,
    At non erepto gloria patre levis.'

XXIII. De statua Bruti hedera circundata

Quid servitutis dexteram immunem gravis
    Hederae coherces vis mala?
An esse Bruti quam tenes nescis manum,
    Nunc quoque tyrannidi asperam,
5   Quamvis iam et ipsae sylvae et invia nemora
    Partes sequimini Caesarum?

XXIV. De Neaerae absentia

Invisus mihi Ianus adest, absente Neaera.
    Ite procul, lusus blanditiaeque leves.
Conveniunt lacrimae tot suspiratibus aegrae
    Aptaque singultu tristia verba meo.
5   Quod tamen in me unum est, cor tecum animusque, Neaera, est,
    Absentem quamvis sors procul atra tenet.

XXV. In Ollum

Graecari quod luctor ais, quod carmina pango:
    Num romanaris, quaeso, quod, Olle, fugis?

XXVI. Ad Neaeram

Quo, quo, dura — tibi, Neaera, dico —
Olim praesidium meum decusque?
An me tu quoque iam facis caballi?
Nam cui, cui iam hominum est fides habenda?
5   Certe tu mea cura, tu voluptas,
Per te non grave erat domo carere,

Greeks, it is little glory to capture an old man, but it is no small glory to rescue one's father."

XXIII. *On the statue of Brutus*[34] *wreathed with ivy*

Evil force of ivy, why do you bind the right hand of Brutus, which was free of heavy servitude? Are you not aware that you restrain the right hand of Brutus, still the bitter enemy of tyranny, although at the present time the very forests and pathless woods follow the party of the Caesars? 5

XXIV. *On the absence of Neaera*

The hated first of January is upon me and Neaera is absent. Away with you, amorous sports and frivolous allurements. Anguished tears befit copious sighs, and sad words are suitable to my sobbing. But one thing remains unchanged: my heart and soul are with you, Neaera, though black fate keep you far from me. 5

XXV. *Against Ollus*

You say I act like a Greek because I stand my ground, and because I write poetry. I ask you, don't you act like a Roman, Ollus, because you run away?

XXVI. *To Neaera*

Why, why are you pitiless—I am speaking to you, Neaera—once my protection and my glory? Are you too going to treat me like a useless nag? In whom can one put one's trust these days? You, at least, my darling and my delight, made it tolerable for me to be 5

Quae nunc tot miserum in malis relinquis
Et nostris frueris superba damnis.
Quod si te mea nec fides, Neaera,
10   Nec suspiria nec movent querelae,
At spera Nemesim deam potentem,
Quae poenas animi istius reposcet.

XXVII. *In Ecnomum*

Lingere carbatinas vult Vection Ecnomus, ipse
   Ut possit trepidas lingere cercolipas.

XXVIII. *De urna in usum fontis versa*

Tu, quicunque meo fontem de marmore sumis,
   Parce, precor, cineri — sum vetus urna — pio.
Vertit in hos usus gelidi rudis accola fontis,
   Nescius, ah, quantum susciperet sceleris.
5   At tu non meritos manes veneratus in urna,
   Hinc quoque tot rerum disce hominumque vices.

XXIX. *In Ecnomum*

Quidam Pelasgos iure questus est suo
   Carere 'inepti' nomine,
Sed id Pelasgum maxima, hercle, iniuria,
   Quis nullus Arpinas foret,
5   Ut doctus, ut vir, ut probus, mille ut alia,
   Si quaeris, id denique genus.
Nam Pulcianos ut Latinus quispiam
   Rudes, scelestos, improbos,
Peculiari sic ἀκαίρους nomine
10   Dixerit et ἀφυέας meus.

without a home, but now you abandon me in my plight, victim of
so many evils, and you haughtily take pleasure in my undoing. But   10
if neither my devotion nor my sighs nor my laments move you,
Neaera, prepare yourself for the powerful goddess, Nemesis, who
will demand vengeance for this haughtiness of yours.

XXVII. *Against Ecnomus*

Ecnomus wants Vettius[35] to lick shoes made of hide so that he
himself can lick quivering hairy monkeys' asses.

XXVIII. *On an urn turned into a fountain*

You, whoever you are, who draw water from my marble, be merci-
ful, I pray you, to these ashes, worthy of respect. I am an old urn.
An ignorant countryman converted me to use as a cool fountain,
ah! not knowing how great a crime he was committing. But you,   5
out of respect for the shades of the dead man in this urn, which
did not merit such a fate, learn also from this of the vicissitudes of
men and things.

XXIX. *Against Ecnomus*

Someone rightly complained that the Greeks did not have a word
for *ineptus*, but the greatest insult to the Greeks is to say that they
did not have a Cicero. If you are looking for erudition, manliness,   5
probity and a thousand other things, that is the nation you want.
For while a certain Italian[36] may have called the people of Mon-
tepulciano ignorant, wicked and dishonest, my fellow Greek would
use the adjectives "ill-suited" and "untalented."   10

XXX. De Andrea Lamponiani

Dum forte Aemathiis Virtus Romana parentat
    Manibus et lacrimis pelluit ossa pia,
Lamponianidae miseras nex perculit aures
    Et subito sensus diriguere gelu.
5 Mox tamen ipsa sui non immemor allevat artus,
    Utque dedit caris annua iusta rogis,
'Brutorum Cassique' inquit 'monumenta, valete,
    Quaeque meis longum fletibus herba vires.
Nos alio revocant nova funera sanctaque nati
10   Sparsa per indignas, hei mihi, membra vias.
Scilicet haec eventa mihi Fortuna reservat,
    Sic quoque sed certe iura tuenda meis.'

XXXI. Ad tabellam

Parva, sed nimium tabella felix,
Quae vultus dominae refers cupitos
Et nunquam mihi dura, acerba nunquam,
Fronte nescio quid nuis serena,
5 Ut te conspicio libens et ora
Mille Amoribus aucta Gratiisque
Agnosco! ut genulas meae puellae,
Ut caros libet intueri ocellos,
Quos dari cuperet sibi Dione!
10 En cape, en violasque cinnamumque
Et mixtas casiae rosas rubentis;
Cape olim tibi destinata serta,
Quae vides lacrimis madere nostris.
Tu suspiria longa, tu dolentis
15 Posthac accipies graves querelas
Et praesens poteris videre flentem,

XXX. On Andrea Lampugnani[37]

As luck would have it, when Roman Virtue was offering sacrifice to the shades of Emathia[38] and bathing the revered bones with tears, news of the death of Lampugnani struck her unhappy ears and suddenly her senses became rigid with cold. Then, not un- 5 mindful of her duties, she lifts his limbs, and as she performed the annual obsequies to the dear remains, she said: "Farewell, tombs of Brutus and Cassius, and grass long verdant with my tears. New funeral rites and the holy limbs of a son scattered, alas! over by- 10 ways unworthy of him call me elsewhere. Clearly Fortune reserves these events for me; in this way the rights of my lieges must be unfailingly protected."

XXXI. To my writing tablet

My small but extremely fortunate writing tablet, you recall the desired visage of my mistress, and never harsh to me, never hostile, with serene brow you seem to nod assent. How gladly I look 5 upon you and recognize your features enhanced by a thousand Cupids and Graces! How pleasant it is to gaze upon the cheeks of my loved one and her dear eyes, which Dione would wish were given to her. Here, take these violets and twigs of cinnamon and 10 red roses mixed with cassia; take these garlands destined for you long ago, which you see are wet with our tears. From now on you will receive long sighs and the tearful laments of a disconsolate 15 lover, and presently you will be able to see one weeping, whom

Quem nec mensa iuvat petita frustra
Nec somnus tegit aut quies ocellos.
At vos interea, labella cara,
20 An est cur ego pressa non resuggo
Et centum fero basiationes?
Sed quis tam subitus refulsit ignis?
Quae te fax, bona, corripit, tabella?
Nosco incendia dura, nosco flammas,
25 Quas de pectore convomo aestuanti.
Mea isthaec, mea culpa; ego scelestus,
Qui te dum temere osculis fatigo
Et iuncto iuvat ore commorari,
Saevo pectoris halitu perussi.

XXXII. De Xysto et herede

Exhausit Xystus bellis et caedibus urbem:
Tercentena heres restituit sobole.

XXXIII. In Posthumum

Quid involato nectis ex auro grave,
Inepte, collum, Posthume?
Hoc est fateri crimen, hoc palam tibi est
Laqueum ominari debitum.

XXXIV. Epitaphium Annibalis

'Cuius hic est tumulus? quae tu, rogo, et unde verendas
Tunsa genas, crinem sic laniata sedes?'
'Annibalis cinerem sacrum aspicis; ast ego Enyo
Fata viri et casus hic queror immeritos,
5 Quem, Roma devicta, odio invidiaque suorum
Tam procul a Lybia terra Libissa tegit:

neither nourishment can alleviate, which he seeks in vain; nor does
sleep or rest cover his eyes. But you in the meantime, dear lips, is   20
there any reason why I should not press my lips upon you and
suck you and give you a hundred kisses? But what was that sud-
den blaze of fire? What torch ignites you, my good writing tablet?
I know these pitiless fires, I know these flames, which I pour out   25
from my impassioned breast. This is my fault, my fault, since as I
recklessly tired you with my kisses and delighted in the closeness
of our lips, I scorched you with the hot breath that issued from
my breast.

XXXII. On Sixtus and his heir[39]

Sixtus exhausted the city with wars and bloodshed: his heir re-
stored it with three-hundred-fold progeny.

XXXIII. Against Postumus

Why do you wreathe and burden your neck with stolen gold, you
fool, Postumus? This is to confess your crime, this is a clear prog-
nostication of the noose you deserve.

XXXIV. Epitaph of Hannibal

"Whose tomb is this? And who are you, I ask, and why do you sit
here, your venerable cheeks bruised and your hair rent in this
way?"—"You behold the sacred ashes of Hannibal, but I am
Enyo,[40] and I lament the fate and undeserved defeat of a great
man, who, after conquering Rome, through the hatred and envy of   5
his own countrymen, now lies buried far from Libya but covered

Non tamen, Annibalis opera nisi et ense superbo,
  Annibalem potuit perdere Parca nocens.'

XXXV. Ad Amorem

Si coelum patria est, puer, beatum,
Si vere peperit Venus benigna,
Si nectar tibi Massicum ministrat,
Si sancta ambrosia est cibus petitus,
5   Quid noctes habitas diesque mecum?
Quid victum face supplicemque aduris?
Quid longam lacrimis sitim repellis?
Quid nostrae dape pasceris medullae?
O vere rabidum genus ferarum!
10 O domo Styge patriaque digne!
Iam levis sumus umbra: quid lacessis?

XXXVI. Ad Amorem

Sancte, qui Memphin, puer, Eriosque
Temperas colles et amoena Cypri
Rura lascivis viola perenni
    Grata Napaeis,

5   Te cano prolem genitoris Aethrae,
Aureae prolem Veneris potentem,
Nobilem flammis et habente certa
    Tela pharetra;

Cuius et tellus et aquae verendum
10 Nomen atque aer veneratur ipse,
Acre cui paret nigra vulneranti
    Aula tyranni.

by Libyssan soil.[41] Nevertheless, were it not for Hannibal's own actions and his proud sword, pernicious fate would not have been able to destroy Hannibal."

XXXV. To Love

If blissful heaven is your place of birth, my child, if it is true that kindly Venus truly brought you forth, if she serves you Massic wine,[42] if holy ambrosia is the food you seek, why do you spend 5 nights and days with me? Why do you burn me, vanquished by your torch and begging for mercy? Why do you stave off your great thirst with my tears? Why do you feast off the marrow of my bones? O truly ravening breed of wild beast, worthy to have the 10 Styx as your home and native land! I am already reduced to an insubstantial shadow. Why do you give me no peace?

XXXVI. To Love

O holy child, who rule Memphis and Mount Eryx[43] and the lovely countryside of Cyprus, dear to the frolicsome woodland nymphs because of its perennial violets, I sing of you, offspring of Aethra,[44] 5 powerful offspring of golden Venus, known for your flaming torches and your quiver with its unerring arrows. Your respected name is held in awe by earth and sea and the very air, and the dark 10 hall of the tyrant[45] obeys you when he is severely wounded by

Quin et hiberna Lycia suisque
Cynthius Delphis genitor relictis,
15 Candidum Admeti pecus et iuvencos
        Pavit heriles,

Cum sub umbroso recubans salicto,
Immemor laudum patrii triumphi,
Flevit immitis leviore plectro
20   Damna sagittae.

Nam quid aut vasti genus acre ponti
Prosequar cete tibi perdomata
Aut in arentis Lybiae leones
        Finibus ictos?

25 Te canit ramo residens virenti
Daulias mater, tibi tollit atrox
Sibilum serpens fera, te iubente
        Regia coniunx

Per iuga et montes vacuosque saltus
30 Errat albenti placitura tauro
Et studet duri thalamis iuvenci
        Digna videri.

XXXVII. De exilio suo

Quid iuvat hostiles totiens fugisse catenas
        Atque animam fatis eripuisse suis?
Non ut cognati restarem sanguinis unus
        Crudelis patriae qui superesse velim,
5   Nec quia non animus lucis contemptor abunde est
        Et velit exilium vertere posse nece,
Sed ne progenies servire antiqua Marulli
        Cogerer indigno tractus ab hoste puer.

Love's arrows. Even the Cynthian god,[46] Apollo, leaving his winter
habitation in Lycia[47] and his home in Delphi to pasture the white   15
flock and the calves of his master Admetus,[48] when he was lying
under shady willows, forgetful of the praises given to his father's
triumph, bewailed in a minor key the injuries he had suffered from   20
Cupid's cruel arrow. Why should I dwell on the fierce race of the
vast sea, where you tamed the sea monster, or tell of the lions you
struck down in the land of parched Libya? The Daulian mother,[49]   25
perched on a green branch sings of you, for you the fierce serpent
suppresses his dreadful hiss, and at your command the king's con-
sort wanders over ridges and mountains and deserted thickets to   30
please the white bull and she is eager to be esteemed worthy of
mating with a ferocious young bull.

XXXVII. On his exile

What good is it to have escaped enemy bondage so many times
and rescued my life from the fate that awaited it? Not that I
should be the only one left of my line and should wish heartlessly
to survive the fall of my native land, nor that I do not thoroughly   5
despise the light of day and would gladly exchange exile for a vio-
lent death, but so that I, offspring of the ancient line of Marulli,
dragged off by a lowly enemy, would not be forced to be a slave. If

Si procul a patria Scythico deprensus in orbe,
10   Heu facinus, Bessi iussa superba fero
Imperiumque ferox patior dominumque potentem,
    Nec nisi libertas nomen inane mea est,
Utilius fuerat duro servire tyranno
    Cumque mea patria cuncta dolenda pati.
15 Est aliquid cineres et tot monumenta suorum
    Cernere et imperiis imperia aucta patrum
Natalique frui, superest dum spiritus, aura,
    Nec procul externis ludibrium esse locis.
Scilicet exuitur generis decus omne domusque,
20   Cum semel ignotam presseris exul humum,
Nec iam nobilitas nec avum generosa propago
    Aut iuvat antiquis fulcta domus titulis.
At certe, patriae quondam dum regna manebant,
    Hospitio totus, qua patet orbis, erat.
25 Tunc, ah, tunc animam pueri exhalare senesque
    Debuimus, tantis nec superesse malis;
Tunc patrii meminisse animi et virtutis avitae
    Inque necem pulchris vulneribus ruere,
Nec libertatem patrio nisi Marte tueri;
30   Haec via quaerendae certa salutis erat.
O pereat numerum primus qui fecit in armis.
    Quantulacunque sat est, dum modo certa manus;
Quantulacunque sat est, patriis ubi miles in armis
    Saevit et adversum non timet ire globos,
35 Et modo coniugium, modo pignora cara domusque
    Excitat, effoeti nunc pia cura patris.
Quis furor est patriam vallatam hostilibus armis
    Tutantem externis credere velle viris
Ignotaque manu confundere civica signa
40   Et sua non Graecis tela putare satis?
Ille, ille hostis erat, ille expugnabat Achivos

far from my native land, captured in the region of Scythia — cruel   10
fate! — I endure the harsh commands of a Bessian[50] and submit to
the fierce authority of a powerful warlord, and liberty is nothing
more than an empty name, it would have been better to serve a
cruel tyrant and suffer every torment with my native country. It is   15
of some comfort to see the tombs and memorials of one's own
people and conquest upon conquest of one's ancestors, to breathe
one's native air, while we still have breath, rather than to be an
object of scorn in a foreign land. Naturally, all dignity of origin
and family is stripped away once you have set foot on unknown   20
soil as an exile, and nobility and glorious lineage and a house
founded on illustrious titles are no longer of any worth.

But certainly, long ago, when the power of our native country
was still intact, the whole world showed us hospitality. That was   25
the time when, young and old, we should have breathed our last
and not survived to see such great calamities; that was the time to
remember the spirit and courage of our ancestors and to rush
headlong to our death bearing glorious wounds. The only way to
defend liberty was with our own armed forces; that was the one   30
sure way to find salvation. Perish the man who first gave impor-
tance to numbers in warfare. Any army, no matter how small, is
sufficient if it is determined; no matter how small, it is sufficient if
the soldier fights ferociously for his native land and is not afraid to
face the close-packed enemy lines, and now his wife, now his dear   35
children, now his home, now dutiful concern for his frail father
spur him on. What madness it is to entrust to strangers the de-
fense of one's native city, besieged by enemy forces, and to defile
the city's banners in unknown hands and to think that Greek   40
forces are not enough! He was the real enemy: *that* soldier de-
feated the Greeks and looted their cities.[51] It was he who impi-

Miles et eversas diripiebat opes,
   Ille deos et fana malis dabat ignibus, ille
   Romanum in Turcas transtulit imperium,
45 Nec nobis tam fata deum, quam culpa luenda est
   Mensque parum prudens consiliumque ducis.
Hanc igitur miseri luimus longumque luemus,
   Dum nos Euxinus et lacrimae minuant.

XXXVIII. In Posthumum

Omnia cum facias, miraris cur facias nil:
   Posthume, rem solam qui facit, ille facit.

XXXIX. In Ecnomum

Quid separatam, vane, suppernas, rogo,
   Alnum Catulli nobilem,
Plebi otiosae scilicet risum parans,
   Oblitus ut soles pedis?

XL. De Autolemo

Dixerat Autolemo flammas consultus aruspex
   Die cavendas postero:
Credidit, et rerum dubius de mane sub amnis
   Delituit Etrusci vadis.
5 Sed neque sic fatum effugit, nam dum innatat Arno,
   Ictus crematur fulmine.

XLI. Ad Alexandram Scalam

Cum versu referas novem sorores,
Vix lustris bene adhuc tribus peractis;
Cum dulci sale seriisque blandis
Ipsum iam superes, puella, patrem,

ously set fire to the gods and their temples, he who delivered the
Roman Empire to the Turks. It is not so much the gods' destiny as   45
our own guilt that must be expiated and the imprudent design and
strategy of our leader. Thus we unhappy creatures expiate and will
continue to expiate our guilt for a long time to come until we are
consumed by the Black Sea and our tears.

XXXVIII. *Against Postumus*

Postumus, you are surprised that you accomplish nothing when
you do everything: it's the man who does one thing that accom-
plishes something.

XXXIX. *Against Ecnomus*

Why, I ask you, you blockhead, do you hamstring the famous
solitary alder of Catullus, providing laughter for the idle crowd,
neglecting the meter, as usual.[52]

XL. *On Autolemus*

The soothsayer consulted by Autolemus told him that he must
avoid flames on the following day. He believed him and being un-
certain what to do, hid himself in the shoals of the Tuscan river
from early morning. But not even this allowed him to escape his   5
fate, for while he was swimming in the Arno he was hit by a light-
ning bolt and consumed by fire.

XLI. *To Alessandra Scala*

Since in your verse you call to mind the nine sisters, although
you have barely completed fifteen years of age; since with pleas-
ing wit and charming sobriety, though still a young girl, you

5 Quo nihil gravius facetiusque est;
Cum nec sit tibi forma nec modestae
Frontis gratia nec decor nec ipse
Suggestus nimii decens capilli
Qui possit nisi coelitus videri,
10 Quid mirum, mea Scala, si decembri
Reddis debita messibus futuris,
Si mittis mediis rosas pruinis,
Natura bene quo voles sequente?

XLII. De Spe et Nemesi

'Quaenam haec, tam semper quae laeta est?' 'Optima rerum,
  Spes bona.' 'Quae lateri iuncta?' 'Potens Nemesis.'
'Dux magis, an comes est?' 'Vindex magis.' 'Unde duabus
  Templa eadem?' 'Speres ne nisi quod liceat.'

XLIII. De Aristomene

Viderat armatas uni dare terga cohortes
  Iuppiter et Martem credidit esse suum.
Mox, ut Aristomenes notis procul agnitus armis
  Et fulsit volucris auxiliaris apex,
5 'Macte,' ait 'o iuvenis, si te mea bella tulissent,
  Non alia coelum tunc eguisset ope.'

XLIV. Ad Amorem

Quid tantum lacrimis meis proterve
Insultas, puer, et semel iacentis
Nequicquam in tenuem furis favillam?
Non sum, non ego, quem putas Marullum.
5 Iam pridem occidit ille, nec superstes

already surpass your father, who is unsurpassed in charm and so- 5
lemnity; since there is no element of your beauty or in the
gracefulness of your modest expression or in your pleasing appear-
ance or in the voluminous masses of your hair so becomingly ar-
ranged that could not seem divinely sent, why should we wonder, 10
my Scala, if in December you absolve your debts to future har-
vests, if in the midst of frost you send forth roses, with nature
gladly following wherever you wish?

XLII. On Hope and Nemesis

"Who is this who is always so happy?" — "The best of all things:
good Hope." — "Who is this next to her?" — "Powerful Nemesis."
— "Is she more a leader or a companion?" — "She is more an
avenger." — "Why do both have the same temple?" — "So that you
hope only for what is allowed."

XLIII. On Aristomenes[53]

Jupiter saw armed cohorts take flight before one man and thought
it was his son Mars. Then, when he recognized Aristomenes from
afar by his well-known armor and the gleaming helmet of an aux-
iliary with its fluttering plumes, he said, "Bravo, young man, if 5
my wars had enlisted you, heaven would not have needed any
other help."

XLIV. To Love

Why, Cupid, do you impudently mock my tears and vent your
rage in vain against the meager ashes of one who lies prostrate
once and for all. I am not the Marullus you think I am. That per- 5
son died long ago and did not survive the separation from his

Carae discidium tulit Neaerae,
Quae nunc tot fluviis procul locisque
Illum nominat, ut ferunt, et illum
Suspirat lacrimis dies et horas,
10 Nequicquam profugum vocans maritum.
Ah, ne tu quoque nos, puella, perde;
Sat, o sat miseri sumus superque!
Quid demens laceras genas? quid ora?
Iam parce aureolis, precor, capillis;
15 Si nescis, meus est, Neaera, sanguis,
Istos quae lacrimae rigant ocellos.
Quod siqua est tibi cura adhuc Marulli
Necdum perditus usquequaque in aevum est,
In te, lux mea, parcere huic memento.

XLV. In Ecnomum

Posse negas dici 'melos,' facunde poeta,
    Atque adeo picas 'nectar' ais 'canere,'
Scilicet huc studio curaque trahente fideli
    Nequando placitum nectar ab ore cadat.
5 Sed neque divinus male μέλος ἄεισεν Homerus,
    Nec, nisi qui laudat, nectar, inepte, canit.

XLVI. De Apolline et Antonio Squarceluppo

Olim superbus Pane devicto, Rhodum
    Qui temperat Phoebus suam,
Tmoli canebat iudicis sententiam
    Iussumque cedere Arcada,
5 Cum Squarceluppi voce perculsus nova
    Ingemuit ad cannas viri,
Vicesque rerum questus, 'Heu, vici deos,
    Nunc cedo' ait 'mortalibus.'

dear Neaera, who now calls upon his name near divers streams and in far-off places, as people say, and sighs for him in tears at every hour, calling in vain upon her exiled husband. Ah! Do not 10 add to our undoing, beloved; we are miserable enough, and more than enough! Why do you tear your cheeks in your frenzy? And your face? Spare your golden hair, I pray you. If you are not aware 15 of it, Neaera, the tears that bathe your eyes are my blood; if you are still concerned about Marullus and he is not lost to you forever, remember to spare him, my light, in yourself.

XLV. *Against Ecnomus*

You claim, eloquent poet, that the word *melos* cannot be used and even say that magpies sing nectar, no doubt because your study and meticulous care convinced you of that meaning, so that the pleasing nectar might not fall from your lips. But the divine Ho- 5 mer was not wrong to sing a *melos*[54] nor does anyone sing "nectar," you idiot, except one who is writing a eulogy.[55]

XLVI. *On Apollo and Antonio Squarcialupi*[56]

Once long ago Apollo, who rules over his beloved Rhodes, arrogant after his defeat of Pan, was singing of the decision of Tmolus[57] and how the Arcadian was ordered to concede the victory, but now struck by the new voice of Squarcialupi, he ut- 5 tered in anguish to the organ pipes, lamenting the vicissitudes of fate: "Alas! I have conquered the gods, and now I surrender to mortals."

XLVII. *Ad Manilium Rhallum*

Malli, nec tepidi grata Favonii
Spirat temperies nec vagus Adria
Secura patitur currere navitam
    Pinu perpetua fide;

5 Non omnis tenui gutture per dies
Integrat volucris carmina Daulias,
Non semper rosa, non lilia vestiunt
    Aut flos terram hiacynthinus.

Nos, Malli, quoque sat, nos quoque sat diu
10 Insignes patria viximus et domo.
Quid mirum, exilio dura per omnia
    Si rerum patimur vices?

Sic Croesum miseris fata potentia
Demersere modis, sic Priamus senex
15 Supplex Iliadum questibus ultimis
    Raptatum petit Hectora,

Sic pastor, neque adhuc gnarus originis,
Tot reges Latius subruit incola,
Quaerendus simili nenia et ipse mox,
20   Annis cuncta trahentibus.

Qui scis an melior nos manet exitus?
Vivendum est lare quocunque libet deis,
Quamvis auspice ego Caesare nec larem
    Despero patrium mihi.

XLVIII. *In Eumelonem*

Indignos vita putat Eumelo, quandoquidem illam
    Et flammis totiens et gladio obiicimus;

XLVII. To Manilius Rhallus

O Malli,[58] the pleasing breezes of warm Favonius are not always
blowing nor does the capricious Adriatic always allow the sailor to
run his course in a safe ship; the nightingale does not renew its   5
song in its tender throat every day nor does the rose or the lily or
the hyacinth always adorn the earth. We too, Malli, yes, we too
have lived long enough, honored men in our country and our   10
home. What marvel is there, then, if we suffer through all the
hardships of exile and the various vicissitudes of life? So in an
atrocious manner the powerful fates cast down Croesus,[59] so old
Priam[60] as a suppliant, begged for the body of Hector that had   15
been violently dragged away, amid the last laments of the Trojan
women, so the simple shepherd of Latium, still ignorant of his
origins, overthrew so many kings, soon to be the object of similar
funeral dirges himself, since time carries all before it. How do you 20
know whether a better fate awaits us? We must live in whatever
home the gods wish, though I have not lost hope that my ancestral
home will be given back to me under the emperor's auspices.

XLVIII. Against Eumelo

Eumelo thinks I am not worthy of life since I expose it so often to
fire and sword, but Eumelo is more unworthy of it since he suffers

Sed magis indignus hac Eumelo, fanda nefanda
    Qui patitur, vitam ne gladio obiiciat.

XLIX. De hirundine

Quid vaga tot terras urbesque emensa volucris,
    Colchidos in saevo nidificas gremio
Pignoribusque tuis credis male sana fidelem,
    Ipsa suos partus quae laniavit atrox,
5 Ni foetus exosa tuos, Pandione nata,
    Phasiaca quaeris perdere saevitia?

L. In Ecnomum

Huc huc, maligna, verte. Quo frustra fugis,
    Vix hoste viso, vipera,
Et iam tenenti frigidam tarde obiicis
    Seram, hostibus fossam velut,
5 Ceu praestet, inter ipse quos nosti mero
    Fregisse noctes improbas?
Quid, quod Pelasgum nomen et patriae decus
    Sub voce mordes 'Graeculi,'
Quasi Pulciana tesqua fodientem patrem
10   Laqueosve fratrum noxios?
Quin quicquid usquam est pestis innatae evome,
    Deprensus in Psylli manu,
Qua tot Latinos principes linguae viros
    Ausus lacessere, tot meos.
15 Agedum, evome, inquam. Iam ne sentis sacrum, iners,
    Sonum et parata verbera?
Rumpere! quid circumspicis frustra? moras
    Quid nectis, obscoenum caput?
Adeste iambi, rapite, caedite, trahite —
20   Sed supplices tendit manus:

the speakable and the unspeakable in order not to expose his life to the sword.

XLIX. On the swallow[61]

Why, after swiftly traversing so many lands and cities in your wanderings, do you make your nest in the savage breast of Medea and unwisely entrust your offspring to one who cruelly butchered her children, unless, child of Pandion,[62] out of hatred for your own 5
children you seek to annihilate them with Colchian[63] savagery?

L. Against Ecnomus

Turn this way, spiteful viper. Why are you fleeing, in vain, having barely caught sight of the enemy, and why, as he is ready to lay hands on you, do you throw a useless bar in his path, too late, like a ditch blocking the enemy, as if it were preferable to pass nights 5
of debauchery and carousing with your friends? What is the meaning of your deriding the Greek name and the glory of Greece with the word "Greekling," as though you were talking about your father digging up the dry clods of Montepulciano[64] or the insidi- 10
ous traps laid by your brothers? Why don't you vomit up whatever congenital poison you possess, with which you dare to harass so many leading Italians and so many of my countrymen. You have fallen into the hands of the Psylli.[65] Come, now, I say, vomit it up. 15
Don't you hear the accursed sound and the readied blows, you impotent fool? Why do you contrive delaying tactics? End your dawdling! Why are you looking around you in vain, you loathsome creature? To the attack, iambs, seize him, strike him, drag him away—but look! he is stretching out his hands in supplication. 20

Bene habet, vomit. Proh, quae lues! verumtamen
Non nisi timenda inertibus.

LI. De Agesilao

'Nuntia magnanimi, volucris, Iovis, ede. Quid urnae
Invicti rostro cudis Agesilei?'
'Ipsa inter volucres quantum caput effero, tantum
Mortales omnis cedere Agesileo.'

LII. De Laurentio Medice Petri Francisci filio

Felix ingenii, felix et gratiae opumque,
Laurus et antiquis non leve nomen avis,
Quaerenti cuidam num plura his optet, 'Ut' inquit
'Et prodesse queam pluribus et cupiam.'

LIII. De Maximiliano Caesare

O felix nimium dies,
Vere digne mihi Threicia nota,
Tandem sospite Caesare,
Qui flexo veluti victima poplite
5   Pene conciderat modo
Tincturus gladios sanguine civicos,
Ni motus prece publica
Fecisset facinus Iuppiter irritum.
Heu, nil cautum homini satis.
10   Nam, quid tela virum, quid miseri Adriae
Vitamus freta turbida
Autumnosque graves febribus annuis,
Si peiora manent domi
Et non tuta suo regia Caesari est?

It's working! He's vomiting. Good God, what a mess! — but one to be feared only by weaklings.

LI. On Agesilaus[66]

"O bird, proclaim the message of noble Jupiter. Why do you pound with your beak on the urn of undefeated Agesilaus?" "As much as I raise my head above all other birds, so must all mortals yield to Agesilaus."

LII. On Lorenzo de' Medici, son of Pierfrancesco

Fortunate in his mental prowess, fortunate in his personal charm and wealth and a name of no little authority stemming from its ancient ancestry, Lorenzo, when asked whether he desired more than that, answered: "That I might be able to be helpful to more people and desire to do so."

LIII. On Emperor Maximilian

O exceptionally happy day, truly deserving, I believe, of an Orphic song. At last Caesar is safe and sound, who like a sacrificial victim, fallen to its knees, was almost brought low,[67] and would have 5 dyed the swords of his fellow citizens with his blood if Jupiter, moved by public prayers, had not rendered the crime ineffectual. Alas! one can never be cautious enough, For what good is it to 10 avoid men's weapons or the turbulent waters of the Adriatic and the unhealthy autumns that bring yearly fevers, if worse things await us at home and even the palace of the emperor is not safe.

15   Quam prope et Pudor et Fides
      Momento periit nudaque Veritas,
  Quam prope Ingenii vigor
      Virtutisque capax dextera splendidae!
  O saltem his superi malis
20   Contenti, facili dehinc ope sospitent
  Tandem vindice dextera
      Purgantem iuvenem tot Nemeis sola,
  Tot praesepibus efferis
      Humano saturis sanguine iam diu!

Liber Quartus

I.

Quartus hic est tibi promissus, bone Laure, libellus,
  Ultima tam brevibus cura futura iocis,
Qui tamen, exiguus quamvis miniique librique est,
  Exiguus forsan non erit ingenii.

II. De Neaera

Tota es candida, tota munda, tota
Succi plenula, tota mollicella,
Tota nequitiaeque amorque, tota
Elegantula, tota delicata,
5   Tota mel, mea vita, sacharumque
Et tota Assyrii Indicique odores.
At sunt qui tamen hanc negent amandam,
Martellusque meus Resorbolusque.
Quid, si idem aut oculos negent amandos

How nearly Honor and Loyalty and naked Truth perished in an 15
instant, how nearly the vigor of Genius and a right hand capable
of outstanding courage almost perished! O may the gods above,
content at least with these evils, provide defense henceforth with 20
their ready help for this young man, who by his avenging right
hand is at last purging the country of so many Nemean monsters,[68]
of wild stables saturated for so long with human blood.

Book IV

I.

This is the fourth little book I promised you, my dear Lorenzo,[1]
which will be the last of my attempts at brief trifles, and although
it may be diminutive in size and graphically unattractive, perhaps
it will not be lacking in inspiration.

II. On Neaera

You are all fair, immaculate, full of vitality, soft and yielding, brim-
ming with love and mischief, supremely elegant, refined, all honey, 5
my life and my sugar and all Assyrian and Indian aromas. But
there are some who say that this woman should not be loved, like
my friends Martelli[2] and Risorboli.[3] Would these same persons

10 Aut siquid magis est amandum ocellis?
   O viros lepidos parum ac molestos!

III. De Daphne et Apolline

Tuta suis monstris et iam nova laurea Daphne,
   Sic quoque amatori sed tamen aspra deo,
'Nunc' ait 'exulta, ramos complexus inanes;
   Ut tua sim, coniunx non ero nempe tua.'

IV. Ad Alexandram Scalam

Felix sorte patris boni,
   Sed multo magis et corporis egregi
Dote et Pieridum sacris,
   Quas non, Scala, modo plurium inutili,
5 Sed morum pariter duces
   Et culti sequeris carminis arbitras,
Hoc Sappho melior mea,
   Cuius facta domi dictaque plurima
Praestans ingenium inquinant.
10   Nam quo tantus amor Castalii chori,
   Si nec lingua pudentior
   Cultu nec melior vita scientia est
Exemploque Aganippidum,
   Olim quas ideo provida virgines
15 Sanxit relligio patrum
   Non visu faciles, non aditu deas,
Nempe nulla quibus fora
   Aut coetus hominum contribuit levis,
Sed curis vacuum nemus
20   Et spelea pigro roscida frigore,
   Culpae materia procul?
   Ergo non epulis magnanimi patris

say that my eyes should not be loved or anything more dear than   10
one's eyes? O what dull and insensitive persons!

III. On Daphne[4] and Apollo

Saved by her miraculous transformation and now become a new
laurel tree, Daphne addressed these harsh words to her divine
lover: "Exult now, as you embrace empty branches; though I be
yours, I shall never be your wife."

IV. To Alessandra Scala

You are blessed by fortune in having a good father, but much more
because of the gift of a striking appearance and the sacred status of
being favored by the Muses, whom, dearest Scala, you follow not
in the useless manner of most people, but as guides to good mor-   5
als and arbiters of refined poetry, in this superior to my beloved
Sappho, whose private life and bad reputation adulterate her out-
standing talent. For of what use is so great a love for the Castalian   10
chorus[5] if one's language is not more restrained through a good
education and one's life not made better through learning, after
the example of the Muses? The farsighted piety of our ancestors   15
consecrated them as virgin goddesses, not exposed to view or eas-
ily approachable, since they had nothing to do with the market
place or the fickle company of men, but their home was the sacred
grove, free of worldly cares, and dewy, frigid grottos far from all   20
occasion of wrongdoing. Therefore they are not present at the
banquets of their magnanimous father nor do they dare stir with

Adsunt aut temere aureae
   Docta fila lyrae sollicitant manu.
25 Ipse dux Patareus chori
   Iussas saepe deum dicere proelia
Et Coeum Aenaria gravem,
   Coram matre licet, vix iterum audiit.
Nam de Pallade mentio
30   Siquando orta, probant caetera, sed neque
Currus et galeas neque
   Tot pugnata probant proelia virgini,
Multoque aptius autumant
   Versari in calathis foeminam inertibus.
35 Quorum iudicio gravi
   Accedis teneris tu quoque ab unguibus,
Non aut divitiarum egens
   Aut morum, male quos saecula perferunt,
Sed felix vacui ingeni
40   Secessu tacito et pectoris artibus,
Integris animi bonis,
   Quae non ulla potest eripere aut dare
Fati iniuria saeviens.
   Ergo tempus erit, cum tua nomina,
45 Cum mores tremulae senes
   Natabus referent multaque pars nurum
Serae ad lumina tedulae
   Hoc sermone graves decipient manus;
Forsan et patrum origine
50   Confusa ac generis legitima nota
Saecli ambagibus inviis,
   Aut Phoebo genitam aut magnanimo Iove,
Musarumque ferent chori
   Unam saecla virum te quoque postera.

skilled fingers the strings of the golden lyre. Although Apollo[6]   25
himself, leader of the chorus of Muses, often called upon them to
sing of the battles of the gods and of Coeus,[7] buried under the isle
of Ischia, he hardly ever heard them again, and only if their
mother was present. For when mention is made of Pallas Athena,
they approve other things, but not chariots and helmets and the   30
many battles in which the virgin goddess[8] was engaged. They
think it much more appropriate that women should be occupied at
home with the wool basket. You have agreed with this severe judg-   35
ment from your earliest years, not because you were wanting in
riches or in that manner of life which the world wrongly upholds,
but because you were happy in the silent reclusion of an undis-
tracted mind and dedicated to artistic pursuits, the unblemished   40
good of the soul, which no wrathful injustice of cruel fate can give
or take away. Therefore there will be a time when trembling old   45
women will recount your fame and exemplary life to their daugh-
ters and many a young woman by the light of the flickering torch
will find solace from her labors in these tales; perhaps when your
family origins and the exact identification of your ancestry will   50
become confused by the pathless windings of time, future genera-
tions will celebrate you as the daughter of Phoebus Apollo or of
great Zeus, or as a member of the chorus of the Muses.

V. Epitaphium Telesillae

Si patriam, patria est Argos, si nomina quaeris
    Scire, Telesillae nobile nomen erat;
At, si artes animosque, vetat pudor hiscere de me,
    Musa sed has, dicent hos Lacedaemonii:
5 Nam, quamvis pudeat Sparten cessisse puellae,
    Vera tamen fari mos Lacedaemoniis.

VI. Ad Ioannem Lascarem

Iane, vatis amor tui,
    Unus qui patria tam procul a domo
Secessu frueris tamen
    Et contentus humo vivis in hospita.
5 Felix, quem neque turbidi
    Bellorum strepitus nec creperae vices
Terrent et gravis alea
    Fortunae indocilis stare loco diu,
Sed sacri medius chori
10   Musarum, facili pectore despicis
Prave quae populus nocens
    Miramur, neque voto neque ponere
Aegris gnari animis modum
    Et res flagitiis solvere non suis.
15 Nam quae tam fera pestilens,
    Quam non ingenio vincimus improbi?
Vel pictas referas licet
    Tygres vel Lybicae immane iecur leae,
Inter se probe obambulant,
20   Nec praedae, nisi dum pulsa abeat fames,
Naturale malum, incubant.
    In diversa furor scilicet omnibus;

V. Epitaph of Telesilla

If you wish to know my country, it is Argos; if you ask my name, it was the noble name of Telesilla;[9] but if you ask me about poetic ability or courage, modesty forbids me to speak of myself; the Muse will testify to one, the Spartans to the other. For although it 5 is shameful for a Spartan to give way to a woman, nevertheless it is the custom of the Spartans to speak the truth.

VI. To Janos Lascaris[10]

Janos, love of your poet friend, you are the only one who, though far removed from your country, still enjoy a secluded retreat and live happily in a hospitable land. You are fortunate, not terrified by 5 the turbulent din of war or uncertain times or the hazards of fortune, which is reluctant to stay very long in one place, but in the midst of the sacred chorus of the Muses you serenely despise what 10 we people wrongfully admire, unable to restrain our desires or our sick minds and to free things from disgraceful actions alien to them. For what wild beast is so savage that we shameless mortals 15 do not surpass it in our inclination to evil? If you call to mind the striped tigers or the brutal rage of the Libyan lioness, they wander about peacefully among themselves, and they are not intent on 20 prey except to satisfy their hunger, a natural evil. All creatures vent their fury on those that differ from themselves; we are the only

Soli mutua vulnera
   Exercemus, atrox soli odium in genus,
25 Indignoque cupidine
   Caeci, iura pii sanguinis, heu, modis
Turbamus miseri omnibus.
   Ergo Ixioneis conditionibus
Versati assidua rota,
30   Pertusa laticem quaerimus amphora
Frustra, quatenus improba
   Mentis cura eadem tempus in ultimum
Imis pectoribus manet,
   Aeque certa foris, certa domi comes,
35 Nec, quae olim veteres pii
   Commenti lacubus sub Stygis ultimae
Cuncta extrema merentibus,
   Sentimus miseri nos mala perpeti.
Nam quid, quaeso, aliud iecurve
40   Obscoenaeque nigri vulturii dapes
Aut saxum capiti imminens
   Impuro et mediis fluminibus sitis,
Quam congesta pecunia
   Forsan deteriori et tituli graves
45 Mentis non satiabilis,
   Pendentis dubiae de studio levi
Plebis usque Quiritium?
   Haec certissima uti sunt, ita nos quoque
Fatemur, bone Lascares—
50   Nam quis lucidum eat inficias diem?—
Acres sed catuli velut
   Latratam semel aut ursam Erymanthino in
Iugo aut multiparam suem,
   Sectamur soliti quae noceant mala,

ones who inflict wounds upon each other, the only ones who bear
fierce hatred against our own species, and blinded by shameless   25
cupidity, miserable creatures that we are, we throw into complete
confusion the laws concerning kindred relations. Therefore like
Ixion,[11] revolving on the endlessly turning wheel, we seek in vain   30
for a drop of water from the perforated amphora,[12] since the same
relentless anxiety remains deep-seated in our breast until the end
of time and is our constant companion both at home and abroad,
and we unhappy souls do not perceive that we suffer the torments   35
which the noble ancient writers devised for those deserving ex-
treme punishment in the pools of the remote Stygian stream.
What else, I ask you, is the liver and the foul repast of the black   40
vulture,[13] or the rock suspended over the impious head,[14] or the
thirst in the midst of flowing water,[15] but money accumulated
perhaps for an evil purpose, and high-sounding titles for an insa-   45
tiable ambition which depends continually on the fickle support of
plebeian voters? Since these things are undeniable, let us admit
they are true, good Lascaris, for who would deny the light of   50
day? But as the fierce whelps pursue the she-bear on Mt. Eryman-
thus,[16] filling the air with their barking, or like the sow that has
given birth to many piglets, we also give chase to the evils that as-

55 Donec — sed prius Herculis
    Olim quos memorat fama laboribus
Infracti — gladio hostico
    Solvamus misera haec membra anima gravi.

VII. *In quendam*

Cum tibi non tacto statuas ex hoste trophaeum,
    Miraris saevam cur abit in Nemesim?

VIII. *Ad Modestum*

Quod nomen titulis novi sepulchri
Quinteri renovas tui, Modeste,
Rem facis, mihi crede, dignam amico,
Te dignam: quid enim fidesque amorque,
5 Quid, pars altera pectoris, sodales,
Si damus cineri ferenda cuncta,
Nec vivi nisi commodique amamur?
Hoc est pectoris ingenique amici,
Ubi olim quoque vivimus sepulti
10 Et nigris stat honos suus favillis.
Quare perge, Modeste, quaeso, perge,
Quem vivum modo amasti, amare ademptum,
Nec parce studiove sumptibusve,
Exemplum memori futurus aevo:
15 Nam qui non amat ossa, non amabat.

IX. *Ad Paulam*

Dura prius cunctis, uni mihi, Paula, benigna,
    Unde aliis facta es blanda, inimica mihi?

sail us until (but only after we have been worn out by Hercules's   55
famed labors of old) by an enemy sword we set free these wretched
limbs from a troubled soul.

VII. *Against a certain person*

Since you are setting up a trophy celebrating victory over an en-
emy you never laid hands on, do you wonder why it turns into
Nemesis?[17]

VIII. *To Modestus*[18]

In restoring the name of your friend, Quinterus, with an inscrip-
tion on a new tomb, you are performing an act worthy of a friend
and worthy of you, Modestus, believe me. For what are faithful-
ness and love, what are bosom friends, our other selves, if we let   5
everything be carried off with their ashes, and if we love each
other only while we are alive and useful to each other? This is the
mark of a true and genuine friend, that one day when we are bur-
ied we are still alive and the honor owed to the dark ashes remains   10
undiminished. Therefore, continue, Modestus, continue, I pray
you, to love one who is taken from you as you loved him when he
was alive. Do not spare devotion or expense, as an example to an
age faithful to his memory: for he who does not love the mortal   15
remains never loved.

IX. *To Paula*

Previously harsh to all, Paula, kind to me alone, why have you
become agreeable to others but hostile to me? Believe me, though

Crede mihi, fingas licet omnia, iam mihi pridem
    Nota es, nunc vero nota quoque es populo.

X. De Quarto et anu

Quartum rogata cur anus salvum velit,
    'Peiora' dixit 'horreo.'

XI. Ad Baptistam Feram

Iam aestas torrida tertium
    Aestatisque parens flava redit Ceres,
Cincta concava tempora
    Foecundae segetis muneribus sacris,
5 Ex quo perditus occidi
    Avulsus dominae, Fera, meae sinu,
Cuius vel Styge naufragus
    Obtutu poteram reddier unico,
Cum per tot nemora interim,
10   Tot sylvas vagus et sicubi pervia
Unis antra patent feris,
    Nequicquam mihi me subripio miser.
Nam quaecunque oculis patent,
    Illic continuo vultus et aurei
15 Occursat capitis decor,
    Et quae nec fugere est lumina nec pati.
Ipsa robora habent genas
    Oris purpurei et pectora eburnea,
Ipsa sibila frondium
20   Carum nomen, et agnosco sub amnibus
Responsantis herae sonum,
    Tam diversa locis quam regio tenet.
Olim fabulam ego impiis
    Terrendis stimulos rebar et asperas

you devise every pretence, you have long been known to me, but now you are known to the common people too.

X. On Quartus[19] and the old woman

Asked why she wanted Quartus alive and well, the old woman replied: "I dread worse things."

XI. To Giambattista Fiera[20]

This is already the third time that scorching summer returns and with it the parent of summer, blond Ceres, her concave temples wreathed with the sacred gifts of the rich harvest, since I came to 5 grief and despair, Fiera, torn away from the bosom of my mistress. At the mere sight of her I could have returned, though ship-wrecked on the river Styx. In the meantime, wandering through endless woods and groves where caves give shelter only to wild 10 beasts, I pitifully try to escape myself in vain. For wherever I turn my glance, her face and the splendor of her golden tresses immedi- 15 ately present themselves to me, and those eyes which I can neither flee nor withstand. The very oak trees reproduce the radiance of her cheeks and her ivory breasts; the rustling of the leaves re- 20 echoes with her dear name, and I recognize the sound of my mis-tress responding to me in the stream although she is in a far differ-ent place. Once I thought that the torments and the fearsome

25 Ultricum Eumenidum faces,
    Sed prorsus nihil est usque adeo leve,
Quod non sensibus intimis
    Admissum moveat sede animum sua.

XII. Epitaphium Constantiae Bentivolae

Bentivola hoc tumulo est Constantia, si modo inanes
    Bentivolae cineres Bentivolam esse damus.
Sed quota Bentivolae pars hic cinis et pigra moles,
    Quae, Mors, ex illa sola tegis tumulo?
5 Nam pudor et, quae ipsa est, artes et vivida honesti
    Cura tenent meritis astra parata suis.

XIII. Ad Faunum

Sylvarum nemorumque Faune cultor,
Unus Naiadum timor sororum,
Seu parant posita lavare veste
Lascivum vitreis latus sub undis,
5 Seu molli recreare membra somno,
Ilex sicubi amica et alta fagus
Excludunt radios potentiores,
Unam, Faune, meam cave lacessas,
Unam, inquam, mihi cariorem ocellis.
10 Quae sit, forsitan, aut ubi, requiris.
Quam cernes mediam novem sororum
Nec voce impare nec decore formae,
Concentu fluvios morantem Etruscos
Ducentemque novo lepore sylvas,
15 Mellita comitante dicta Suada,
Hanc unam, precor, o benigne, castus

torches of the avenging Furies were a fable meant to inspire terror   25
in the impious, but now there is nothing so insignificant that does
not affect my innermost feelings and throw my mind into utter
turmoil.

XII. Epitaph of Costanza Bentivoglio[21]

This is the tomb of Costanza Bentivoglio, if we grant that the
empty ashes of Bentivoglio are Bentivoglio. But how small a part
of Bentivoglio are these ashes and lifeless stone, which are the only
parts of her that you cover in a tomb, O Death! For her modesty   5
and her behavior and her vigorous cultivation of virtue, an integral
part of her, dwell among the stars made ready for her through her
merits.

XIII. To Faunus[22]

Faunus, dweller in woods and forests, the one source of fear for
the Naiad sisters,[23] whether after taking off their clothes they pre-
pare to wash their voluptuous limbs in the glittering waves, or re-   5
store their bodies in soft slumber wherever a friendly ilex tree or
tall beech shuts out the more powerful rays of the sun, take care,
Faunus, not to harass my sweetheart, my only one, who is dearer
to me than my very eyes. Who is she, or where, perhaps you ask.   10
She is the one whom you will see in the midst of the nine Muses,
their equal in quality of voice and comeliness of form, halting the
course of Tuscan streams with her harmonious song, beguiling
the woodlands with a new charm, with the honeyed goddess of   15
persuasion accompanying her words. This one young woman, I

Castam praetereas et integellus,
Aversis oculisque vultibusque,
Siquando acciderit tibi videnda;
20   Nam timet mea Scala non latere,
Neu nos fraude mala deus lacessas.
Sic Nais tibi amica, sic Dianae
Mitis dextera et irritae sagittae
Sectanti comitum choros suarum!

XIV. In quendam

Et vere et belle te nullum decipere inquis:
    Neminem enim, cunctos fallere, decipere est.

XV. In Ecnomum

'Dic aliquem sodes, dic, Ecnome, quaeso, colorem.'
    'Haeremus almis occupati legibus.'
'Quid de legatis Falcidia, dic age, sancit?'
    'Sophiam magistri, iura non exponimus.'
5   'Ecquid stare potest sola virtute beatus?'
    'Virtutem inertem omitte, naturam inspice.'
'Cur raro Arctois bacchantur fulmina lucis?'
    'Atqui libellos novimus, non fulmina.'
'Quos, agedum, si fas, quos, Ecnome, quaeso, libellos?'
10   'Medicos, peritos syderum et id alios genus.'
'Fas ne paroxysmi febrem curare diebus?'
    'Ego ne valens de febribus verbum loquar?'
'Num licet infaustos signorum avertere cursus?'
    'Quin, his relictis, ad studia vetera redi!'

pray, O kindly one, that you honorably and chastely pass her by, respecting her chastity, and turn away your eyes and your face if perchance you happen to see her, for my beloved Scala is afraid 20 that she is not hidden, and that as a god you torment us with trickery. So may Nais be friendly to you, and may Diana's right hand be merciful and her arrows ineffectual as you follow in the train of her companions.

XIV. Against a certain person

It is both true and clever of you to say that you have never played a trick on anyone, for to deceive everyone is to deceive no one.

XV. Against Ecnomus

"Give us, if you please, Ecnomus, I beg of you, some rhetorical gem." — "We hold fast and stand by the laws that nurtured us." — "Tell us, what does the Lex Falcidia[24] prescribe about ambassadors?" — "We do not explain the wisdom of the magistrate nor the laws." — "Can one be blessed possessing virtue alone?" — "Pay 5 no regard to useless virtue, examine nature." — "Why do lightning bolts seldom strike groves in the far north?" — "Our subject is books, not lightning bolts." — "Ecnomus, if I may, what books, I ask you?" — "Medical books and those that treat of the stars and 10 others of that nature." — "Is it lawful to cure a fever on the days when a patient has convulsions?" — "Am I, a man in good health, able to speak about fevers?" — "Is it permitted to change the unlucky direction of the heavenly bodies?" — "Let's drop this subject

15 'Incipe, sic capiti semper pater adsit Iachus!'
        'Non, Daphni, matutinus redis huc neve alius.'
    'Atqui non pes hic, non, Ecnome, sermo Latinus.'
        'Abi, homo, minuta haec spernimus docti viri.'

XVI. De Biliotto astrologo

Dum cavet astrologus perituris sydera amicis,
    Dum sibi boletos non cavet, ipse perit.

XVII. De laudibus Rhacusae

Rhacusa, multis gens Epidauria,
Sicana pubes pluribus, at mihi,
    Ut nomen incertum genusque,
        Grande soli decus urbiumque

5   Quascunque longus subluit Adria,
    Quo te merentem carmine prosequar,
        Non falsus aut somno petita
            Materia, sine teste, inani?

    Amica quondam dulcis, ubi puer
10 Primas querelas et miseri exili
        Lamenta de tristi profudi
            Pectore non inimicus hospes.

    Hinc me locorum vis rapit aspera
    Evicta cultu saxaque mollibus
15   Servire Phaeacum viretis
            Iussa virum docili labore

    Et cuncta Cressa vite nitentia,
    Qua longa Sercus brachia porrigit,

and return to the study of antiquity." — "Begin, and may father 15
Iachus[25] be ever at your side." — "You won't return here in the
morning, Daphnis,[26] and neither will anyone else." — "But the
meter is faulty, and it's not Latin, Ecnomus." — "Off with you, fel-
low, we learned men despise such trivia."

XVI. On Biliotti, the astrologer[27]

While he cautions friends, doomed to die, about the stars, while
he is not on his guard against mushrooms, he himself dies.

XVII. On the praises of Ragusa[28]

Ragusa, known to many as the people of Epidaurum,[29] to many
others as of Sicilian origin, but to me, though your name and race
be uncertain, as the great glory of the land and cities washed by the 5
far-reaching Adriatic, with what poetry shall I proceed to praise
you as you deserve, not using falsification or unsubstantial material
acquired in sleep, without direct testimony? At one time you were
my dear friend, when as a boy I poured out from my sad heart the 10
first complaints and lamentations of an unhappy exile, though I
was not regarded as an enemy, but as a guest. From this place a
harsh force carries me off to lands tamed by cultivation and rocks
compelled by the skillful labor of man to serve the soft meadows 15
of the Phaeacians[30] and the whole land thriving with Cretan vines,
where Mt. Srdj[31] extends its long arms, acting as a barrier to the
wintry frosts and protecting the people from the North wind. 20

    Obiectus hibernis pruinis,
20   Et Boream populis tuetur;

Hinc tuta passim sponte deum freta
Littusque foetum portubus et bonis
    Gens laeta convectis utroque
        Limine flammiferentis astri;

25 Hinc ipsa muro moenia duplici
Educta coelo — pars licet altera
    Natura et abrupti superbit
        Rupibus aeriis profundi —

Complexa portus mole Cyclopea
30 Urbisque quantas divitias neque
    Mater Syracusae tulere
        Nec gemino mare dives Isthmos.

Etsi ista — quanquam maxima, nec nisi
Concessa raris munere coelitum —
35   Virtutis et laudum tuarum
        Vera loqui quota pars volenti,

Cum morem et urbis saepe animo sacra
Tot iura mecum cogito, cum decus
    Pulchramque libertatem avorum
40   Perpetua serie retentam

Interque Turcas et Venetum asperum
Et inquietae regna Neapolis,
    Vix qualis Aetneo profundo
        Unda freti natat aestuosi?

45 Heu, quae suetum nec patitur iugum
Nec, si carendum sit, ferat otium,

Here there are safe inlets dispersed here and there by the will of the gods and a shoreline abounding with ports, people happy with goods brought from one end to the other of the flaming sun's trajectory. Here the walls themselves rise to the heavens in double file 25 while the other part is provided by nature and prides itself in its soaring heights and sheer precipices. With the Cyclopean massiveness of the port and the city you embrace riches that the mother 30 city Syracuse and the rich Isthmus[32] that connects two seas never possessed. And yet what a small part of your virtue and merits are all these things, great as they are and granted only to the few by the favor of the gods, for one who wishes to tell the truth. When 35 I reflect within myself on the traditions and sacred laws of the city and the dignity and noble liberty of your ancestors, continuously 40 preserved amid the Turks and the oppressive Venetians and the kingdom of turbulent Naples,[33] my praise could scarcely be compared to a wave of the seething Straits of Messina in the Sicilian depths. Alas! Naples, which neither tolerates the customary yoke 45 nor, if it were set free, would bear tranquility, uncertain of what it

       Incerta votorum suisque
         Exitio totiens futura!

      Nam quae remotis usque adeo iacet
50   Gens ulla terris, quod mare tam procul
        Ignotum acerbis Appulorum
          Exiliis Calabrumque cladi?

      Non his beati quaeritur artibus
      Quies honesti, non bona strenuae
55   Virtutis et frugi parata
         Regna domi populique pace!

      Sed haec silenti non patiens amor,
      Tu vero coeptis artibus, optima,
        Rem auge decusque et nationum,
60   Ut merita es, caput usque vive.

XVIII. *Ad Alexandram Scalam*

      Quod tam tota decens formosaque, tota venusta,
        Rara quidem, sed non unica, Scala mea, es.
      At quod casta decens, at quod formosa pudica,
        Dispeream si non unica, Scala mea, es.
5   Nam, cum Pieridum reputo commertia sacra,
        Iam non ulterius unica, Scala: dea es.

XIX. *De Philippo duce Burgundiae*

      Olim cum Maries audisset morte Philippum
        Matrem vocantem 'Patria!',
      'Nate,' ait 'et patriae mox idem altorque paterque,
        Quid nomine erras tam pio?
5   Nec tibi me praeter genitrix et, Caesare salvo,
        Lugere cuiquam ingens nefas.'

wants and often a source of destruction to its own people! For 50
what people, even those who live in the remotest parts of the
earth, what sea is so distant that it is untouched by the cruel exiles
of the Apulians and the slaughter of the Calabrians? It is not by
these methods that we seek the tranquility of moral rectitude, the
blessing of unfaltering virtue and power honestly procured with 55
the people's approval! These are the words of love, which cannot
be silenced, but you, noble Ragusa, through undertaking artistic
pursuits, increase your prosperity and your glory, and as a leader
of nations, as you have deserved, may you enjoy long life. 60

XVIII. To Alessandra Scala

Since you are supremely beautiful and attractive, so entirely en-
chanting, my dear Scala, you are a rare, but not unique beauty.
But since you are chastely attractive and modest in your beauty,
may I perish if you are not unique, my dear Scala. For when I 5
consider your sacred commerce with the Muses, then you are no
longer unique, my beloved Scala: you are a goddess.

XIX. On Philip, Duke of Burgundy[34]

When Mary[35] heard Philip calling his mother on her deathbed
"My country!" she said, "My son, soon one and the same person
will be the support and the father of the country.[36] Why do you
err in pronouncing such a venerable name? You have no mother 5
but me, and while the Emperor is alive, it is a grievous wrong for
anyone to be in mourning."

XX. Epitaphium Bracci Perusini

Braccius hic situs est. Quaeris genus actaque: utrunque
  Ni teneas dicto nomine, nil teneas.

XXI. Ad Somnum

Somne, pax animi quiesque lassi,
Curarum fuga, Somne, saevientum,
Unus qui recreas fovesque saecla,
Idem regibus et popello inerti:
5 Ecquid, Somne pater, meremur uni,
Cur nos vel fugias adire prorsus
Vel, siquando venis, graves dolorem,
Usque saevior aspriorque amanti?
An non scilicet est satis, maligne,
10 Quod vivi domina caremus, heheu,
Necdum pectus iners ferimus ense,
Ni tu nos quoque, Somne, territando
Tot horrentibus eneces figuris?
Nam nunc dente ferae petita iniquo
15 Frustra poscere opem, modo videtur
Nostris exanimis iacere in ulnis;
Nunc, aut montibus aviis relicta
Aut sylvis, lacrimis replere cuncta;
Nunc, vasti maris obrui procellis,
20 Aut ultro mediae insilire flammae
Tandem duritiem execrans priorem,
Aut ferro dare pectus hauriendum.
Quae si, Somne, diu putas ferenda,
Nescis, ah, nimias faces Amoris

XX. Epitaph of Fortebraccio of Perugia[37]

Fortebraccio is buried here. You inquire about his family and his deeds. If you do not comprehend them both at the mention of his name, you will not comprehend anything.

XXI. To Sleep

Sleep, peace and quiet of the weary mind, refuge from raging cares, O Sleep, who alone restore and refresh mortal men, both kings and the indolent masses, why am I the only one, Father 5 Sleep, to deserve that you either avoid visiting me altogether or, if you do come, aggravate my sorrow, ever more cruel and pitiless to a lover? Is it not enough, O heartless one, that while I am living I 10 am deprived of my mistress, alas! and have not yet plunged the sword into my lifeless breast, but that you too, O Sleep, must annihilate me, terrifying me with horrible apparitions? For at one moment she seems to be the prey of the ferocious jaws of a wild beast, begging in vain for help; at another time she lies lifeless in 15 my arms; now, abandoned on remote mountains or in trackless woods, she fills the air with her cries; now she is overwhelmed by the storms of the vast sea, or she is ready to leap into the midst of 20 the flames, cursing her previous hardheartedness in despair, or poised to plunge the knife into her breast. O Sleep, if you think such torments can be endured for long, you do not know the

25 Et quid certa fides queat mariti,
   Nescis quam miseris molesta vita est,
   Quae laetis quoque saepe finienda.

XXII. De Mathia Corvino rege Ungariae

Legibus imperioque aucto bellique domique,
   Vix reliquus laudi iam locus ullus erat;
At, postquam Aonidum studia accessere benigna,
   'Ulterius' dixi 'nil dare cura potest.'
5 Ulterius das ipse tamen, crescenteque passim
   Plebe nova, e proprio tecta domosque paras.
Sic ope, sancte, tua, patriae pater, undique leges
   Crescunt, regna, artes, plebs nova, tecta nova.

XXIII. Epitaphium Mariae Martellae Bracci filiae

Hoc Maria in tumulo Bracci iacet: et putat, heheu,
   Esse aliquis curae saecla hominesque deis?
Nam quo tantus honos formae et mens virgine maior,
   Si praematuris tot bona danda rogis?
5 Quid, quod praecipiti delapsu extincta puella
   Invidiam fatis hac quoque parte facit?
Ipsa tamen felix quotiens, comprendere non est,
   Tam cito de vitae rapta puella malis,
Quae partam in patriam vita meritisque recepta,
10   Laeta deum fruitur commodiore solo.
At nobis non longa dies, non commoda tota
   Aeternam hanc dement pectore amaritiem.

power of love's fires and what the unfailing devotion of a husband   25
can do, you do not know how distressing life is for the unfortu-
nate, when even those who are happy must put an end to it.

XXII. On Matthias Corvinus, King of Hungary[38]

After your great success in the establishment of law and dominion
both in war and in peace, there was hardly any room for further
praise. But after the beneficial pursuits of literature and the arts
were added to this, I said, "His conduct of affairs cannot possi-
bly produce further results." Yet you make further progress, and   5
as new populations increase everywhere, you provide homes and
dwellings from your own property. So by your help, holy father of
the country, everywhere laws, kingdoms, arts, new people, new
dwellings come into existence.

XXIII. Epitaph of Maria Martelli, daughter of Braccio[39]

In this tomb lies Maria, daughter of Braccio; and can anyone
think, alas! that the gods have care for the affairs of men? What
was the purpose of such sheer beauty and intelligence beyond that
of a young girl, if so many blessings must be surrendered to an
early death? Is it possible that the death of a girl from a headlong   5
fall arouses the envy of the fates even in this? Yet one cannot know
what happiness awaits the young girl so suddenly snatched from
the evils of life, who is received into that native country which she
has gained by her life and merits, and happily enjoys the more fa-   10
vorable land of the gods. But for us neither length of days nor
every blessing will take away the unending bitterness from our
hearts.

XXIV. De perfidia puellari

Sylvae Morelli, non nisi beluis
Mihique, sed iam plus quoque cognitae
    Mihique lamentisque nostris
        Quam patriis catulis ferarum;

5 Et tu dolentis non semel auctior
Fletu, Remagi, ex quo placitum deis
    Cnidique reginae potenti
        Mergere nos Stygio baratro;

Vos sol et aurae et conscia—proh dolor!—
10 Ardoris olim sydera mutui;
    Adeste supremum ultimisque,
        Si merui, date vim querelis.

Nam quo aestuantis deinde novissima
Servantur oris verba, semel mori
15   Si iam necesse est? quin suprema
        Cor tumidum satiamus ira?

Non sic capaci vis furit ignea
Fornace clusa aut fulmineus vapor,
    Austroque nimbosoque Cauro
20   Aetherias glomerante nubes.

Haec, haec fides est, hoc meruit meus
Ardor! Quid ultra spe miseri improbae
    Torquemur incassumque amantes
        Quod cupimus, meruisse avemus?

25 An quisquam inanem vanius aera
Captet dolosis retibus aut iubar
    Solare consertis fenestris,
        Quam meritis animos puellae?

XXIV. On a young woman's perfidy

Woods of Monte Morello,[40] known only to wild beasts and to me,
but by this time more to me and to my laments than to the young
cubs who dwell there; and you, Rimaggio,[41] more than once in-   5
creased in volume by the tears of a grieving lover since the time it
pleased the gods and the powerful queen of Cnidus[42] to send me
down into the Stygian pit; O sun and upper winds, O stars once
privy — oh sorrow! — to our mutual passion, assist me in this last   10
moment and, if I have merited it, give strength to my last lamenta-
tion. Why withhold the final words of my seething eloquence, if I   15
must die once and for all? Why not gratify my bursting heart with
a last eruption of anger? The fiery fury shut up in a capacious
furnace is not so great nor the flashes of heat lightning when the
south and the stormy northwest winds concentrate the rain clouds   20
coming from the sky. This, this is your faithfulness, this is the
recompense for my ardor! Why am I still tortured by exces-
sive hope to win over a depraved woman? Why, squandering
my love, am I eager to be granted what I desire? Is it any more   25
futile for someone to capture the empty air with deceitful nets or
the rays of the sun in a closed window than to win the heart of a

Crudele saeclum, quas neque amor movet
30   Precesque, et ipsis de lacrimis virum,
      Ceu rore vocales cicadae,
        Exhilarant male fida corda!

Ergo, dum inanis pectore spiritus
Curvaeque qualiscunque sonus lyrae,
35   Chaosque et ultrices sorores
       Perfidiae memores precabor.

Quanquam quid amens, heu, precor aut cui?
Digna est, fatemur, quae pereat male;
     Sed ipse non iccirco dignus
40   Qui precer haec modo tantum amatae:

Quin vivat et nos nunc quoque sentiat
Ingrata amicos et facinus suum
     Virtute de nostra fideque
       Colligat et fateatur ultro!

45 At ipse longae perfidiae memor,
Tandem solutus compede dispari,
     Votumque persolvam potenti
       Iustitiae Nemesique sanctae.

XXV. *Epitaphium Innocentii octavi*

Spurcicies, gula, avaritia atque ignavia deses
   Hoc, Octave, iacent, quo tegeris, tumulo.

XXVI. *Ad Carolum regem Francorum*

Si tibi, rex, longinqua dies ac tempus amicos
   Praestat et hic unus sensibus haeret amor,
Quis negat extremis numerandum infraque receptos,
   Cuius adhuc notum vix bene nomen habes?

woman by his merits? O cruel race, which cannot be moved by
love or prayers, and like cicadas making shrill sounds in the morn-
ing dew, they gladden their faithless hearts with men's tears. There-
fore, while there is still some feeble breath remaining to me and
the sound of the curved lyre, such as it is, I shall invoke Chaos and
the avenging sisters, who are mindful of treachery. And yet, what
do I pray for in my frenzy? And against whom? She deserves to
die an awful death, I admit, but it would not be worthy of me to
pray for this for a woman I loved so much only recently. Rather let
her live and let this ungrateful woman know that I am her friend
even now and let her recognize her wickedness from my virtue and
fidelity and admit to it of her own will! But mindful of her long
perfidy, finally liberated from the fetters that affected only one of us,
I shall discharge my vow to powerful justice and holy Nemesis.

30

35

40

45

XXV. Epitaph of Innocent VIII[43]

Filth, gluttony, avarice and sluggish sloth lie in this tomb, Innocent
VIII, where you are buried.

XXVI. To Charles, king of the French[44]

If length of days and time generate friends for you, O king, and
this is the only love that remains fixed in your senses, who can
deny that he whose name is still hardly known to you should be
numbered among the least of your friends and should be inferior

5 At, si certus amor moresque in amante probantur
      Et placet in duris nobilitata fides,
  Crede mihi, quamvis addas, rex optime, primis,
      Ille novus primis non inhonestus ero.

XXVII. Ad Paulum

Quod tam saepe gravi torqueris, Paule, dolore
      Et secat indignos saeva podagra pedes,
Non ultrix poena haec meriti, sed scilicet unus
      Neve hominum felix neu sine labe fores.
5 Tu tamen, insanos animo superante dolores,
      Hoc magis invictum tollis in astra caput.

XXVIII. Ad puellam Etruscam

Puella Etrusca, quae meum
Pectus tot annos perdite
Torsisti amore mutuo,
Nunc nacta inanes discidi
5 Causas, novis amoribus
Servire inepta sustines
Sacrique vatis in locum
Ascisti amantis nobiles,
Usura quos pascit gravis
10 Et institura patria,
Qualis decebat scilicet
Quam di deaeque tam improbi
Sceleris, ut aequum est, puniunt.
Vale, puella perfida,
15 Olim Marulli ocellule,
Indigna nostris ignibus,
Indigna tam certa fide!

to those already admitted? But if a true love and upright character   5
are recognized as good qualities in a lover and if a fidelity proven
in difficult conditions deserves commendation, believe me, most
noble king, even were you to add me to your first friends, as a
newcomer, I shall not be a cause of dishonor to them.

XXVII. To Paolo

That you are so often afflicted with severe pain, Paolo, and the
cruel gout torments your guiltless feet, this is not an avenging pain
which you have merited, but simply that you are a man with your
share of misfortune and not without physical defects. But if you   5
have the courage to overcome this maddening pain, you raise your
head high toward the stars, all the more undefeated.

XXVIII. To a Tuscan girl

Tuscan girl, who tortured my heart to the point of desperation for
so many years in a mutual love affair, now inventing a specious
cause for separation, you foolishly submit to be a slave to new   5
amours and in place of a sacred poet you have taken to yourself
aristocratic lovers, who are maintained by exorbitant usury and a   10
country that will give them high positions, the kind of person
whom the gods and goddesses punish, with good reason, for such
a shameless crime. Farewell, perfidious maiden, once the darling of   15
Marullus, unworthy of my affections, unworthy of such abiding

Me, post Neaeram, foemina
Vel nulla — quod magis velim —
20 Vel certe habebit firmior.
Tu spreta, tunc demum scies
Quantum profani et sordidi
Distent Marulli amoribus.

XXIX. Epitaphium Pauli Tarchaniotae avunculi

Quod procul Inachiis tegeris, carissime, ab oris,
    Desine de fato, Tarchaniota, queri.
Una eadem terra est, quam cernis, ubique locorum,
    Nec magis Elysium hinc aut minus inde viae;
5 Nam nobis mandata satisque superque dedisti,
    Tot rerum invictus pondere et exilii.

XXX. Ad Camillam

Odi te, mihi crede, quantacunque es,
Odi, confiteor, Camilla, sed quam
Et odi et magis in dies magisque
Velim odisse, sequi atque amare cogor.
5 Sic me amor retrahit tuus trahitque,
Sic quem saevitia fugas proterva,
Tam rarae revocas decore formae.

XXXI. Epitaphium Ioannis Pici

Occidis aetatis media quod, Pice, iuventa,
    Ultima Socraticae flenda ruina domus,
Nec vel nobilitas vel opes vel gratia formae
    Profuit aut animi tot bona rara tui,
5 Non hoc, crede mihi, naturae iniuria matris,
    Larga vel imprimis quae fuit una tibi,

trust! After Neaera either no woman — which I would prefer — or   20
certainly a more loyal woman will have me. Only when you are
spurned will you know how different profane and sordid lovers are
from the love of Marullus.

XXIX. Epitaph of his uncle Paul Tarchaniota

Cease lamenting your fate of being buried far from Greek lands,
dearest uncle, Tarchaniota. All the land you see around you is one
and the same, and the road to Elysium is not shorter or longer
from any one place; for the instructions your gave us are enough   5
and more than enough, you who remained undefeated by the
weight of so much ill-fortune and exile.

XXX. To Camilla

I hate you, believe me, no matter how beautiful you are; I hate
you, I confess, Camilla, but the more I hate you and wish to hate
you more and more, day by day, I am forced to follow after you
and love you. So does my love for you draw me back again and   5
again, and though you drive me away with shameless cruelty, you
call me back by your exotic beauty.

XXXI. Epitaph of Giovanni Pico

With your death while still a young man, Pico, we must mourn
the final extinction of the house of Socrates. Neither nobility nor
wealth nor physical beauty was of any avail, nor such a multitude
of intellectual gifts. This was not, believe me, a wrong inflicted by   5
Mother Nature, which was singularly generous to you, perhaps

Sed vitae documenta hominum et quam fluxa sit ollis
Forma, genus, dotes ingenii, imperia.

XXXII. Ad Carolum regem Franciae

Invicte, Magni, rex, Caroli genus,
Quem tot virorum, tot superum piae
    Sortes iacentis vindicemque
      Iustitiae fideique poscunt,

5 Quem moesta tellus Ausonis hinc vocat,
Illinc solutis Graecia crinibus,
    Et quicquid immanis profanat
      Turca Asiae Syriaeque pinguis,

Olim virorum patria et artium
10 Sedesque vera ac relligio deum,
    Nunc Christianae servitutis
      Dedecus obprobriumque turpe.

Quid coelitum ultro fata vocantia
Morare segnis? non ideo tibi
15   Victoriarum tot repente
      Di facilem tribuere palmam,

Primisque in annis et puero et patris
Favore casso tot populos feros,
    Adusque pugnaces Britannos
20   Alpibus Allobrogum ab nivosis,

Iussere victos tendere brachia.
Si te decori gloria splendidi
    Nil tangit immensumque in aevum
      Nomina per populos itura,

more than with any other person, but it was an example of the life of men, how fleeting are beauty, good birth, gifts of genius, empires.

XXXII. To King Charles of France[45]

Invincible king, descendant of Charlemagne, whom the sacred destinies of so many men and so many gods invoke as the avenger of justice and good faith that have been brought low, whom the unhappy land of Ausonia[46] calls upon from here, and from there Greece with its hair disheveled, and all the lands of Asia Minor and fertile Syria which the savage Turk profanes, once the land of heroes and of art and the true seat and sanctuary of the gods, now the shame of Christian servitude and a source of disgraceful reproach. Why do you delay fulfilling the destiny of the gods, which summons you onward? It was not for this that they granted you so many easy and rapid victories, and in your early years as a young man without the support of a father willed that so many fierce peoples from the snowy Alps of the Allobroges[47] to the warlike Britons should surrender in defeat to you. If you are not moved by the prospect of a splendid victory and a name that will be on the

25 At supplicantum tot miserae exulum
  Sordesque tangant et lacrimae piae,
    At Christianorum relicta
      Ossa tot, heu, canibus lupisque,

  Foedisque tangat relligio modis
30 Spurcata Christi, sospite Galliae
    Rectore te nobis potentis,
      Cuius avum proavumque clara

  Virtus furentem barbariem unice
  Et Sarracenos contudit impetus,
35   Cum, saeva tempestas repente
      Missa quasi illuviesque campis,

  Non occupatae finibus Africae
  Contenti, Hiberi non opibus soli,
    Sperare iam Gallos et ipsum
40   Ausi animis Rhodanum superbis.

  Sed nec bonorum tunc superum favor
  Desideratus, nec tibi tam pia
    In bella eunti defuturus,
      Carle: moras modo mitte inertis,

45 Occasionem et, quam tribuunt, cape,
  Aeque nocentis, dissimiles licet,
    Gnarus, patrantem, quique, possit
      Cum, scelus haud prohibet patrari.

XXXIII. *Epitaphium Beatricis Estensis*

Solverat Eridanus tumidarum flumina aquarum.
  Solverat, et populis non levis horror erat,
Quippe gravis Pyrrhae metuentes tempora cladis,
  Credebant simili crescere flumen aqua.

184

lips of men for centuries to come, perhaps you will be moved by   25
the miserable squalor and pitiful tears of countless suppliant exiles
who implore your compassion, or by the vast number of bones of
Christians left to wolves and dogs, and by the shameless defile-   30
ment of the Christian religion, while you in full vigor, king of
powerful France, remain our champion. The illustrious valor of
your ancestors, unaided, subdued the furious barbarity of the
Saracen attacks when, like a raging storm which suddenly floods   35
the plains, not satisfied with having occupied Africa or with the
riches of Spain, they dared in their arrogance to have hopes of   40
conquering the French and the Rhone itself. But the favor of the
gods was not lacking then and will not be lacking to you now,
Charles, as you set out for this holy war. Cast off sluggish procras-
tination and seize the opportunity the gods offer you, bearing in   45
mind, that though distinct from one another, he who commits a
crime and he who does not prevent it from being committed are
equally guilty.

XXXIII. *Epitaph of Beatrice d'Este*[48]

The Po had unleashed floods of tumid water. It had unleashed
them, and the population was stricken with terror since they were
afraid the time of the terrible disaster of Pyrrha[49] had returned

5　Ille dolor fuerat saevus lacrimaeque futuri
　　　Funeris et iustis dona paranda novis:
　　Scilicet et fluvios tangunt tua acerba, Beatrix,
　　　Funera, nedum homines moestaque corda viri.

XXXIV. Ad Ianum Medicen Petri Francisci filium

　　Amorem ocellis insidentem fulgidis
　　　Vidi beatae Ruverae
　　Charitesque circum et Dionen auream,
　　　Spretis Cytheris dulcibus.
5　Hic me volentem aut arma principis mei
　　　Devota fari patriae
　　Tuasve laudes, Iane, et antiquum decus,
　　　'Quo raperis, imprudens?' ait.
　　'Tun tot virorum, tot poeta virginum
10　　Meusque longum signifer,
　　Unam relinques Ruveram indictam meam?
　　　O immemor nostrae facis!
　　An post Neaerae funera et tristes rogos
　　　Tu quoque iam Amorem negligis?
15　Habuit, fatemur, illa et ardentes faces
　　　Et nostra secum spicula
　　Multosque saepe matre, multos impotens
　　　Me quoque vetante torserat;
　　Verum ipsa coelo dignior tandem suo
20　　Templis deorum internitet.
　　Nos tot beatis utpote excussi bonis,
　　　Quae nulla reddent tempora,
　　Moesti tenebris egimus vitam diu,
　　　Acturi in omne saeculum,

and that the waters would reach those levels. The grief was intense   5
and there were tears for future funeral rites and gifts had to be
prepared for the new obsequies. It is evident that your untimely
death touches the rivers, Beatrice, not to speak of mankind and
the sad heart of your husband.

XXXIV. To Giovanni de' Medici, son of Pierfrancesco[50]

I saw Love residing in the radiant eyes of the fair della Rovere,[51]
and around her were the Graces and golden Dione,[52] spurning her
sweet Cythera. As I stood there, wishing to speak of the military   5
exploits of my prince[53] in behalf of his native land or of your
virtues, Giovanni, and your ancestral glories, Love said to me:
"Where are you being carried away, without your knowing it?
Will you, a poet who sang of so many men and so many young
women and were long my standard-bearer, leave only my beloved   10
della Rovere unsung, forgetful of our torch? After the death and
sad funeral rites of Neaera, are you now indifferent to Love as
well? She, I admit, had our flaming torches and arrows with her   15
and often tortured many men with uncontrolled savagery, though
my mother and I forbade it; but now finally, more worthy of
heaven, she dwells resplendent in the temples of the gods. As for   20
us, since we have been deprived of so many blessings that time
will not restore to us, we have passed our lives in darkness for a
long time, mourning our loss, and we would have continued for-

25 Ni paeti ocelli Ruverae et flavus decor
　　Collo iacentum crinium
　Vultusque, quales mater aut matris soror
　　Pallas velit Tritonia,
　Sceptris honorem reddidissent, imparem
30　　Fateor, pigendum non tamen.
　Nam quid decori pectoris papillulas
　　Latusque dignum coelite,
　Quid cilia dicam Bistonum aemula arcubus,
　　Cum prima tentant proelia?
35 Iam colla eburnea, iam Indicos elenchulos
　　Oris ferasque turbidas
　Mulcere nata verba et amnis sistere
　　Altis citatos cursibus,
　Iunone dignas iam manus, iam caetera
40　　Egregia paucis exequi,
　Formam Cytherae matris et laudes meae
　　Est velle paucis exequi.
　Sed haec caduci cuncta flos aevi brevis
　　Aeque rosetis gemmeis,
45 Quae mane ripis Sileris aprici nova,
　　Surgente marcent vespere,
　Ni tu rogatus dulcibus, vates meus,
　　Tuis Camaenis subvenis,
　Quae mortis atrae legibus, quae temporis
50　　Potentiores invidi,
　Vivos, sepultos, quos volunt, raptos humo,
　　Per ora mittunt gentium.
　Quod si petenti nec ego nec mater tibi
　　Unquam Cythere defuit,
55 Si Septimillam, si dedi Glyceren piam,
　　Quamvis petitam tot procis,

ever if the alluring glances of della Rovere and her beautiful blonde 25
tresses cascading over her shoulders, and the features of which my
mother or my mother's sister, Pallas Tritonia,[54] would be envious,
had not given to my scepter an honor that was not the equal of
Neaera, but certainly not to be despised. For what shall I say of 30
the nipples of her divine breast and her loins, worthy of a god-
dess? What shall I say of her eyebrows, rivals of Thracian bows
when they enter into their first battles? To speak of her ivory neck, 35
her teeth, which are like Indian pearls, her speech that can soothe
savage beasts and stop rivers in their course, hands worthy of Juno,
and all her other excellent qualities, would be like attempting to 40
sum up in a few words the beauty and the praises of my mother,
Cythera. But all of this is but the brief flowering of fleeting time,
like the jewellike rose gardens that open anew in the morning on 45
the banks of the sunny Sele[55] and wither at the approach of eve-
ning, unless you, my loyal poet, in answer to my request, come to
my aid with your sweet Muses who, more powerful than the laws 50
of black death and envious time, snatch from the earth whoever
they wish, alive or buried, and bring them back to life on people's
lips. But if neither I nor my mother Cythera have ever denied your
prayers, if I gave you Septimilla, or loyal Glycera, although she 55

Si ipsam Neaeram specimen humanae unicum
    Naturae et exactum decus,
Neaeram, honestum nomen aeternum mihi,
60   Vires Neaeram Cypridos,
Cuius quotannis moesta nunc tumulo quoque
    Charis capillum demetit,
Per sacra Phoebi quae sacerdos fers tui
    Novemque Musas numina,
65 Per siquid est, quod tela adhuc possunt mea
    Sat tibi superque cognita,
Oro: malignis eripe hanc tenebris quoque
    Oblivionis luridae,
Famae levatam curribus vivacibus,
70   Musa novante saecula.'
Haec ille. Sed mihi redditae Antoni mei
    Urgentiores litterae
Alpes citatis passibus transcendere
    Ad Galliae motum iubent.
75 Quare monenti, Iane, tu pare deo,
    Ego sequar arma principis.

was sought after by many suitors, if I gave you Neaera herself, a
unique specimen of human nature and an exemplar of perfect
beauty, Neaera, a name I shall hold in honor forever, Neaera, the   60
life force of Venus, at whose tomb every year Grace sadly cuts off
one of her locks, by the sacred rites which you celebrate as a priest
of your beloved Phoebus Apollo, and by the divinities of the nine
Muses, by whatever powers my shafts, so well known to you, still   65
retain, I pray you: rescue her also from the malevolent darkness of
pale oblivion, raising her up on the long-lived chariot of fame,
thanks to the Muse who renews the ages." Thus he spoke to me.   70
But a more urgent letter has come to me from my good friend
Antonio, which bids me to cross the Alps with all speed to join
the French forces. Therefore, Giovanni, you obey God's command   75
and I shall join the military campaign of the prince.

HYMNORUM NATURALIUM

Ad Antonellum Sanctoseverinum principem Salernitanum

Si tuus est vates, si cuncta volumina vatis,
  Quaeris praecipue cur tuus iste liber?
Sol quoque cuncta regit, solis tamen unica sedes:
  Haec eadem regum est, quae superum est ratio.

HYMNS TO NATURE

To Antonello Sanseverino, prince of Salerno

If the poet is yours, if all the poet's volumes are yours, do you ask why this book is peculiarly yours? The sun governs all things, yet it has only one abode: kings conduct themselves in the same way as gods.[1]

Liber Primus

I. Iovi Optimo Maximo

Ab Iove principium, Iovis est quodcunque movemus;
Prima mihi graviore sono dicenda potestas
Est Iovis. Hinc magni divum tot numina mundi,
Hinc rerum natura parens, hinc lucidus aether,
5   Quaeque sub incurvo variantur plurima coelo.
Sed neque Pieridum praesentia vatibus antra
Nec tu, care, satis nostris, Pimplee, Camaenis
Parnasusque biceps facundaque flumina largae
Phocidos. Ipse animum vati, mentem ipse ministra,
10 Sancte pater, sive aetherio delapsus Olympo
Enthea divino praecordia concutis oestro
Ignotasque vias aperis teque ipse recludis
Sive iubes cinctum solis caput igne tuentem,
Ingenio mentisque oculis ad inane levatis,
15 Eminus informi quaesitum ostendere in umbra
Effigiemque tuam primos et ducere vultus.
Nam, quamvis solusque reples solusque gubernas
Omnia et occasus aeque moderaris et ortus,
Quamvis quicquid adest, quodcunque ubicunque videmus,
20 Ipse idem es penitusque nihil nisi Iuppiter usquam,
Quis tamen infirmi comprendat pectoris haustu,
Quem mare, quem tellus, vacui quem nubila coeli
Non capiunt sanctique patens plaga lucida regni?
Effugit humanos divina potentia fines
25 Mortalesque hebetat captus et pectora pigra,
Ex quo coelicolae, natali sede relicta,
Invalidos artus terrenaque membra subimus,
Corpoream iussi molem compage tueri.

Book I

I. To Jupiter, Greatest and Best

From Jupiter is our beginning,[2] to Jupiter belongs all that we do; the first power to be celebrated in solemn tones is that of Jupiter. From him proceed the many divinities of the vast universe, from him comes nature, mother of all things, from him luminous Aether and the multiplicity of things that change form beneath the vault 5 of heaven. But neither the caves of the Pierides,[3] propitious to poets, nor you, dear Pimpleus,[4] suffice unto my song, nor twin-peaked Parnassus and the eloquent streams of bounteous Phocis.[5] Give inspiration to the poet, give him understanding, O holy fa- 10 ther, whether descending from high Olympus you arouse his en-raptured feelings with divine ecstasy and open unknown paths and reveal yourself to him or bid him contemplate the sun's head en-circled with fire, elevating his spirit and the eyes of his mind to the void, to show forth what he sought from afar in formless shadows 15 and to trace your image and the first rudimentary features of your countenance.

For though you alone fill and you alone govern all things and justly regulate their rise and fall, though all that exists and all that we see around us is yourself and nothing but Jupiter exists any- 20 where, who could comprehend with the breath of his feeble intel-ligence him whom the sea, the land, the clouds of the vacant heavens, and the vast shining expanse of your heavenly kingdom cannot contain? Divine power surpasses human limitations and 25 dulls mortal understanding and our sluggish hearts ever since, though once heaven-dwellers, we left our native home and took on feeble limbs and earthly members, and were commanded to look after the framework of our burdensome body. For as soon as we

Nam, simulac tenebris et inerti carcere clausi
30 Mortiferum Stygiae somnum potavimus undae,
Excidit offecto solidum de pectore verum,
Pro rebusque leves nequicquam amplectimur umbras,
Antiquae patriae ac verae rationis inanes.
Hinc rapit ambitio, rapit hinc furiosa libido,
35 Inde metus bella aspra movent et gaudia et irae
Raraque in humanis non mendax gloria rebus.
Ipsi, inter facies simulachraque mille ferarum
Impia Circaeae depasti pocula mensae,
Obscoenis stabulamur haris, nec tecta paterna
40 Respicimus dulcemque Ithaco de culmine fumum,
Iam pridem in foedas dociles transire figuras.
Sed te moly tamen nobis tribuente beatum,
Securi dominae atque dapis, qua numina monstrant,
Nitimur immensum venerari carmine puro,
45 Et rerum auctorem dominumque agnoscimus aethrae,
Quem non principium, non ulla extrema fatigant,
Expertem ortus atque obitus; qui cuncta gubernas
Nescius imperii totusque in te ipse vicesque
Despicis aeternus et tempora sufficis aevo,
50 Unigenam sancto prolem complexus amore
Aeterno aeternam et perfectam, labe carente,
Cui rerum late custodia tradita cessit
Et regni tutela tui, consorsque potestas
Temperat acceptas sine fine et tempore habenas;
55 Qui varios rebus tribuis nascentibus ortus,
Qui sua naturae praescribis iura potenti,
Qui terras, coelum, aera, aquas, vertisque regisque
Contentusque tua varias quaecunque quiete,
Mille per augustum spargens miracula mundum.
60 Nam, cum tota gravi torperet machina acervo
Noxque Chaos densis circumdaret atra tenebris

were enclosed in the darkness of this dreary prison[6] and drank the   30
deadly sleep of the Stygian wave, solid truth abandoned our ob-
structed mental faculties, and in place of real things we vainly
embrace fleeting shadows, deprived of our ancient homeland and
true reason. On one side ambition seizes us, on another raging
lust, next cruel wars arise, brought on by fear, and pleasures and   35
anger, and that which is rarely without deceit in human affairs,
glory. And in the midst of a thousand apparitions and images of
wild beasts, after quaffing the impious cups of Circe's table, we are
stabled in obscene pig sties, and we do not look back to our pater-
nal dwelling and the pleasant smoke issuing from an Ithacan roof-   40
top, by now resigned to turn into hideous shapes.[7] But since you
give us the gift of moly,[8] the beatific herb, forgetful of mistress and
banquet, and following the indications of the gods, we strive to
worship the infinite in a pure song, and we acknowledge you as the   45
author of creation and lord of the ether, constrained by no begin-
ning and no end, exempt from birth and death; who govern all
things and are ruled by none, sufficient unto yourself, and you
disdain all change, being eternal, and assign portions of time to
eternity, embracing your only begotten offspring[9] with holy and   50
eternal love, and she is eternal and perfect, without stain, to whom
the care of the vast universe and the protection of your kingdom
has been confided. Sharing your power,[10] she controls the reins
she has received without limit of time or space, but it is you who   55
assign various origins to each thing that comes into the world,
who prescribe the laws for powerful nature, who set in motion and
rule the lands, the heavens, the air, the waters, and happy in your
repose, diversify all things, spreading a thousand wonders over the
august universe.

For when the whole fabric of the universe[11] lay torpid in a pon-   60
derous mass and black night surrounded Chaos with thick shad-

Perque superiectas volitaret spiritus undas,
Mole recens orta, et vacuum sola inane teneret,
Primus opes bonus ipse bonas partiris in orbem
65 Squallentemque novo massam fulgore serenas
Et tenebras luce et tenebris lucem eximis atris
Appellasque diem et nocti sua nomina ponis,
Primus aquis secernis aquas coelumque profundum
Erigis aequoreasque iubes discludere moles.
70 Tum mare substernis tumidum, tum lege verenda
Imponis finesque suos et littora Nereo
Aridaque ostentas mediis sola prodiga in undis.
Apparent subitae, dictu mirabile, terrae,
Divitiisque suis capitur iustissima Tellus
75 Atque animum facies movet et variantia rerum,
Nanque videbat uti modo coelum tangeret ipsum
Rupibus aeriis, ima modo valle dehiscens
Infernum Chaos et nigrantes proderet umbras,
Nunc sola pacato diffunderet aemula ponto
80 Temperie verisque opibus foecunda benigni,
Seque repentinis fluviorum spectat in undis.
Tum nova suspendis rutilanti sydera mundo
Anguesque volucresque et Pleadas Atlanteas,
Utque pruinosis lunares noctibus axes,
85 Portantem Aurorae praeponis lumina Solem,
Solem sydereae moderantem frena choreae,
Obliquuumque iubes currus agitare per orbem.
Tum liquidum mutis foecundas piscibus aequor
Aeriumque leves spargis per inane volucres,
90 Tum latas replere iubes animalia sylvas
Deque solo genus humanum producis inerti
Et mentem inspiras melioris origine formae,
Cui quicquid mare, quicquid habent sola subiicis ipsa,
Exutosque olim terrenae pondera molis

ows and the spirit hovered over the surface of the waters, as soon
as the mass of primeval matter emerged, and empty space occu-
pied what would soon become land, you in your goodness are the
first to distribute the good riches to the world and brighten the   65
earth's formless mass with your new lightning and remove dark-
ness from light and light from black darkness and you call it day
and you give night its name, and you are the first to separate the
waters from the waters and the first to raise up the boundless sky
and command the watery masses to separate out into parts. Then   70
you spread out the swollen sea, then with hallowed law you im-
pose boundaries and coastlines on Nereus[12] and you make the dry
land appear, prodigal in its riches, in the midst of the waves. Sud-
denly tracts of land appear, marvelous to relate, and the most just
Earth[13] is fascinated by its riches and the beauty and variety of   75
things moves her soul, for she saw how at one moment she
touched the sky itself with her cliffs that reached high into the air,
and how at another moment, splitting open into a deep valley, she
revealed infernal Chaos and the dark shades; now she spread out
the plains that rivaled the placid sea, fertile, thanks to the mild   80
climate and the rich abundance of benign spring, and she is re-
flected in the waves of the rivers that suddenly spring into being.
Then you suspend new constellations in the glowing firmament
and serpents and birds and the Pleiades,[14] daughters of Atlas, and
as you set the moon's chariot over the frigid nights, so you put the   85
Sun, light-bearer, in charge over the dawn, the Sun who keeps in
check the dance of the stars, and you order it to drive its chariot
over the slanting earth. Then you make the liquid sea abound with
mute fish and you disperse the nimble birds through the empty
air, then you order the broad forests to fill up with living things,   90
and from the inert soil you produce the human race and breathe
into it a mind of better form in its origins, to which you make the
expanse of the sea and land subject, and when they have put off

95   Rursus in antiquam patriam das posse reverti,
      Unde hominum curas tot despectemus inanes
      Incertasque vices rerum metuendaque fata
      Et quanta mortale genus nox occupet umbra.
      Salve, sancte parens, vere pater optime rerum,
100   Vere opifex, terraeque mala compage gravatos
      Dum data vincla nefas dirumpere carceris atri,
      Eripe tot pelagi iactatos tristibus undis,
      Tot caecis pressos tenebris, pater, exue vota
      Impia: nil vanum, nil admiremur inane,
105   Antiquae memores patriae, et quem corporis aegri
      Non licet, ingenii quaeramus lumine puro.

II. Palladi

    Te te, suprema maximi proles Iovis,
        Innupta Pallas, invoco,
    Hastae potentem nobilis viraginem,
        Quam Phorcis asperat ferox,
5   Cum multilingue sibilis quassans caput
        Procul profanos submovet.
    O sola rerum, o lucidi domina aetheris,
        O coelitum sanctum decus,
    Huc huc duelli, pacis huc ades potens,
10   Seu te tyrannicum solum et
    Vicina templa rupibus Telonicis
        Seu fertilis Nilus tenet,
    Sive alta Itoni saxa sive argenteis
        Vorticibus Inachus pater,
15   Sive in remotis optimi regnis patris,
        Dignata mortales parum,

the weight of their earthly substance, you give them leave to return   95
to their ancient homeland, whence we can look down on the
empty cares of men and the uncertain vicissitudes of life and the
fearsome fates and see what great darkness the night spreads over
the mortal race.

Hail, holy parent, verily supreme father of all creation, verily   100
the architect of the universe, and deliver us, weighed down by the
evil framework of the earth, while it is forbidden us to break asun-
der the bonds of this dark prison that have been laid upon us, save
us from the somber waves of the sea on which we are tossed, from
the gloomy shadows that press upon us, O father; rid us of impi-
ous desires, may we not admire what is vain and empty, mindful of   105
our ancient homeland, and let us seek with the pure light of intel-
lect him whom we cannot seek with the forces of our weak body.

II. To Pallas

You, Pallas, great offspring of greatest Jupiter, you, unwedded Pal-
las, I invoke, warrior goddess exulting in the noble lance,[15] whom
fierce Medusa[16] makes terrible in appearance when, with hissing   5
sounds and shaking her many-tongued heads, she keeps the pro-
fane at a distance. O sole sovereign of creation and of the lumi-
nous ether, O sacred glory of the heavenly dwellers, hither come,
powerful goddess of war and peace, whether a tyrannical land[17]   10
holds you or the temple near the steep Telonic cliffs[18] or the fertile
Nile,[19] or the rocky heights of Itonus[20] or the silvery whirlpools of
father Inachus,[21] or whether in the remote kingdom of your excel-   15

Aevum beata ducis et nutu omnia
　　Heres paterna temperas.
Quo non Metus, non inquies penetrat Dolor
20　　Dubiisve Senium gressibus
Aut sydus anni noxium aut Auster gravis
　　Morbis domesticis sinum,
Sed cuncta vere germinant semper novo
　　Vicis malignae nescia,
25　Et nunc fluentis irrigantur lacteis
　　Nunc melle passim Hymetio.
At ipsa curru flammeo septemiugo,
　　Ter auream quassans comam,
Longum citatas huc et huc agis rotas
30　　Ausis tremenda masculis.
Subsidit aether ipse, contremit fretum,
　　Emota respondent sola.
At, quae trecentae virginis stipant latus
　　Olea revinctae candida,
35　Pars haeret uno fixa in obtutu deae,
　　Tam forti ab ore pendula,
Aliae aut recenti lilio aut spargunt rosis,
　　Quod quaeque potis est conferens.
Has pater Homerus inter atque Orpheus pater,
40　　Uterque plectro adamantino,
Partum Chariclus subsecuti nobilem,
　　Laudes heriles concinunt:
Ut sola patris vertice ex ipso edita,
　　Hominumque origo et coelitum,
45　Prima et nefandos aggeres disieceris
　　Audax paternis ignibus,
Ipsumque fratrum maxime Enceladum trucem,
　　Non ante equestris cognita,

202

lent father, showing little regard for mortals, you lead a blessed life
and by a mere sign govern all things as your father's heir. There
neither fear nor disquieting sorrow nor old age with uncertain   20
steps nor the unhealthy season of the Dog Star nor the sirocco, its
bosom heavy with the usual maladies, can make their way, but all
things germinate in a perpetually renewed spring, ignorant of the
barren time of year, now watered by rivers of milk, now with free-   25
flowing Hymettian honey.[22] But from your flaming chariot borne
by seven horses,[23] shaking your golden locks three times, you steer
this way and that the wheels that have traveled many miles, fear-   30
some for your masculine feats of daring. The ether itself stands
still, the sea trembles, the earth responds with tremors. But three
hundred attendants surround the virgin girded with pale green
olive branches, some of whom remain fixed in pure contemplation   35
of the goddess, their eyes riveted on her heroic features, others
sprinkle her with freshly placed lilies or with roses, each contribut-
ing what she can. In their midst is father Homer[24] and father Or-
pheus, both with adamantine plectrum following in the steps of   40
the noble offspring of Chariclo.[25] They sing the praises of their
mistress, how you alone, sprung from the very head of Jupiter, you
the origin of men and heavenly beings, were the first to smash the   45
impious earthworks, daring to wield your father's thunderbolts,
and you hurled the fiercest of the brothers, Enceladus himself,[26]

Stagnis profundi Tartari demiseris,
50   Mirante monstrum patruo.
Prima inquietis gentibus certas domos
        Stabilemque dederis patriam,
Prima arce, prima moenibus ditaveris,
        Prima optimis tot artibus.
55 Tu sancta prima iura, tu legem invenis,
        Commenta vim dignam malis,
Tu prima mentes compari nectis iugo,
        Tu propria tribuis pignora,
Tu celsa raptos tollis ad templa aetheris,
60   Tu patriam antiquam doces
Coelumque patrem maximum rerum omnium
        Curis caducis subiicis.
Salve, beati lucidum germen patris,
        Vere Phaneta splendide,
65 Eadem virago, mas eadem, eadem furor,
        Sapientiaque eadem et quies,
Animisque nostris ades et atra nubila
        Discute tua immensa face.

III. Amori

Alme coelestum genitor potensque
Aetheris lati volucer Cupido,
Splendidum sydus geminaeque duplex
        Gloria matris,

5   Quem modo insanis agitata ventis
Stagna delectant mediisque in undis
Improbus Phorci nimia puellas
        Lampade aduris,

down to the stagnant waters of deepest Tartarus, although you
were never known previously to be a skilled equestrian, while your   50
uncle[27] stood aghast at the sight of the monster. You were the first
to give to restless peoples a secure dwelling and a stable homeland,[28]
the first to give them a citadel and ramparts, the first to give them
so many excellent arts. You first discovered sacred rights and law,   55
and devised adequate punishment for the wicked, you were the
first to unite minds under an equal yoke and grant them their le-
gitimate offspring, you carry us off and lift us to the high regions
of the ether, you teach us about our ancient homeland and put   60
heaven, the mighty father of all things, in the place of fleeting
cares. Greetings, luminous child of a fortunate father, truly splen-
did Phanes,[29] woman and man and madness, and at the same time   65
wisdom and repose, assist our minds and disperse the dark clouds
with your immense torch.

III. To Love

Gracious parent of the heavenly beings and powerful lord of the
vast ether, winged Cupid, brilliant star and double glory of a
double-natured mother,[30] who now take pleasure in the wide ex-   5
panses of the sea stirred up by furious winds and in the midst of
the waves mischievously enflame the daughters of Phorcus[31] with

Nunc ab extremo peragrans Eoo
10   Ultimas Gades Lybiamque et Arcton
Dulcibus rixis et amico amaro
      Pectora versas.

Saepe magnorum medius deorum
Aethera immensumque tenes Olympum,
15   Hic ubi missa superos sagitta
      Flectis et ipsum

Arbitrum rerum dominumque patrem,
Cuius auditum procul omnis horret
Coelitum pubes, procul omnis horret
20   Machina nomen.

Quid, quod et novas Chaos in figuras
Digeris primus docilemque rerum
Mutuis nectis seriem catenis
      Pace rebelli?

25   Quid, quod, antiqua superata Anance,
Suscipis mundum placidum regendum?
Quid, quod et leges et habenda iura
      Figis inermis,

Quod peregrinas animas caducae
30   Devocas massae populumque inertem
Edoces terris hominum salubres
      Iungere coetus,

Quod pias magnum per inane mentes
Aureae sistis gremio parentis,
35   Gratiarum inter comites choreas
      Servaque fata?

your burning torch, now traveling from the Far East to Cadiz at 10
land's end and to Libya and the Arctic region you torment hearts
with sweet quarrels and friendly bitterness. Often in the company
of the great gods you hold sway in the upper air and immense
Olympus, where with your shafts you bend the gods to your will, 15
even the arbiter of all things, lord and father, at the sound of
whose name, heard from afar, all the inhabitants of heaven trem-
ble, from afar the whole mechanism of the world trembles. And 20
what of your separating Chaos into new forms for the first time
and your joining together of the docile succession of things with
common chains in peaceful rebellion?[32] And what of your triumph 25
over ancient Necessity and your assuming the task of ruling the
world in peace?[33] And what of the laws and rights that must be
respected, which you introduce without recourse to arms? And 30
that you call down peregrine souls to dwell in perishable matter
and teach the ignorant multitude to form salutary alliances on
earth, and that you place pious minds dispersed through the great
void[34] in the lap of your golden mother, amidst the choruses of 35
the Graces,[35] her companions, and the docile fates? O peace, O

O quies magnae reparatioque
Grata naturae columenque rerum,
O adoratum mihi rite primis
40   Numen ab annis,

Huc ades tandem, puer o beate,
Dexter, et caecos miseratus aegri
Pectoris motus, agedum, profanis
    Exime curis.

IV. Coelitibus

Audi, beatum sancta coelitum cohors,
    Quae templa Olympi possides
Stabileque in aevum lucidas ambis Iovis
    Rota domos novemplici,
5 Rutilis verenda vultibus, rutilis genis,
    Comaque rutila et vestibus,
Tereti diurnae lampados qualis face
    Nubes coruscat obvia
Aut cum, cubile frigidum linquens, diem
10   Aurora sub novum rubet,
Quotiens reductis excitat laboribus
    Mortalium aegra pectora,
Quae dulcis olim presserat somno quies
    Curis soluta edacibus.
15 Audi, beata imago Pallados bonae,
    Templum beatum Pallados,
Cuius secuta qua licet vestigia,
    Sequentibus ducem exhibes
Nostrisque vinclis libera atque onere gravi,
20   Quo premimur infirmum genus,
Supra malignae servitutis terminos
    Coeli pererras ardua,

pleasant renewal of great nature, cornerstone of all creation, O
divinity, whom I have worshipped devoutly from my earliest years,   40
come down, I pray, O blessed child, propitiously, and taking pity
on the blind passions of a sick heart, come swiftly and deliver me
from profane cares!

IV. To the heavenly beings

Listen, O holy court of the blessed in heaven, who possess the
sacred precincts of Olympus, and steadfast for all eternity revolve
around the bright dwelling of Jupiter on a nine-circled wheel, in-   5
spiring awe by your radiant visages, your radiant cheeks, your radi-
ant locks and vesture, as a cloud that reflects the rays of the round
fiery globe of the sun, lamp of the day, or when, leaving her cold
bed, Aurora glows at the approach of the new day each time she   10
awakens the weary hearts of mortals to return to their labors,
which a short time ago found relief in sweet repose, free of carking
cares. Hearken to us, blessed image of good Pallas, blessed temple   15
of Pallas, a guide to those who have followed in your footsteps as
far as possible, and free us from our chains and from the heavy
burden that oppresses us, weak race that we are. Transcending the   20
confines of our base servitude, you traverse the heights of heaven,

Utcunque constans firmitate mascula,
    Cedente nunquam pectore.
25 Et nunc labores et caduca protinus
    Sceptra miserata gentium,
Modo labantis sustines Atlantico
    Gravia ruinae pondera;
Nunc mille inertes excitas mysteriis,
30   Ignara livoris mali,
Caecoque mentes involutas carcere
    Nota profani submoves;
Iam tum procellis debitam furentibus
    Benigna sublevans ratem,
35 Mediisque nimbis et freti fragoribus
    Arcton serenas candidam.
Verum huc, beata coelitum, huc ades, virum
    Sanctissima expiatio,
Tuaque fotos optima tandem face
40   In mystica coopta tua.

V. Aeternitati

Ipsa mihi vocem atque adamantina suffice plectra,
Dum caneris, propiorque ausis ingentibus adsis,
Immensi regina aevi, quae lucida templa
Aetheris augustosque tenes, augusta, recessus,
5 Pace tua late pollens teque ipsa beata,
Quam pariter flavos crines intonsa Iuventa
Ambit et indomitum nitens Virtus pede aeneo,
Altera divinis epulis assistere mensae
Purpureaque manu iuvenile infundere nectar,
10 Haec largas defendere opes et pectore firmo
Tutari melior fixos in saecula fines
Hostilesque minas regno propellere herili.

ever constant, with a masculine firmness, your courage never fail-
ing. And now, taking pity on labors and kingdoms here below,   25
doomed soon to fall, like Atlas, you sustain the ponderous weight
of the tottering ruins; at other times you rouse the indolent with
countless secret rites since you are free of all envy, and you remove   30
minds enclosed in their dark prisons from the stigma of impiety;
in your great kindness you rescue the ship already at the mercy of
raging tempests, and in the midst of storm clouds and the roar of   35
the sea you brighten up the Northern Sky. But come, come here,
blessed and most holy purification of heavenly beings and of men,
and admit at last to your mystical rites those whom you have
warmed with your beneficial torch.   40

V. To Eternity

You yourself lend me voice and adamantine plectrum as I sing of
you, and come nearer to assist me in this vast, daring enterprise, O
queen of infinite time, who inhabit the bright regions and the au-
gust recesses of the ether, O august one, exercising broad powers   5
in your calm serenity and supremely happy in yourself, surrounded
by unshorn Youth[36] with her flowing blonde locks and side by side
with Virtue who stands firm with her bronze foot, the one god-
dess more suited to assist at the divine banquets and to pour the
nectar of youth with rosy hand, while the other better defends   10
your vast dominion and with sturdy courage watches over bound-
aries fixed for all time and wards off hostile attacks from the king-

Pone tamen, quamvis longo, pone, intervallo,
Omniferens Natura subit curvaque verendus
15 Falce senex spatiisque breves aequalibus Horae
Atque idem totiens Annus remeansque meansque,
Lubrica servato relegens vestigia gressu.
Ipsa autem, divum circumstipante caterva,
Regales illusa sinus auro atque argento,
20 Celsa sedes solioque alte subnixa perenni
Das leges et iura polo coelestiaque aegris
Dividis et certa firmas aeterna quiete,
Aerumnis privata malis, privata periclis.
Tum senium totis excludis provida regnis
25 Perpetuoque adamante ligas fugientia saecla,
Amfractus aevi varios venturaque lapsis
Intermixta legens praesenti inclusa fideli,
Diversosque dies obtutu colligis uno.
Ipsa eadem pars, totum eadem; sine fine, sine ortu,
30 Tota ortus finisque aeque; discrimine nullo
Tota teres, nullaque tui non consona parte.
Salve, magna parens late radiantis Olympi,
Magna deum, precibusque piis non dura rogari,
Aspice nos — hoc tantum! — et, si haud indigna precamur
35 Coelestique olim sancta de stirpe creati,
Adsis, o, propior, cognatoque adiice coelo.

VI. Baccho

Agedum, canite patrem, Thespiades, mihi Bromium,
Sobolem igneam Iovis, quem peperit bona Semele
Puerum coma praesignem et radiantibus oculis.
Euoe! sonant furenti mihi pectora rabie

dom of her mistress. Behind her, though separated by a great distance, comes Nature, who produces all things, and the feared old 15
man with his curved sickle, and at equal distances the fleeting Hours[37] and the Year, which comes and goes, always the same, retracing his slippery path with measured step.

And you, surrounded by a throng of divinities, your regal breast adorned with gold and silver, seated on high upon your eternal 20
throne, issue laws and rules to the universe, separate heavenly from earthly things and establish eternal things in a fixed, everlasting peace, free of evil afflictions, free of dangers. Then, prudently, you exclude old age from all your realms and unite the fleeing ages 25
with unyielding adamant, gathering together the various twisting courses of time, commingling past and future, joining them in a uniform present, and with a single glance you bring together the different days. You yourself are at the same time the part and the whole; without end, without beginning, equally beginning and 30
end; without distinction you are perfectly rounded, harmonious in every part. Hail, great mother of wide-ranging Olympus, great mother of the gods, and do not turn a deaf ear to our pious prayers. Look upon us—this only we ask—and if we pray for things that are not unworthy and were once created from a heav- 35
enly and holy stock, assist us by your presence, ever nearer, and lead us back to our celestial origins.

VI. To Bacchus[38]

Come now, Muses,[39] sing to me of father Bromius,[40] fiery offspring of Jupiter,[41] whom the good Semele brought forth, the boy distinguished by his locks and his radiant eyes. Euoe![42] My breast sends

5   Nimioque deo plenus concutitur gravis animus.
     Euoe! date cymbalum huc, huc date cornua querula,
     Cingat virentem mihi taenia viperea comam,
     Comam diffusam animis Aeoliis hederigeram,
     Quam hinc mille secutae atque illinc trepidante pede sacro,
10   Ululent citatis Edonides usque tripudiis
     Valido sub thyrso iacientes vi capita fera,
     Euoe! sessore pandi geminante quadrupedis.
     At ipse vagus, anhelans, animo duce nimio,
     Totus nova plenus mente, per avia nemora
15   Orgia praecedam acutis celebrans ululatibus,
     Orgia verendis arcana recondita calathis,
     Penitus quae sanctis frustra captes sine initiis,
     Novies perpessus sacra Castalidos vada vitreae.
     Iam iam citatis terrae reboant sola pedibus
20   Oculisque negat medium nubes pulverea diem,
     Gregibus cinctutis euantum deproperantibus.
     Fugiunt deserta turbatae per nemora ferae,
     Regio volucres nec sustinet aetheria suas.
     Euoe! impotenti thyrso gravis, alme Dionyse,
25   Martie, bicornis, rex, omnipotens, femorigena,
     Mystice, Thioneu, ultor, solivage, Euie, satyre,
     Genitor deorum idem atque idem germen amabile,
     Nyctelie, multiformis, hymeneie, nomie,
     Gemine, hospitalis, Liber, pater optime maxime.
30   Domitus quem Ganges, quem gemmea marmora pelagi
     Sensere primi, cui cessit terrigena cohors
     Rhoetusque Mimasque, qui Penthea, qui male nimium
     Adigis Lycurgum tandem sua pendere scelera
     Ausosque deum in tenero nautas fallere puero.

forth a sound emanating from a frenzied rage and my soul, over- 5
flowing with the god, is shaken. Euoe! give me the cymbals, give
me the plaintive horns, and may a headband of vipers gird my
youthful locks, my locks adorned with ivy, fluttering in the breeze,
and in my train may a thousand Edonian women[43] follow after, 10
their sacred feet trembling, with shrill ululations and dancing the
wild tripudium,[44] violently shaking their ferine heads under the
powerful thyrsus,[45] while the rider on his stooped mount repeats
the cry "euoe"! But I myself, wandering aimlessly, gasping for
breath, led on by overpowering feelings, totally filled with a new
spirit, press forward into the pathless woodlands, celebrating the 15
orgies of Bacchus with piercing shrieks, the secret *orgia*[46] hidden
away in a venerated basket, which you would try to touch in vain
without a sacred initiation, or without having received nine times
the sacred waters of transparent Castalia. Already the soil echoes
with the sound of hurrying footsteps and a cloud of dust blots out 20
the midday sun, while troupes of Bacchantes clad in loincloths
hasten along. Frightened wild beasts flee through the deserted
woods, and the region of the sky cannot support its winged crea-
tures. Euoe! Weighed down by the wild thyrsus, O life-giving Di-
onysus, martial, two-horned king,[47] almighty one, born from the 25
thigh,[48] initiate in the sacred mysteries, son of Thyone,[49] avenger,
wandering alone, Euius,[50] Satyr, at once father of the gods and
loveable infant, nocturnal,[51] multiform, god of marriage, shepherd,
twofold, hospitable, Liber,[52] greatest and best father. You are the 30
one whom the vanquished Ganges,[53] whom the crystalline marble
surface of the sea was the first to recognize, before whom the
earthborn cohort and Rhoetus and Mimas[54] retreated; the one
who constrained Pentheus[55] and the excessively repressive Lycur-
gus[56] to pay for their crimes and the pirates who dared to deceive

35 Nam, quid corymbis surgentia stamina subitis
    Dominasque dicam nequicquam denique trepidas
    Sceleri quaerentes per noctis opaca latibula?
    Quid, sera licet, non neglecta piacula Acrisii?
    Tu, sancte, flectis amnes truculentaque maria,
40 Ruptisque rotas decurrentia Chia lapidibus,
    Tu mella primus nova colligis ilice sterili,
    Tibi vomer uncus debet, tibi spicifera Ceres,
    Tibi iura, tibi urbes, tibi mens bona nescia sceleris,
    Tibi impotentis male perpetiens animus heri.
45 Tu robur consilio addis, tu numina supero
    Reperis Olympo primus, tibi sancta Mimallonum
    Cohors insomni lustrant gelidam pede Rhodopen,
    Nimio divulsos raptantes impete vitulos,
    Tibi mille vatum praecordia sortilega fremunt,
50 Tibi ager viret almus, tu florea prata tepentibus
    Zephyris coloras, tu dissona seminia ligas,
    Tu saecla mundo semper fugientia reparas
    Longa iuventa, tu libras pondera machinae
    Medioque terram suspendis in aere stabilem.
55 Per te remota coeli procul ardua colimus,
    Nimio diffusi praecordia nectare gravia,
    Tu das deorum sanctis accumbere dapibus.
    Salve, benigne lychnita, deum et pater hominum,
    Animoque dexter tua mystica rite colentibus
60 Adsis, tuis non sine amoribus et Themide bona,
    Themide nympharum stipata Coricidum choris.

the god in the frail child.[57] Why shall I speak of the threads of the   35
distaff that suddenly became clusters of ivy, and the women trem-
bling in vain as they sought a hiding place for their crime in the
darkness of the night?[58] And why speak of the tardy, but not ne-
glected punishment of Acrisius?[59] It is you, O holy one, who bend
the rivers and the truculent seas, who split open the rocks to make   40
the Chian wine flow;[60] you are the first to collect new honey from
the sterile ilex, to you is owed the curved plowshare, to you Ceres,
bearing ears of wheat, is indebted, to you laws, to you cities, to
you the pure heart, ignorant of crime, to you the spirit that does
not suffer a despotic master. You add force to judgment; you are   45
the first to discover the gods on high Olympus, for you the sacred
band of the Bacchantes[61] traverses the frozen Rhodope[62] on sleep-
less foot, dragging off young calves and tearing them apart in their
mad fury; for you the oracular hearts of a thousand prophets
rumble, for you the fruitful fields are verdant, you color the flower-   50
ing meadows with your warm zephyrs, you join diverse seeds
together, you recover for the world the ever-fleeing generations
through long-lasting youth, you balance the weight of the world
machine and suspend the earth in the middle of the air in a firm
position. Through you we inhabit the remote heights of the heav-   55
ens, our heavy hearts cheered with too much nectar, you allow us
to take our places at the tables of the gods.

Hail, benignant source of light,[63] father of gods and men, in
your benevolence give aid to those who piously celebrate your mys-
teries, together with your loved one, good Themis,[64] Themis sur-   60
rounded by the dancing choruses of the Corycian nymphs.

Liber Secundus

I. Pani

Divae, supremi progenies Iovis,
Tuque, o choreae, Pieri, dux sacrae,
   Sortita frondosum cacumen,
      Calliope, nemorosi Olympi,

5 Adsis canori pectinis arbitra,
Sive hoc sub antro sive sub ilice hac
   Motura concentus loquaces,
      Dum medio tacet aura sole,

Quos foeta tygris, quos leo Parthicus,
10 Mixti maritis innocui gregis,
   Mirentur, offensae prioris
      Immemores solitaeque praedae,

Ruptoque praeceps Arnus ab aggere
Sistat citatum cursibus impetum
15   Longis, et ad vocem resultent
      Carminis aeriae cupressus,

Seu tu Gigantas fulmine praepeti
Coelo repulsos dicere seu velis
   Cantare Latonae potentem
20   Progeniem celeris sagittae

Seu bellicosae Pallados aegida
Victas et urbes seu potius iugis
   Gaudentem intonsi Lycaei
      Pana, vagi pecoris magistrum,

25 Qui per nivosi devia verticis,
Qua nulla presso stat pede semita,

Book II

I. To Pan

O goddesses, offspring of Jupiter most high, and you, Calliope, the
Muse who leads the sacred dance, Calliope,[1] to whom belongs the 5
leafy peak of wooded Olympus, be present, mistress of the tuneful
lyre, either in this grotto or under this ilex tree to intone the fluent
harmonies, while the breeze lies quiet under the noonday sun,[2]
melodies that will charm the tigress that has just given birth and 10
the Parthian lion,[3] both mixed in with the males of the harmless
flock, unmindful of previous offenses and of their usual prey. And
may the Arno, rushing headlong after the collapse of the dam,
check the swift impetus of its lengthy course, and may the tower- 15
ing cypresses reecho the sound of the melody, whether you wish to
sing of the Giants cast down from the heavens by the whirling
thunderbolt or to sing of the offspring of Latona,[4] master of the 20
swift arrow, or of the shield of warlike Pallas Athena and the cit-
ies she conquered, or rather of Pan enjoying the slopes of sylvan
Mt. Lycaeus,[5] guide of the ranging herd,[6] who through the solitary 25

Rupesque inaccessas capellis
Virgineas agitat choreas,

Novisque semper concitus ignibus
30 Blandum novena cantat arundine,
Auditus a primis Eoi
Sedibus Hesperio colono,

Quod nec virenti tecta sub arbore
Aequet volucris garrula nec citas
35 Cantando consuetae morari
Voce rates triplici puellae.

At, cum renidens Hesperus os sacrum
De matris unda Tethyos extulit
Spargitque Lethaeos per orbem
40 Nox tenebris adoperta somnos,

Tum vero quantus coelicolis patet
Modo huc citatis curribus, huc modo,
Quaecunque sub coelo salubri
Mente pater peragrat fovetque!

45 Quem pone longo scilicet ordine
Ingens deorum subsequitur chorus,
Censi sub undenis magistris,
Aede bonam remorante Vestam;

Donec sereni verticibus sacris
50 Accepti Olympi, corpora de via
Lassata succussuque longo
Ambrosiae dapibus refirmant.

Illic vicissim nunc epulis diem
Terunt, soluti morsibus asperis

regions of the snowy mountain peaks, where there is no trace of footprints, and over crags where no goat has gone, leads the dances of the nymphs, and constantly inspired by new fires, plays sweetly   30 on his nine-reeded instrument, heard from the furthest dwelling of the East to the farmer in the land of the evening star. It is a song unrivalled by the garrulous bird[7] sheltered under a green tree   35 or the three young women[8] who by their singing stop the swift ships passing by.

But when the resplendent evening star has lifted its sacred face from the waters of its mother, Tethys,[9] and night, veiled in darkness, has spread its Lethean slumber through the world, then he   40 reveals his true grandeur to the denizens of the sky, and urging his chariot now here, now there, the father traverses all the regions   45 that lie beneath the sky and nurtures them with his salubrious presence! Behind him, in a long line, follows the immense choir of the gods, ranked under the eleven principal gods, but good Vesta[10] remains in her temple, until they are greeted on the summits of   50 serene Olympus, where they refresh their bodies, tired from the journey and the jolting of the chariot, with an ambrosial feast.

55   Curarum et insomnis querelae,
       Nunc pateras iterant capaces,

Largoque blandi nectare carminis
Donante vires, te recinunt patrem
    Terraeque ventosique Nerei,
60   Pan bone, te genialis Aethrae.

At ipse inertis nunc pigra machinae
Fulcisque alisque et foedere mutuo
    Triplex et hinc triplex per artus
       Fusus habes agitasque molem,

65 Nunc consonanti dissona semina
Quiete firmas, nunc nitida infimis
    Diversa non una catena
       Consolidas et aquarum et aurae,

Nunc plena Baccho pectora fertilis
70 Chaos tenebris multivolum explicas,
    Nunc caeca tot mundi malignis
       Membra modis operosus ornas,

Cunctisque largus, nec tamen ullius,
Fixis coherces omnia legibus,
75   Nec fine finis nec priore
       Seminio, pater omnium idem.

Salve, deorum maxime, Pan pater,
Pan rite et idem rite Diespiter,
    Molisque securis caducae
80   Da, pater, ingenium salubre.

There they spend part of the day in banqueting, free from the bit- 55
ter pangs of anxiety and sleepless sorrow; at other times they
continue to fill the capacious goblets, and sustained by the plenti-
ful nectar that gives them the strength to sing a pleasant song,
they take turns in singing of you, good Pan, father of the earth
and of the windy sea and the fecund Aether. 60

But you also sustain and nourish the sluggish mass of the inert
world machine, and by a mutual pact in triple form,[11] then dif-
fused triply through its members, you hold and set the entire mass 65
in motion. Now you consolidate the dissonant seeds in a conso-
nant peace,[12] now you consolidate the brilliant luminaries and the
baser elements with more than one chain of water and air; now, 70
your spirit filled with Bacchus, made fertile, you free anarchic[13]
chaos from the darkness, now you adorn painstakingly the various
parts of the world which are concealed from sight in so many hos-
tile ways. Generous to all, without being partial to any, you keep 75
them all together with fixed laws, without limiting them by any
boundary or by priority of procreation, common father of all.
Hail, greatest of gods, father Pan, ritually Pan and ritually
Diespiter;[14] to those who are unmindful of the weight of perish- 80
able mortality give, O father, a sane spirit.

II. Coelo

Audi, felix patria superum,
Omnia ferens, omnia continens,
Munde pater, sedes alta Iovis,
Qui par nulli, similis uni,
5   In te totus, tuus es totus,
Qui fine carens, terminus omnium,
Longo terras circuis ambitu
Opibusque late pollens tuis
Sortis degis nescius aegrae;
10 Qui Naturae sancta potentis
Ipsos vocas sub iuga coelites;
Qui totus teres undique et integer
Sua cunctis semina dividis.
Tu prona, pater, saecula parturis
15 Indefessam terens orbitam,
Tu perpetua cuncta catena
Prima sollers nectis ab aethra,
Pater incertum rexne melior.
O sanctissime deorum pater,
20 Pater Naturae, adsis, precor, et,
Utcunque mihi rite vocatus,
Tua dexter nos ope sospita.

III. Stellis

O saepe rerum perpetuas vices
Mirata mecum, dic, agedum, dea,
   Stellas et influxu tenaci
      Cuncta iubar variare pollens.

5 Nam, sive mundi prima orientis et
Ruptis creatos ilicibus viros,

II. To Heaven

Listen, happy homeland of the gods, producing all things, contain-
ing all things, father Cosmos,[15] lofty dwelling of Jupiter, you to
whom nothing is equal, who are like unto the One,[16] totally con- 5
tained in yourself, you are all your own. Without limits, the end
point of all things, you circle the lands in a long orbit and exerting
your influence far and wide, you lead an existence free of all ills.
You summon the heavenly beings themselves to submit to the holy 10
yoke of powerful Nature. Perfectly rounded on all sides and intact
in every aspect, you distribute generative seeds to all things, to
each as required. It is you, father, who give birth to the fleeting
centuries, tirelessly traversing your orbit; you bind together all 15
things skillfully in an unending chain, beginning with the ether,
O father, or perhaps better, king. O most holy father of the gods,
Father of Nature, assist us, I pray, and in whatever way I have rit- 20
ually addressed you, graciously keep us safe by your good help.[17]

III. To the stars

O thou who often marveled with me at the perpetual cycles of
things, tell me, O goddess,[18] I pray, of the stars and their radiance
that has the power through its continuing influence to cause all
things to fluctuate. For whether we go back to the beginnings of 5

Cum primum in ignotas recessit
   Gleba recens animata formas,

Seu longa deinceps saecla revolvimus,
10 Hinc omne principium omnibus, hinc modus,
    Quaecunque vitali sub aura
      Sol videt exoriens cadensve.

Hinc tot beatis terra nitet bonis,
Hinc inquietis semina fluctibus,
15   Hinc ros et hymbres, hinc sororum
      Stamina perpetienda cunctis.

Nam, cur inerti numina nenia
Et nocte frustra obtundimus et die
    Iovemque ridentem precesque
20   Totque supervacuas querelas?

Colendus ille est, sed trahit omnia
Vis saeva fati turbinis in modum aut
    De monte torrentis nivali
      Praecipites rapientis ornos,

25 Ipsoque patrum semine protinus
Haurimus aevi laeta dolenda, nec
    Discedit a prima supremus
      Lege dies variatve discors.

Atque hic paterno gaudet humum bove
30 Vertisse et ulmis nectere pampinos,
    Hic arma sectatur tubasque,
      Hic Cypriae melior carinae;

Alter benignis syderibus potens
Repente clarum tollit humo caput,

the emerging world and man issuing from the split ilex trees,[19] when for the first time the glebe was endowed with life and passed into unknown forms, or whether we reflect on the long run of the centuries, it is from the stars that all things under the life-giving air that the sun sees in its rising and setting have their beginning and their mode of being. It is they who make the earth thrive with such abundance of good things, they who give seeds to the restless waters; from them come dew and rain and the thread of the sisters[20] to which we must all be subject. Why, therefore do we din our inept refrains into the ears of the gods night and day, in vain, and harass Jupiter, who laughs at our prayers and our useless laments? He must be worshipped, but the cruel force of destiny carries all before it like a whirlwind or a torrent that comes rushing down from the snowy peaks and carries off the ash trees in headlong flight. Straight from the seed of our fathers we derive the joys and sorrows of life, and the last day does not depart from the initial law or show any variation. One man takes joy in turning up the soil with his father's oxen and training the vine shoots on the elms, another follows in the pursuit of arms and trumpets, another is better suited for Cyprian ships;[21] yet another, enjoying the favor of the stars, suddenly raises his glorious head from the

35   Daturus exemplum ruina
        Forsitan immoderatae habenae.

    Ille, ominosa sic rapiente vi
    Astrorum, honestos dedecorat patres
        Et parta maiorum labore
40   Dilacerat male faustus heres.

    At ipsa coelo lucida sydera
    Affixa cursus deproperant suos,
        Secura privati laboris,
        Dum stet opus solida catena

45   Naturae et aeterni imperium Iovis
    Fixum per omnes lege dies data,
        Gaudentque nil prorsus relinqui
        Alterius moderandum habenis.

    Gaudete, Noctis progenies sacra,
50   Stellae beatae: nos procul a domo
        Quae fata nascenti dedistis
        Interea miseri feremus.

IV. Saturno

    Saturni celebres dies
        Adsunt et resonant cuncta mero simul,
    Simul laeta licentia
        Aetatis memori scilicet aureae.
5   Nos sicci tamen, ac velut
        Nunc demum patriae moenia fax voret,
    Cessamus neque tempora
        Et pronos miseri respicimus dies.
    Profer, Hylle puer, cadum,
10   Da vati cytharam. Pecten ubi aureus,

earth, perhaps destined to give example by his ruin of uncontrolled 35
conduct. Another, carried away by the ominous force of the stars, 40
dishonors his noble parents and dissipates the fruits of his ances-
tors' labors, an ill-fated heir. But they, the shining stars, fixed in
the firmament, hurry along their course with no labor of their
own, as long as the work of Nature and the rule of Jupiter remain 45
fixed in a solid chain, with one law assigned for all time, and they
rejoice that absolutely nothing is left to be directed by the reins of
others. Rejoice, sacred offspring of the night,[22] blessed stars: we, in 50
the meantime, far from our homeland, will endure in misery the
destinies you gave us at our birth.

IV. To Saturn

The feast days of Saturn[23] are upon us and everything resounds
with wine and joyous license, obviously in commemoration of the
Golden Age. But I have remained sober, and as if at precisely this 5
moment fires devoured the ramparts of my native city, I am idle
and pay no attention in my misery to the moments or the hours
that fly past. Garçon! Hyllus, bring me a bottle; give the poet his 10

Lauri mnemosynum mei,
    Et blandum resonans par lyra pectini?
Nil insigne nisi iuvat
    Indictumque. Iuvat dicere saecula
15 Fortunata dei ac sua
    Crescentem Cererem sponte, nec annuae
Curae debita semina,
    Et lactis nivei flumina, flumina
Larga nectaris Attici,
20   Cum Pax atque Fides casta per oppida
Visebant hominum domos,
    Nec possessa diu imperia hospiti
Pigebat dare strenuo.
    Nam, quid maius habent coelicolae patre
25 Saturno Iovis optimi,
    Eodem magnanimo patre Iovis, Rheae
Eodem coniuge maximo,
    Quam de taurisono bellipotens sinu
Pater Protogonus dedit
30   Terrarumque parentem et liquidi aetheris?
Quis aeque est alius potens,
    Idem cuncta dare atque idem alere omnia,
Idem, cum libet, omnia
    Parcarum memori lege resolvere?
35 Quis foecundior ingeni
    Largitor, solidae quis retinentiae,
Quis et pauperiem pati
    Et niti melior cum duce, par duci?
Hic, seu casta magis iuvant,
40   Felix casta sequi, seu taciturnitas
Et tenax animus sui,
    Observare bonus tuta silentia.

cithara. Where is my gold plectrum, souvenir of my poetic prize, and the sweet-sounding lyre, companion of the plectrum? Nothing pleases me except what is exceptional and never said before. I like to sing of the blessed centuries of the god and of the wheat 15 that grew spontaneously, and the seed that was not owed to the year's labors, and the rivers of snow-white milk, the wide rivers of Attic nectar, when Peace and Faith visited the houses of men in 20 the chaste cities, and one did not suffer the anguish of surrendering long possessed territories to an intrusive stranger. What greater thing do the heavenly dwellers possess than Saturn, father 25 of great Jupiter, the magnanimous father of Jupiter and the great spouse of Rhea,[24] to whom her father Protogonos,[25] the bull-roarer, powerful in war, gave birth, and she became mother of lands and 30 the limpid ether? Who else is equally powerful, able to give everything and nourish everything and likewise, if he pleases, to undo everything according to the relentless law of the Fates? Who is a 35 more generous bestower of genius, of retentive memory; who is more capable of suffering poverty and of tolerating fatigue at the side of a leader, equally unyielding? If chastity is preferred, he is 40 happy to favor chastity; if quietude and steadfastness, he main-

Hic suspendere fertili
    Sollers vomere agros, hic sua semina
45 Doctus fertilibus dare
    Terris et veteres Chaonias dapes
Blandis vertere frugibus.
    Quin, quamvis senio debilis et situ
Annorum, nihilominus
50   Et fundare domos strenuus et semel
Collectam rabiem impigre
    Exercere modis omnibus efficax.
Saturne, optime maxime,
    Saturne omnipotens progenitor deum,
55 Absint hinc procul, o, procul,
    Et lugubre odium, sancte, precor, tuum
Et vis saeva: alios minae
    Importunae, alios ira premat tua.

                    V. Iovi

Iuppiter pie, Iuppiter
Benigne, optime Iuppiter,
Qui tuo nitidum aethera
    Ambis igne beato,

5 Te cano placidum patrem
Terrarum, placidum aequoris,
Largum, quicquid ubique adest,
    Fertili dare dextra,

Sive augere libet novis
10 Glebas seminibus rudes
Sive enata salubribus
    Fortunare alimentis.

tains secure silence. He is skillful in turning over the soil with a
fertile plow, expert in distributing the proper seed to the fertile   45
lands and in transforming the ancient Chaonian repasts[26] into
fruitful harvests. Moreover, despite the weakness of old age and
the physical deterioration caused by increasing years, he has the   50
energy to establish dwellings, and once he has summoned up his
anger, he is capable of exercising it energetically in every way. Sat-
urn, best and greatest, Saturn, all-powerful progenitor of the gods,
keep far, far from us your gloomy hatred, holy one, I pray, and   55
your cruel violence: reserve for others your grim threats and your
anger.

V. To Jupiter[27]

Loyal Jupiter, benign Jupiter, best Jupiter, who surround the shin-
ing firmament with your blessed light, I sing of you, serene father   5
of earth, serene father of the sea, generous in bestowing your gifts
on all things, wherever they may be, with your life-giving right
hand, whether it please you to give increase with new seeds to the   10
uncultivated clods of earth, or with healthy nourishment to make

Et nunc saeva repellere
Sylvis flabra virentibus,
15   Nunc laetum sata commodo
    Culta spargere rore,

Nunc rigentia flumina
Dura solvere compede,
Nunc defendere Syrium
20   Aegris pulverulentum

Terris et pecori mala
Momenta, arboribus mala,
Cum semel rabiem improbam
    Tellus syderis hausit.

25   Sed nec vere novo thima
Complecti numero queam
Aut quas saevus Atabolus
    Olim torquet arenas,

Nec, si lingua adamantina
30   Sonet, vox adamantina,
Tuas expediam tamen
    Laudes et benefacta,

Aut cum falciferi patris
Almo sydere temperas
35   Minas et rabiem feram,
    Quo non saevior alter,

Seu libet misera lue
Urbes polluere integras
Sive fasque nefasque gravi
40   Involvisse ruina;

the sprouting plants prosper. Now you take pleasure in repelling
the violent winds from the verdant forests, now in sprinkling the   15
cultivated fields with beneficial dew; now you liberate the frozen
rivers from their harsh fetters, now you protect the weary lands
from dusty Sirius[28] and the flocks and trees from harmful astral   20
influences, once the earth has absorbed the relentless ferocity of
the star. But even if I were to count the sprigs of thyme in spring   25
or the sands which the violent sirocco[29] churns up, or speak with
an adamantine tongue or an adamantine voice, would I be able to   30
relate your praises and benefactions, either when with your kindly
star you appease the threats and savage rage of your sickle-bearing
father,[30] who has no equal in cruelty, whether it be his whim to   35
infest entire cities with a loathsome plague or envelop right and
wrong in common destruction; or when, after driving off wicked-   40

Aut cum, fraude procul mala
Pulsa, nequitia procul,
Idem legibus omnia,
    Idem moribus ornas.

45 At lugubre nefas vada
Horret tristificae Stygis
Rotamque et capiti improbo
    Imminentia saxa.

O coeli decus, o potens
50 Votorum et triplicis boni,
Salve, rite vocantibus
    Felix, Iuppiter alme.

VI. Marti

Antiqua Codri progenies, licet
Hinc arva bubus mille teras tuis,
    Hinc dite seponas in arca
        Quicquid Arabs vehit aestuosus,

5 Frustra clientum dinumeres greges
Et consulari praemia purpurae,
    Frustra renidentes curules
        Et veterum decora alta patrum,

Ni cuncta prudens dis referas bonis:
10 Hos nocte, castis hos precibus die
    Supplex adores, hos in omne
        Tempus opem veniamque poscas;

Nec vero, siquid durius accidit —
Quae multa vitae fert varius tenor —
15   Spem praeter, iccirco labare
        Relligio pietasque debet.

ness and deceit, you provide law and good morals for all things. But sullen injustice shudders before the shallows of the hateful 45 Styx[31] and the wheel[32] and the rocks[33] that hang over the shameless head. O glory of the heavens, O arbiter of vows and of the 50 triple blessing, greetings, propitious to those who call upon you fittingly, kindly Jupiter.

VI. To Mars

O ancient offspring of Codrus,[34] though you plow your fields with a thousand oxen and store up in rich coffers all the goods that torrid Arabia transports, in vain would you count the crowds of clients and the privileges of consular purple, in vain the resplendent 5 curule chairs and the lofty dignities of the ancient fathers, if you do not wisely attribute all of this to the good gods and humbly adore them, day and night, with holy prayers and implore help and 10 pardon at all times; and if something difficult to bear, contrary to your hopes, befalls you—for the varied vicissitudes of life bring many such hardships—religion and piety must not waver. For not 15

Nam nec perenni terra viret coma
Et saepe sudo nunc capimur brevi,
    Nunc frustra inundantes procellae
20   Terrificant redeunte sole.

Quare, tot olim quanquam opibus patrum
Excussi Etrusco carpimur otio,
    Dic, sancta, dic, Clio, parentum
        Laude patrem solita Gradivum,

25 Heu, tot suorum quem miserae iuvant
Clades, repulso Strymone Thracio
    Tectisque Byzanti superbis,
        Tristia dum fovet arma Turcae.

Sed quid benignae non faciunt preces?
30 Forsan minarum desinet hic quoque
    Iam tandem et oblitus peracti
        Respiciet propior nepotes.

Tunc me nec Orpheus carminibus pater
Aequet canentem nec pecorum deo
35   Laudatus aestiva sub umbra,
            Multiloquae fidicen Camaenae,

Quanquam sonoris hic fidibus rudes
Duxisset ornos et vaga flumina
    Frenasset, hunc dignatus ipse
40   Ultro epulis decimaque Phoebus.

Sed plena solvens pectora numine,
Dicam arma, plectro dicam adamantino
    Currus et adversa iacentem
        Cuspide terrigenam cohortem,

238

even the earth is always green and flowering and often we are deceived by a brief period of good weather, and then the drenching storms terrify us, but in vain, for the sun returns. Therefore, although bereft long ago of the wealth of our fathers, we lead a tranquil existence here in Tuscany. Sing, holy Clio,[35] in words of praise used by our ancestors, of father Gradivus,[36] although, alas! he takes delight in the deplorable slaughter of his own kind, abandoning the Thracian Strymon[37] and the proud dwellings of Byzantium while he promotes the grim warfare of the Turks.

And yet, what can devout prayers not accomplish? Perhaps he too will at last desist from his threats and forgetting the past will look with more favor upon his descendants. Then neither father Orpheus will equal me in song nor the lyre player of the eloquent Camenae,[38] praised by the god of herd animals in the summer shade, though the one with his melodious lyre drew after him the rugged ash trees and checked the course of the wandering streams, and the other[39] was deemed worthy of banquets and largesse by Phoebus Apollo himself. But giving free rein to my breast, filled with the divinity, I will sing of arms, I will sing with my adamantine plectrum of chariots and of the cohort of earthborn Titans prostrate on the ground with their spears still turned against the

45 Cum, saeva cunctis bella timentibus
    Superque moles molibus additas —
        Sic prima nil virtus perhorret! —
            Mars cuperet tamen arma solus,

    Mars tunc Olympo primum oculis patris
50 Admissus, alta sub Rhodope puer
        Haemoque adhuc suetus leones
            Cominus exagitare aprosque.

    Ut vero cunctos ancipitis mali
    Concussit horror Terraque partubus
55   Superba crescebat sereno
            Iam propior propiorque coelo,

    'Quid, o, quid annos digeritis rudes?
    An sic creari nil' ait 'ab Iove est'
        Paean, 'o aeternum carentes
60   Morte dei et bone rex deorum?'

    Simulque et ensem dat puero et galeam
    Aeratam et hamis undique nexilem
        Auroque loricam trilicem,
            Aeolii Steropis laborem.

65 Excepit omnis regia plausibus,
    Primusque nutu Iuppiter annuens
        Terrasque concussitque coelum,
            Cynthe, tua domina invidente.

    Et iam profanae versae acies retro,
70 Iam Terra monstris ipsa suis gravis,
        Aeterna quid distent caducis
            Senserat et manibus Tonantis

enemy. When all were in fear of cruel war and mountains were 45
piled upon mountains,[40] Mars alone longed for the fight—since
youthful courage fears nothing!—Mars was then admitted for the
first time to Olympus under the gaze of his father, while he was
still a boy, accustomed to pursue lions and wild boars at close
quarters under the peaks of Mt. Rhodope and Mt. Haemus.[41] 50
When all were stricken with fear of the impending evil and Earth,
proud of her offspring, rose nearer and nearer to the cloudless 55
heavens, the god Paean[42] cried out, "What is this? Why do you
count his tender years? Is it nothing to have been created by Jupi-
ter, O gods eternally exempt from death and you, good king of 60
the gods?" And forthwith he gives a sword and a bronze helmet to
the boy and a cuirass woven with chain mail and triple-threaded
gold, the work of Aeolian Sterope.[43] The whole palace welcomed 65
him with applause and Jupiter, first of all, nodding in assent,
shook the heavens and the earth,[44] though, Mount Cynthus,[45]
your mistress looked on with discontent.[46] And when the ranks of
the impious invaders were already repulsed, Earth, weighed down 70
by her monstrous progeny, had become aware of the distance that
separated eternal from temporal things and the difference between
the lightning bolts hurled by the hand of the god of thunder and

Contorta Rhoeti fulmina fraxinis,
Iam laeta signo sancta deum cohors
    75   Redibat audito receptus,
          Arma Iovis pariter canentes.

At non receptus ille nec imperi
Audit verendi signa, sed improba
      In caede perstabat ferocum
    80   Impatiens animorum et irae,

Ni iam tum et annos et pueri Venus
Mirata dextram, nec faciem minus,
      Complexa germanum benignis
      Aurea continuisset ulnis.

85 Salve, et virorum Mars pater et pater
Armorum, et olim — si merui modo —
      Da, quaeso, da, Gradive, pulchraque
      Ob patriam atque inopina fata.

VII. *Veneri*

Iam sat huc illuc, Erato, vagata,
Arte concussas moderante habenas,
    Dum per et tractus et inane Olympi
      Curris apertum,

5 Flecte vocales, agedum, quadrigas,
Sancta qua vocat genitrix Amorum,
    Flecte. Quis neget genitrici Amorum
      Carmina danda?

Nunc et auratos bene pone crines,
10 Tortulum myrto cohibente cirrum,
    Nunc et Eois opibus gravatas
      Indue vestes,

the ash spears of the giant Rhoetus, and now the holy army of the
gods, after hearing the trumpet sound the retreat, was returning, 75
joyfully singing in chorus of the armed might of Jupiter. But Mars
did not hear the signal for retreat or the command that was to be
obeyed, but would have pressed on in the horrendous slaughter,
unable to control his ferocious spirit and his wrath, had not golden 80
Venus, admiring even then his youthful years and his strong right
arm as well as his beauty, held back her brother in her tender em-
brace. Hail, Mars, father of heroes and father of arms, and one 85
day — provided I have merited it — grant, I pray you, O Gradivus,
beautiful and unexpected destinies to my native land.

VII. To Venus

Having wandered sufficiently here and there, Erato,[47] with the art
of poetry holding the reins, as you course through the regions and
the empty expanse of Olympus, come! steer your resounding 5
chariot to the place where the holy mother of the Cupids calls.
Who would refuse to offer songs to the mother of the Cupids?
And now arrange carefully your golden hair with myrtle,[48] which 10
keeps your rebellious curls in place, and now put on the garments

Qualis exortu serieque prima
Diceris rerum Veneris parentis
15 Donaque et largas cecinisse blando
    Pectine laudes.

Ante nec terrae facies inerti
Nec suus stellis honor et sine ullis
Aura torpebat zephyris, sine ullis
20   Piscibus unda.

Prima de patris gremio Cythere
Caeca Naturae miserata membra,
Solvit antiquam minimum pigendo
    Foedere litem.

25 Illa supremis spatiis removit
Lucidum hunc ignem mediasque terras
Arte suspendit pelagusque molles
    Inter et auras.

Tunc et immenso micuere primum
30 Signa tot coelo et sua flamina aer
Cepit, admirans volucrum proterva
    Proelia fratrum;

Tunc repentinis freta visa monstris
Fervere et nova facie novoque
35 Flore diffusos aperire tellus
    Daedala vultus.

Iam greges passim varios boumque ar-
Menta, iam pictas volucres ferasque
Surgere emotis erat hic et illic
40   Cernere glebis.

laden with Oriental riches, just as they say you were at the birth
and the first stages of creation when you sang on your sweet lyre   15
of the gifts and the abundant merits of mother Venus. Before that,
neither did the inert earth have any beauty nor did the stars have
their splendor and the air was torpid without any breezes, the   20
waves without fish. Venus,[49] born from her father's loins, was the
first to take pity on the formless members of nature and resolved
the ancient discord with a pact that caused no discontent. It   25
was she who removed this bright, fiery star from upper space and
with art suspended the earth between the deep sea and the soft
breezes. Then for the first time myriads of constellations gleamed   30
in the immense heavens and the air acquired its winds and gazed
in wonder at the violent battles of winged brethren; then the sea
was seen suddenly to seethe with monstrous creatures and the
daedalian[50] earth took on a new beauty and scattered new flow-   35
ers over its surface. Now various flocks and herds of oxen could
be seen everywhere, varicolored birds and wild beasts arose here
and there from the tilled soil. But the sickly common herd of   40

At virum, quamvis etiam labante
Aegra plebs genu, meditari et urbes
Tectaque et iam tum sociorum amicos
    Iungere coetus.

45 Quos ferox inter medios Cupido
Acer it, fratrum comitante turba,
Callidus quondam petiisse certa
    Quenque sagitta,

Seu libet magnae genitricis alta
50 Templa semota peragrare cura,
Seu procellosae per aperta vitae
    Flectere gressum,

Sive, mutato iaculis veneno,
Mutuis tactos penitus favillis
55 Carpere et gentis breve ver parata
    Prole novare.

Ipsa lascivo Venus alma partu
Laeta, nunc iunctis vehitur columbis,
Eriosque altos et opima Cypri
60   Templa revisens.

Ridet et tellus veniente diva
Carpathi et rident freta, nec sereno
Sibilat coelo nisi blandientis
    Aura Favoni.

65 Nunc, novis sanctum caput impedita
Floribus, plausasque levis choreas
Ducit et passim violis scatentem
    Ter pede nudo

men, their knees still wobbly, began to contemplate cities and
dwellings and to join friendly alliances with their fellows. In their   45
midst fierce Cupid makes his way, accompanied by a band of his
companions, cunning, as always, in striking his victims with un-
erring arrow, whether it be his pleasure to traverse the lofty tem-   50
ples of his great mother, where all cares are excluded, or to direct
his steps to the open spaces of storm-ridden existence, or changing
the poison of his arrows,[51] to touch two persons and then con-
sume them with mutual flames to renew the brief spring of human   55
life with new offspring.

Kindly Venus[52] herself, content with her mischievous child, is
borne aloft by her team of doves to visit the heights of Mt. Eryx[53]
and the rich temples of Cyprus.[54] And the earth laughs with joy   60
at the arrival of the goddess and the Carpathian Sea[55] laughs,
and from the serene sky there is no sound save for the caressing
breezes of Favonius.[56] Now, her holy head garlanded with fresh   65
flowers, she nimbly leads the dance to a clapped rhythm and beats
the earth bursting with violets three times with her bare foot.

Concutit terram; sequitur Iuventa
70 Fervidum spirans, sequitur Voluptas
Prodiga et zonis Charitum renidens
  Turba solutis.

Spectat occulto latitans roseto
Mars pater simulque cupit videri
75 Et timet, simul velut igne cera ex-
  Udat abitque.

Nunc ubi currus, ubi amica quondam
Hasta? quid tecum, bone dux, roseto?
Nempe iam sordent galeae aptiorque
80   Crinibus herba est.

Illa tormentisque deique amore
Pulchrior, quam dissimulat videre,
Hoc mage occulta placuisse quaerit,
  Callida, ab arte.

85 Et modo suras teretes reducta
Veste, dum saltat, studiosa nudat,
Et modo pectus retegit statimque
  Claudit eburneum.

Sed, Venus regina, Iovis propago
90 Aurea, huc adsis, precor, et maligna
Nocte discussa tua da beata
  Visere templa.

VIII. *Mercurio*

Ergo restabat mihi—proh, deorum
Rex bone!—hoc fatis etiam malignis,
Patria ut Graecus sacra non Pelasga
  Voce referrem,

248

Lusty Youth comes next and after her prodigal Pleasure and the   70
resplendent Graces, their cinctures loosened. Hidden away in a
concealed rose garden Mars looks on and both wishes and fears to   75
be seen, and like wax in the fire, glows and dissolves. Where now
is your chariot, where your spear, once your friend? What do you
have to do with a rose garden, great warrior? Clearly, helmets
seem squalid to you now and grass is more becoming to your   80
hair.

   She, rendered more beautiful by her torment and love for the
god, the more she feigns not to see him, the more she shrewdly
seeks to please him with her subtle stratagems. Now she reveals   85
her smooth calves, studiously drawing up her dress as she dances,
and now she bares her ivory breasts and quickly covers them again.
But, queen Venus, golden offspring of Jupiter,[57] come to my aid, I   90
pray you, and dispelling the malignant night, permit me to visit
your sacred shrines.

VIII. To Mercury

So it was my destiny — ah! good king of the gods — so this too
was willed by the spiteful fates — that I, a Greek, should nar-
rate the sacred things of my country in a non-Hellenic voice,

5 Quique tot saeclis tripodas silentes
   Primus Orpheo pede rite movi,
   Exul Etrusci streperem sonanda
       Vallibus Arni.

   Sed tamen Delphisque meis habenda
10 Gratia et Maia genito beata:
   Ille nec turpem exilio nec unquam
       Passus inertem,

   Perque tot terras, mala tot secutus
   Per freta huc fatis agitatum et illuc,
15 Largus et Scythae dedit et Latini
       Pectinis usum.

   Forsitan, vanus nisi fallor augur,
   Et decus labente daturus aevo
   Exuli, magni invideant quod olim
20   Saepe tyranni.

   Interim, si non patriae beata
   Voce, qua grato licitum cadente
   Te canam Phoebo, tibi substrepemus
       Syderis ortu,

25 O potens vatum geminique mundi,
   Mercuri, interpres, pater, unde primum
   Fluxit et nervis honor et decorae
       Copia linguae,

   Arte dum blanda populos recentes
30 Caede deterres solita suisque
   Providus sylvis, meliora tandem
       Quaerere suasos,

and that I, who first roused the tripods,[58] silent for so many cen- 5
turies, in an orphic rhythm, as an exile, should make the valleys of
the Etruscan Arno resound with my loud song. But I must thank
my Delphi and the son of blessed Maia,[59] for he never permitted 10
that my exile should be shameful or idle, and following me through
many lands and over rough seas, as I was tossed about here and
there by the fates, generously conceded to me the use of the Scyth- 15
ian[60] and the Latin plectrum. Perhaps, if I am not a false prophet,
as time passes, he will also grant honor to the exile, which one day
great monarchs will envy. In the meantime, if not in the blessed 20
language of my country, I shall sing of you in the language that is
permitted me, at the pleasant hour of sunset, and I will whisper to
you at break of day, O lord of poets and of both worlds,[61] Mer- 25
cury, messenger, father, from whom honor first flowed to the lyre
and abundance to beautiful language, while you with seductive art
discouraged recently formed peoples from their customary carnage 30
and providently drew them out of the forest to seek a better life,

Inque crescentes facis ire muros
Marmora ad vocem cytharae bicornis,
35   Dulce subsultim tremuli insecuta
        Pollicis ictum.

Nam, quid et leges positas et acris
Ingeni commenta loquar benigna,
Quis sine incassum steterant relictis
40   Oppida sylvis?

Tu procellosa vagus hospes alno
Adriae curris freta, tu remotos
Gadibus Seras gelidisque donas
        Bactra Britannis

45   Impiger mercator, ut omnia omnes
Gentibus terraeque ferant et aurae.
Te tuus Ianusque forumque supplex
        Orat avarum,

Quique vel penna trepidis vel extis
50   Doctus eventura videre quique
Fluctibus sollers numerosque vastae
        Ponit arenae,

Sive quis Graia nitidus palestra,
Barbarae miratus opes olivae,
55   Vara Pisaeo redeunte nudat
        Brachia lustro

Sive quis cura meliore felix
Aethera atque ipsas animo capaci
Concipit stellas positusque coelo et
60   Nomina dicit.

and made marble blocks change into rising walls at the sound of
your two-horned lyre,[62] as they follow by leaps and bounds the   35
sweet sound of your vibrating thumb. And why speak of the laws[63]
you established and of the beneficent inventions of your acute ge-
nius, without which towns would have risen in vain after the for-   40
est was abandoned? An errant stranger, you cross the stormy seas
of the Adriatic, and as a tireless merchant you bring gifts from
China to Cadiz, and from Bactria to the shivering Britons, so that   45
all lands and all winds bring all types of merchandise to all peo-
ples. Your dear Janus[64] and the greedy forum pray and implore
you, and he who through winged flight or palpitating entrails has   50
learned to see the future, and he who cleverly can count the waves
or the grains of sand of the vast desert. The oiled athlete in the
Greek palaestra also prays to you, marveling at the rich resources
of the barbarian wild olive tree, and baring his curved arms at the 55
return of the Pisan Olympiads,[65] or the one who, happy in his
more noble activity, conceives in his capacious mind the ether and
the very stars and their positions in the sky and tells their names. 60

Iam leves somnos dare, iam negare,
Vestrum opus; vestrum, pater Argicida,
Nocte sopitis aperire divum
    Condita fata,

65 Vestrum et aurata revocare virga
Sedibus functas animas sepultis,
Vestrum et invisi spatiis iniquis
    Reddere Averni.

Salve, io, verum decus exilique
70 Dulce lenimen patriaeque victae,
Commodus peraeque animoque gnavo et
    Rebus agendis.

Liber Tertius

I. Soli

Quis novus hic animis furor incidit? unde repente
Mens fremit horrentique sonant praecordia motu?
Quis tantus quatit ossa tremor? Procul este, profani,
Este! movent imis delubra excussa cavernis
5 Adventante deo et mons circum immane remugit.
Scilicet antiquas tanto post tempore sedes
Dignatur tamen atque situ marcentia longo
Antra subit consueta, deum confessus, Apollo,
Inspiratque graves animos et pectore magnum
10 Saevit, agens oestro, furiataque corda fatigat
Bacchantum rabie atque agitatu mentis anhelo.
Iam mihi, discussa mortali pectore nube,
Parcarum reseratur opus; iam panditur ingens

To allot light sleep or to refuse it is your task; yours it is, father, slayer of Argos,[66] to reveal the fates decided by gods to those asleep at night, and it is your function also to call back dead souls 65 from their place of burial with your golden wand[67] and to return them to the unfriendly spaces of hated Avernus.[68] Hail, true glory 70 and sweet solace of exile and of my conquered native land, equally propitious to the diligent spirit and to the conduct of human affairs.

Book III

I. To the Sun

What new divine inspiration invades my spirit? Whence comes suddenly this frenzied feeling in my soul and the terrible turmoil that reverberates in my breast? What great trembling shakes my bones?[1] Keep your distance, profane crowd, stay away! The sanctuaries move, shaken from the subterranean caverns at the advent 5 of the god, and the surrounding mountain[2] responds with a tremendous roar. It is evident that after so many years, considering his ancient dwelling worthy, Apollo finally enters into the customary caves, dilapidated from long neglect,[3] manifesting himself as a god, and inspires powerful feelings in me, and rages mightily in my 10 breast, filling it with divine frenzy, and exhausts my delirious fervor with the fury of the Bacchantes and the panting agitation of the mind. Now that the cloud is dissipated in my mortal breast,

Annorum series et longum interprete cassa
15 Certatim tenebris quaerunt erumpere fata,
Angustumque premunt pariter tot saecula pectus.
Iam mutat vigor atque hominem desuevimus aegrum,
Admissi supera depascere lumina luce,
Praesentesque deos propius ipsumque tuemur,
20 Solus inexhausta qui lampade cuncta gubernat,
Sol pater — unde etiam Solem dixere priores —
Et patria longe moderatur imagine mundum,
Idem rex hominum atque deum, pater omnibus idem,
Candida quem Thia, ut perhibent, Hyperione magno
25 Conceptum rapidas Acheloi fudit ad undas,
Ingentem ingenti et radiantem luce paterna.
    Nam, cum coelicolis Hyperion cognitus unis
Degeret, humanis contingi captibus exsors,
Qui nisi de bruto nequeunt capere augmina sensu,
30 Et tamen ignotus nollet per saecla latere,
Auricomum genitor foecundo lumine Solem
Edidit effigiemque sui formavit ad ipsam,
Per quem sublimes possimus tollere mentes
Metirique animo et conferre incognita notis,
35 Utpote naturae tantum qui visilis anteit
Omnia, quam divos inter pater emicat omnis
Infra seque premit magnorum saecla deorum.
Neve loco terras non conveniente vaporet,
In media medium mundi regione locatum,
40 Umbrarum iussit, iussit confinia habere
Lucis et ignitos hac exercere iugales,
Unde queat propius tenebrosa accendere flammis
Et dare vicinum germanae lumen opacae.
Hunc dextra laevaque Anni Mensesque Diesque
45 Circumstant nutusque observant Tempora heriles.
Ipse gravis quatiens gemmarum pondere habenas,

the workings of the fates are revealed to me; now the great se-
quence of the years is opened up and the fates, long deprived of an   15
interpreter, strive with one another to burst forth from the dark-
ness, and so many centuries press upon my narrow consciousness.
Now our strength changes and we have put off human frailty,
permitted to feast our eyes upon the light emanating from a light
on high, and we contemplate the gods face to face, close by, and   20
that *sole* god who with his inexhaustible lamp governs all things,
father Sun — that is why the ancients called him Sun[4] — and in the
image of his father guides the world from afar, king of men and of
gods, and father equally to all, who they say, generated by great
Hyperion,[5] issued forth from the womb of the fair Theia[6] into the   25
fast-flowing Achelous,[7] immense from immense and radiant with
his father's light.

In fact, when Hyperion was known only to the inhabitants of
heaven, inaccessible to the understanding of humans, who cannot
acquire new knowledge[8] except through the brute senses, and yet   30
did not wish to remain unknown all through the centuries, the
parent engendered the golden-haired Sun through fecund light
and formed him after his own image, so that through him we
might elevate our minds to greater heights and mentally measure
and compare the unknown to the known, since by his visibility[9] he   35
surpasses all things in nature, as much as his father stands out
among the other gods, and submerges the generations of the great
gods. In order that he would not scorch the earth if he were put in
an unsuitable position, he placed him in the middle of the middle
region of the universe and commanded that he be situated on the   40
boundary of darkness and light, and in this way he could lead his
fiery steeds and be able to set fire to dark places in closer proximity
and give neighboring light to his sister, devoid of light. Around
him on the right and on the left stand the years, the months and
the days, and the seasons observe the signs of their master. He,   45
shaking the reins weighted with precious gems, makes his entrance

Ingreditur superis curru spectabilis aureo,
Qua patet obliquum medium via secta per orbem,
Certa premens certus vestigia. Cedit eunti
50 Continuo flectitque loco turba obvia divum,
Regales propius veriti contingere gressus,
Munificus licet immensi partitur honores
Inque ipsos mundi moderamina dividit ultro,
Commodus imperium multis tenuisse secundis,
55 Non tamen ut summae rerum invigilare suetus
Naturae partem totius negligat ullam.
Nam sublima inferna salutifer omnia flammis
Ipse suis lustrat lustrataque servat et auget,
Complexus terram atque auras coelumque profundum
60 Et quae mortales maria appellare solemus;
Permixtusque tamen rebus contagia nulla
Accipit et cunctis visus dumtaxat inhaeret.
    Hinc et Sidonii, stellis genus acre tuendis,
Fecerunt capti vicino errore ruinas
65 Luciferumque omni privarunt corpore fontem,
Esse rati purae nimirum et simplicis actum
Mentis de propria mittentis lumina sede,
Ipsa etiam lux quandoquidem sit corpore cassa.
Nec vero, in morem rapidi cum fluminis acta
70 Omnia, materia faciente cupidine rerum,
Crescendoque fluant totiens crescantque fluendo,
Aut alio donante novas potuere sub auras
Surgere et aetatis contingere lumina laeta
Aut offecta mali volvendis mensibus anni
75 Rursus in antiquam posito squallore iuventam
Luxuriare novasque iterum sibi sumere vires,
Cum primum tepidi sub tempora verna Favoni
Aura suum terris genitalem exuscitat auctum
Adventuque dei gemmantia prata colorat.

258

on his golden chariot, in full sight of the gods, where the path[10] traced through the middle of the circle extends obliquely, tracing fixed trajectories at fixed times. The throng of gods that goes out 50 to meet him makes way for him and turns aside, fearing to tread too close to his royal steps, even though he generously apportions the duties of ruling immense space and willingly shares with them the governance of the universe, content to delegate power to subalterns, but not in such a way as, being accustomed to watching over 55 the totality of matter, to neglect any part of all of nature. For as conveyer of well-being he illumines with his flames the heights and the depths, and having illumined them preserves and strengthens them, embracing the earth and the air and the deep sky and 60 what we mortals are accustomed to call seas; and though interfused with things,[11] he has no contact with them but inheres in them only in appearance.

For this reason the Phoenicians, a people very skilled in observing the stars, victims of a similar error, went wrong totally and 65 deprived the source of light of all corporality, thinking that it was an act of a pure, simple spirit which emits light from its own being, since light itself was devoid of a body. But since all things are swept along like a rushing torrent, and matter, impelled by desire, 70 causes them to flow as they increase and increase as they flow, they would not be able through the gift of another to rise up into the fresh breezes and arrive at the joyous light of life nor, impeded by the arrival of the months of the bad part of the year, could 75 they shed their squalor and flourish again in their former youth and recover new strength as soon as, in the springtime of warm Favonius, the air awakens in the earth its creative growth and at the approach of the god colors the flowering meadows.

80 At pecudum genus omne viget, genus omne virorum,
Perculsi teneras anni dulcedine mentes,
Concurruntque obnixi inter se frontibus hedi
Et nova lascivo persultant pabula motu,
Nec liquidum tremulis concentibus aera cessant
85 Mulcere et laetum volucres Paeana sonare,
Contectae nemorum viridantibus undique ramis,
Et cum mane novo terras Sol exit Eoo
Visurus thalamo et cum seros vespere currus
Solvit et oceano viduas commendat habenas,
90 Donec in humentes spatiis declivibus Austros
Paulatim flexo secum trahat omnia gyro
Detque locum letho et rursum regna altera mundi
Atque alio terras longe beet orbe repostas,
Natura prohibente moras rerumque suaque.
95 Nam neque res, alia non deficiente vicissim,
Ulla potest dulces invisere luminis auras
Crescendoque aevum capere atque assumere vires,
Et vita coram—quid enim nisi vivida rerum
Vita satorque animarum aeternus Sol pater et fons?—
100 Esse locum siquis letho putat, avius errat
Naturae procul a vera ratione vagatus.
Ergo, corporibus ne tandem exhausta creandis
Sylva cadat naturae aut Sol pater omnibus idem
Occupet in parti totis bona debita terris,
105 Alterno temone, cavi modo brachia Cancri
Ignit et aestivam rectus ferit inde Syenen,
Nunc pressum Aegocerota, gelu regna horrida longo
Saturni visit senis ignavaque pruina
Pigros exhortatur equos et verbere saevit.
110 Interea medius magnum permensus Olympum,
In coetum vocat atque imis annexa suprema
Componit docilis blandi dulcedine plectri

But every race of animals flourishes too, and the race of men, their   80
tender minds stricken by the sweetness of the season, and the
young goats run together, butting each other with their horns and
romping about playfully, prancing over the new pastures, and the
birds never cease caressing the limpid air with their tremulous
harmonies and intone a glad paean to the sun, sheltered by the   85
green branches everywhere in the woods, both in the early morn-
ing when the Sun rises up from his bedchamber in the east to visit
the earth, and when late in the evening he unharnesses his chariot
and commits to the ocean the reins he has cast away, until through   90
spaces sloping toward the humid South winds, bending his course
little by little, he drags everything along with him and gives place
to death and gladdens in turn the other kingdoms of the world
and the far-off lands in another orbit, since the nature of things
and his own nature forbid delay.

For nothing, if another being does not in its turn fade away, can   95
visit the sweet breezes of light and progress in age and gather
strength, and if anyone think in the presence of life—for what else
is the eternal Sun, father and fountainhead, but the vivifying life
of things and the progenitor of souls?—that there is room for   100
death, he has wandered far from the true principles of nature.
Then, in order that the matter of nature does not eventually de-
generate, exhausted by the creation of bodies, or that the Sun, fa-
ther of all things equally, should confine in one single part of the
earth the benefits owed to all of them, changing the direction of
his chariot, at one time he warms the claws of concave Cancer, and   105
then in summer beats down on Assuan in a straight vertical line;
at another time he visits sunken Capricorn,[12] the realm of old
Saturn, shivering from the enervating cold, and he urges on his
horses, paralyzed by the cold, and snaps his whip cruelly.

In the meantime, having traveled halfway through the great sky,   110
he calls together and joins the highest with the lowest, which are
responsive to the sweetness of his seductive lyre, and unites the

Diversasque uno partis tamen intertextu
Unit ab unius genitoris imagine magni.
115 Et toto pater exercet commertia mundo,
Non tantum gravitate carentia pondere pressis
Aut sicca innectens humore fluentibus aut quae
Igne calent multo glacie torpentibus acri,
Verum etiam mortalibus aeterna atque caducis,
120 Omnia, qua patet immensi plaga lucida regni,
Complexus stabili per mutua vincla catena,
Unde parens Natura et amica daedala lite
Semina, de pulchro revocato imitamine coelo,
Tot facies volucrum varias, tot saecla ferarum
125 Concipiunt, tot marmoreo monstra humida ponto,
Diffusasque beant cornu praedivite terras.
    Nam mentis vim divinam mortalibus aegris
Quis non aetherio de Sole intelligat esse,
Nunc quoque terrena videat cum mole gravatos
130 Mutari tamen ad mutati lumina Solis
Et pariter motusque omnis speciesque novare
Ad nutum patris et variari tempus in omne?
Ille genus vivat mortale, ille omnia sancta
Luce replet, visumque oculis rebusque colorem
135 Sufficiens, ligat ille benigna quaeque catena
Atque modis unit late bonus omnia miris,
Ille vices variatque annorum et gentibus aegris
Tempora metitur simul idem atque explicat idem
Fatorum seriem et non exorabile pensum,
140 Lucida perlapsus coeli duodena per astra,
Permutatque vices et amaris prospera miscet,
Nunc felix mihi, nunc alii. Neque enim bona semper
Publica privatas possunt admittere curas
Et quid quisque sibi prudens fugiatve petatve,
145 Sed, qua sancta trahunt divinae commoda summae,

two diverse elements in one interlacement, in the image of his
one great progenitor. As father he establishes relationships in the 115
whole universe, interweaving not only things devoid of weight
with those that are weighed down by great masses, or dry sub-
stances with those saturated with liquids, or things flaming hot
with those paralyzed by biting cold, but also eternal things with
mortal and transitory things, all the elements throughout the shin- 120
ing expanse of his vast realm, he folds into his embrace with a firm
chain joining the various links together. Then Mother Nature and
productive seeds, in friendly rivalry, in imitation of the beautiful
heavens, produce infinite forms of birds and of beasts, and wet 125
monsters of the marble sea, and gladden the widespread lands
with their rich cornucopia.

As for the divine force of the mind, who would not understand
that it came to sick mortals from the ethereal Sun, when one sees
that even now, though burdened by their earthly bodies, they 130
change according to the changing light of the Sun and at the same
time transform all their movements and appearances at a sign
from the father, and constantly vary?[13] He vivifies the race of mor-
tals; he fills them with a holy light; he gives light to the eyes and
color to things; he links all things together with a beneficent chain 135
and in marvelous ways unites all things in his great goodness; he
varies the times of the year and in like manner he measures out
the length of time for sick mortals; and it is he who unfolds the
sequence of the fates and the inexorable allotment of wool to be
spun by the fates, as he glides past the brilliant twelve constella- 140
tions one by one, and alternates the lot of each individual, mixing
the good with the bitter, now favorable to me, now to another. For
the public welfare cannot always be made compatible with private
interests or with what each one, consulting his own interests,
should avoid or pursue, but rather, in whatever direction the sa- 145

Ipse artes, ipse ingenium censusque viritim
Partitur variatque modis. Nunc infima rerum
Tollere humo populique potens imponere habenis
Detractos opera atque alieni pondere aratri,
150 Nunc solio insignes patrio sceptrisque beatos
Deturbare loco et praesens damnare ruinae;
Aut alacres raptare in bella virilia Martis
Et studio immani fusi exercere cruoris,
Aut caeci desideriis infamibus auri
155 Incoquere. Hos animi exigui et rationis inanes
Desidia miseroque agitare cupidine rerum,
Hos cantu mulcere levi et suspendere hiantes
Solis ad armenta atque inclusos utribus Euros
Infamesque dapes sociorum Ithacensis Ulyxei.
160 Saepe animis inflare tumentibus aspera corda
Vicinoque ciere duello et pascere praeda
Nec leges nec dignatos communia iura,
Saepe modo ventri pecudum dare nequitiaeque
Et damnare leves stactae bene olentibus auris;
165 Aut inopes, regno extorres, formidine lethi,
Heu, miseros variis tamen exagitare latebris,
Bithynamque fidem et Ponti male tuta quaerentes
Hospitia — usque adeo paucis mors optima rerum
Intellecta atque illudit vitae improba Syren! —
170 Aut cocco rapere immodico pictaeque nitore
Vestis honorati praestantes corporis auctu,
Sed nimios tamen et plebis formidine laetos.
Interdum sine more, sine ordine mittere quosdam
In scelus omne, novas laetantes nectere clades
175 Cladibus insanaque hominum incrudescere caede
Et praedas vectare et saevis tradere flammis
Omnia nec gnaros sociis nec parcere amicis.
Interdum facilesque animi morumque benignos

cred purposes of the divine mind lead him, he distributes talents, genius and riches among men in various ways. At times he is capable of raising up from the ground the lowliest of creatures and can entrust the reins of power to men whom he has taken away from their labors and from the weight of another man's plow; at other times he can depose from their position men distinguished by the appanage of an ancestral throne and royal scepters and suddenly condemn them to ruin, or he can drag eager young men into the manly wars of Mars and exhaust them in the savage pursuit of bloodshed, or consume them with the detestable desire for gold, which renders them blind. Those with petty minds, devoid of reason, he drives to their laziness and pathetic cupidity; others he beguiles with sweet singing and holds them in a state of uncertainty as they gape at the herds of the Sun and the east winds enclosed in the leather bags[14] and the infamous banquets[15] of the companions of Ithacan Ulysses. Often he puffs up arrogant spirits with violent feelings and incites them to a duel with their neighbor and sates with plunder those who disregard laws and common rights; often he gives men over to the belly like beasts and to debauchery, and condemns frivolous souls to the sweet-smelling perfumes of myrrh. Or he harasses the poor, banned from their country, terrified, alas! by the fear of death, from their various hiding places, and those seeking Bithynian good faith[16] and the treacherous hospitality of Pontus — so few understand that death is the most desirable of all things and are deluded by the deceitful Siren of life! — or entices with extravagant scarlet and the splendor of a richly embroidered garment those who are conspicuous for their physical appearance,[17] but are puffed up and happy to be respected by the crowd. Sometimes he instigates certain people without morals or principles to commit all kinds of crimes, who take pleasure in adding new disasters to present disasters and revel in mad massacres, who haul off booty and consign everything to the fury of the flames, sparing neither friends nor allies. Sometimes he makes

150

155

160

165

170

175

Clarare et trutina pendentes omnia iusta,
180 Et quibus indignum tenui insultare clienti
Et perferre malis turbantes quaeque rapinis.
Nunc alios premere indecores nec nomine multo
Nec dignos fama et tamen intra tecta timendos,
Et quorum imperiosa domi fortuna paternae,
185 Quique sibi plaudant nimio plus et sua tantum
Mirati nil praeterea admittantve probentve,
Ignari prorsus parere et cedere cuiquam.
Nunc alios foedare libidine turpiter actos,
Non patriae natosve parentibus atque propinquis,
190 Non sociis, non ipsa vocatae in foedera lecti,
Spectaclis potius sed inanibus et male frugi
Pigritiae tantumque mero indulgere paratos
Atque ioco et vacuos captantes undique risus.
    Iam quotiens aut regifico de culmine coeli
195 Vagitusque hausit primos et inertia membra
Fusa solo domina excepit miseratus ab arce
Aut roseo iam tum exoriens prospexit ab ortu
Aureus et primo nascentem afflavit Eoo,
Ipse manu laeta deductum ad limina regum
200 Hortaturque animisque replet, ipse excitat acri
Spe dubiumque etiam rerum incertumque futuri
Insinuatque aulae atque inter regesque ducesque
Versantem nunc divitiis attollit opimis,
Nunc ultro fascesque fluunt dominaeque secures
205 Purpuraque ac missum externis de finibus aurum
Undantesque clientelae et fastigia rerum
Spem supra votumque animi. Quin aspera saepe
Signa virum, saepe innumerae stupuere catervae
Ductantem rigidos insana in bella maniplos,
210 Praesertim adverso Atlantis si littore fulsit
Iuppiter et, summum coeli Mavorte tenente,

famous those of docile spirit and of benevolent character who weigh everything on the scales of justice, who think it shameful to 180 insult an indigent client or tolerate those who throw everything into confusion through their depraved acts of plunder. Now he crushes base individuals, neither renowned nor worthy of renown, yet who inspire fear within their own family, and dictate the law in the paternal household, and who congratulate themselves in an 185 insufferable manner and admire only their own accomplishments, without acknowledging or approving anything else, completely incapable of obeying or yielding to anyone. Now he defiles those shamefully driven by lust, who were born neither for their country nor for their parents and relatives, nor for their companions, nor 190 for the one designated to share their bed, but instead are eager to take pleasure in vain spectacles and useless idleness and indulge only in wine and gambling and seek to arouse empty laughter at every opportunity.

Whenever either from the regal heights of heaven he has heard the first cries of a newborn child and seen its helpless body lying 195 on the ground, taking pity on it from his sovereign citadel, he took it under his care, or when rising in his golden splendor from the rose-colored East, he saw and breathed upon a newborn child at break of dawn, he conducts him with his own joyous hand to the thresholds of kings and encourages him and inspires him with 200 confidence, and he himself animates him with ardent hope, and though the child is still hesitant and uncertain of the future, he leads him into the palace, where he mingles with kings and princes. Now he exalts him with sumptuous riches, now fasces and lordly axes spontaneously rain down in abundance, and purple 205 and gold sent from foreign lands and waves of clients and pinnacles of power beyond the hopes and desires of the mind. Furthermore, often fierce lines of soldiers, often innumerable squadrons were filled with awe before one who led rugged maniples into senseless wars, especially if the planet Jupiter shone from the shore 210

Ipsa quoque angello quovis arrisit ab uno
Luna vaporifera radiorum lampade plena.
Nam neque tum fluvii obiecti nec barbara claustra
215 Armatum tenuere audacisve agmina Pori:
Qua via nulla, ruit praeceps et fulminis instar
Victor ad extremum ferro metit obvia Gangen,
Unus homo terris natus dare iura subactis.
At frustra ingentes iras, frustra aspra potentum
220 Declines odia, infelix, generique tibique,
Et tantum aerumnae prima damnatus ab hora,
Herculeo quotiens pronus mare vespere sero
Natalem infecit, dum iam iuga solvere prima
Nocte parat fessus caecis subeuntibus umbris,
225 Sudoremque viae puro lavit aequoris amne,
Suspensus cura fumantum totus equorum.
Tunc animi vitia exundant ingentia iniqui
Multiplicesque doli, tunc felle madentia corda
Pallentesque artus aegroque in corpore febris
230 Assidua et subitae fortunae exempla ruinae.
Omnia quae ut rapidi tamen inclementia Martis
Saturnique auget tardum iubar — utpote uterque
Infandisque hominum vitiis laetique ruina —
Avertit Venus et sancti Iovis aureus ardor
235 Lunaque partiliter positu radiata benigno;
Nec tantum avertunt, verum et praedivite fama
Nobilitant censuque beant et fascibus auctos.
    Ipse gravis tantumque aspectu optandus amico,
Si tamen ex imo depressae cardine terrae
240 Viderit hoc coelum tunc primum haurire parantem,
Ne tibi rem tenuem, ne primae incommoda vitae
Suspira, puer, et meritis quod gratia nullis

opposite Atlas, with Mars high in the sky, and if the full moon
herself smiled from a tiny corner[18] with her vaporous halo of rays.
At that moment neither the rivers[19] that stood in his way nor the
barriers of barbarian lands[20] nor the troops of audacious Porus[21]   215
could stop the armed man: where there is no path he swoops
down headlong and like a bolt of lightning, triumphantly mows
down with his sword all that he encounters as far as the distant
Ganges, the one man born to give laws to the lands he subdued.
But in vain would you try to turn aside the immense anger and the   220
bitter hatred of the powerful from your family line and from your-
self, ill-fated hero, condemned to trying labors with no respite
from your first hour, from the moment the Sun, descending upon
the Herculean Sea[22] in the late evening, tainted your birthday,
while he was preparing wearily to unyoke his team of horses at the
beginning of the night, as dark shadows approach, and he washes   225
away the sweat of the journey in the pure stream of Ocean, en-
tirely taken up with the care of his steaming horses. Then the
enormous vices of the unjust soul gush forth and multiple arti-
fices, then hearts dripping with gall and pale limbs appear and re-
current fevers in a sick body and moments of unforeseen reversals   230
of fortune. All of these evils are augmented by the severity of the
swiftly moving planet Mars and the late glow of Saturn — for both
of them rejoice in the unspeakable vices of men and their destruc-
tion — but Venus and the golden fires of holy Jupiter turn them
away, and the Moon's rays, partially, when it is in a favorable posi-   235
tion. Not only do they turn away these evils but they also enno-
ble men with extravagant renown and bless them with riches and
honors.

As for the Sun himself, an august deity, to be approached only
when he is positioned in a favorable aspect, if he has spied you
preparing yourself from the lowest axis of the low-lying earth to   240
drink in with the mind the glory of the heavens for the first time,
do not lament your poverty or the difficulties of your earlier life,

Respondet quaesita. Aderit sors laetior olim,
Cum te compositum iam tandem cana senectus
245 Excipiet sortisque hylarem votique potentem
Longaque pensantem fortunae vulnera laetis.
Interea damna atque aetatis mille labores
Disce aequis perferre animis nec acerba parentis
Fata nec effusi iacturam horresce peculi,
250 Aut contra magnum impatiens contendere Solem
Perge, animosi Euri quem horrent et signa sequuntur
Sudumque pluviaeque et grandinis impetus acer,
Neu spera thure et multa prece flectere posse
Ferrea constanter servantem pensa Sororum,
255 Quamvis immeritos supremo tempore casus
Graiorumque animo miserans modo tristia fata,
Avertit terris oculos confessaque luctum
Signa dedit moesta tenebrarum nocte volutus,
Tantum oculis scelus indignatus cernere rectis.
260 Ergo non pietas illos, non inclyta facta
Virtutesque artesque et coelo cura vagata
Texerunt: cessere malis tot moenia flammis
Versa solo, tot coelicolum templa aurea divum,
Gensque virum terris et ponto nata tenendo
265 Proiecti misere foedas pavere volucres.
Et dubitem sancti in terris nihil esse fateri?
Ipsi, quos patriae excidio sors ultima rerum
Subduxit, tumulis proavorum avellimur, heheu,
Fortuna graviore et toto spargimur orbe,
270 Humanae exemplum vitae sortisque futuri.
   Quod si non regisque mei natique benigna
Cura sit, ipsa ruat divinae gratia linguae,
Ipsae artes tantoque virum sacrata labore
Nomina Lethaeis abeant immersa lacunis.
275 Illi relliquias monumentaque sancta Pelasgum

young lad,[23] or that favor does not respond to your merits when you seek it. A happier lot will be yours one day when white old age will find you serene, happy with your lot, having fulfilled your desires and counterbalancing the long-lasting ills of fortune with happy events. For the present learn to support tribulation and the countless anxieties of life with a calm spirit and do not be alarmed at the cruel fate of your mother[24] or the loss and dispersal of your savings, or do not protest impatiently against the great Sun, whom the blustering east winds fear and the constellations obey and the clear bright sky and the rains and the fierce onset of hail; and do not hope to be able to assuage with incense and many prayers him who unswervingly guards the inflexible spinning of the Fates, although at the final moment taking pity in his heart on the unmerited catastrophe and sad fate of the Greeks, he averted his glance from the earth and manifested his grief by enveloping himself in a dark night of mourning, not deigning to look directly upon such great infamy.[25] Thus neither their piety nor their glorious exploits, their virtues, their talents and their inquiry into the heavens protected them; so many ramparts surrendered to the pernicious flames, tumbling to the ground; so many golden temples of the celestial gods, and a race of heroes, born to dominate land and sea, lay prostrate and became the food of filthy birds. Should I hesitate to affirm that there is nothing sacred on earth? We ourselves, who were rescued from the destruction of our country by the final chance turn of events, suffered the even heavier misfortune of being torn away from the tombs of our ancestors, alas! and dispersed throughout the world to be an example of human life and destiny.

But if it were not for the kind solicitude of my king and his son,[26] even the grace of the divine language would have gone to ruin, even the arts and the names of the heroes made sacred by so much toil would have been lost, immersed in the depths of Lethe. They strive with one another to collect these remnants and sacred

245

250

255

260

265

270

275

Colligere et saevis certant subducere fatis
Tantorum saltem decus ingeniumque virorum
Scriptaque divinas animi testantia curas,
Mortales supra captus mentemque caducam,
280 Praesidium soboli certum quandoque renatae.
Sol pater, et siquis misero deus aethere in alto est
Praeterea, nec cuncta carent mea pondere vota,
Hos saltem cinerum patriae excidiique misertos
Felices iuvenemque suis servate patremque
285 Sedibus, immunes odii indecorumque laborum
Fortunae: at siquid gravius, pater, imminet, in nos
Vertite nec vita dignos nec luminis aura!

II. Lunae

Colles Etrusci, vosque non ultra meas
    Sensura voces flumina,
Totiensque dicta iam mihi Florentia,
    Adeste supremum, rogo,
5 Dum pauca vobis, grata sed grati, ultimo
    Mandata discessu damus,
Testati amica civium commertia
    Et Medicis hospitium mei.
O fida quondam tot cohors sodalium,
10   Duri levamen exili,
Ego ne, relictis, heu miser, vobis, queam
    Exilia perpeti altera?
Sed fati acerba vis ferenda fortiter!
    Duc, Hylle, mannos ocius,
15 Dum mane primus subrubet oriens novo.
    Amo ego viatorem impigrum.

memorials of the Greeks and to rescue from the cruel Fates at least the honor and genius of such great men and the writings that attest to the divine pursuits of the mind, which are beyond human capacity and the perishable mind, a sure safeguard to generations 280 which will one day be born again.[27] O father Sun, and if there be any other deity in the high ether to aid the unfortunate and to ensure that all my prayers may not be without effect, conserve in prosperity at least these men, father and son, who had pity on the ashes and annihilation of my country; keep them secure in their dwelling place, free from the hatred and the inglorious ordeals in- 285 flicted on us by fortune; but if some other more grievous misfortune is impending, turn it upon us, who are worthy neither of life nor of the radiance of the light.

II. To the Moon

Etruscan hills, and you streams of water who will no longer hear my voice, and Florence, so often sung of by me, assist me for the last time, I pray you, while in my final departure I address these 5 few but grateful words to you, issuing from a grateful heart in recognition of the friendly exchanges with your citizens and the hospitality of my dear friend, de' Medici.[28] O faithful company of so many good friends in past times, solace of a harsh exile, shall 10 I, miserable wretch, be able to endure another exile when I have left you? But the cruel force of destiny must be suffered courageously! Lead out the packhorses more quickly, Hyllus, while the 15 East is tinged with red in the early morning light. I love the inde-

Interea amicis hinc et hinc sermonibus
    Viae levanda incommoda,
Vel tu virorum fortium aut laudes Deum
20   Incipe; canentem subsequar.

Hyllus

Miles Gradivum cantat, upilio Palen,
    Udus Lyaeum vinitor,
Cererem perustus messor aestivo die,
    Mercator undarum patrem,
25 Nos tot per alta nemora, per sylvas vagi,
    Nemorum potentem Deliam.

Marullus

Enses Gradivus sufficit, pascua Pales,
    Libera Lyaeus pocula,
Pingues aristas flava gentibus Ceres,
30   Opes pater tridentifer,
Hunc lucis haustum Delia et sanctum iubar,
    Lucina dicta matribus.

Hyllus

Levisomna pubes, navitae, umbras temnite,
    Temnite, viatores vagi;
35 At vos sub ima fugite — si sapitis — vada,
    Vis, helluones, humida,
Dum noctis atrum Delia horrorem excutit
    Et plena replet omnia.

fatigable traveler. In the meantime we will relieve the ennui of the
journey with friendly, alternating conversations. You may begin, if   20
you wish, by singing the praise of brave heroes or gods, and I will
respond to your song.

Hyllus

The soldier sings of Mars, the shepherd of Pales,[29] the drunken
vineyard worker of Bacchus, the sunburned harvester of Ceres on
a summer's day, the merchant of the father of the waves, while we,   25
wandering through these deep woods and groves, sing of Delia,
mistress of groves.[30]

Marullus

Mars supplies the sword, Pales the pasturelands, Bacchus abun-
dant draughts, blonde Ceres provides mankind with rich har-
vests, the father who bears the trident dispenses great riches, this   30
draught of light and sacred radiance is the gift of Delia, called
Lucina[31] by mothers.

Hyllus

O sailors, young men of light sleep, and you, wandering travelers,
scorn the shadows of night, but you, drunkards, slaves of drink,   35
flee to the depths of the sea, if you are wise, while the full moon
drives away the dark horrors of the night and fills everything with
light.

Marullus

Carpite cupita gaudia et fructus breves
40   Lacrimarum, amantes, carpite,
Nec tu laborem differ, agricola impiger,
     Sylvaeque lignator sciens,
Dum fratris almo Delia amplexu silet
     Tenebrisque densat omnia.

Hyllus

45 Quid tot figuras Carpathi, quaeso, senis
     Miraris, hospes candide?
Non est leones, non sues miraculum
     Induere, non rapidas faces,
Sed hanc eandem, nunquam eandem quae prius,
50   Lucere cunctis gentibus.

Marullus

Esto bimater, esto, Bacche candide,
     De patrio femore editus,
Esto iuventae flore perpetuo nitens,
     Imberbis annis omnibus,
55 Cum mense semper dum nova exurgat novo
     Totiens renata Delia!

Hyllus

Zanclaea tellus, sive tu Messenia
     Mavis vocari, seu utraque,
Ecquid tot aestus saevientis aequoris
60   Vicina cum videas freto,
Nostrae potestas quanta sit sentis deae
     Oceani in ultima aequora?

Marullus

Seize, lovers, your desired joys and the short-lived fruits of your 40
tears, and you tireless farmer, do not put off your labor, nor you,
woodsman, master of the forest, while Delia in the loving embrace
of her brother, the sun, is silent and involves everything in thick
darkness.

Hyllus

Why, innocent stranger, do you marvel at the various shapes of the 45
old man of Carpathus?[32] It is no miracle to take on the form of a
lion or a pig, or of devouring torches, but it is a miracle that Delia,
always the same but never the same as before, emits her light to all 50
people.

Marullus

You may have been born of two mothers, fair Bacchus, issued
from the thigh of your father; you may be resplendent in the
flower of perpetual youth, beardless at every age, as long as Delia, 55
forever reborn, will rise anew with every new month.

Hyllus

O land of Zancle,[33] whether you prefer to be called Messina, or be
invoked with both names, surely when you see the raging sea
foaming in the strait nearby, you sense how great is the power of 60
our goddess to the far ends of the vast ocean?

Marullus

Facunde, magni, Mercuri, Atlantis nepos,
    Cui limina utraque pervia,
65 Ecquid nigrantis regna cum peragres soli,
    Cum lucidum unus aethera,
Nostrae potestas quanta sit sentis deae
    Geminae potentis machinae?

Sed haec triformi sat deae. Nunc iter, age,
70   Coeptum sequamur ocius,
Vias precati prosperas tamen prius
    Laetam viarum Deliam.

Liber Quartus

I. Aetheri

Iam fessa longa, Pieri, nenia
Duraeque planctu, Melpomene, fugae,
    Concede poscenti sorori
      Barbiton in breve multichordem,

5 Dum, post supremi regna Iovis bona
Ipsumque et olim lucida sydera
    Cantata, nunc rerum benignum
      Aethera concinimus parentem.

Magnum nec ulli auditum opus antehac:
10 Sed me volentem nomina patriae
    Hortantur attentata nulli
      Antra sequi vacuosque saltus,

Marullus

O Mercury, eloquent grandson of great Atlas, to whom passage to
both realms is accessible, when you traverse the kingdom of the   65
shadowy land or when, alone, you wander through the lumi-
nous ether, do you sense how great is the power of our goddess,
mistress of both worlds? But this will suffice for the triform god-
dess.[34] Now let us pursue more swiftly the journey we have begun,   70
but not without first praying for a prosperous journey from her
who is propitious to travelers, Delia.

Book IV

I. To Aether

By now weary of the long dirge, O Muse, and of the lamentations
about my cruel exile, Melpomene,[1] surrender for a moment to
your sister,[2] who requests it, the many-stringed lute, while after   5
singing of the bounteous kingdom of highest Jupiter and the god
himself and the luminous stars, I now sing of Aether, benign fa-
ther of all things. This is a great undertaking, unheard of by any-
one until now: but the reputation of my native land exhorts me,   10
and I accept gladly to seek out caves never before explored and
deserted woodlands. I have no desire to drive my chariot, sprung

Pigetque trita vatibus orbita
Versare cretos semine Pegasi
15   Currus, paternarum viarum
        Immemores volucrisque pennae.

Nam quo Pelasgi gloria sanguinis,
Si non futuri gens quoque temporis
    Agnoscit auditos et ipsa
20   Voce probat sibi teste Graios?

Verum unde primum exordia carminis
Sumenda coepti, quod medium mihi,
    Quae rebus in tantis canenti
        Ultima erit quasi meta laudum?

25 Chaos ne caecum prosequar et rude
Rerum volumen, cum mare, cum sola
    Ignesque et aurarum potestas
        Mixta pigro iacuere acervo,

Donec malignis conditionibus
30 Offensus Aether molis inutilis,
    Levatus in sublima mundi
        Constituit sua membra rebus?

An nunc ut udum versus in aera
Transit, figuras sumere quas velit
35   Sciens, modo algentes coactus
        In fluvios latices perennat,

Idemque posto rore friabilis
Turres Cybele sustinet arduas,
    Idem peracto rursus orbe
40   In solitos remeat vapores?

from the seed of Pegasus,[3] over wheel tracks traversed by poets, 15
forgetful of the father's paths and his fleet wings. For what good is
the glory of Greek blood if people of future generations do not
also recognize Greeks when they hear them and identify them by 20
their voice? But where shall I begin my song, what will be the
central part and the final goal, as it were, of my eulogies on such
great themes? Shall I describe blind Chaos and the formless con- 25
volution of things, when the sea, the lands and the fires and the
power of the winds lay mixed together in an inert mass until
Aether, displeased by the precarious state of this useless pile, 30
raised himself up to the heights of heaven and assigned each ele-
ment its place?[4]

Or shall I tell how he changes into humid air, able to assume
whatever shapes he wishes, and then condensed into cold rivers, 35
preserves the waters, and then, putting aside its liquid form of
dew, becomes friable and in the guise of Cybele sustains high tow-
ers; then, this cycle completed, returns to the usual vapors? Or 40

An ut fluentis semina machinae
Complexus aequis undique nexibus,
   Diesque et aetates per omnis
      Versat agens variatque cuncta,

45 Longoque rerum commodus ambitu,
Quae pigra quondam attollit et augmine
   Foecundat inter se iugata
      Materiae male viva membra,

Unde haec, perenni fonte velut scatens,
50 Tot saeculorum daedala copia,
   Tot rerum ab excelso petita
      Seminii meliore parte,

Et quae benignos frugiferae sinus
Telluris et quae stagna liquentia
55   Latumque pendenti volatu
      Aera quae decorant volucres?

Nanque ipse cunctis ut pater et pius
Altor peregre, sic penitus domi
   Nequicquam anhelos inter aestus
60   Crescere quid patiensve oriri,

Felix abunde simplicis imperi
Nitentis una laude domestica
   Formaeque de nullis petitae
      Illecebris aliunde rerum.

65 Verum sequentem, par uti, singula
Dies volucris deficit interim,
   Vocatque iamdudum coruscans
      Iuppiter in sua sacra vatem;

how, embracing the seeds of the fluid world machine with equally
distributed connections, he modifies and varies all that is, each day
and each season, and opportunely circling things in a wide orbit,   45
raises up elements that were formerly inert and adds to their num-
ber and makes fertile the lifeless components of matter, after join-
ing them together. From this, as from a perpetually gushing foun-
tain, comes this intricately varied abundance of so many species,   50
so many things acquired from on high from the best part of the
seeds; and those things that adorn the fecund cavities of the rich
earth, and those that adorn the liquid pools, and the winged crea-   55
tures that adorn the immensity of the air in suspended flight? As
he is father and faithful nurturer of all things outside his realm, so
deep within his domain in the midst of stifling heat he does not
allow anything to grow or be born, abundantly happy with his   60
simple dominion, which shines with its own native loveliness,
happy also in the beauty not sought elsewhere from any entice-
ments of things.

But, as I pursue each point, as is fit, the fleeting day is fading,   65
and gleaming Jupiter has long been calling upon the poet to cele-

Quare, precati gentibus, o bone
70   Aether, benignum te prius — ut facis —
      Laetumque, vocalis quod instat
          Exequar Aonidum sacerdos.

II. Iovi Fulgeratori

Dicturus Iovis optimi
    Laudes eximias, sume animos, age,
Vates, et Iove maximo
    Dignum prome chely multiloqua sonum,
5 Si quaeris volucrem fugam
    Annorum et strepitus morte potentior
Amnis spernere luridi,
    Ascitus meritis Pieridum choris.
O Ithomie maxime,
10   Sancti progenies alma Hyperionis,
Quem mater genuit Rhea
    Olim fagiferis rupibus Arcadum,
Mox quamvis metuens scelus
    Servandum Losiis virginibus dedit,
15 Lascivique pedis Nedae
    Thisoaeque bonae, et quae iaculo leves
Misso figere dorcadas
    Agno docta, chori virginei decus.
Nam, coelo solitus quia
20   Natos inserere et concilio deum
Clam consorte tori, pater
    Vesci pignoribus creditus est suis:
Nec vicinia garrula
    Deerant et famuli, vaniloquum genus —
25 Rara saepe adeo fides! —
    Firmantes oculis singula testibus.

brate his sacred rites. Therefore, O kindly Aether, after praying   70
that you show your favor to mankind, as you do, I shall fulfill the
duty that presses upon me as an inspired priest of the Muses.

II. To Jupiter, hurler of the thunderbolt[5]

To sing the outstanding praises of good Jupiter, summon your
courage, poet, and bring forth a sound worthy of greatest Jupiter
from your many-voiced lyre, if overcoming death, you wish to   5
show your disdain for the swift passage of time and the horrid
sounds of the ghastly river and to be admitted deservedly into the
choruses of the Muses. O great offspring from Mount Ithome,[6]
benevolent son of holy Hyperion, whom your mother Rhea   10
brought forth in olden times in the beech groves among the crags
of Arcadia, who then, although fearing some misfortune, entrusted
you to the care of the nymphs of the Lusius river[7]and to Neda,[8]   15
fond of dancing, and to the good Theisoa,[9] and to Agno,[10] skillful
in hurling the javelin and piercing the swift gazelles, glory of the
virgin chorus. The fact is that since the father was accustomed
to introduce his children into heaven and into the council of the   20
gods without his wife's knowledge, it was thought that he de-
voured his own children, and the gossip of the neighbors and
the servants, a race of prattlers, was not lacking—loyalty is a rare   25
quality—who affirmed that they were eyewitnesses of every de-

Ergo muneris anxiae
    Nymphae, quas dubias hinc amor, hinc metus
Angit, non sibi virgines
30   Ausae, consiliis credere non suis,
In partem socios spei
    Curetas, iuvenes Gnosiacos, vocant,
Curetas neque dextera
    Segnes nec vigili pectore inutiles,
35 Quorum multa domi licet
    Maior militiae gloria splendidae,
Ii certaminis impares,
    Quod possunt—quid enim contra Hyperionem
Mortales aliud queant?—
40   Infantem violis tectum et amaraco
Nymphis dant alere abditum
    Secretis latebris Creteaci specus.
Ipsi, ne rudis artium
    Vagor consilium ponat in irrito,
45 Patris proditus auribus,
    Armati in numerum ter choreas leves
Plaudunt, ter cava cymbala
    Pulsant in numerum tentaque tympana.
Et iam lampade torrida
50   Fulgebat medio Sol pater aethere
Fraudum coniugis inscius,
    Cum fessos choreis assiduis sopor
Tandem languidus occupat,
    Hic omnis iuvenum effusus abit labor.
55 Nanque audita simul patris
    Vox aures pepulit, pene simul, puer,
In fumos volucer fugis,
    Sublatus nebularum ex oculis modo.

tail. Therefore the nymphs, worried about their task and torn be-
tween love and fear, not daring—being but maidens—to trust   30
themselves or their own judgment, call upon the Curetes,[11] young
men of Knossos, to share their hopes, the Curetes, who were not
wanting in physical strength or in loyal vigilance. But though their   35
glory is great in peace and even greater for their splendid victories
in war, they are unequal to the contest. They do what they can—
for what else can mortals do against Hyperion?—they give the   40
child covered with violets and marjoram to the nymphs to be
raised in secret in the hidden recesses of a cave in Cretea.[12] They
themselves, lest the cries of the innocent child render their plan
ineffective if they should reach the ears of his father, donning   45
their armor, clap their hands three times in rhythm to accompany
their nimble dancing, three times they strike rhythmically the hol-
low cymbals and the taut drums. And by now with his scorching
lamp father Sun was shining in the middle of the ether, ignorant   50
of the ruses of his spouse when, tired from their unceasing dances,
languid sleep at length overpowers them. At this point all the ef-
fort expended by the young men is lost. For as soon as the sound   55
of the voice struck the father's ears, almost instantly, O child, you
flee swiftly and disappear, removed from sight, like a cloud. The

Planxerunt facinus deae,
60   Planxit Creteaque et Sithonia nive
Lycaeus pater albicans
    Plangebantque deae moestaque Cretea:
Cuncta nox adeo premit!
    Ipse flammiferis per liquidum aera
65 Purgatus radiis patris,
    Qualis deposita vere nitet novo
Serpens pelle decentior,
    Aegris iura viris, iura dabas deis
Subnixus solio aureo.

70   Hic, cum saeva manu fulmina traderet
Venturi genitor sciens,
    'His terras' ait, 'his, nate, potentia
Olim concuties freta
    Iratus, scelera his impia vindices
75 Titanum et rabidas minas
    Immanisque Gigae et Purpurei trucis,
Cum coelum manus impia
    Audebit sceleris poscere praemium.
Magnorum neque enim deum
80   Quanquam sceptra tenes, quanquam hominum genus
Unus et regis et iuvas,
    Tantum flagitii aut consiliis tuis
Flectes aut reverentia.
    Utendum valido fulmine, nate, erit.
85 Hoste sed tamen impigre op—
    Presso et flagitii auctoribus, ut decens,
Digno supplicio datis,
    Ne saevi, moneo, progenies mea,
Ultra, neve puta magis
90   Quicquam et rege hominum et coelicolum patre
Dignum quam cupere omnia

288

goddesses mourned the episode, and Cretea wept and the Lycaean 60
father,[13] white with Sithonian[14] snow, and the goddesses wept, and
sad Cretea. Night weighs so heavily on the world!

But you in the limpid air, purified by the flaming rays of your
father, like a serpent in spring that shines more brilliantly when 65
it has sloughed off its skin, prescribed laws to unhappy mankind
and to the gods, seated upon your golden throne. Then, as he 70
transmitted the cruel thunderbolts into your hand, your father,
who knows the future, said: "With these one day you will shake
the lands in your anger, with these the powerful seas; with these
you will avenge the impious crimes of the Titans and the raging 75
threats of monstrous Gyges and savage Porphyrion,[15] when the
impious band will dare to ask heaven for a reward for their crime.
Though you rule with your scepter over the great gods, though 80
you alone guide and aid the human race, you will not curb such
infamy, neither by your wise decisions nor by fear. You will have to
use the force of the thunderbolt, my son. However, once the en- 85
emy has been forcefully subdued and you have meted out to the
authors of the crime the punishment they deserve, as is fitting, do
not unleash your fury any further, I admonish you, my child, and
do not think that there is anything more worthy of the king of 90

Servare atque adeo ignoscere plurimis.
Iam quae gloria fulmina
Torquenti, invalidum in vulgum animis rapi,
95 Nec saltem Lybicae modo
Exemploque leae parcere segnibus,
Cum stent alta Ceraunia
Inconcussa iugis, cum aeriae undique
Tot quercus nemora occupent
100 Vicinisque negent roboribus diem,
Tot delubra minantia
Ipsis syderibus, tot pateant sacrae
Moles turribus arduis,
Quis et tela queas et validam manum
105 Exercere decentius
Multo vel Phlegyam perdere quam trucem?
Illuc horrida fulmina
Torquenda et validis viribus ignium
Rumpendae aeriae minae
110 Saxorum, scopulis ut scopulos suis
Disiectasque procul graves
Tot moles subiti turbinis impetu
Gens mirata virum sciant
Et regnare Iovem et mittere fulmina,
115 Exemploque simul deum
Assuescant miseris parcere civibus.
Quin, siquando deum minae,
Ut fit, vis gravior siqua duellica
Aegris gentibus imminet,
120 Tunc et deciduo sydere rem palam
Signare et vacuum aera
Nunc ignire facis fulgure splendidae
Memento, modo fertilis
In morem paleae accendere, quam catus

men and father of gods than to wish to preserve all things intact
and therefore to pardon a great number of persons. What glory
would there be for one who hurls thunderbolts to vent his anger
against the defenseless crowd rather than like the Libyan lioness to   95
pardon at least the sluggish, while the towering Ceraunia[16] rise up
unshaken on their summits, and while everywhere countless oak
trees, reaching high into the air, occupy the woodlands and deny   100
daylight to the neighboring smaller oaks, and so many sacred
shrines that threaten even the stars stretch out over the horizon,
so many execrable piles with their lofty towers against which you
can employ your weapons and your powerful hand in a much   105
more fitting manner than even in destroying the fierce Phlegyas?[17]
It is there that you should hurl your terrible thunderbolts and the
menacing pinnacles of the rocks should be shattered by the potent
force of fire so that when the race of men see great piles of rocks   110
torn away from the mountainside and massive boulders thrown
great distances by the violent impetus of a sudden whirlwind, they
will know that Jupiter reigns and hurls his thunderbolts, and at   115
the same time may learn from the example of the gods to be mer-
ciful to their unfortunate fellow citizens. Moreover, if some day
threats come from the gods, as often happens, or if some excep-
tionally grave threat of war impends over weary mankind, re-   120
member to give a clear sign of disaster through a falling star, and
at times to ignite the empty air with a fiery meteor or to set it

125   Dulces saepe reconditas
      Post messes subitis agricola ignibus
  Olim tradit inutilem,
      Nunc alta gelidi de Boreae domo
  Dirum immittere coelitus
130   Omen, sanguineae triste iubar comae.
  Non tu, nate, graves vices
      Regnantum — neque enim fas — miserarier,
  Quos quandoque animus nocens
      In praeceps ita aget sanguine civico
135   Devotos patriis deis
      Et nullis hominum de spoliis minor
  Argenti sitis improba,
      Nullum non licitum, quod libuit, nefas.
  Adde pectora inertia
140   Expertesque animos et reverentiae
  Divum et iustitiae sacrae,
      Quaeque est sancta bonis usque adeo fides,
  Ut iam non homines magis
      Dicendi, gelidae quam Scythiae horrida
145   Quae dumeta colunt ferae.
      Hoc sed, nate, magis, tam meritam nihil
  Plebem commiseratus et
      Damnatos populos servitio gravi,
  Saltem commonitu Iovis
150   Assuescant lacrimas ebibere ut suas!'
  Dixit, et subitis pater
      Avertit lacrimis ora madentia.
  At tu, seu Capitolii
      Rupes sive tenes flumina Olympiae
155 Saturnique patris iugum,
      Mitis, sancte, precor, Iuppiter, huc ades.

ablaze like the plentiful straw which the prudent farmer quickly   125
burns after the rich harvest has been gathered in, since it is of no
use, and at other times to send down from the sky a dire omen
from the home of the freezing north wind, the ill-boding radiance   130
of a bloodred comet.

"But you, my son, do not take pity—for it is not allowed—on
the grave vicissitudes of kings, whose guilty mind will sooner or
later drive them to the brink, accursed by their ancestral gods be-   135
cause of their shedding of citizens' blood no less than for their in-
satiable thirst for money, which drives them to plunder their sub-
jects, since no crime that pleases them is forbidden. Add to this
their insensitive hearts and their minds devoid of respect for the   140
gods and of sacred justice and of that loyalty which is hallowed by
good men, to such a degree that they are no more to be called men
than the wild beasts that inhabit the rugged steppes of savage   145
Scythia. But, my son, have pity rather on the common people,
who do not deserve their lot, and on those nations condemned to
harsh servitude, so that, warned by Jupiter, they at least learn to   150
swallow their tears as something they have merited." So he spoke,
and his father turned away his face, bathed in a sudden rush of
tears. But you, whether you command the heights of the Capito-
line[18] or the rivers of Olympia and the mountain of your fa-   155
ther,[19] Saturn, O holy Jupiter, I pray you, assist me, in your great
kindness.

III. *Iunoni*

Iunonem canimus, deae,
    Iunoni meritum dicite, quaesumus,
Carmen, vos licet innubae,
    Consors illa tori magnanimi Iovis,
5 Quamvis ipsa quoque innuba
    Mansisset, studium sed nimium obstitit
Et matris pietas Rheae.
    Saepe illi genitor 'O mihi me magis
Cara, iam puerilium
10   Tandem desine' ait. 'Quid, genus aetheris
Et iam fertilibus tori
    Tempestiva bonis, languida adhuc tamen
Lassas brachia Tameni,
    Et matris residens in gremio senis
15 Geronteia Punica
    Tractas, bima velut? Sunt sua singulis
Annis tempora, sunt sui
    Mores, nec, decuit quicquid heri, decet.
Quin, iam si sapis, indue
20   Quam gestura deam, nec Pheneum polo
Praefer aut monitis meis
    Matris degeneres blanditias tuae.'
Illa non ideo magis
    Assueto potis avellier est sinu,
25 Materna sed enim modo
    Picta veste manu, saepe cohercitis
In nodum aut Zephyro datis
    Aut flexis tenues ordine in anulos
Per vices varias comis
30   Gaudens, coelicolum commoda negligit,
Quamvis nec leporem sequi

III. To Juno

We sing of Juno, O goddesses;[20] to Juno sing the song she merits,
I pray you, though you be unwed, while she shares the marriage
bed of magnanimous Jupiter. Yet she too would have remained 5
unmarried, but the great affection and religious scruples of her
mother Rhea opposed this desire. Often her father would say to
her: "O my child, dearer to me than my own self, it is time that 10
you have done with childish things. Why is it, descendant of
Aether, now at the age for the fecund blessings of the marriage
bed, you continue to tire the enfeebled arms of Temenos,[21] and
seated on the knees of your aged mother play with the pomegran- 15
ates[22] from Mt. Geronteion,[23] like a two-year-old child? Each age
has its own moments, each its own activities, and what was fitting
yesterday is not fitting today. Come now, if you are wise, play the
role of the goddess you are destined to become, and do not prefer 20
Pheneus[24] to the sky or the soft blandishments of your mother to
my counsel." Nonetheless, she is no more able than before to tear
herself away from the habitual comfort of her mother's breast, but 25
takes joy in a dress embroidered by her mother's hand, or in her
hair fastened in a knot or flowing freely in the breeze or crimped
and ordered into thin curls in various styles, ignoring the advan- 30
tages of heaven dwellers, although she does not forgo pursuing a

Interdum et celeres per iuga capreas
Nec ignava liquentibus
    Stymphali tenerum mersa latus vadis
35 Sudorem lavere impigrum.
    Et tunc forte, deum sic voluentibus
Fatis, nuda Erasiniis
    Pellucebat aquis quale ebur Indicum
Inclusum tenui vitro,
40   Cum vidit simul hanc et cupiit simul
Frater; sed nimium tamen
    Festinata verens tempore non suo
Interrumpere gaudia,
    Primis spem latitans distulit in rubis,
45 Donec lassula aquis dea
    Vicina posuit sub platano latus.
Tum vero exiliit, lupus
    Ceu quondam procul aspecta ove Martius
Aut Gangetica belua
50 Scymnorum trepidum sicubi nacta prae —
Datorem. Illa dolore diu
    Amens marmoreae persimilis stetit,
At mens est ubi reddita
    Et cum mente nefas ante oculos fuit,
55 Materno ne puella metu
    Incertum mage confusa pudore ne,
Involvitque diem nigrae
    Obtentu nebulae et septa pigerrimo
Circumclauditur aere
60   Mortis certa, nisi Pithyius omnia ex
Alto prospiciens pater
    Avertisset atrox propositum deae,
Sublatam aetheriis plagis
    Solatus: nihil hic aut odio aut dolo

hare on occasion or fleet-footed goats over the mountains or im-
mersing her tender body in the limpid Stymphalian waters[25] and   35
washing off the sweat produced by her exertions.

And once, as the fates of the gods unrolled, it happened that
she was shimmering naked in the waters of Erasinus[26] like Indian
ivory enclosed in thin glass, when her brother saw her and imme-   40
diately desired her. But fearing he would spoil his pleasure by ex-
cessive, ill-timed haste, hiding in the nearby bushes, he deferred
his hopes until, weary from her bathing, the goddess stretched out 45
her limbs under a plane tree. Then he leaped out like a wolf of
Mars at the sight of a sheep in the distance or like a Ganges tiger
when it has come upon the terrified ravisher of its young. She,   50
beside herself with pain and anguish, for a long time stood fixed
like a marble statue, but when she regained her senses and the
impious act stood before her eyes, whether confused by fear of her 55
mother or by shame it is not known, she conceals the light of day
by veiling it in a dark cloud and encircles and encloses herself in
completely motionless air, resolved to die, if the Pythian father,[27]   60
surveying the whole scene from on high, had not averted the ter-
rible resolution of the goddess, and taking her up into the regions

65 Admissum, omnia sanguinis
        Fraterni atque adeo plena fide bona;
    Nec vero pelagi arbitro
        Amphitritem aliter aut aliter datam
    Tethyn Oceano seni;
70   Tantum ne thalami nomina caelibis
    Demirata, aliud scelus
        Quam extremum et populi flagitium levis
    Detestabile crederet,
        Naturae placitis non dare brachia.
75 'An tu' inquit, 'rogo, munere
        Materno edita, non quod prior accipis
    Porges grata sequentibus,
        Integro veluti fessula lampadem,
    Fraudabisque sui, impia,
80   Aevi parte, parens, sic tua viscera?
    Quid, quod haud nisi protinus
        Defectus sterile est, nec numeris sine
    Virtus stare potest suis?
        Nam, siquis Venerem omnem oderit, ut bono
85 Quaerendo hinc melius vacet
        Nec transversus eat, non animis semel
    Congressus paribus deae,
        Iam virtutis iners deseruit locum,
    Nec frustra videt inspici
90   Naturam et varias seminii vices,
    Frustra stelligeras domos
        Dimotumque procul visibus aethera,
    Ni tanto studio erutum,
        Unde idcunque libet, denique saeculi
95 Sanctis cesserit usibus.
        Tantum commoditas publica habet boni,

of the ether, consoled her, assuring her that nothing had been   65
permitted to happen either through hatred or guile, but all was
owing to fraternal blood and entirely in good faith. He explained
to her that in no other way was Amphitrite[28] given to the ruler of
the sea or Tethys to old Oceanus; that her shock at the loss of her   70
reputation for chastity should not prevent her from believing that
there was any other crime so detestable as that of the fickle popu-
lace, namely, not yielding to the decrees of nature.

"I ask you," he said, "Will you, who by the gift of your mother   75
came into the world, not gratefully transmit what you once re-
ceived to those who come after you, as a tired runner passes on
the torch to a fresh one, and will you thus cheat, impious mother,
your own womb of its part in life? Is it not true that only what   80
is deficient from the very beginning is sterile, and that virtue can-
not subsist without plurality? For if anyone despises Venus alto-
gether in order to devote himself better to the pursuit of the good   85
and not go astray, never united to the goddess by like sentiments,
he has unfeelingly deserted the place of virtue, and does not see   90
that one studies nature and the various cycles of the elements
in vain, and in vain observes the starry dwellings and the ether,
far removed from sight, if what he has unearthed through so much
study, whatever its source, does not contribute to the holy uses   95
of human life. Public utility has the capacity for so much good,

Haec quamvis hominum tamen,
Quos terrena gravant nubila pectoris.
Nam quis, quaeso, ferat deum ae —
100   Ternum aut iustitia quaerere prodita
Virtutem aut, medium nisi,
Si quicquam modo sit, credere quod decet?'
Sic fatus gremio pater
Impostae oscula libavit. Et ecce iam
105   Germanus quoque venerat
Facturus thalamo criminibus satis,
Torve quem licet intuens,
Sensit nescio quid plus solito tepens
Imis pectoribus dea:
110   Sed non dum tamen aut humor abit genis
Aut suspiria pectore,
Quae longe radiis pulsa pater suis
In ventos animat leves
Paulatim et varios distribuit locis.
115   Illi ortus memores sui
Circumstant dominam nunc quoque seduli,
Siquando varias Iovis
Plorantem insidias furtaque viderint,
Quamvis plurima dissident,
120   Nec mens omnibus aut consilium est idem.
Nanque hic aestifero die
Excitus lacrimas nubilus aggravat,
Ille durior ingeni
Solaturque deam et nubila discutit
125   Frontis aut lacrimas gelat
Grata fulgidulis virginibus nive.
Pars ipsi pelago gravis,
Per quod vecta suo Sidonis est bove:

even if it benefits mankind, whose hearts are weighed down by earthly clouds. For I ask you, who would tolerate that an eternal god, by betraying justice, should either seek after virtue or not believe that virtue is nothing but a mean, supposing there to be one?"

After saying this, the god drew her to his bosom and kissed her.[29] And now her brother also came to make satisfaction by marriage for his transgression. Still giving him severe looks, the goddess felt feelings of warmth in her breast that were more intense than usual, but the wet tears had not yet left her cheeks nor the sighs her breast, which the father of gods disperses with his rays and converts into light breezes, and little by little distributes them to various places. But they, mindful of their origin, surround their mistress, still filled with solicitude, whenever they see her crying over the various ruses and betrayals of Jupiter, although they are in great disagreement, and do not have the same attitude or the same opinion. One of them, roused up by the sultry day, brings clouds and increases her tears; another, of more solid character, consoles the goddess and removes the clouds from her brow or freezes her tears in the snow, which so pleases the dazzling young maidens. Others ruffle the sea, over which the Sidonian maid[30]

Ipsis multiparae solis
130   Terrae, semina quae et materiam novis
Blanda nutrit amoribus,
    Aut flabris ruit aut praecipiti omnia
Sternit grandinis agmine
    Et foedam illuviem nube rotat cava.
135 Moerent prataque roscida
    Vastata et nemorum strage virentium
Passim squallida stant sola;
    Ipsi, nunc humeros nunc latera ardua
Pulsati, aerii undique
140   Montes vix capiti pestiferam luem
Defendunt dubii geli,
    Impexam laceri sic quoque non semel
Menti canitiem hispidi
    Et collo positam multiiugo comam.
145 Salve, maxima coelitum,
    Iuno sancta, eadem digna Iove optimo
Coniunx atque eadem soror,
    Humanumque genus, quandoquidem omnium
Pollens, tum pecus et sata
150   Et stirpes facilis laetaque sospita.

IV. Oceano

Quo te, profundi rector, Oceane, aequoris,
    Rerum pater sanctissime,
Quo carmine, inquam, nunc mihi, quibus vocem
    Gratus Camaenarum sonis,
5 Impar, tot olim solvar in linguas licet,
    Quot ipse in alta flumina?
Verum nec ipsi visa coelitum patri
    Indigna Baucis hospita,

was transported by her bull; they are oppressive also to the soil of
the fertile land, which nourishes the seeds and the woodlands in-   130
spiring new loves, or swoop down with their blasts or level every-
thing with a violent downfall of hail and stir up slimy mud with a
tornado. The dewy meadows lie in pitiful ruin, and with the de-   135
struction of the green forest the land lies barren everywhere. The
towering mountains themselves, their lofty shoulders and steep
slopes battered on every side, barely fend off the ruinous calamity   140
of the dangerous ice from their peaks, the white hairs of their un-
kempt beard disfigured more than once and the foliage on their
multiple ridges devastated.

Greetings, greatest of the goddesses, holy Juno, worthy to be   145
both Jupiter's spouse and sister, since you are all-powerful, and in
your kind benevolence protect the human race and beasts and the   150
sown fields and the plants.

IV. To Ocean

With what song, Ocean, master of the deep, most holy father of
things, with what song, I say, with what sounds of the Camenae
shall I invoke you to win your favor, since I am unequal to the   5
task, though for some time now I express myself in as many styles
as you do in deep streams? But the hospitality of Baucis[31] did not
seem unworthy to the father of the gods himself, even if many

Cum supplicarent plurimi passim aureo
10   Cratere et extis pinguibus.
O quadriformis machinae altor unice,
      Seu fonte iugi profluis
Ipsisque terris editus terras alis
      Gemino cohercens ambitu,
15 Stagnante nutris cuncta seu potius vado
      Tot saeculis tamen manens,
Nec te perusti minuit aut fervor soli
      Divesque arenarum Aethiops
Aut ipse sanctis pastus aestuariis
20   Aether tot ignium face.
Nam quid Charybdis impias dicam minas
      Ausisque Rhoeti par scelus,
Cum bis resorbens cuncta adhuc tegens fretum,
      Bis Nereo extrema minitans,
25 Non ante visa tot aetheri ostendit sola,
      Iam pene votorum rea,
Ni tertio haustu faucibus patentibus
      Instar Laconici specus,
Misso tridente guttur horrendum ferae
30   Fixisset aequoris arbiter?
Illa et dolore percita et rabie sua,
      Hostem acrius contra movens,
Haustumque pontum evomuit et telum simul
      In ora bellantis dei.
35 Quod ni canorae buccinae obiectu patrem
      Triton obumbrasset citus,
Insignis ille clade funesta dies
      Neptunno et undis fulserat.
Tunc fama primum cognitum littus salo
40   Visosque Nereo margines,

people made offerings everywhere to him with golden mixing
bowls and fat victims. O sole nourisher of the quadriform uni- 10
verse, whether you flow down from an inexhaustible source or else
nourish the earth, gushing up from the very soil, encircling it in a
twofold direction, or rather nurture all things with still waters, 15
remaining unchanged through the centuries, undiminished by the
heat of the scorched soil or the land of the Ethiopians rich in sand
or Aether itself, with its torch of multiple fires, nourished in the 20
sacred tidal basins.

And why should I speak of the impious threats of Charybdis[32]
and of her crime, equal to the audacity of Rhoetus,[33] when twice
swallowing up the sea, which up to that time covered everything,
twice menacing Nereus[34] with the worst of evils, she revealed so 25
many lands that Aether had not yet seen? Her desire was almost
granted if it were not that, as she was about to swallow the seas for
the third time with her gaping jaws,[35] like the cave in Laconia,[36]
the lord of the seas hurled his trident and transfixed the monster's 30
horrid gullet.

Stricken with pain and rage, advancing ferociously toward her
enemy, she vomited forth both the sea that she had swallowed and
the trident into the face of her divine opponent. But if Triton[37] 35
had not quickly screened his father, throwing his loud trumpet in
the way, that day would have dawned as fatally disastrous for Nep-
tune and the waves. It is said that on that day the open sea saw the
shoreline for the first time and Nereus saw his boundaries, for in 40

Nam saeva pugnae damna praeter asperae
    Gravavit et Tethys malum,
Quae clade monstri territa inopina novi
    Sibique iam timens dea,
45 Vastis aquarum septa circum molibus
    Terrarum in ima fugerat.
Nam mox maritae et ipse Neptunnus prece,
    Quanquam repressa belua—
Quid non venena uxoria atque artes queunt?—
50   Huc vim liquentum transtulit
Locumque Phoebo cuncta turbandi dedit
    Amore Terrae saucio,
Seu mallet aequor rapere seu corrumpere
    Flammis perustum torridis,
55 Donec tot aegra patrui Phoebe malis,
    Postquam monendo haud proficit,
Conversa in iras 'Ecquid et nos contra' ait
    'Artes valebunt pellicis?
Quod nisi alienis abstinet frater manus,
60   Sciet esse non uni iecur.
Non sic profana sacra miscuit dies
    Errorque longus coelitum,
Ut ipsa quoque iam regna Saturni senis
    Cedant probrosis noctibus.'
65 Sic fata, aquarum concitabat agmina
    Rogantia ultro ut duceret,
Tantum impotentis imperi Phoebus sibi
    Odiique et irae fecerat!
Sed vetuit ultra Carpathi procedere
70   Prudens futurorum senex,
Virtute multum qui ducis pro tempore
    Sermone laudata gravi,

addition to the cruel losses suffered in the fierce battle, Thetis[38]
aggravated the trouble. Terrified by the unforeseen destruction
caused by the new monster, the goddess, fearing for her own
safety, surrounded by the immense bodies of water, had fled into   45
the depths of the earth. Hereupon, Neptune in his turn, at the
entreaty of his wife — what can the seductive charm and artifices
of a wife not obtain? — though the beast had been subdued, trans-   50
ferred the force of the liquid elements into the Earth and gave
Phoebus, who was smitten with love for the earth, the opportu-
nity of throwing everything into disorder, whether it was his in-
tent to carry off or evaporate the sea, scorched by torrid flames. At   55
this point, Phoebe,[39] distressed by the villainous actions of her
uncle and seeing that her advice was ignored, was moved to anger.
"Will the artifices of a concubine succeed against me also?" she
said. "If my brother cannot keep his hands off the property of oth-
ers, he will find out that he is not the only one to have passions.   60
Time and the long wanderings of the heavenly bodies have not
confounded the sacred and the profane to such an extent that now
even the kingdoms of ancient Saturn cede to shameless nights."

After saying this she assembled the battalion of waters, who of   65
their own accord asked that she be their leader, such was the ha-
tred and anger that Phoebus aroused by his wanton dominion!
But the old man of Carpathos,[40] knowing the future, forbade the   70
waters to proceed any further, and after duly praising the courage
of their leader in a weighty discourse, as the occasion demanded,

Iussisque posthac fluctibus meritam optime
    Quocunque Phoeben subsequi.
75 Olim haec deorum debita docuit omnia
    Fatis moveri nesciis:
Neque enim vel aras aliter aeternis deis
    Vel thura sperandum pia
Meritisque tandem victimas dignas suis,
80   Longis dierum amfractibus.
'Quin te quoque' inquit versus ad ducem 'manent,
    Manent honores debiti,
Potensque Deli dicta, non tamen potens
    Deli fereris unius.'
85 Haec ille, et altum desilit in aequor senex,
    Parentibus cunctis deo.
At tu, beate Oceane, pars rerum optima,
    Idem creator omnium,
Idem altor, adsis dexter et precantium
90   Benignus exaudi preces.

V. Terrae

Extrema est dea Terra mihi quoque iure canenda,
Ultima, sed meritis quae primos aequet honores,
Turriferens, foecunda, potens, quam nomine Magnae
Sacrarunt veteres adyto monstrante Parentis,
5 Sive quod inde hominum gnavum genus, inde ferarum,
Quaeque virent campis herbae, quaeque ardua sylvae
Taygeta horrentisque tenent pineta Lycaei,
Unde animale genus generatim vivit adauctum,
Sive quod, omnia cum interdum mortalibus aegris
10 Irasci atque modo soleant furere acta novercae,
Una pios tenet affectus sine fine parentis
Indulgetque suis, una exagitata quiescit

he ordered the waves to follow Phoebe henceforth wherever she
led them, since she had merited their gratitude. He taught that   75
everything that we ordinarily attribute to the gods is set in mo-
tion by the blind fates; otherwise the eternal gods should not ex-
pect altars or pious incense or sacrificial victims worthy of their
merits in the long succession of days. "Yes, and for you also," he   80
said, turning to their leader, "fitting honor is reserved; you who are
called mistress of Delos, will not be called mistress of Delos
alone." Thus spoke the old man and he plunged into the deep, and   85
all gave obedience to the god. But you, blessed Ocean, excellent
part of creation and at the same time creator and sustainer of all
things, assist us with your favor and graciously hear the prayers of   90
those who call upon you.

V. To Earth

As a last labor the goddess Earth also must rightly be the subject
of my song—last, but worthy by her merits of being awarded the
first honors. Tower-bearing,[41] fecund, powerful, whom the an-
cients consecrated with the name of Great Mother, as the inner
sanctum of her temple reveals, whether because from her comes   5
the diligent race of men, from her wild beasts and the verdant
grasses of the fields, and the woods that cover the heights of Mt.
Taygetus,[42] and the pine groves of spiny Mt. Lycaeus,[43] where ev-
ery race of living creatures lives and increases, each according to its
kind; or whether because, while all things from time to time be-
come angry and enraged with sick mortals, driven on in the man-   10
ner of a stepmother, she alone endlessly preserves the pious affec-

Scrutandosque sinus impune et viscera praebet—
Usque adeo scelera interdum leve ferre suorum est!—
15 Quamvis utiliter Stygio tegat illa baratro
Plurima, materiem tantarum haud inscia cladum.
      Hinc neque deformes iunxerunt curribus ursos
Nec grege de molli capreas cervosque fugaces,
Sed fulvis horrenda iubis generosa leonum
20 Colla, quod egregiis quantum quisque eminet ausis,
Aequius hoc debet senium grave ferre parentum.
Nam biiugis invecta, nihil nisi vincula bina
Aurarumque profundarum laticisque liquentis
Significat terras atque inter lucida templa,
25 Quis innixa suo medio est neque pondere pressa
Desinit a fuso circum pendere ligatu,
Undique flammarum spatiis distantibus aeque.
Nec vero sine consilio causaque potenti
Omniparae steriles matri servire catervas
30 Crediderim, neque enim curam gerat ille parentum,
Interea stimulis viroque agitatus amoris
Siquis, et ingratos qui ponere nesciat ignes.
Adde quod, ut superos, ipsos quoque sola parentes
Delectant pura, a superis qui proximus ordo est;
35 Adde quod officium natis praestamus habendis
Nostra sponte bona—quis enim hoc dubitaverit unquam?—
Nec nisi Naturae memores plerumque novercae,
At matri quaecunque accepta rependimus ante.
Ingrati prorsus, nec vitae munere digni,
40 Siquos progenies sperataque cura nepotum
Ubera quam matrisque piae studiumque fidele
Plus movet et decimum in mensem tolerata pericla,
Ante repentino coeli quam territus haustu

tions of a mother and is indulgent toward her children; she alone, though troubled, remains calm; she offers her breasts and her entrails freely to be explored — so easy is it at times to put up with the crimes of one's children — although she prudently conceals 15 many things in the abyss of the Styx, since she knows they can cause great calamities.

That is why they did not join to her chariot formless bears[44] or goats from the gentle flock or deer, prone to run away, but the 20 noble necks of lions, bristling with tawny manes, because the more anyone stands out for his audacious deeds, the more equitably should he support the burdensome old age of his parents. That she is transported by a two-horsed chariot signifies nothing more than the twofold bonds of the boundless air and the liquid waters between the earth and the luminous region of the sky. Supported 25 by them, she holds the middle position and without being oppressed by her weight she never ceases to be suspended between the bonds that surround her; in all directions the distance to the flaming heavenly regions is the same. It is not without design or 30 without good reason, I should think, that the mother who brings forth all things is attended by bands of sterile followers, for one who was aroused by the goads and poison of love, unable to lay aside these ungrateful fires, would not be able to take care of his parents. Add to this that like the gods above, parents, who are to be ranked closest to the gods, also take delight only in pure things; add also that we perform the duty of procreating children of our 35 spontaneous good will — who could ever doubt it? — mindful only of Nature, who for the most part acts as a stepmother,[45] but to our dutiful mother we repay all the gifts we received previously. Ungrateful, certainly, and unworthy of the gift of life are those who 40 are moved more by the prospect of children and the hope of caring for grandchildren than they are by the breasts and the faithful care given by a pious mother and the risks incurred for nine full months before the newborn child, terrified by the sudden intake

Vagiat aetheriam in lucem novus editus infans,
45   Cum proiectus humi nudus iacet, indigus, exsors
Auxilii, infirmusque pedum infirmusque palati,
Atque uno non tantum infelix, quod sua damna
Non capit et quantum superat perferre laborum.
Et dubitem caris debere parentibus omnia?
50   Aut aliud totque aera putem crepitantia velle
Aeribus armatasque manus et cymbala circum,
Quam partes armis maternaque iura tuenda,
Nullius in nostras admissis vocibus aures?
Quid, quod Oaxeis contectus Iuppiter antris
55   Ereptumque patri ius et tam prompta iuventus
Curetum contra Saturni regia iussa,   ,
De plano monet, interdum vel morte parata
Tormentisque piae matris commissa tegenda?
Tantus honor sancti reverentia nominis haec est,
60   Ipsum quo rectorem etiam appellare deorum
Non piget atque hominum magnum usurpare parentem.
    Verum quid iuvat eximie iam vocibus uti,
Si pia tam foedis sceleramus nomina factis
Turbamusque malis inter nos quaeque rapinis,
65   Partiri communem ausi per vulnera matrem?
Hinc versum fas atque nefas scelerataque bella
Invasere, tenet furor exitialis habendi
Luxuriesque, nec imperii spe turbidi inanis
Cessamus placidam gentis turbare quietem,
70   Immemores eadem in terra mox esse cubandum
Omnibus, assueta ducibus confundere egenos
Affectuque pari natos quoscunque fovere
Materno exceptos gremio per saecula longa.
At tu, magna parens, quando omnis adempta quietis
75   Spes aliter, iam tandem adsis et nos quoque humatis
Adiice, tot duros genitrix miserata labores.

of air, newly brought forth into the light of day, wails and when   45
cast upon the ground lies there naked, needy, helpless, unable to
walk or eat, fortunate in only one respect, that it does not under-
stand its plight and all the trials it has yet to suffer.[46] Am I to
doubt that I owe everything to my dear parents? And what is the   50
meaning of bronze clashing against bronze and armed bands of
men and cymbals but that we must defend by force of arms the
cause and the rights of our mother without letting any other voice
enter our ears? What shall we say of the hiding of Jupiter in the
cave of the Oaxes,[47] the right wrested from his father, and the   55
young band of Curetes[48] ready to disobey the royal orders of Sat-
urn—do they not remind us clearly that sometimes even in the
face of torture and death we must guard the secrets confided to us
by a pious mother? This reverence for a holy name is such a great   60
honor that we do not hesitate to address the ruler of the gods by
this name and call him the great parent of men.

But what good is it to use high-sounding words if we defile pi-
ous names by such shameful acts and throw everything into tur-
moil among ourselves by impious pillaging, daring to dismember   65
our common mother by inflicting wounds upon her? As a conse-
quence just and unjust have been reversed and wicked wars have
descended upon us; a fatal fury of avidity and love of luxury has
taken hold of us, and agitated by the hope of empty power, we
never cease to disturb the peace of tranquil people, forgetting that   70
soon we must all lie in the same earth, which is accustomed to
confound prince and pauper and to warm with equal affection all
the children, whoever they may be, that she has received into her
bosom in the course of the long centuries. But you, great mother,
since all hope of any other peace has been taken away from us,
now at last assist us and add us also to those who are buried, tak-   75
ing pity, mother, on our many harsh labors.

NENIARUM

Liber Primus

I. De acerbitate fortunae

Nos circum Medio freto
    Cyrnus pulsa tenet vix Boreae truci
Ereptos ope coelitum,
    Olim Cyrnus avis Romulidis potens,
5 Nunc pubes Nomadum fera
    Natura referens saevitiem loci;
Et iam quarta videt dies
    Aut vulsis male radicibus improbam
Solantes misere famem
10   Aut, quos clausa tenent aequora, piscibus.
Tu pugnas quereris tamen,
    Infelix anime, et te sine proelia
Gesta tot Caroli tui,
    Dum speras itiner commodius freto,
15 Qui, si non mihi nuntii
    Vani, iam Tyberim et moenia Romuli
Etruscis domitis tenet
    Campanisque ferox imminet hostibus.
Quanquam haec haud nova, denique
20   nunc sors flenda mihi, nam paries velut
Aevo exesus et imbribus
    Inclinatus abit quo semel incipit
Praeceps, sic miseri altera
    In fata ex aliis mittimur — heu dolorem
25 Indignum! — neque iam quies
    Aut spes effugii urgentibus est deis.

POEMS OF LAMENT

Book I[1]

I. On the harshness of fortune

Barely rescued from the fierce blasts of the North wind by the
help of the gods, we are here on the island of Corsica,[2] battered on
all sides by the Mediterranean — Corsica, once powerful with its
Roman heritage, now a wild population of nomads who resemble   5
in nature the savageness of their surroundings; and now it is the
fourth day that we desperately relieve our relentless hunger with
roots crudely pulled up out of the earth or fish from inlets. But   10
you, unhappy soul, complain about the skirmishes and the many
pitched battles waged without you by your beloved Charles,[3] while
you await a more favorable crossing over the sea. If messages that   15
have come to me are not in error, he already holds the Tiber and
the walls of Rome after subduing the Tuscan forces, and he poses
a fierce threat to his enemies in Campania.[4] Although these things
are not new, in the end I must bewail my fate, for as the wall, eaten   20
away by age and bent over by the rains, collapses headlong into
rubble, so we miserable mortals are tossed from one fate to an-
other — alas! what undeserved suffering! — and there is no longer   25

Nam quae non gravior mihi
　　Lux effulsit et hesterna inimicior,
Ex quo primum utero editus
30　　Materno iubar hoc hausi oculis puer?
Mitto nunc patriae graves
　　Occasus miser infandaque funera,
Mitto tot solo ab ultimo
　　Urbes, tot populos excidio datos;
35　Quae gravissima scilicet,
　　Haud privata queror, non equidem inscius
Quam foedi ingenii sua
　　Solari mala communiter asperis.
Sed quis est ita perditus,
40　　Unus qui patriae et civibus optimis
Dedignetur idem pati
　　Communemque deum non ferat aequiter?
Nos Fortuna nocens rogo
　　Ereptos patriae et fletibus ultimis,
45　Humanis grave vivere
　　Exemplum dedit, heu, rebus, ubi improba
Noctes luderet et dies,
　　Incertum volucri nixa pedem rotae;
Et nec flectere eam domus
50　　Infandus cinis et funera adhuc queunt,
Nec tot exilia aspera
　　Et regum atque ducum saeva odia ac minae
Servatam egregie ob fidem.
　　Quin ipsas quoque iam affligere contumax
55　Ecce amicitias parat
　　Et Lauri immeritam clade nova mei
Funestavit atrox domum,
　　Erepto gemini pignoris altero.

any respite or hope of escape, as the gods press hard upon us. What day has not dawned on me more oppressive or hostile than the last since I first issued from my mother's womb and saw the light of day as a child? I won't mention now in my despondency the calamitous fall of my native country and unspeakable massacres; I pass over so many cities razed to the ground, so many peoples doomed to destruction. I won't complain of personal misfortunes, grave though they may be, for I am not unaware how shameful it is to find comfort for one's own ills in shared adversity. But who is so depraved as to be the only one who disdains to share the sufferings of his country and its leading citizens and will not abide equally a god common to all? Baneful Fortune in saving us from the funeral pyre of our country and final laments for its fall gave us a stern example of how to live, alas! in the midst of human affairs, in which she wantonly rests her uncertain foot on the swiftly turning wheel; and she is not moved by the horrible ashes and ruin of a house, nor by harsh exile nor by the savage hatred and threats of kings and princes in payment for preservation of good faith. In fact, behold, she is now getting ready spitefully to bring distress on my friendships and has cruelly brought death into the undeserving household of my good friend Lorenzo with a new disaster, carrying off one of his twin offspring. Ill-fated

Infelix Averardule,
60   Non iam delitiae, sed miseri patris
Aeternae lacrimae et dolor,
    Quae te, care puer, vis rapit effera
Nil miserta parentium,
    Huius praecipui, tot proceres tuos
65 Inter, dia Fluentia,
    Illius genitae sanguine regio.
Nil domus, miseris modis
    Quae tota attonita atque igne Iovis velut
Tacta moeret inutilis,
70   Aeque praesidium quondam inopi aut reo,
Aeque dulce decus deum
    Laetis sorte bona, seu genus hospites
Sive illi patriae domo
    Partes et generis pignora civici!
75 At pater miser, ah miser,
    Ponendis superum divitias suas
Tot templis pius erogat
    Nequicquam et veterum certat opes patrum
Largis vincere sumptibus
80   Nequicquam. Quis enim praeterea neget
Humana omnia casibus
    Incertis fluere atque impete herae levis,
Quae mortalia provehi
    Iam pridem invidia, saeva, vetat deum?
85 Nam quot spes ea publicas
    Tecum, quas rapuit magnanimae indolis
Scintillas, patruo ac patre
    Dignas! Ut miserae non pueriliter
Perpessus spatium luis,
90   Vix ingressus adhuc ver breve septimum!

Averardolo,⁵ no longer the joy of his hapless father, but a source of   60
endless tears and sorrow, what savage violence carried you off, dear
child, taking no pity on your parents, especially that outstanding
person among all your great leaders, divine Florence, and your   65
mother, born of royal blood;⁶ it had no pity on the household,
which, shocked in the most appalling manner, as if struck by Jupi-
ter's lightning bolt, mourns in vain, at one time both a refuge to   70
the needy and the felon, and a cherished glory of the gods for
those blessed with good fortune, whether they be guests or mem-
bers of the ancestral household and scions of the city's race. But   75
the unfortunate father, O so unfortunate! piously expends his
great riches in building temples to the gods, in vain, and strives to
surpass the resources of his ancestors with huge expenditures, in
vain. Besides, who will deny that all human events slip by with   80
uncertain outcome and at the impulse of a fickle mistress, who for
so long now through envy of the gods prohibits humanity from
making progress? For how many hopes of the people she carried   85
off with you, what sparks of a noble character, worthy of his uncle
and his father! How you tolerated to the end the duration of that
terrible pestilence in no childish manner, when you had hardly   90

Ut matris lacrimas piae
  Solatus, tenera saepe etiam manu
Trivisti irriguas genas!
  Ut solem hunc miseris gentibus et diem
95 Tam carum, puer, haud semel
  Sprevisti, utpote cui maior erat vigor
Iam tum, mens erat altior
  Humana! Neque enim conditionibus
Nobiscum huc paribus, puer,
100   Missus de patria coelite veneras,
Hac ut mole videlicet
  Clausus corporea et carcere terreo,
Errorum male penderes
  Poenas primigeni nil meritus patris,
105 Sed terris breve inertibus
  Ostensus, liquidi rursus in aetheris
Sancta templa recederes,
  Consors ambrosiae et nectaris aurei.
Illinc spes hominum leves
110   Et caecos animi despicis impetus —
Incertum miserans magis
  Irridensne, puer, factaque dictaque
Tot nostra — et superum vides
  Quam nil munere adhuc est — homini datum,
115 Nec longa miserum magis
  Vita nec celeri morte beatius.

II. Nenia

Haec certe patriae dulcia littora
Contra saxa iacent, haec pelage impete
Huc propulsa gravi Bosphorici freti
  Plangunt Hesperium latus.

entered upon your seventh year! How you consoled your pious mother's tears; often you even dried her wet cheek with your tender hand! How you spurned more than once this sun and this light of day so dear to miserable mortals, my child, as one might   95 expect from one whose vigor already at that age was greater and whose mind loftier than those of an ordinary person! For, sent   100 from our heavenly country, you did not come here on equal terms with us, that is, confined in this corporeal mass and earthly prison, to pay the penalty, undeservedly, of the sins of our primal parent, but manifested for a brief time to the inert earth, you were des-   105 tined to return again to the holy realms of the liquid ether, to partake of ambrosia and golden nectar. From there you disdain the fickle hopes of mankind and the blind impulses of the mind — it is   110 uncertain whether you are more inclined to take pity or to laugh at all our words and deeds — and you see that nothing has been given to man up to now by the gift of the gods, and that nothing is more   115 miserable than a long life and nothing more blessed than a quick death.

II. Laments

Surely, opposite these rocks lie the dear shores of my native land, and these waves, driven here by the swell of the Bosporus, beat

5 Ipsae nonne vides mitius aurulae
   Ut spirant memores unde videlicet
   Tantum innata potest rebus in omnibus
       Natura et patrium solum?

   Quid, tantis spatiis monstriferi aequoris,
10 Tanto tempore post lassulae, adhuc tamen
   Halant nescio quid, quod patrium et novis
       Mulcet aera odoribus?

   Felices nimium, vespere quae domo
   Egressae redeunt mane Aquilonibus
15 Versis, nec peregre perpetuo exigunt
       Aetatem exilio gravem;

   Felices sed enim multo etiam magis,
   Si tantum patriae fluminibus suae
   Et primi solita littoris algula
20   Contentae lateant domi,

   Nec longinqua velint flumina visere
   Et terrae varios et pelagi sinus,
   Quae multum referant deinde rogantibus
       Vergentem usque sororibus

25 Ad noctem. Quis enim suavia nesciat
   Auditu et vacuis apposita auribus,
   Quae diversa locis alter et hic refert
       Mille exhausta laboribus?

   Inter quae memorant mutua dum invicem
30 Quaeruntque, admonitae forsitan et mei,
   Narrant nunc Boreae sedibus intimis
       Visum, qua vagus alluit

against the western shore. Do you not see how the breezes them- 5
selves blow more softly, obviously recalling where they came from,
where nature and the native soil is so powerful in all things? How,
though exhausted after the long crossing over the monster-infested
sea, they still exhale a certain indefinable perfume, which fills the 10
air with new aromas? Exceeding happy breezes, leaving their home
at eventide, they return in the morning when the north wind
changes direction and do not pass their melancholy lives in unend- 15
ing exile; but much happier still if they could remain safely at
home, content with the streams of their native land and the famil- 20
iar algae that line the edges of the shoreline, with no desire to visit
distant rivers and various inlets of land and sea in order to de-
scribe them to their sister breezes, who question them on their
return long into the night. For who does not know the pleasure of 25
listening with avid attention to the exploits, accomplished at the
cost of countless hardships in sundry lands, narrated by one per-
son or another? And as they relate these accounts, each in turn,
and their audience plies them with questions, perhaps mention is 30
made of me, and now they recount that they saw me in the far
north where the meandering Mesta river[7] waters the region inhab-

Rhodos Mesta suos, nunc Byce lintea
Dantem plena, modo littora Dacica
35 Scrutantem et veterum saepe etiam patrum
      Curae impervia plurima,

Interdum Galatas sive Britannias
Seu quae lata serunt aequora Teutones,
Interdum Buduae moenia nobilis
40   Et nondum domitam Bragam.

Sed nec ruricolam messe recondita
Tam laetum aut patrio denique navitam
Portu nec teneram flavi ita coniugis
      Gaudentem gremio nurum,

45 Quantum haec terra meis grata laboribus,
Extremos cupiam condere ubi dies,
Iam nec militiae nec satis amplius
      Viae erroribus utilis.

Quamvis nescio quae coelicolum impia
50 Arcent fata procul, nam totiens quia
Victores cadimus rursus et invicem
      Parta linquere cogimur?

Cernis qui populos vexat agens furor,
Quae nomen rabies publica Belgicum
55 Contra tot superos suppliciter piis
      Orantum precibus modo.

Non haec, non temere insania gentibus.
Nimirum populos magnae agitant minae
Coelestum et Stygiam Thesiphone ferox
60   Saevit concutiens facem,

ited by the Thracians, now sailing over Lake Byce[8] or exploring
the Dacian[9] coast and many other places that were inaccessible to   35
our ancestors, or at times among the Gauls or the Britons or tra-
versing the vast plains cultivated by the Teutons, or at other times
within the walls of noble Budua[10] and still unconquered Brazza.[11]   40
But neither the joy of the farmer who has stored the harvest in his
granary nor of the sailor when he has finally reached his home
port nor of the young wife rejoicing in the embrace of her blonde
spouse can equal my love of that land, scene of my many labors,   45
where I would wish to spend my last days, when I am no longer fit
for military life and aimless wanderings. And yet some impious   50
destiny willed by the gods keeps me far away from it, for every
time we are victorious we fall again and are forced to abandon all
that we have won. You see what a compulsive fury plagues nations,
what public hatred there is against the French name, which only   55
recently was the object of so many suppliant prayers to the gods.
This madness among nations has not come about by chance. Evi-
dently great threats from the gods stir up the people and fierce
Tisiphone[12] rages wildly, shaking her Stygian torch, ever since a   60

Ex quo terra potens ubere agri, potens
Armorum atque virum, pars merito optima
Terrarum, studio partis et improba
    Inter se invidia ducum,

65 Imploravit opes primitus exteras,
Nec Normanna modo nec iuga Bethica
Et fastus domini ferre Suevici
    Turpe credidit Italae.

Heheu, quae video bella resurgere!
70 Quanto sanguine, quis funeribus lues
Infelix geminae perfidiae nefas,
    Iam non Parthenope amplius,

Olim quae totiens maluit emori
Quam servare minus fortiter ac decet
75 Urbem tot meritis egregiam patrum,
    Inconcussam animo fidem!

Est in gente nocens culpa — quis hoc neget? —
Sunt exempla feris commoda beluis,
Sed non propterea regi ita protinus
80   Succensendum erat optimo.

Verum nos soliti monstra pati diu,
Culpamus facilem principis in suos
Naturam et vitio vertimus improbe
    Quae miranda opibus magis

85 In tantis, neque enim est sanguine cetea
Humano et volucres pascere regium
Nec punire statim pleraque pulchrius,
    Quam ferendo retundere.

land powerful because of its rich soil, powerful in men and arms, justly considered a privileged part of the world, driven by party factions and by shameless feelings of envy among princes, im- 65 plored for the first time the help of foreigners, and did not think it disgraceful for Italy to endure the Norman or Spanish yoke or the arrogance of a Swabian prince.[13] Alas! What wars I see arising! With how much bloodshed, with how many funeral rites will you 70 atone for the ill-fated crime of double perfidy, no longer that Naples which once preferred to die many times rather than not maintain an unshakable fidelity, as befits a city famed for the many 75 merits of its ancestors. Heavy guilt lies with the people—who would deny it?—atrocities worthy of wild beasts were committed, but that was no reason for a noble king to have given in immediately to such anger. But we, who have long been used to support- 80 ing monstrous cruelties, criticize a prince for being indulgent toward his subjects, and we wickedly treat as a fault that which in a man of such wealth should instead merit our admiration. For it is 85 not worthy of a king to feed human blood to sea monsters and rapacious birds, nor is it more honorable to punish immediately a great number of persons rather than subdue them by forbearance.

III. De Morte Ioannis Medicis

At nos senectae praesidium gravis —
Proh sortem iniquam! — et Pieridum chori,
    Condigna sperabamus in te
        Praemia tot studiis reposta.

5   Nam quis te adempto iam locus artibus?
Quae spes amico est? Occidis, occidis,
    Hortator exemplumque laudum,
        Ante diem mihi, Iane, raptus.

Quamvis ruinis obstrepo publicis
10 Privata lugens, qualiter Insuber
    Cultor paterni damna agelli,
        Tecta Pado rapiente et urbes.

Nam nec cadentis Graecia Achillei
Sic fracta letho est nec cito tam suum
15   Desideravit Iulianum
        Roma, fero minitante Partho,

Qualis minaces pertulit impetus
Orbata tanto praeside Tuscia,
    Confessa nunc demum quid esses,
20   Invidiam superante laude.

Nam quis iuventam ploret amabilem
Condigne et ipso tempore egentibus,
    In nulla non momenta opesque,
        Divitias studiumque promptum?

25 Nunc illa duri mens subit exili
Invicta damnis, nunc reditus pii
    Iraeque condonatae amori
        Et patriae meritis benignae,

III. *On the death of Giovanni de' Medici*[14]

But we hoped in you for a bulwark of burdensome old age—alas!
unfair fate!—and of the chorus of the Muses, a fitting reward re-
served for so many studious pursuits. But with your loss, what   5
place is there for the arts now? What hope is there for your
friend? You are gone, you are gone, advocate and example of excel-
lence, snatched from me, Giovanni, before your time. And yet in
the midst of public ruin I loudly protest, mourning private losses,   10
like the Lombard farmer who grieves over the damage to his fam-
ily plot of land when the Po carries away houses and cities. Greece
was not so crushed in spirit at the death of Achilles nor did Rome   15
so quickly feel the absence of Julius Caesar when the warlike Par-
thians threatened their borders as Tuscany, deprived of such a bul-
wark, has endured threatening attacks, only now admitting what
you were, as praise won out over envy. For who could lament his   20
youth in a fitting manner, charitable as he was to the needy in
their time of need, always ready to come to their aid with his abun-
dant resources and dedication? Now I conjure up that resolute   25
mind, undaunted by the privations of harsh exile, now his faithful
return and his anger turned to love and generosity toward his

Nunc cura patri provida publici
30 Furorque plebis saepe domestica
       Lenitus impensa famesque,
          Alpe vias dare vi coacta.

Ergo senatus delitias suas,
Spem vulgus, artes praesidia uniter
35   Amissa plorantes in uno,
          Perpetuant sine fine questus,

Multique, laudes dum memorant tuas,
'At nos deorum scilicet' inquiunt
       'Curae futuri, quisquis ista
40   Imperio moderatur unus!'

Simulque abortis fletibus arduos
Tulere vultus ad fera sydera,
       Coelumque Fortunamque questi
          Et pretium meritis negatum.

45 Nam quid relicti te sine lacrimas
Fratris, quid orbam praesidio domum
       Dicam, nec aspectus heriles
          Adveniens subituram in aevum?

Felix, decennis Petre, puertiae,
50 Tot damna non dum qui tua concipis,
       Nec quid sit amissum per annos
          Scire potes patruo cadente,

Implumis olim qualis acredula
Ignara matris, quam calamo ferox
55   Auceps prehensam febrienti
          Forte dapem dedit esse nato.

country, now his provident care of public funds and his allaying the 30
anger and hunger of the people at his own expense, when he had
to force his way across the Alps. Therefore the Senate mourns the
loss of their favorite, the people are bereft of their hope, and the 35
arts with one voice, mourning their protector, continue their la-
ments without end, and many, as they narrate your praises, say, "It
is clear that we will be in the care of the gods, whatever individual 40
governs us." And together, with tears welling up, they turned their
uplifted faces to the cruel stars, protesting against the gods and
Fortune that they had been denied the reward owed to their mer-
its. What shall I say of the tears of your brother, left behind with- 45
out you, or of the house deprived of its guardian that will not see
the master's son in a succeeding age? Happy in your boyhood, ten-
year-old Piero,[15] while you do not yet conceive of the extent of 50
your losses, nor can you know what has been lost over the years
after your uncle died, like the unfledged lark that never knew its
mother, which a brutal fowler caught with his lime-twig and by 55

Nos terque et ultra, nos miseri ingeni
Sensusque, quis—heu!—vivere nec licet,
    Amice, iam tecum nec ultra
60   Esse libet sine te relictis,

Sed, longa vitae tempora inutilis
Querendo, noctes carpimur et dies,
    Post ista securi deorum
        Invidiae Nemesisque acerbae.

IV. Ad Carolum Regem Francorum

Dum tu fugaces, rex, catulis feras
Sectaris altum per nemus et diem ex
    Die trahendo cara perdis
        Tempora non redeuntis anni,

5 Heheu, rebelles quam vereor minas
Ne fractus hostis cornuaque interim
    Resumat in foedam ruentis
        Imperii populique cladem.

Nam nec tuorum iniuriae et improba
10 Vis cessat in quoscunque sine hostium
    Delectu amicorumve, ut ipsi
        Iam noceant magis hoste amici,

Et ille sollers temporis occupat
Recte gerendi singula momina,
15   Nec praeterire occasionem
        Praecipitis sinit acer horae.

Hinc illi amici, praesidia hinc nova
Crescunt, nec aut iam Sfortia spiritus
    In te rebelles Pontifexque
20   Dissimulant odiumve celant

chance gave to eat to his feverish child. We, three times and more, are stricken in mind and feelings and alas! it is not given to us to live with you any longer, friend, and we have no desire to live, left 60 without you. But lamenting the long duration of a useless life, we are consumed day and night, from now on indifferent to the envy of the gods and of cruel Nemesis.

IV. To Charles, King of France

While you, O King, pursue the fleeing prey with your hounds through the deep woods and day after day waste the precious time of a year that will not return, alas! I fear that the defeated enemy 5 will in the meantime resume their rebellious threats and reorganize their battalions to bring about the shameful downfall of a collapsing empire and people. For the wrongs inflicted by your men and their unrelenting violence that does not distinguish be- 10 tween friend and foe never ceases, so that by now friends do more harm than the enemy, and he cleverly seizes every opportune moment and shrewdly does not let any occasion of swiftly passing 15 time go by. In this way friends and new alliances increase, and now Sforza and the Pope do not dissimulate their rebellious feelings 20

Aut ipse Hiberus. Nam Venetos tibi
Iam pridem acerbos tutemet efficis,
    Persuasus infidis tuorum
        Consiliis male venditisque.

25 Ergo modo excors et pariter deis
Mortalibusque infensus et omnibus
    Exutus armis, regno, amicis,
        In solium rediit paternum,

Ipsoque iam nunc plura fere tenet
30 Victore victus, quae tamen — heu pudor! —
    Tenere non confisus olim
        Integer imperiique opumque.

Quod siqua regni, tot tibi principum
Ducumque siqua est, siqua tot urbium
35   Vestrarum, honesti splendidique
        Siqua animo tibi cura demum,

Iam te precamur, sume, age, spiritus
Dignos et istam, invicte, moram exue.
    Quid fraudolentam crastinando
40   Das cinerem Boreae movere?

Nil de repente est cernere maximum.
Curandus aeger, dum medicabilis
    Est plaga, nec totos per artus
        Mortiferum subiit venenum.

45 At ipse demens, heu, patriam quoque
Fingebam et alti moenia Bosphori
    Quandoque visurum, fugata
        Auspice te Scythia superba.

against you or hide their hatred, nor does Spain.[16] For a long time
now you have been making Venice your bitter enemy, persuaded
by the untrustworthy advice of your venal courtiers. Therefore, 25
only recently, in an insensate manner equally hateful to gods and
men, stripped of all his military might, his kingdom and his
friends, he has returned to his father's throne, and though de- 30
feated, now occupies almost more land than the victor, which, for
shame! he did not dare to seize when his power and resources
were intact. But if you have any concern for your kingdom, for the
many princes and dukes, for the many cities that belong to you, 35
for what is honorable and glorious, if finally you have any concern
at all, we pray you now, take courage, as befits you, and firm of
purpose, cast off delay. Why do you allow the North Wind to stir 40
up the treacherous ashes by procrastinating? Important decisions
cannot be made suddenly. The sick patient must be cured while
the wound is still curable, before the deadly poison has penetrated
into all his limbs. But I myself in my madness, alas! imagined that 45
I would one day see my native land and the walls that tower over
the deep Bosporus, after the proud Scythians had been routed

Nunc parta nostro sanguine linquimus
50 Hosti tenenda et, quod pudeat magis,
    Lucro imputamus, siquis aegre
      Consuluit fugiendo vitae.

I nunc, tuorum, Carle, potentiam
Regnorum et armis Belgica robora
55   Mirare, dum Campana caede
      Luxurient sata Gallicana!

Ut nempe vincas, denique quae tibi
Vicisse, amicis, gloria, perditis?
    Feris ne tradendae tot urbes,
60   Exitio populis tributis,

Qui te suorum sanguine, qui suo
Fecere, si non ipse vetas, herum
    Non Rhosiarum Caucasique,
      Italiae sed enim beatae?

65 Hos destinatus, nunc vacuam sinis
Si praedam et armis obiicis hostium,
    Servando cum sis debeasque,
      Non homines tibi defuisse

Deosve, sed — quod dicere abominer! —
70 Scies amicos, iura, fidem, deos,
    Fas, famam, honestatem, decorum,
      Denique te tibi destitutum.

V. Ad Antonium Baldracanum

Baldracane, Aganippidum
    Custos sancte, quid est tam meritum optime
De teque et patria senem
    Et, quas saecula amant, perdere turpiter

under your leadership. Now we leave possessions acquired by our
own blood in the hands of the enemy and, what is more shameful,   50
we count it as gain if anyone unwillingly took thought for his life
by fleeing. Go now, Charles, and marvel at the power of your king-
doms and the armed might of France, while the crops of Campa-   55
nia thrive on Gallic blood! Even if you should win, what glory is
there in winning if your friends are sacrificed? Must so many cities
be abandoned to wild beasts, peoples consigned to their doom,
who by the blood of their children and their own blood — if you   60
yourself do not prevent it — made you lord not of Russia and the
Caucasus, but of prosperous Italy? Having marked them out for   65
their doom, if you allow your prey to go free and leave them at the
mercy of enemy troops when it is your duty to preserve them from
death, you will find out that it was neither men nor the gods who
failed you, but — may the gods forgive me! — you who have de-   70
serted friends, rights, trust, the gods, divine law, fame, honor,
glory, and finally yourself.

V. To Antonio Baldraccano[17]

Baldraccano, holy guardian of the Muses, why suffer in a shameful
manner the loss of an old man who deserved so well of you and

5   Artes ingenii impigri?
      Cur non flere die, non venientibus
    Astris desinis aureis,
      Et Manes lacrimis sollicitas patris?
    Non est, crede mihi, ut putas,
10   Baldracane, pium de superum queri
    Decreto neque debitam
      Naturae atque deo sortem animantibus
    Cunctis ferre modestius.
      An tu, tantus homo, vel sapientiae
15   Doctrinaeque putas tuae
      Nulla quaerere ope rem reparabilem,
    Vel non foeminei ingeni
      Absumi misere fletibus improbis?
    Vixit pene dies Pyli
20   Felix, sive genus nobile respicis,
    Seu casti sociam tori,
      Seu, quos rara solet sors dare fortibus,
    Dignos se patre liberos.
      Nam quid tot memorem principibus fidem
25   Laudatam atque animi integri
      Dotes saecla super degenerantia
    Aetatis male masculae?
      Nunc, conviva velut, quod fuerat super
    Mortali genio satur
30   Vitae, si revolat patrium ad aethera,
    Nil hic, non modo quod fleas,
      Sed cur non potius iudice gaudeas
    Aequo, qualis Olympiae
      Olim victor, ubi, pulvere strenuo
35   Decurso spatii sacri,
      Laetus fronde comam pressit amabili.

his country and impair the skills of a tireless genius that will 5
please future ages? Why do you not cease to weep during the day
and again at night when the shining stars appear; why harass your
father's departed spirit[18] with your tears? It is not, believe me, an
act of filial piety, as you think, Baldraccano, to complain of the 10
decisions of the gods and not to bear with more moderation the
destiny owed to nature and to god by all living beings. Or do you,
a man of such renown, think it is worthy of your wisdom and
learning to seek in vain after something that cannot be recovered 15
by any human resources, or to be piteously consumed by shameful
tears more fitting to a woman? He lived almost as long as Nestor,
fortunate in every way, whether you consider his noble race or the 20
partner who shared his chaste bed or, what fate rarely accords the
brave, children worthy of their father. Why should I mention his
loyalty, praised by so many leaders and the qualities of an upright 25
spirit superior to the degenerating times of an age lacking in viril-
ity? Now, like a guest at table, since he has had his fill of life and
satisfied his mortal Genius,[19] if he flies back to his heavenly home, 30
there is nothing for you to weep over; why not rather rejoice in the
decision of a fair judge, just as a victor at Olympia, when he has
run the race vigorously in the dust of the sacred space, happily 35
places the longed-for wreath upon his head?

EPIGRAMMATA VARIA

I. Ad Ecnomum

Quaeris qua niteat docto coma parte Catullo:
    Proximus Arcturo fulgor et Erigone est.
'Virginis et saevi contingens nanque Leonis
    Lumina, Calisto iuncta Lycaoniae,
5 Flectit in occasum, tardum dux ante Bootem,
    Qui vix sero alto mergitur Oceano.'
Quae tu si relegens, ubi sit coma regia quaeris,
    Ecnome, aquas medio quaeris in Oceano.
Quamvis quid relegas, vitiis miser invidiaque
10   Perditus? Ingeniis candor inesse solet.
Ergo, dum omnia conturbas, dum credere doctis
    Negligis et per te nil sapis ipse tamen,
Fecisti Oarionem ex Erigone, ex Arcturo
    Hydrochoum: iam quod monstrum erit ipsa coma?

II. In Monillum

Versus scribere nos putat Monillus
Quam nimis faciles, parum disertos,
Nec quales lepidi sonent Cetegi,
Quos noster probat unicos Monillus.
5 Atqui non lepidis ego Cetegis,
Si nescis — quid enim, venuste, mecum
Ante tot, rogo, saecla funeratis? —
Verum annis studeo meis placere,
Notus vel studeo labore nullo,
10 Exemplo monitus tui Cetegi,
Quem tecum probo, non loquor, Monille.

MISCELLANEOUS EPIGRAMS

I. To Ecnomus[1]

You ask where the lock shines in the learned Catullus.[2] Its effulgence is near Arcturus[3] and Erigone.[4] "Bordering on the constellations of Virgo and fierce Leo, close to Callisto, daughter of Lycaon,[5] she inclines toward her setting, leading the way for slow 5
Boötes, who sinks late into the deep Ocean."[6] If you reread these lines, and seek where the royal lock is, Ecnomus, you are looking for water in the middle of the Ocean. Yet what is the use of rereading, you miserable creature, victim of your vices and of envy? Men of talent are distinguished by their clarity. Therefore, while 10
you confuse everything and refuse to believe learned men and yet know nothing yourself, you made Erigone into Oarion and Arcturus into Hydrochous.[7] What kind of a monster will this lock become?[8]

II. To Monillus

Monillus is of the opinion that I write verse that is too facile and not very learned, without the sonority of the charming Cethegus,[9] the only poetry that our good friend Monillus approves of. But I 5
am not eager to please people like Cethegus, in case you don't know it—for what do I have to do, I ask you, my charming friend, with those who have been buried so many years ago—but I wish to please people of my own time or to become well-known without much effort, instructed by the example of your Cethegus, 10
whom I approve together with you, Monillus, but do not speak of.

Nam Suadae populis medulla dictus,
Nil Remo dedit optimus legendum.

III. Ad Isabettam Gonzagam ducem Urbini

Quod nomen taceam tuum, Isabetta,
Et vix tot bona saeculis priorum
Ulli nobilibus parata curis—
Nedum istis miseris meis in annis,
5   In quis nec pudor aestimatur assis
Nec mos ingeniumve, quod solebat
Tunc ire imperia ante et ante honores—
Non est cur ideo nihil merenti
Irasci gravius velis Marullo,
10 Qui, prius quoque non bonus poeta,
Nunc vero et serie diu laborum
Infractus, timet, ah, timet, fatemur,
In te tot bona saeculi, tot artes
Et dignam Paphiae decore formam,
15 Culpa deterere ingeni minoris.

IV. In sacerdotum avaritiam

Quis male Virginea gladium suspendit in aede
    Telaque non hominum tincta cruore semel?
Ista parens pietatis et impia facta perosa,
    Amovet a templis ipsa suis Maria;
5   Et tamen haec recipitque libens laudatque sacerdos:
    Nimirum laudat, quae capit ipse sibi.

V. In Cominium

Servatus modo naufragio cum mercibus Anglis,
    Gratus opum partem das, Comini, superis,

342

For though people called him the marrow of persuasiveness,[10] at his best he gave Rome nothing to read.

III. To Elizabeth Gonzaga, Duchess of Urbino[11]

Although I make no mention of your name, Elizabeth, and the prosperity you have attained by your outstanding administration, which none of your predecessors achieved—to say nothing of these tragic years, in which no value is attributed to decency or 5 tradition or talent, once more valued than empires or honors— there is no reason why you should be so angry with Marullus, who is not deserving of blame. While he was not a good poet previ- 10 ously, now debilitated by a succession of labors over a long period of time, he fears, ah yes! he fears that because of his inferior talent he will detract from these many blessings of the age bestowed on you, your many artistic achievements and a beauty worthy of Ve- 15 nus herself.

IV. Against the avarice of priests

Who unwisely hung a sword and weapons stained more than once with men's blood in the church of the Blessed Virgin? The mother of piety, Mary herself, who hates impious acts, keeps such things far from her shrines; and yet the priest accepts these things will- 5 ingly and praises them: of course he praises things that he takes for himself.

V. Against Cominius

Saved just now from shipwreck with a store of English goods, Cominius, you gratefully give part of your wealth to the gods, and

Divitiasque tuas templisque arisque deorum
    Congeris et credis sic satis his facere.
5 Infelix, quid enim sperasti numina mundi
    Magna tuis donis et stipe posse capi?
  Fas, Comini, rectumque deis pietasque sacranda est,
    Si nescis: hominum caetera, non Superum.

VI. De filio Auli

Quae lux progeniem optatam dedit, abstulit Aulo,
    Sed gravior luctus luctibus ipse modus.
Nam bene vix contacta infans vagiverat aura,
    Afflatus subito cum Iovis igne perit.
5 At mater 'Quanto ante' inquit, 'miser, ante crematus,
    Finisses nostras tecum etiam lacrimas!'

VII. De Diogene et Aristippo

Nudus Aristippo nudo Canis obvius umbris
    Sub Stygiis 'Ubi nunc aurum' ait 'est Siculum?
Nunc saltem illecebris disces luxuque carere
    Teque Hiro cuivis esse putare parem.'
5 Ille senis laeva barbam et sordentia vellens
    Menta 'Pares si non viximus, hoc satis est!'

VIII. Ad Hylam

Ore prius pleno solitus laudare iugatos,
    Cur nunc laudator caelibis es thalami,
Quodque magis mirum, cum morem et coniugis artes,
    Cum faciem coelo laudibus ipse feras?

you pile up your riches in churches and on the altars of the gods and think that in this way you render them due service. Foolish 5 man, did you hope that the great divinities of the universe could be won over by your gifts and miserable sums of money? Moral principles, uprightness and piety must be consecrated to the gods, Cominius, if you would like to know: other things pertain to humans, not to the gods.

VI. On the son of Aulus

The day that gave Aulus his desired offspring also took it away from him, but the manner of his grief was more grievous than the grief itself. For scarcely had the child uttered his first wail as he breathed in the air when, suddenly stricken by Jupiter's lightning bolt, he perished. But the mother said, 'Poor child, if you had 5 been consumed by fire only a little earlier, you would have brought an end to our tears along with your life!'

VII. On Diogenes and Aristippus

When the naked Diogenes[12] met the naked Aristippus[13] in the Stygian shades, he said to him, "Where is your Sicilian gold now? Now at least you will learn how to do without allurements and luxury and consider yourself equal to any beggar."[14] The other old 5 man, grabbing him by his beard and his filthy chin with his left hand, retorted, "As long as I didn't live like you, that is enough!"

VIII. To Hylas

You used to praise married people loudly; why do you now praise the state of celibacy? And what is more surprising, when you praise to the skies the obedience, skills and good looks of your mate?

5   Crede mihi, non ista tori, non culpa maritae est:
       Sed quis, Hyla, natas sex, rogo, pauper amet?

IX. In Posthumum

Aedificare, canesque et equos et pascere mimas,
       Promptum iter ad nudam est, Posthume, pauperiem.

X. De miseria vitae

Heraclite et Democrite, hic ridere paratus,
       Tu contra lacrimis cuncta rigare tuis,
Dicite: quo vitam mortalem auctore deorum
       Tam bene iudicio dispari uterque notat?
5   Certe equidem reputans mortalia vos ego scire,
       Pace dei, solos vos puto ego sapere.

XI. Divo Georgio

Loricam, thoracam, ocreas, coxalia, conum
       Campanum et, rarum Massagae opus, galeam,
Atque lacertale utrunque atque humerale litamque
       Hastam auro geminae tegminaque ipsa manus,
5   Et gladium et mentale, tibi hic dico fixa, Georgi,
       Pertaesus saecli militiam sterilem.

XII. De Domillo caeco ferente claudum

Claudi iuvatus lumine impositi humeris,
Caecus Domillus huc et illuc per vias
Urbisque tantae flexuosa compita
Graditur inoffensus, et acerba incommoda
5   Alterius alter commodo pensat suo,
Defecta membra sublevantes invicem.
Sic nec Domillus caecus atque ille ambulans,

Believe me, the marriage bed or the wife is not to blame: but I ask 5
you, Hylas, what pauper is going to love six female offspring?

IX. Against Postumus

To be in the building business and to maintain dogs, horses and
dancing girls is a quick road to abject poverty, Postumus.

X. On life's misery

Heraclitus and Democritus,[15] one of you ready to laugh and the
other, on the contrary, bathing everything with your tears, tell me,
by what god's authority does each of you criticize mortal affairs so
well, each with contrasting views? At all events, when I reflect that 5
you know what mortality is, with all due respect to god, I think
only you are wise.

XI. To Saint George

My cuirass, my breast plate, my greaves, my thigh guards, my
Campanian bronze crest and my helmet, a rare example of Scyth-
ian workmanship, and my arm guards and shoulder guards and
my golden spear, and both of my gauntlets and my sword and chin 5
guard—all of these I hang up here and dedicate to you, George,
weary of the unprofitable military service of this age.[16]

XII. On the blind man Domillus carrying a cripple[17]

With the aid of the vision of a lame man placed on his shoulders
the blind Domillus walks without obstruction hither and thither
through the streets and the winding crossroads of the great city,
and one makes up for the harsh disadvantages of the other through 5
his own advantages, each aiding the physical defects of the other.
In this way Domillus is not blind and the other one is walking.

Nil non docente pervicacis ingeni
Necessitate et improba indigentia.
10   Oedipode dignum aenigma, mancus utpote
Neuterque uterque, uterque neuterque integer.

XIII. De Carolo Francorum rege

Placatus mitisque suis, ubi multa nefanda
    Censura Carolus vidit egere sua,
'Cur regno aut vita non possum cedere honeste,
    Dummodo cum regno cedam' ait 'et gladiis?'
5   Dixerat, heu, subito carae cum coniugis ulnis
    Concidit atque animum reddidit, ut petiit.
Crudeles superi semperque in dira parati:
    Optatis neque vis nec deus utilibus.

XIV. Epitaphium eiusdem

Post maria et terras domitas restabat Olympus:
    Hunc quoque, sed nimium, rex, petis ante diem.

This is the lesson taught by the determined nature of necessity and shameless indigence. It is an enigma worthy of Oedipus, see- 10 ing that neither of them, yet each of them is crippled, and neither, yet each of them is of sound body.

XIII. On Charles, King of France

Reconciled and at peace with his family, when Charles saw that his many wicked deeds were free of censure, he said: "Why can I not withdraw honorably from my kingdom and life, as long as I withdraw with my kingdom and my sword?" He had no sooner 5 spoken when alas! he suddenly fell into the arms of his dear spouse and rendered up his spirit,[18] as he asked this question. The gods are cruel and always ready to accomplish dreadful things: there is no power or god for useful wishes.

XIV. Epitaph of the same

After sea and land were subdued, Olympus remained: this too you seek, O king, but too early.

INSTITUTIONUM PRINCIPALIUM

Liber Primus

Ab Iove principium rursus cape carminis orsi,
Musa. Decet vatem nil non Iove rite vocato
Moliri et sanctum praefari in singula nomen,
Praesertim regem egregium bellique domique
5   Dum damus et primo paulatim a luminis ortu
Crescentem varios rerum formamus in usus,
Experti quanto imperia et vis nescia recti
Stent populis cassique animi ratione potentum.
    Tu modo, si meriti Delphos tot saecla silentes
10 Cortinamque tuam et sacrata recludimus antra,
Adsis, o Thymbraee, favens, pater, aviaque ausis
Pande novum nemus et nulli sacra nota priorum.
Primus ego, veterum damnato more parentum,
Phoebeo vetitos culpavi in carmine lusus,
15 Primus inexpertum mundi per inane vagatus,
Perpetuam seriem tractus Telluris ad ipsos
Ab Iove deduxi servatoque ordine rerum
Suspendi solidam naturae ex aere catenam.
Et nunc arma strepant duri licet undique Martis
20 Proque levi dextram calamo gravis hasta fatiget
Et terat inclusum vatis caput aerea cassis,
Non tamen Aonidum conceptus pectore cessit
Dulcis amor. Iuvat irriguos accedere fontes
Rursus et intacta crinem contexere lauro
25 Inventumque deum, divini carminis usum,
Post superos ipsumque Iovem, post semina prima,

THE EDUCATION OF A PRINCE

Book I[1]

From Jupiter begin again a new poem,[2] O Muse. A poet should
not undertake anything without ritually calling upon Jupiter and
mentioning his holy name before every endeavor, especially since 5
we are describing a king, preeminent in war and peace, and form-
ing him for his various duties little by little from the day of his
birth and through the years of his growing to manhood, having
learned how much it costs populations to be subject to rule and
power ignorant of what is right and to minds of the powerful de-
void of reason.

But you, Thymbraean father,[3] be present with your favor if I 10
am worthy to reopen Delphi, which has lain silent for so many
centuries,[4] and your cauldron and sacred caverns, and as I venture
into untrodden paths, open wide the new grove and holy rites
known to none of my forebears. Rejecting the practices of my an-
cestors, I first found fault with obscene themes, prohibited in an 15
Apollonian poem; I was the first to explore the unfamiliar void of
the universe, and to establish an unbroken series beginning with
Jupiter, extending to the confines of the earth itself, and preserving
the order of things, I suspended a solid chain of nature from the
vault of heaven. And although now the weapons of pitiless Mars 20
resound on all sides[5] and instead of the light pen a heavy spear
burdens my right arm and a bronze helmet presses on the head of
the poet enclosed within it, nevertheless the sweet love of the
Muses conceived in my heart never ceases. It is a joy to approach
the gushing fountains again and to wreath my hair with untouched 25
laurel and to turn from the themes of the gods, the subject of di-
vine song, after the celestial beings and Jupiter himself, after the

Dicendas merito regum convertere in artes.
Mox tamen egregias virtutes actaque vestra
Exequar et latum effundam, vir magne, per orbem
30 Exemplisque tuis saecla illustrabo futura.
     Principio gravidam, cum primum menstrua sextum
Viderit et pleno Phoebe radiaverit igni —
Nam quae deinde subit, vitali innoxia partu
Interdum, numeri natura adiuta potentis —
35 Iam tum cura vigil carae nutricis habendae
Excitet et, quando illecebris luxuque profano
Exuimus iam pridem animum affectusque parentum
Et pudet in dulces distendere pectora natos,
At saltem pretioque dato donisque paranda,
40 Materno siqua ingenio velit aegra subire
Obsequia et blandi fastidia ferre laboris.
Hanc neque non validam patiar, ne regius infans
Contactu culpam trahat et spem fallat avorum,
Nec placet aut iam tum vergenti ignava papilla
45 Aut contra rudis et prima quae foeta iuventa
Nesciat infirmi nutrix mala taedia alumni
Sponte pati et querulo vagitu rumpere somnos.
Adsint praecipue mores vitaeque probatae
Compositus tenor et qualem decet esse pudentis
50 Matronae: neque enim interdum minus ubere blandae
Nutricis pueri attrahimus, quam semine ab ipso
Matris et antiqua ductorum ab origine patrum.
Ac veluti sylvae laudataque poma sapores
Degenerant patriumque solum mutata recusant
55 Ferre genus notum et consuetos arbore succos,
Sic hominum ruit in peius generosa propago
Alturae vitio indignae et, nisi cura resistat,
Naturamque novam atque externas degener artes

primeval substances, to the conduct of kings, worthy to be the
subject of poetry. Then I shall narrate your outstanding virtues
and exploits, great hero, and send them forth into the wide world   30
and shall enlighten future ages with your example.

First of all, when the moon has run its monthly course six
times and has radiated its light at its brightest—for the next
moon, strengthened by the properties of the powerful number   35
seven, is not harmful to the newly born—the pregnant woman
must take care to find a loving wet nurse, and since through
worldly luxury and enticements we have forgotten the feelings and
affections of parents and are ashamed to extend the breasts to our
sweet offspring, at least with money and gifts we can procure the   40
services of a woman with maternal instincts who will be willing to
undertake this difficult task and suffer the tedious monotony of a
pleasant duty. I would not allow that she be a woman of poor
health, lest the royal child contract some disease from her and dis-
appoint the hopes of his ancestors, and I do not want, on the one   45
hand, one lacking physical energy and already flabby-breasted nor,
on the other hand, do I want one who is inexperienced and bore
children when she was very young and does not know how to put
up willingly with the annoyances of a sick child and be robbed of
her sleep by loud wailings. She must be possessed of good morals,
especially, and exhibit an orderly and upright way of life, as befits   50
a modest matron, for as children we often inherit just as much
from the breast of a kindly nurse as from the race of our mother
or the ancient lineage of our fathers. And just as trees degenerate
and prized fruits lose their flavor and when transplanted from   55
their native soil refuse to bear a well-known variety and produce
the usual juices, so a noble stock of men quickly degenerates
through faulty upbringing, and if proper care is not employed, it

Induat et gentem paulatim exudet avitam.
60   Atque ideo frugique animorum acrisque iuventae
Insignem prius exquirunt, tum deinde salubri
Disponunt habilem ventura ad munia victu
Dilutique mero Bacchi, licet humida vina
Ipse parum credam succis differre cicutae
65 In puero, nisi septenis iam solibus actis
Decoxit tenera conceptum aetate fluorem.
Nam geminam mox post hyemem rude poscere 'pappa'
Incipiat puroque buas de fonte petitas.
Ante reformidant quaeque et, quod saepe videmus,
70 Siquando solito candens liquor ubere desit,
Horrent lac quoque non suetum et ieiunia durant—
Tantum usus valet in teneris!—notasque papillas
Poscunt et sicco nequicquam gutture lambunt
Vagituque replent puerili concava tecta.
75 Quod nisi, quam primum causa morboque reperto,
Occurris culpae et mammarum claustra relaxas,
Nequicquam pius infantes miserabere questus
Flaventique voles miseris succurrere capra,
Praesertim si conceptus properataque damno
80 Est Venus et non ulla uteri spes arte levandi.
Verum, haec ut teneris metuenda infantibus aevi
Ignarisque cibi, sic, postquam firmior aetas
Naturae iam praesidio et muniverit armis,
Proderit invitos etiam multumque rebelles
85 Intempestivo lactis depellere ab usu—
Paulatim tamen et nequa vim sentiat infans!—
Sordentique luto et tactu picis ubera nigra
Porgenda aut aloes occulto infecta sapore,
Sponte sua blandum ut nectar desuescat amare,
90 Offensus totiens supposti fraude veneni.
      Illud in his moneo repetens, nequando solutum

becomes degenerate, taking on a new nature and extraneous characteristics and gradually casts off its ancestral race.   60

Therefore they shall search for one who is honest by nature and remarkable for her youthful vigor, one who through her healthful diet and sober consumption of diluted wine will be ready for her future duties, although in my opinion watered-down wine is little   65 different than the juice of the hemlock in a boy, unless in his eighth year he has eliminated the harmful liquid he consumed at a tender age. Soon after his second year he should begin to ask for baby food and drink from a pure source. Before that they shun   70 everything and, as we often see, when the white liquid from the accustomed breasts is lacking, they shrink from any other milk and suffer hunger — so powerful is habit in young children — and seek the familiar breasts and lick in vain with dry throats and fill   75 the empty rooms with their cries. Once you have discovered the cause of the malady, if you do not take measures to deal with the problem and give access once again to the breasts, in vain will you take pity on the poor child's laments and wish to assist it with the milk of a yellow goat, especially if you have conceived again and   80 engaged in sexual intercourse too quickly and there is no hope of aborting the fetus. We must take these precautions when the child is of tender age and is not able to eat food, but when they become stronger of body and nature has provided them with protection and they begin to teethe, it will be beneficial to wean them from   85 milk when it is no longer appropriate, even if they are unwilling and resist, but this should only be done gradually so that the child does not sense any violence. And you will offer them breasts that are smeared with mud or black pitch or impregnated secretly with the taste of aloes so that the child will become disaccustomed of   90 its own accord to the desire for the sweet nectar, disgusted by the repeated deceitful stratagem of the substituted bitter drink.

I repeat this advice: that when you unwrap the child from his

Nexibus et tepido perfusum corpora rore
Aut tenues vestis mutatum atque humida lina,
Ante crepundillis properes involvere suetis
95   Et solitis arctare modis undantia membra,
Bracchia quam surasque breves et cerea nati
Crura locis aptes studio composta fideli.
Nam saepe, incautae culpa nutricis inerti,
Vidi ego mendoso foedam distorta plicatu
100   Membra notam serae traxisse in tarda senectae
Tempora, nec medicae potuere avertere curae,
Hippocratesque senex et Pergameus Galenus,
Nec suspensa deis miserandae vota parentis.
      Quid dicam, undantem quae porrectura papillam
105   Mollibus e stratis gnavum levat impigra corpus,
Nec gremio exceptum carum nisi lactat alumnum,
Ne superincumbens miti decepta quiete
Suffocet infirmum et nequicquam vana moventem?
Quid, quae pensilibus cunis stans ubera praebet,
110   Ne tunc illa quidem aut cubito secura gravato
Inniti sociave gravem sine fallere noctem —
Tanta est humanis taciti pellacia somni! —
At, cum plena satur iam duxerit ubera natus
Inque vicem blandus sopor aggravat, ecce sororem
115   Advocat et parvi curam commendat alumni.
Illa sedens dextra cunas movet et simul ore
Invitat tenues modulata ad carmina somnos.
Nam puero modo Nestoreae longaeva senectae
Saecla optat, nunc Pellaei ducis inclyta regno
120   Nomina, Achilleae nunc fortia proelia dextrae.
'Hunc non Cliniades facie, non voce Pericles
Vincat, in hoc plebes firmet sua vota patresque,

swaddling clothes and give him a warm bath, or change his wet
diapers, before you hasten to wind him in his usual wrappings and   95
confine his dripping limbs in the usual way, arrange his arms and
the little calves and delicate thighs of the child with great care in
the proper manner. For I have often seen limbs distorted through   100
the negligence and ineptitude of a careless nurse in wrapping the
child, an ugly deformation that continued into advanced old age,
which medical remedies were not able to eliminate, neither hoary
Hippocrates[6] nor Galen of Pergamum[7] nor the votive tablets to
the gods hung on the walls by a pitiful parent.

What shall I say of the nurse who as she is about to offer her   105
full breasts to the child lifts herself up energetically from the soft
bed and does not hold the child in her lap unless she is nursing
him, lest while lying on him she is deceived by soft sleep and suf-
focates the weak child, who thrashes about in vain? What shall I   110
say of the nurse who gives suck while she is standing up and the
child is in a hanging cradle? Let her not be negligent even then
when leaning on her elbow, weighed down with fatigue, or without
a companion to beguile the wearisome night — so great is the se-
ductiveness of silent sleep to mortals! But when the child has
drunk his full from the full breasts and sweet sleep conquers him   115
in turn, behold, she summons her sister and commends to her the
care of the tiny child. Sitting down, she rocks the cradle with her
right hand and at the same time invites light sleep by singing a
melodious song. At one moment she wishes a life as long as that
of Nestor for the boy, at other times she mentions the name of   120
the famous king of Pella,[8] now the courageous battles of Achilles.
"May Alcibiades,[9] son of Clinias, not surpass him in beauty, nor
Pericles in speech; in him may the people and senators confirm

Ignotique velint populi potuisse videre.'
Interea placida vagit si forte quiete
125 Eccitus, accurrit subito et plena ubera porgit
Aut pictam ostentat volucrem aut laquearia tecti
Aurata ac densum crepitantem ex aere canoro
Bracteolam et lacrimas spectaclo avertit inani.
Nam mihi ne, quaeso, quisquam laudaverit illam,
130 Quae personatum puero ostentare Cyclopa
Gaudet et hirsuta Antiphatae terrere figura
Crescentesque animos puerili in pectore frangit
Indignaque replens cura miseroque pavore,
Nescia quanta superstitio mortalibus aegris
135 Damna ferat primisque haustum grave virus ab annis.
Quo magis et tenebras et caeca silentia noctis
Formandi et strepitus iam tum contemnere inanes,
Frigoraque innocuisque pati Spartana lavacri
Artubus atque habili membris dare robora ludo,
140 Sub Iove detectum victa cohibente capillum,
Nec quicquam tactu horrendum gustuve putare,
Quod non pernitiem temptantibus afferat ullam.
    Nam, quanquam antiquo veterum de semine patrum
Multa modis multis caeca ratione videmus
145 Influere interdum et seros revocare nepotes
Naturam gentisque notas ac signa referre,
Pleraque sunt tamen alturae, nec inutilis aegri
Usque adeo quisquam est animi, qui cernere murem
Exiguum non sustineat, quem brassica tacta
150 Laedat et aspectu vilis pallescat echinni
Aut rutam horreat halantem atque Cytorida buxum,
Delitias regum et viridantis nomina sylvae,
Multaque praeterea non dissona talia monstris,
Si non vana parens et nutrix vanior illa,
155 Dum cupido affectant similem ostentare parenti

their hopes, and may foreign peoples wish they had been able to see him."

In the meantime, if the child is awakened from his peaceful sleep and cries, she runs to him immediately and extends her full breasts or she shows him a picture of a bird or the golden coffers of the ceiling or copper sheets that make a rattling noise and averts tears with empty show. But, I beseech you, let no one recommend to me a nurse who enjoys showing masks of the Cyclops to the child and terrifying him with a figure of shaggy Antiphates[10] and weakens the developing courageous spirit in a child's heart, filling it with inappropriate anxiety and distressing fear, unmindful of how much damage superstition, a virulent poison imbibed in early years, inflicts on unhappy mortals. They must be trained all the more at that age to have no fear of darkness and the gloomy silence of the night and empty noises and to endure cold Spartan baths without doing any harm to the body and to strengthen their limbs in agile sports, to stay out in the open air naked with only a band holding their hair together, to consider nothing abhorrent to touch or taste as long as it does not bring any serious harm to those who try it.

For although we see that many things influence us in many ways from our ancestral parentage in a mysterious manner, and that later distant descendants recall the characteristics of their family and call to mind their features and qualities, many things also result from upbringing. No one is so stupid and fearful that he cannot bear the sight of a tiny mouse or the feel of cabbage or grows pale at the sight of a simple sea urchin or shudders at a smelly rue or a Mt. Cytorus box tree,[11] the delight of kings and glory of the verdant woods, and many other similar apparitions, if it were not that his foolish mother or even more foolish

125

130

135

140

145

150

155

    Maternumque probant utero grave teste pudorem,
    Singula rimatae cerei inclinamina alumni,
    Ingererent multa atque alerent, ea saepe probando,
    Quae crescente dehinc animo, crescentibus annis,
160 Praesertim veteri exemplo subnixa suorum,
    Paulatim assumunt vires et robore adepto
    Ima penetrali radice in pectora tendunt
    Possessumque agitant hominem versantque premendo.
    Qualis ubi saepe ignoto commissus adhaesit
165 Surculus aut platani trunco aut frondentis olivae,
    Ille quidem primo rudis impatiensque laborum
    Et tantum attactu excussus prope simplice euntum,
    At, si foecundis adolevit robur ab annis,
    Securus tempestatum coelique ruinae
170 Explicat ingentes ramos sinuosaque pandit
    Bracchia nativumque alte nemus occupat umbra
    Largus opum regnatque immoto robore victor.
    Nam cur arva iuvat gnavus versata colonus
    Pomaque coguntur iussos dare mitia succos,
175 Cur cadit ingenii vis insita deside vita,
    Si contra augeri nequit et mitescere cultu,
    Nec doctrina potest speratum infundere rectum?
    Scilicet aeria solitus regione vagari
    Falco levis, studio assiduo tamen atque labore
180 Assuescit vigilem paulatim ferre magistrum,
    Deiectaque procul celsa de nube volucre,
    Rursus in obsequium solitum et sua vincla redire.
    Nos hominem foeta ecceptum de matre cadentem
    Ignarumque sui et tantum ad monstrata paratum,
185 Speramus non admonitu, non posse moveri
    Exemplo et primae blanda assuetudine vitae,
    Si modo non vana accedat cultura regentis?
    Nam cui non Cybele est collo vectata leonum

nurse try to show that he resembles his ambitious father and testi-
fies to his mother's chastity by the indisputable testimony of the
womb. Scrutinizing every inclination of the impressionable child,
they speak of them frequently and encourage and approve their
development, and as the child grows up, in spirit and in years,   160
these characteristics, with the support of the long-standing exam-
ple of the child's ancestors, little by little acquire strength and
vigor, penetrate deeply into the personality, take possession of the
individual and exercise a troubling influence over him. So it often 165
happens that when a cutting is grafted on to a different type of
tree, whether it be the trunk of a plane tree or a leafy olive tree, at
first it is imperfectly formed and resists the farmer's efforts and is
knocked off merely by the simple contact with passersby, but if it
reaches maturity and grows to full strength, resistant to storms   170
and the fury of the heavens, it spreads its huge branches and
twisted arms and fills its native grove with its thick shade and
bears abundant fruit and with unshaken power reigns victoriously.
Why does the hardworking farmer improve the land by turning
over the soil and why do the cultivated fruit trees produce the de- 175
sired juices, and why does the inborn vigor of the mind diminish
through an idle way of life if it is not developed and matured
through cultivation, and if instruction is not able to instill the
hoped for moral rectitude?

The nimble falcon, accustomed to roam through the regions of   180
the sky, is trained little by little through much effort and dedica-
tion to obey its watchful master, and after it has brought down its
prey from high up in the heavens, to return to its habitual obedi-
ence and its bonds. Can we not hope that a child, lifted up after it
has fallen from its mother's womb, having no self-knowledge and   185
only capable of doing what it is taught, can be influenced by ad-
monition and example and the repeated gentle routines of early
childhood, if only no foolish training is imparted by the one who
guides him? For who is not familiar with Cybele, borne along on

Nota, quis Eoae nescit certamina gentis
190 Impositasque arces nigrantis tergore belvae?
Ipse greges inter memini atque armenta Sclavena,
Qua deserta rhoas etiam nunc moenia monstrant,
Indigenam vidisse lupum, quem matre perempta
Nutritumque sero et foetae canis ubere pastor
195 Miscuerat levibus Serbis fidisque Molossis.
Ille inter teneros versari innoxius hedos
Custodisque modo foetas ambire capellas
Aut sylvis errare vagus semperque cruentus,
Nec nisi raptata praedae cum parte redire.
200 Cura tamen princeps, lupus agnitus. Hunc ubi primum
Sensit adesse, animis hostilibus ilicet ire
Obvius et morsu primus dare vulnera, primus
Sternere humi prensum atque hosti insultare iacenti
Cognataeque ferox laetari sanguine caedis.
205 Tantum humana potest longa experientia cura!
Quo magis, o, monitis huc quisque advertite mentem,
Infantesque animos monstratorumque capaces
Artibus et placido iam inde exercete decoro,
Servili dicto procul exemploque remoto
210 Degeneri, ne commentis exercita vanis
Concidat in primo surgens nova pectore virtus
Immanemque notam venientibus afferat annis.
Talis, Achaemenium quae regem Perside in alta
Eduxit populisque Asiae regnisque verendum,
215 Spaco, et Romuleis multum laudata Latinis
Acca parens, gratoque pii quae munere alumni
Nunc quoque in Hesperia nomen tenet advena terra.
Talis et ipsa, sinu quae quondam exerta parato,
Ithome, gravida tunc primum matris ab alvo

362

her team of lions,[12] or the battles waged among peoples of the   190
East and the towers placed on the backs of black elephants?

I myself remember seeing among the flocks and herds of the
Slavs, where streams still run through the abandoned walls, a na-
tive wolf, which after losing its mother and being later nourished   195
by the teats of a pregnant bitch, was mixed in with swift, faithful
Serbian Molossian hounds by the shepherd.[13] It lived among the
young goats harmlessly and circled around the pregnant she-goats
like a watchdog or would go wandering off in the woods, always
bloodstained and never returned without part of the prey it had   200
seized. Its chief care was to catch the scent of a wolf. As soon as it
sensed that one was present, it took off immediately in a frenzy to
face it and was the first to inflict wounds, biting it, and first to
seize it and throw it to the ground, leaping on its prostrate foe and   205
taking fierce joy in the blood of his slaughtered kin. So powerful is
human skill combined with long devoted attention! For all the
more reason let everyone turn his attention to these examples and
train young children and impressionable minds in skills and good
manners from an early age. Keep far from them all vulgar expres-   210
sions and ignoble behavior lest right from the start newly acquired
virtue, rising up in their hearts, fall victim to vain falsehoods and
leave ugly traces in future years. So did Spaco act, who brought up   215
the Achaemenian king in upper Persia,[14] a monarch revered by the
peoples and kingdoms of Asia, and Acca Larentia,[15] much praised
by the Latin race, descendants of Romulus, and she who, though a
foreigner, still enjoys a good reputation in the land of Italy by the

220 Eccepitque Iovem venientem atque ubera parvo,
Ubera nectareis porsit rorantia guttis.
    Et tamen, exacto Pisaei pulvere lustri,
Haec quoque pellenda est sensim tibi seque movenda
Tradendusque puer iam tum vitaeque magistro
225 Spectatae et simul eloquii rerumque perito,
Qui gravis et dudum nervoso incoctus honesto,
Hinc arte ingenioque, illinc praestantibus actae
Aetatis iuvet exemplis, nec vita refutet
Doctrinam serpantque animis contagia foeda.
230 Nam, licet egregie magnis doctrina decori
Regibus et prudens sollertis gratia linguae
Hortandisque animis deterrendisque suorum
Militiaeque domique et, sicubi flagitat usus,
Legatum affari venientem, sicubi amicos
235 Alloqui et infenso socios ex hoste parare,
Malo tamen Curiosque rudes parcumque loquendi
Spartanum; malo hinnitus praeponere equinos
Assuetum cytharae aut siquid vetus attulit aetas
Horridius, quam Caesareae nitida agmina linguae
240 Errantemque annum deprensa ad signa vocatum,
Si vitae quoque cum tantis mihi dotibus affers
Flagitia atque malo conturbas mella veneno.
Hinc ausi studium multi damnare politi
Oris et Aonios animi contemnere cultus,
245 Scilicet utilius multo mala gentibus aegris
Ignorare rati, quam splendida noscere factu,
In peius quando proni sumus ipsaque damno
Notitia est, si non superat respectus honesti
Relligioque deum fandi memorum atque nefandi,
250 Quis sine nec primi quondam potuere coire
Illi hominum coetus veniens nec crescere in aevum:
Nam leges qui fixerunt plerumque refigunt

grateful gift of her nursling.[16] And so also was Ithome,[17] who once   220
readily offered her breasts, running over with drops of nectar, to
Jupiter who had just issued from the womb of his mother.

However, when the child has reached his fifth year, you must
gradually remove the nurse and send her away and the boy must   225
be handed over at this point to a teacher of unblemished life,
skilled in speech and with much experience, a man of earnestness,
endowed with a natural, vigorous sense of honor, who will be ben-
eficial both by his skill and talent and by the outstanding example
of his life, and his own conduct must not contradict his teaching   230
and in this way allow a foul pollution to seep into the mind of his
charge. For although outstanding learning and the subtle charm of
clever speech enable kings to exhort or discourage their subjects in
war and peace, and when necessity requires it, to welcome the visit   235
of an ambassador, and as the occasion demands, address friends or
make allies of a bitter foe, nevertheless, I prefer rugged men like
Curius[18] and the Spartan, spare of speech; one who prefers the
whinnying of horses to the cithara, and the rough language of an
earlier age to the elegant flow of courtly speech and the art of   240
dividing up the year according to the movements of the stars, if
together with so many gifts you bring a dishonorable life and lace
the honey with deadly poison. For this reason many have dared
to condemn the pursuit of polished speaking and to despise   245
the cultivation of the Muses, evidently thinking that it is much
more advantageous for the miserable lot of mankind not to know
bad things than for them to know about splendid accomplish-
ments, since we are all prone to evil and knowledge in itself is
detrimental if respect for honor and reverence for the gods, who   250
are mindful of good and evil, do not prevail, without whom an-
cient societies could not have come together nor developed through

Liberaque est illis libiti usurpata facultas.
Ac, dum prima etiam titubat nunc sensibus aetas,
255   Nec capit impatiens animus maiora laborum,
Profuerit tabulis virtutem et pariete picto
Ostentare patrum et decora enumerare parata,
Siqua domi: nam praecipue mentem illa remordent
Cognataeque adhibent stimulos imitamine laudis.
260   Sed tamen et clari tumulo generosus Achillis
Ploravit Macedo, Marathoniaque acta soporem
Rumpebant auso patriam mutare carinis,
Nec frustra tot facta virum effigiesque priorum
Caelantes auro et Gangeo elephanto
265   Servabantque foro veteres ipsoque senatu.
Atque illum Geticum victa de gente vocarunt,
Hunc Scythicum, Cretensem alium; sic Dalmata fractus,
Sic titulis cessit victorum Alemanicus axis,
Sic totiens Persis nuribus funesta Latinis.
270   Omne adeo genus exempli certamine pulchro
Eccitat egregiasque animas spe replet honesti:
Qualis ubi Eleo sonipes de carcere missus
Corripuit spatium atque ipso discrimine palmae
Tum demum accendit vires seque increpat ipse
275   Successu admonitus subeuntis et ilia tendit
Impatiens culpae ac vinci dolet aemula virtus.
     Interea studiis Musarum assuesce volentem
Paulatim, blandique ediscat imagine multa
Commenti quae Pierio nisi tecta lepore
280   Horret adhuc animus tener ingeniumque recusat.
Aspera enim via virtutum acclivisque recessus
Ducendusque puer quasi versicolora per arva,
Ac veluti intexendi aditus foliisque rosaque
Fallendusque labor vario oblectamine rerum:
285   Ceu cum littoribus vacuis innupta puella

the ages. For those who established the laws often undo them and arrogate to themselves the power of changing them as they wish. While the child's mental faculties are still insecure and he is not capable of greater things, it would be beneficial to show him the excellent qualities of his forefathers in paintings and murals and relate their honorable exploits, if there are such objects in the home, for these examples make an impression on the mind and incite imitation of family virtues. And yet the noble-spirited Macedonian king wept over the tomb of glorious Achilles,[19] and the battle of Marathon robbed Themistocles of his sleep,[20] who dared to exchange his city with the hulls of ships.[21] It was not without reason that men of old carved images of the exploits of their heroes in gold and Indian ivory and conserved them in the forum and the senate house. And they called one general "Geticus"[22] after the people that he conquered, and another "Scythicus" and another "Cretensis."[23] So were the Dalmatians vanquished,[24] so the Alemannic region[25] yielded a title to the victors as did the Parthians,[26] so often a cause of mourning to young Roman brides. So true is it that every type of example excites people to glorious combat and fills noble souls with hope of honor. In this same way, a steed at Elis rushes out from the barriers and races over the track and at the decisive moment of gaining the victory spurs itself on and, rejecting failure, when it senses that its rival is gaining ground, stretches its flanks, and its competitive spirit is rankled to suffer defeat.

In the meantime, accustom the boy little by little to the study of literature if he shows interest, and by making use of cajoling verbal representations have him learn by heart many things which a still tender mind shrinks from and rejects unless they are coated with the charm of the Muses. For the path to virtue is arduous and it is an upward climb,[27] and the boy must be led, as it were, through brightly colored fields and the approach must be intertwined with leaves and roses and the labor must be disguised by various de-

255

260

265

270

275

280

285

Processit longe et comites matremque reliquit
Imprudens, ludo intenta attritisque lapillis,
Nec, revocata nisi, errorem vix denique sensit.
Adde quod et numerus multum modulataque pollet
290 Iunctura illabique animo atque illapsa teneri.
    Tu modo non tantum obscoenos, obprobria Phoebi,
Edico, procul, o, vates, procul inde relega,
Dignos qui scelerum persolvant sanguine poenas
Aut vivi terrae infossi aut vivi ignibus hausti,
295 Sed quoscunque olim nihil in commune referre
Videris et versus apinis implere sonoros.
Nam quae foeda viro iactura in principe plus est
Temporis aut tam nulla hominum reparabilis arte,
Cui centum hinc aures pateant licet indeque centum
300 Lernaeique modo geminet capita undique monstri,
Vix ideo fuerit rebus satis unus agendis,
Nec facile imbutus nugis queat inde revelli
Vanaque multiloquae deponere gaudia linguae?
    Nam, siquis putet utilibus conferre cavenda
305 Et velit oppositis rectum cognoscere ab ipsis,
Id tamen haud prius, exactis nisi mollibus annis,
Audeat, et longo compostis moribus usu;
Quamvis tunc quoque non ullis praesentibus aures
Inquinet. Ipse legat moneo quae multa relatu
310 Foeda, nec admisso violet male teste pudorem.
Nonne vides vitaque graves et moribus olim
Inter se licet alterno sermone remissos,
Non nisi contecto quaedam capite inque voluto
Dicere? tanta bonis servandi cura modesti est!
315 Aut nanque est fugienda omnis lascivia prorsus
Aut sic attingenda, velut qui castra sequutus

lightful distractions, as when an unmarried girl has wandered far off on a deserted shore and foolishly left her companions and mother behind, intent on playing and collecting smooth pebbles, and barely recognizes at last that she has wandered off when she is called back. At this age rhythm and melodic combinations of syllables are very effective and once insinuated into the mind remain there. 290

And you, teacher, I adjure you, banish far, far away not only obscene poets, a disgrace to Apollo, who deserve to pay the penalty for their crimes with their blood or be buried alive or consumed alive in the flames, but also all those who you see contribute nothing useful and fill their high-sounding verses with nonsense. For what is a more shameful waste of time for a prince or what vice is more irredeemable by any human skill? Even if he had on one side a hundred ears and on the other another hundred, and like the Lernean monster[28] could generate two heads for each one cut off, he would not be able to withstand them by himself, and it would not be easy, once he has imbibed this rubbish, to be torn away therefrom and put aside the vain pleasures of a garrulous tongue. 295 300

If anyone thinks he can compare things that should be avoided to things that are useful and wishes to discover moral rectitude from these two opposites, he should not attempt to do this until the impressionable years are at an end and the child's character has been formed through long practice. Though even then he should not befoul his ears in the presence of others. I advise that he read stories with indecent content by himself and not violate decency in front of another. Don't you see that when men of great sobriety and stern morals sometimes engage in relaxed conversation with one another, they say certain things only with their head covered and veiled? So much attention do good men give to the preservation of modesty! Either all licentious behavior must be avoided altogether or be indulged in like a soldier who comes upon 305 310 315

Hostica barbarici explorat catus agmina valli,
Militiaeque acri primis consuetus ab annis
Marcentes epulis passim luxuque fluentes,
320 Scortaque craterasque inter patriosque ululatus,
Ridet, et in longum mentem vovet hostibus illam.
      Forsitan et Satyros ponam qua parte requiris.
Utile nimirum est virtutem audire loquentes,
Si modo virtutem, non pessima quaeque loquuntur
325 Flagitia et foedant etiam bona siqua pudendis.
Nam qui multa negat linguae reticenda modestae
Et putat in solis crimen consistere rebus
Aut hominem populo ceu poma feracia testae
Inserit, ah, tenerae ne se mihi perditus auri
330 Insinuet pulchrumque pudens canis ore lacessat.
Nec gnarus naturae hominum, quae turpia visu
Abdidit amovitque oculis latitantia nostris,
Provida in exemplum atque imitamina gentibus aegris,
Nec Phoebi Aonidumque novem sortisque professae.
335 Nam quis non videat sacrum, coelestia dona,
Carmen et ex ipsis adytis quandoque profectum,
Non homini tribuisse deos, ne scilicet error
Devius et culpae scelerum praecone carerent,
Sed neu relligio divum contempta iaceret,
340 Neu virtus laudata parum, neu semina prima
Ignorata vicesque astrorum et legifer axis
Et quid quisque sibi aut patriae, quid debet amicis?
      Sed neque vere novo quot sese floribus arbor
Induat autumno refert, nisi mitia servat
345 Et totidem ramis suspendit poma gravatis,
Nec quantum tener egregia puer indole possit,
Si non, Socraticae mox inflammatus amore
Pallados, Aoniis non transfuga manserit antris

the enemy encampment and cautiously reconnoiters the barbarian lines behind the palisades, and as one accustomed from early years to the harshness of military life, he laughs at them idling away their time at banquets, indulging themselves in soft living in the midst of harlots and bowls of wine and barbaric yelps, and prays they will maintain this mentality for a long time to come.

Perhaps you will ask what role I assign to writers of satire. Without a doubt it is profitable to hear people talking about virtue, provided it is true virtue and they are not talking about the basest of human conduct and defile even good things with their indecent harangues. He who says that a man of temperate language need not refrain from saying many things and thinks that wrongdoing consists only in acting or sticks a man among the people like juicy fruit into a crock, ah! may such a scoundrel not instill his ideas into innocent ears and like a barking dog challenge decency and morality. Such a person does not know man's nature, which hid and removed repulsive things from our eyes, careful to provide sick mortals with good examples for our imitation, and he is not aware of Apollo and the nine Muses and the priestess who gave oracular responses. For who does not see that sacred song, a gift from heaven, which once emanated from the innermost part of the temple, was not given to men by the gods so that devious error and wrongdoing would not lack someone to publicize their crimes, but so that respect for the gods would not be held in contempt and virtue would not go uncommended, and so that there would not be ignorance of the first seeds of things and the movements of the stars and the majesty of the heavens and the duties everyone owes to himself or his native land, and his friends?

But it doesn't matter how many flowers adorn the tree in spring if in autumn it does not produce an equal amount of sweet fruit on its fruit-laden branches, nor does it matter how gifted a young man may be if later he is not enflamed with the love of Socratic wisdom and does not spend a good part of his youth in the grot-

Aetatis partem haud minimam, vetera acta priorum
350 Evolvens vitamque educens inde futuram.
Quoque modo servet laudatum ad cuncta decorum —
Nec facilis servare labor, nisi deligis artem
Vivendi finemque animo proponis habendum —
Quoque suos actus signo quasi dirigat omnes,
355 Virtutis pulchrae memor atque unius honesti,
Ne velut Ionio deprensus nocte silenti,
Ignarus coeli atque aurae, dum dextera laevis
Perturbat, longo huc fluctu iactatus et illuc
Actus eat pelago et saevis ludibria ventis,
360 Donec inhaerentem scopuli eccepere Ceraunei,
Frustra iam implorantem undas et fata querentem
Seque accusantem, ah miserum! et delicta fatentem.
　　　At vitae instituat quam quis genus, ante necesse est
Ingeniumque capax pueri penitusque videre
365 Naturam et quales animorum in singula vires,
Quid iam tum eximie, quid non feliciter audet.
Hic salibus melior blandis, vitae ille severae,
Ambitione alius magis applausuque Quiritum
Temptatur studioque aurae popularis inani.
370 Nonne vides ille ut galeas et splendida tantum
Tractet tela manu, placidam probet ille quietem,
Ille nihil non dissimulet parvosque sodales
Iam tum fallat, hic ingenue putet omnia agenda,
Indignans vicisse, palam nisi vicerit hostem
375 Congressus campoque audax concurrerit aequo?
Has leges fatale animis venientibus astrum
Imposuit coelique ascendens hora potentis,
Tempore quo primum gravidae pigra pondera matris
Formamus miseri atque alto descendere Olympo
380 Cogimur, humanae passuri incommoda vitae.

toes of the Muses, turning over in his mind the deeds of men of 350
old and drawing from them the goals of his future life. He will
reflect on how he will preserve honor in all circumstances — no
easy task unless you choose a definite way of life and propose a
fixed goal — and to what star he will direct, as it were, all his ac- 355
tions, mindful only of noble virtue and honor, lest, like one caught
in the Ionian sea[29] in the silent night, unfamiliar with the heavens
and the winds, confusing east and west, he be tossed about hither
and yon in the endless storm and be driven over the sea, a play- 360
thing of the raging winds, until he crashes against the Ceraunian
reefs,[30] imploring the waves in vain and lamenting his fate and ac-
cusing himself — ah wretched creature! and confessing his crimes.

Before deciding the kind of life for which the boy is suited, the
tutor must know his capabilities and be thoroughly familiar with 365
his character and his particular strengths, what things he under-
takes with exceptional success and what he attempts unsuccess-
fully. One excels in clever witticisms, another is of a more severe
character, and yet another is tempted by ambition and the ap-
plause of the crowd and the empty desire for popular approval. Do 370
you not notice how one only handles helmets and flashing swords,
another prefers peaceful quiet; another never reveals his true feel-
ings and is already at work deceiving his young companions; an-
other thinks that everything should be done honorably and resents 375
winning unless he has defeated his enemy openly and boldly in a
fair contest? These laws were imposed on souls at their entrance
into life by their fatal star when it is in the ascendant at the mo-
ment of our birth, when we miserable creatures first constitute a
heavy burden to our pregnant mother and are forced to come 380
down from high Olympus to endure the tribulations of human
life.

373

Ergo, ubi naturam penitus perspexeris omnem
Ingenitasque artes pueri et clinamina prima,
Quamvis multa magis fortasse aliena placebunt,
Nativis tamen insistendum dotibus atque
385 Audendum nihil omnino pugnante Minerva.
Quippe sequi id demum insipere est, quodcunque nequimus
Assequi et egregia nostrum cum laude tueri.
Nam quid in Isthmiaco diversum agitare iuvencos
Pulvere et affusae risum praebere coronae
390 Aut terram Argei generosis scindere alumnis?
Siqua tamen vitiosa—ferunt nam multa novales
Ipsae etiam vitiosa, nec est teres undique quicquam—
Siqua igitur vitiosa, omni de pectore cura
Depellenda procul vel, si minus id licet omne,
395 Flectenda in melius, rerum discrimine parvo
Saepe malis dirimente brevi bona calle propinqua,
Pleraque vivendo minuenda interque legenda,
Ante tamen vires mora quam exitiosa diesque
Afferat et fibras penetret cacoethes in imas
400 Mortiferum, agricolae cura monstrante sagaci,
Agricolae, qui primum olim lactentibus herbis
Lappas et lolium atque infelices paliuros
Persequitur sterilemque vetat succrescere sylvam,
Assiduus terram rastris operaque fatigans
405 Foeminea. It magnum latis longo ordine campis
Agmen et incurvum solatur voce laborem,
At procul aspiciens credit pecus ire viator.
Imprimis sedandae hyemes quasi totaque mentis
Tempestas motusque omnes sub signa vocandi
410 Constanti ratione et certa lege domandi,
Ne, velut effuso sessore equa trima, vagati
Longius abiiciant rerum finemque modumque
Transversumque ferant hominem, nec dicta parati

Therefore when you have fully perceived the nature and the in-
born qualities of the boy and his first inclinations, although per-
haps many other qualities will please you more, you must concen-   385
trate your attention on his native gifts and not venture upon
anything else against the boy's natural bent. In the end it is fool-
ishness to follow after something we cannot attain and regard as
our own with high praise. For it is no different than driving young   390
bulls in the Isthmian dust[31] and arousing the laughter of the spec-
tators, or cleaving the soil in Argos with thoroughbred foals. If,
however, some moral defects are present — for even newly plowed
fields contain many imperfections and nothing is entirely perfect
— if, as I say, some moral defects exist, take care that they be   395
driven far from his heart, or if they cannot be completely eradi-
cated, that they be changed for the better, for sometimes a tiny
line or a narrow path divides the good from the bad, and as the
child grows up, many things have to be pulled out and extirpated
before a fatal delay lends them strength and a deadly incurable   400
disease penetrates into his inner fiber. The sagacious remedy of
the farmer is instructive, who, when the sap is first flowing in the
plants, roots out the weeds, darnel and harmful thorns and does
not allow sterile brushwood to invade the crops, and indefatigably   405
batters the earth with a drag hoe with help from women workers.
A long line of people in a body moves through the wide field and
they console their backbreaking labor with singing, but a traveler
looking on from a distance thinks it is a flock of sheep.

Above all, outbursts of anger must be quelled, which in a man-
ner of speaking are like a storm that envelops the whole mind, and   410
all the emotions must be brought under control through the con-
stant exercise of reason and subdued according to fixed rules lest,
as when a three-year-old mare throws off the rider, they wander
off into the distance and disregard all bounds and restraints and

Eccipere et iussas trocleis intendere funes
415 Nec nati dare, natura prohibente recurva,
Providaque e summa puppi torquere guberna,
Sed pecudum fugere atque sequi nimis omnia ritu
Inconsulte, incomposite, nec pectora tantum
Atque intus turbare animum, verum extima saepe
420 Membra quoque ac vocem et vultus mutare priores.
Quod nisi commoti dominatrix certa furoris
Adsit et excussos ratio pulcherrima frenos
Ore remordere ac iussis parere lupatis
Cogat, eant nulla in praeceps tardante ruina
425 Perque enses et tela immissosque urbibus ignes,
Non secus atque olim noto rectore soluti
Flammiferi Phaetontis equi, cum foedera rerum
Triste chaos veteremque expavit machina acervum
Audaci culpa unius votoque protervo,
430 Respexitque suum, Phlegrae post fulmina, telum
Iuppiter et missis solvit pater ignibus ignes.
    Nam, ceu corporis in membris sua munera cuique
Sunt data, nec partes oculi pedis aut oculorum
Bracchia, non humeri poscunt pulmonis anheli,
435 Sed contenta bonis naturae singula degunt,
Sic, animi quoniam varia est vis atque potestas,
Una etenim imperio, geminae parere tributae ,
Cuique suae usurpandae artes, nec sorte movendum
Decretoque Iovis praescripta et lege Promethei.
440 Nam perhibent, perfecta hominis compage, Prometheum
Continuo admisisse deos ipsumque Tonantem
Regali luxu acceptos epulisque paratis.
Forte aderant triplices praestanti aetate sorores,
Cura quibus mensas struere et dare brutia nigra.
445 Sed patria Logus hanc olim pietate receptam

carry a man off course. They are neither willing to take orders and   415
tighten the ropes on the windlasses, as ordered, nor were they
born to give orders, since their deformed nature impedes them,
and to guide the rudder competently at the stern of the ship, but
like a herd of sheep they run away and follow everything in a
thoughtless and disorderly manner and not only throw their hearts   420
and minds into confusion, but often alter their external appear-
ance and voice and usual facial expression. If the ruling force of
noble reason is not present to control this aroused frenzy and force
it to take between its teeth the bit that has been shaken off and to
submit to the jagged-toothed bit, they will run headlong to their   425
destruction with nothing to stop them, through swords and weap-
ons and fires set to cities, just as the fiery horses of Phaethon[32]
once did when they were loosed from their usual master when the
fabric of the universe stood in fear of gloomy chaos and primitive
confusion because of the criminal daring and reckless desire of one   430
person, and Jupiter looked around and saw his weapon, which he
had previously used at Phlegra,[33] and hurling his fiery thunder-
bolts, put out the fire.

For just as each member of the body was given its role to per-
form,[34] so that the eyes do not ask for the function of the foot or
the arms for that of the eyes, and the shoulders do not ask for that   435
of the gasping lungs, but each is happy with fulfilling its own task,
so with the soul, which has various capacities and powers. One is
given full command and the other two must lend obedience. Each
fulfills its own function and must not deviate from its assigned lot
or from the decree of Jupiter or the law prescribed by Prometheus.   440
For they say that Prometheus, after forming man, immediately
invited the gods and Jupiter himself to a banquet of regal opu-
lence. It happened that three sisters in the flower of youth were
present who were charged with setting the table and serving dark   445
beer.[35] But Reason had once given shelter to one of them with
paternal affection and had accustomed her to partake of divine

Ambrosiae assuerat divinae et nectaris haustu,
Illas lacte ferae Scythicis aluere sub antris.
Hic opere eximie laudato atque arte magistra,
'Immo age,' coelicolum pater 'has quoque, docte Prometheu,
450 Adiice' ait, 'nec te labor aut cura ulla retardet,
Quin opus egregium atque aevum mirabile in omne
Tergeminis his virginibus quasi civibus ornes.
Sed, ne forte duae — neque enim leve pectoris hausti
Crimen habent referuntque Estetea fronte parentem —
455 Omnem animis molem exturbent, praecordia subter
Ponito ventorumque dato regione secunda
Ferre vices magni praeclaro imitamine mundi.
Hanc autem, motos componere sola tumultus
Quae sciat et placida late regere omnia pace,
460 Mandatricem operum media procul arce locato.'
Commento applausere dei, imprimisque Prometheus —
Sensit enim quantum aeternis immane caduca
Concedant — orat precibus rata dicta manere.
    Ergo omni exercendae opera et sua cuique facultas
465 Agnoscenda usu et rerum assuetudine certa.
Nanque dabunt animos paulatim infractaque iusso
Colla iugo dominamque ediscent ferre volentes;
Frena tamen retinenda manu pressaeque catenae.
Nam neque sessor equo, longa licet arte manuque
470 Edomito, totas ideo concedit habenas,
Sed gressus regit et stimulis saepe acribus urget
Exploratque fidem et cogit meminisse magistrum.
Nam saepe insurgunt domitae et solito arma capescunt
Acrius, extremum annixae quasi corpore venae
475 Aut cum deficiente alimento flamma repente
Emicuit luce et subita tectum omne replevit.
Hoc ubi, dura magis contendere vincla memento

ambrosia and nectar, while the other two had been nursed by wild beasts in Scythian caves. At this point the father of the gods, after lavishing great praise on Prometheus's handiwork and masterful art, said, "Come now, learned Prometheus, add these also to your 450 accomplishments, and spare no labor or care in beautifying your splendid creation, a marvel for all ages to come, with these three young women as fellow citizens. But in the case of the other two—for they are liable to no small reproach and they bear a re- 455 semblance to their father Aisthesis in their countenance—lest they disturb the entire soul by their haughty airs, place them un- der the diaphragm and allow them to perform the function of the winds in a less important part of the body, in imitation of the great universe. The first of them, however, who is the only one 460 who knows how to calm disturbances and to govern everything peacefully, place far away in the middle of the citadel as the one who issues commands about what must be done." The gods ap- plauded the proposal, Prometheus most of all—for he knew how infinitely inferior transitory things are to eternal—begged that these words be approved.

Therefore each faculty must be put to its own proper use 465 through repeated practice. Little by little the two sisters will be- come docile and will learn to bend their necks under the yoke and willingly accept their mistress, but the bridle must be held fast and restraints enforced. For the rider does not totally relax the reins 470 even with a horse that has been trained by long skill and experi- ence, but he controls his pace and often urges him on with sharp goading and tests his obedience and makes it remember who is master. Often the sisters, though subdued, rise up and take up arms more fiercely than usual, exerting themselves to the full, 475 like veins in the body, or as a flame when the fuel is running out suddenly makes a bright flicker and fills the house with light. When this happens, remember to draw the harsh reins tighter

Spemque resistendi eripere et compellere primis
Impetibus veniam orare erroremque fateri,
480 Dum servata sequi carae vestigia tandem
Assuescunt dominae et mandata capescere aventes.
    Praecipue fugienda procul memorantia culpae
Omnis et indecorum turpes fomenta ministri,
Nec quisquam sine delectu sine iudice certo
485 Convictu temere cari admittendus alumni.
Ipse autem teneris iam tum mihi laetus ab annis
Mirari senium et parere monentibus ultro
Aetatemque rudem fulcire aetate magistra
Ac similem quandoque deos sibi poscere mentem.
490 Nunc multos blande affari atque incessere castis
Interdum salibus, modo respondere benigne
Omnibus et nullum non tempore laedere dicto.
Nam neque compellare isdem sermonibus omnes,
Sed bello super atque armis rogitare magistros
495 Bellandi, nautas super aequore, denique laetos
Sementum de messe, canes nutrire paratos
De canibus, peregre venientes quae loca et urbes,
Quos fluvios, quid quisque ignoto viderit orbe,
Alteriusque memor facti dictique probator
500 Raro nec ingenue de se nisi nota profari,
Quamvis expositae cutis idem animique reposti
Et blando illustris famae perculsus amore,
Praeferat obscuris Pelidae funera canis
Praereptamque sibi laudem gemat acta parentis,
505 Degener haud propria regni virtute parati.
    Interea servare vicem atque alterna modestus
Alloquia et coeptis finem quoque ponere verbis
Pluraque narratis audire et condita habere
Pectore, nec linguae temere indulgere volucri

and to snatch away any hope of resistance and compel them to ask   480
pardon for their previous onslaught and confess their error until
they finally become accustomed to follow the good example of
their dear mistress and accept her commands willingly.

Anything that might call to mind some wrongdoing must be
sedulously avoided as well as servants guilty of disgraceful behav-
ior, who are an instigation to shameful actions, and no one should   485
be rashly admitted to close association with the pupil without
careful choice and reliable advice. The boy himself in my opinion
should have respect for old age from his earliest years and willingly
listen to advice and support his inexperienced youth with the wis-
dom of a man of more mature years, and ask the gods to grant   490
him a similar wisdom one day. Now he should be taught how to
address others politely and sometimes indulge in harmless witti-
cisms, to answer in a friendly manner to all and not to give offense
by any untimely words. He should not address everyone in the
same manner, but concerning war and armor he should ask ques-   495
tions of those expert in the art of war, sailors concerning the sea;
of those who are successful in the sowing of crops he will ask
about harvests, from experts in the raising of dogs he will ask
about dogs, of those who travel abroad he will ask what places and
cities, what rivers they saw and about their adventures in foreign
lands. He should remember other people's deeds and approve of   500
their words but of himself he will speak rarely and not too can-
didly, and then only well-known facts. Although his exterior lies
open to people's gaze, his feelings should remain hidden; and over-
whelmed by the cogent desire for glorious renown, he should pre-
fer the early death of Achilles to an obscure old age and regret that   505
the famous deeds of his parent have robbed him of praise and feel
unworthy of a kingdom not acquired through his own prowess.

He should await his turn in conversations and modestly allow
others to speak, and put an end to his own words and listen to the

510 Aut studio respondendi pellectus inani
    Denudare palam melius quae multa latebant.
    Multum adeo placidae comis pellacia vitae
    Blandaque personae vox maiestate retenta
    Saepe movent, nec vero alia magis arte tot annos
515 Vidimus — infandum — duro servire tyranno
    Italiam et pelagi tabo freta marcida Etrusci
    Volvendisque ducum miserandae stragis acervis.
    Et dabat occultae documenta haud mollia mentis
    Ille quidem toto longinqui tempore regni,
520 Sed quotus alterius melior sibi quisque periclo est?
    Quo magis est reputandum animo, quae denique recti
    Ipsius vis, tanta potest ubi fucus inanis
    Tantum umbra sibi virtutis promittere vana
    Atque animis hominum sese insinuare repostis.
525 Quod siquis nihil ad speciem quod spectet honesti
    Negligat atque decens nulla non parte requirat,
    In motu quoque non minimum gestuque virili
    Ponet et indignos removebit corpore comptus
    Illecebrasque supervacuas et Gange petitam
530 Luxurie stactam imbellem costique liquores,
    Iudice vix teneris mare non prohibenda puellis.
    Nam quid malobrocho et myrrha perfusus olenti
    Vir praestare queat quique emollire venenis
    Corpus et Ispanae pellem de more maritae
535 Quaerat? Amat propria spectari laude virilis
    Forma, nec Assyrium quam se magis optat olere.
        Est etiam pars vestitus non ultima habenda,
    Non boream modo uti defendat iniquaque flagra
    Corporibus dubiasque vices mutabilis anni,
540 Sed quia non aliter fortunae oculisque tuentum
    Fit satis, et tanta maiestas regia dote
    Prodita plebeo vilis sordescit amictu.

stories told and keep them stored away in his heart, and he must   510
not give free rein to a loose tongue or be tempted to give glib an-
swers and openly reveal many things that would have better re-
mained hidden. The sweet seduction of a peaceful life and per-
suasive speech forcibly detained by a monarch often have great
influence, and we have seen that in no other way — I shrink from   515
saying it — Italy was the slave for many years of a cruel tyrant[36] and
the waters of the Tyrrhenian Sea were fetid with putrid matter
and heaps of washed up corpses of leaders, victims of a horri-
ble slaughter. And during the entire time of his long reign he   520
gave forceful examples of his secret purpose, but how few are there
who become better through the danger to which another is ex-
posed? All the more must one consider how great is the power of
moral rectitude itself when empty hypocrisy can promise so much
merely through false shadows of virtue and insinuate itself deeply   525
into men's minds. But if anyone neglects nothing that befits the
outward appearance of an honorable man and on every occasion
strives after what is appropriate, he will give great importance also
to his deportment and his manly gestures and will reject all adorn-
ment not worthy of his character and superfluous frills and un-   530
manly myrrh and nard, which in male judgment may scarcely be
allowed to delicate young girls. For what can we expect of a man
drenched with aromatic myrrh, who wishes to enervate his body
with poisons and have skin like a Spanish doña? Manly beauty   535
finds pleasure in being admired for its own excellence and a real
man prefers to smell more like himself than like an Assyrian.

The importance of dress should not be underestimated, not
only to ward off the cruel lashings of the North wind from our
bodies and the uncertain phases of the changing seasons, but also   540
because in no other way is it possible to satisfy one's high position
and the eyes of the onlookers, and once a king has divested him-

Nam, qui iudicium de se et communia vota
Negligit aut metui potius quam quaerit amari,
545 Demens, nec videt imperium popularibus auris
Praecipue et solido vulgi constare favore —
Qualis erat modo qui regni non ante ruinam
Sensit, quam subitis fractus successibus hostis
Privato caput exilio rex obtulit ultro —
550 Aut nescit contempta semel vanescere regna
Fortunamque quati, male maiestate soluta,
Nec vero ratione alia lita templa metallo
Quaesitaeque olim ducibus sellaeque rotaeque
Tot pictae, tot palmatae sceptrique superbum
555 Insigne et collo pendentes divite gemmae.
      Sed modus optimus in rebus: tantum extera desit
Seu levitas seu luxuria advectusque peregre
Ornatus novitasque animo non digna modesto.
Nam cytharae cantusque atque enervantia mentem
560 Instrumenta lyrae et priscis quoque tibia probro,
Illa quidem mensis interdum adhibenda potentum
Virtutesque virum memorandae et splendida facta,
Sed non attingenda etiam, aut sine testibus ullis
Attingenda domi, nec honor quaerendus ab illis,
565 Sed requies curae brevis ingenioque levamen.
Sed neque sub crotalo tenerum latus arte movere
Regnator meus et morum quandoque futurus
Arbiter Aethiopum discat saltare puellas
Atque Agarena sequi molles ad tympana motus,
570 Aetatis licet obprobrio corrupta reclamet
Nobilitas choreasque assueti plaudere reges.
      Nam quid iam miseri non vidimus, impius ex quo
Havarus et Gotthis Herulus permixtus et Unnis
Et rabies Longobarda et Germanicus Albis
575 Irrupit Latio, fatisque exercita tandem

self of his regal splendor he becomes mean and squalid in plebeian garb. For he who neglects public opinion of himself and the general wishes of the people or seeks to be feared rather than loved[37]   545 is insane, and does not see that dominion consists chiefly of popular favor and the solid support of the common people. This was illustrated recently by the king who only realized this after the destruction of his kingdom. Crushed by the sudden successes of his enemy, he offered voluntarily to go into exile as a private citi-   550 zen.[38] Such a man does not understand that when his majestic grandeur has come to an end, his hated rule vanishes with it and his fortune is shaken. For no other reason were churches covered with gold and specially painted chairs and wheels were sought af-   555 ter, and togas embroidered with palm leaves and the proud symbol of the scepter and gems that hung around the necks of the rich.

But moderation is best in all things. External frivolity or luxury or adornment imported from far-off places or novelty is unworthy of a modest mind. The cithara and song and the lyre, which ener-   560 vates the mind, and the flute, which was regarded with suspicion in antiquity, are sometimes employed at the tables of the mighty and the virtues and splendid deeds of heroes are narrated, but one must not take up these instruments or play them at home with no   565 one present, nor should one seek honor from them but only brief respite from cares and as a solace to the spirit. But the ruler and future arbiter of morals I envisage should not learn how to sway his hips and dance skillfully to the accompaniment of castanets like Aethiopian damsels or follow the sensual rhythms of Saracen   570 drums, although the nobility of our day, corrupted by scandalous fashions, protest against constraints, and kings applaud round dances.

What have we miserable mortals not witnessed since the impious Avars[39] and the Herulians,[40] mixed in with the Goths[41] and the Huns[42] and the wild Lombards[43] and Germans from the   575 Elbe, rushed into Latium and in the end, beleaguered by fate,

Roma sacerdotum patuit miseranda rapinis,
Perque nefas divisa ereptaque venditaque auro
Imperia et partes armis variantibus ortae,
Atque animi, invidia inflammati odiisque suorum,
580 Externas sibi quaerere opes peregrinaque malle
Regna pati quam desertis concedere fractos
Partibus et fastus gentilis ferre tyranni.
Hinc veluti sordes tota rate plurimaque hausti
Aequoris illuvies imum petit atque suopte
585 Sentinam facit ingenio, sic undique culpae
Contractae transversum animos egere priores
Virtutesque mares corrupit mollior hospes
Atque nefas fasque impune et sacra versa profanis.
      Tantum autem culpasse omnes mirabile non est
590 Nequitiam Venerisque malos damnasse furores.
Nam neque deiiciat quod nos pecudum atque ferarum
Naturae quicquam magis aut penetralibus imis
Excutiens aeque et mentem de sede revellens,
Nec tot confluxere aegris mala gentibus unde
595 Atque neces atque exilia atque incendia saepe
Regnorum, et simul Europae funesta Asiaeque
Arma decennali ducentia quaeque ruina,
Heu, male speratis Lacedaemoniis hymeneis.
Nam quid ego, veterum repetens exempla, revolvam
600 Tarquinios Appique nefas immane furentis
Aut infelicis Messenae tristia bella
Virtutesque tot egregias bellique domique
Demetri et rarum divinae mentis acumen
Spurcicia miseraeque sepulta libidine vitae?
605 Quid Scyllas, quid Medeas, quid Gnosida turpem,
Cum deserta etiam post tanto Ispania bellis
Monstret adhuc fera foemineae monumenta rapinae,

wretched Rome was plundered by priests, and through heinous
wickedness high offices were divided up and seized and sold for
gold, and parties sprang up through the various fluctuations of
war, and minds enflamed with envy and hatred for their own kind   580
sought external support and preferred to suffer foreign domination
rather than surrender to the parties they had deserted and suffer
the arrogance of a local tyrant. As a result, just as filth floods the
whole ship and the muck of the sea water that has been let in goes   585
to the bottom and turns into bilgewater, so guilt contracted from
various sources drove previous animosities in the opposite direc-
tion and a more effeminate guest corrupted masculine virtues and
wrong turned into right and the sacred into the profane with im-
punity.

It is no wonder that everyone has denounced depravity and   590
condemned the harmful madness of Venus. For there is nothing
that debases us more to the nature of animals and wild beasts or
drives us from the innermost shrines of the gods and tears our
mind from its dwelling place, nor have so many evils come together 595
to afflict sick mortals, whence come murders and exile and the fi-
ery destruction of kingdoms and deadly hostilities between Eu-
rope and Asia[44] that led to a tragic ten-year war, alas! because of a
sinfully desired Spartan wedding. Why need I revert to ancient   600
examples, to the Tarquins[45] and the horrible crime of the mad Ap-
pius[46] or the disastrous wars over Messene,[47] the outstanding feats
of Demetrius[48] in war and peace and the rare acumen of his divine
intelligence, buried by the foul lust of a miserable life? Why   605
should I mention Scylla or Medea or the shameful maiden of
Knossos,[49] since even today Spain, ravaged by wars, still testifies to
the cruel consequences of a kidnapped woman,[50] when the misfor-

387

Cum Malatestarum pateant mala, cum tua, Guido
Infelix, cum Manfredi miserandus iniqui
610 Exitus et furiis Ianarum exercitus orbis
Atque huc atque illuc confusaque saecla ruina?
    Atque ideo puerum a coetu et muliebribus arcent
Illecebris residesque avertunt pectore curas
Aut duro illum venatu castoque labore
615 Sylvarum exercentes aut insultibus acris
Aemathii, non Gnosiaca contendere cornu
Arte rudem visamque procul fixisse volucrem,
Non torquere manu validam iuveniliter hastam
Aclidaque intorto stridentem aptare flagello.
620 Saepe etiam saltu quatiunt durantque palaestra
Actaea pugnaeque assuescunt membra futurae,
Sive lacessere opus sive hostem exire necesse.
Tum boream aestivosque docent contemnere soles
Sub Iove Spartanumque Eurotam ferre decembri,
625 Nec sudore famem nisi nec nisi pulvere somnos
Velle pati, et iam tunc invento pascere frugi
Naturam modicis contentam et sponte paratis.
    Atque haec cuncta puer primis mihi regius annis
Audeat egregiamque animi vim suscitet usu
630 Virtutemque ultro atque instantes ferre labores.
Nam, quamvis sponte ingenii generosus honestum
Appetit agnoscitque omnis, tamen aurea si non
Accedit doctrina et promovet insita cultus,
Aegrescit praeclara habitu natura maligno
635 Paulatim, culpaeque premunt bene pectora nata
Atque omnem captum eripiunt, ceu febre gravatus
Cum iacet et venis iam se haud capit igneus ardor,
Ille tamen panacenque bonam Phoebeaque vina
Aversus fugit et sensu contraria poscit

tunes of the Malatesta family[51] are plainly evident, and yours, poor 610
Guido,[52] and the pitiful end of the treacherous Manfredi[53] and the
fury of the two Joans[54] that shook the world from its founda-
tions?

And therefore they keep the boy away from crowds and the
enticements of women and remove languid cares from his mind,
either training him in the rugged discipline of the hunt and the 615
chaste hardship of the woods, getting him used to the leaping up
of the Macedonian hound, but not to compete with the Cretan
bow while he has not yet received instruction in that skill, and to
shoot at birds in the distance, not to hurl the sturdy spear while
still a young boy or fit the whirring javelin to the twisted thong. 620
Often too they train the boy in jumping and harden him in the
Attic palaestra and accustom his limbs for future fighting, whether
it be necessary to challenge or escape the enemy. Then they teach
him to withstand the north wind and the summer heat and to 625
swim the Spartan Eurotas river in December, and to surrender to
hunger only after great exertions and to sleep only when exhausted
and to nourish himself with whatever he finds and to be satisfied
with simple fare prepared by himself.

All these things the prince should undertake in his early years 630
and he should stimulate this exceptional manly capacity by prac-
tice and be able to support pressing hardships. For even if every
young man of good breeding spontaneously strives after virtue,
nevertheless, if it is not accompanied by golden learning, which
takes root in him and advances his education, little by little his 635
outstanding nature becomes sick through bad habit, and moral
defects oppress his wellborn character and rob him of all his po-
tentialities, as when one stricken with fever is confined to bed, and
the veins cannot contain the fiery heat. But he refuses beneficial

640 Corrupto miser atque odit meliora loquutos.
　　Nec tibi sit solum curae exercere, sed una
　　Delige quos socios studiorum adiungere possis
　　Aequales, quos monstratis puer artibus ante
　　Ire velit contraque obniti intentius acer.
645 Quin etiam pharetraeque leves atque aurea frena
　　Victori statuenda probrosaque praemia victo,
　　Ut quem verus honor nondum eccitat, eccitet aeger
　　Hunc dolor alteriusque humeris splendentia dona,
　　Acceptamque notam reputans secum, aggravet ipse
650 Dedecus et segnem lacrimis sese increpet ultro
　　Incendatque pudore animos et suscitet ira:
　　Qualis, Cecropii Eridani aut prope curva fluenta
　　Ludentis totiensque Nedae vada laeta plicantis,
　　Armento pulsus patrio regnisque iuvencus
655 Moeret inexhaustum exilia et rivalis amari
　　Successus, plagarumque immemor atque laboris
　　Unam secum ignominiam amissosque hymeneos
　　Mente agitat, quernoque obnixus cornua trunco
　　Iam tum hostem vocat in pugnam Martemque lacessit,
660 Ipsam animam dare iam pulchra pro laude paratus.
　　　　Quod siquando ducem—neque enim non tristibus armis
　　Miscendus iam tum et vallum assuescendus amare—
　　Ergo ducem emissis siquando praeficis alis
　　Atque inimica iubes duro quatere oppida bello,
665 Non illum magno Annibali aut oppone Gilippo,
　　Nec sine pugnacem primis incessere Thracam
　　Auspiciis. Lybiae manus et magis apta vehendis
　　Mercibus Aegypto Venetum est caedenda iuventus,
　　Paulatimque augendi animi et quasi Sarmata falco
670 Ducendus, superando facillima quaeque, gradatim.
　　Nam facile exultantem animum compescere rerum
　　Notitia docilique accessu fertilis aevi,

medicine and the wine Asclepius[55] prescribes and no longer in his   640
right senses the poor man asks for what will harm him and hates
those who give better advice.

It is not only your duty to look after him, but choose compan-
ions of his same age to compete with him in his activities, whom   645
he will wish to excel in the skills that he has learned. You must
award light quivers and golden bridles to the victor and booby
prizes to the loser so that if he is not yet motivated to win true
honors, the embarrassment will spur him on, and when he sees
the gifts gleaming on another's shoulders, reflecting on the dis-   650
grace he has suffered, he himself will exaggerate the dishonor and
will reproach himself with tears for his sluggishness, and shame
and anger will rouse his spirits — just as the young bull, near the
winding stream of the Eridanus[56] in Attica[57] and the Neda,[58]
which delights in its meandering waters, driven from his master's   655
herd, mourns indefatigably his exile and the success of his bitter
rival, and unmindful of its wounds and fatigues thinks only of its
disgrace and its defeat in finding a mate and thrusts its horns
against the trunk of an oak tree and again calls to his rival and
challenges him to a warring battle, ready to give up his life for such   660
a beautiful reward.

But if ever — for even at that age he must be involved in grim
warfare and must have a liking for the earthworks — if ever, as I
say, you put him in charge of squadrons sent out on a mission and
order him to batter the walls of some enemy town in a ruthless
war, do not set him against the great Hannibal or Gylippus[59] or   665
allow him to attack the fierce Thracians in his initial campaigns.
Better that Libyan troops and Venetian youth, more suited for
transporting merchandise from Egypt, be cut down, and that his
courage be increased gradually and that he be trained like a Sar-
matian falcon by easy stages, surmounting tasks that give no diffi-   670

Et quantum humanis hera possit Adrastea rebus,
Nec quisquam audax est adeo, praesentia quem non
675 Concutiant horrenda et durae mortis imago,
Ante oculos faciem exertantis putridaque ora
Sanguine et huic aurae supremum Acherunta minantis.
Nam contemnere opes superum et Iovis acta lacertis
Fulmina, nec scopuli venientem horrere ruinam,
680 Et nulla ratione enses ruere inter et ignem,
Desipere id demum, quamvis plerumque videmus
Ante tubam tales et adhuc procul hoste manente
Turpia vicino foede dare terga periclo,
Nec sufferre oculis venientem cernere contra.
685 Ergo ubi regrediendum homini, quoque usque videndum,
Haud quia non cuicunque animanti optabile dulcem
Conservasse animam et multis quoque saepe tributum
Eximiae laudi fato cessisse ruenti,
Nec posuisse leves rumores ante salutem,
690 Sed quod multa dies varius volvendaque rerum
Fert series, cum seu patriae poscente iuvandae
Officio seu tutandorum forte suorum
Vitandaeve notae, turpe est sibi parcere forti
Et vitam egregio non impendisse decoro.

culty. For it is easy to restrain an enthusiastic spirit by practical experience and the wisdom of mature years, and to teach him how much power the goddess Nemesis[60] has in human affairs. And no one is so reckless as not to be shaken by the terrible presence and 675 image of pitiless death, which thrusts its face and its mouth, dripping with putrefied blood, before our eyes, threatening this world with the doom of Acheron.[61] It is foolish to disregard the power of the gods and the thunderbolts hurled by Jupiter's arm, or not to 680 shudder before the imminent collapse of a projecting rock, and to rush heedlessly into the fires of war, although we often see certain people, before the bugle is blown, while the enemy are still at a distance, basely turn tail when the enemy draws near, who cannot bear looking at them as they approach. Therefore when one must 685 retreat, one should carefully consider how far, not that it is unnatural to save one's life — in fact, some have even been praised for yielding to the onslaught of fate and not giving more importance to calumny than to their own lives.[62] But because the succession of 690 days and the revolving sequence of events bring many alternations of fortune, whether duty demands that we aid our country or it chances that we must protect our own kin or avoid disgrace, then it is a base thing for a brave man not to sacrifice his life to attain illustrious renown.

APPENDIX
TWO LETTERS OF MARULLUS

: I :

Michael Marull(us) Ioanni Pico suo salutem.

1 Magna me voluptate affecerunt litterae tuae, nam post discessum tuum ex Urbe, nihil ad <nos de> te non suspectum, nihil omnino <non> periculosum afferebatur. Accedebat summa inimicorum malignitas, maxima potentia, quae etiam tutissima quaeque maxime faciebant timenda. Quo magis libet mirari magnitudinem animi tui, qui, tot difficultatibus circumventus, tot periculis, ita tuam dignitatem, ita auctoritatem tutatus es, quasi veteranus aliquis et in excipiendis cavendisque Fortunae ictibus egregie artifex, non quasi adolescens ab ineunte aetate in otio isto et litteraria, ut ita dicam, umbra versatus. Sed haec quo minus abs te expectabantur, hoc certe et admirabiliora et iocundiora sunt nobis, ut interdum libeat exclamare Christianum illud: Felix culpa, quae tantum meruit redemptorem! Nisi enim inimicitiae istae intercessissent, litteras tuas sciremus sane, ut scimus; constantiam, animi magnitudinem omnino nesciremus. Sed de his hactenus.

2 Quod vero ad epigramma pertinet, quo te dicis fraudatum, etsi vehementer doleo desiderari abs te aliquod officium meum, cui pro summa in me humanitate et benivolentia nihil est quod non debeo, tamen delectat nescio quomodo requisitio ista et frequens

APPENDIX
TWO LETTERS OF MARULLUS

: I :

Michael Marullus to his good friend Giovanni Pico, greetings.

Your letter gave me great delight, for after your departure from 1
Rome no news concerning you was communicated to me that was
not suspect, nothing at all that was not dangerous. Added to that
was the extraordinary malice of your enemies and their immense
power, which caused even the most innocent matters greatly to be
feared. Hence it is all the more pleasant to admire your greatness
of spirit, since, beset by so many difficulties and so many perils,
you defended your dignity and authority like a veteran soldier and
showed extraordinary skill in accepting and averting the blows of
fortune, not like a young man engaged from your earliest years in
leisurely pursuits and the shelter of letters, so to speak. But the
less we expected these things of you, the more worthy of admira-
tion and gratification they are to us, so that at times we are in-
clined to utter that Christian saying, "O happy fault, which gained
for us so great a redeemer!"[1] For if these enmities had not inter-
vened, we would know about your literary works, to be sure, as we
know them, but we would not know anything about your firm-
ness of character and your greatness of soul. But enough on this
subject.

As far as the epigram is concerned, where you say that you were 2
defrauded, I am sorely afflicted that you, to whom there is nothing
that I do not owe in return for your great kindness and benevo-
lence to me, should be in need of some service of mine. Neverthe-

395

flagitatio tua; neque enim ita desiderares, nisi etiam probares. Ea
vero demum est, ut ille inquit, laus vera, laudari a laudato viro.
Sed ego, qui tuas virtutes quanti faciam optime mihi sum conscius,
longe honestius putavi nihil de te, ut de Carthagine inquit Salus-
tius, quam pauca dicere. Rem itaque distuli in aliud tempus et
quidem non temere, quod feci etiam in Ioanne Petri Francisci, cui
ego quantum debeam nemo mortalium est qui nesciat.

3   Quod vero de ista secessione Etrusca scribis, utinam, mi Pice,
ea tempora essent, ut et secedere tecum et otiari mihi liceret!
Nam, ut omittam iucundissimam tuam consuetudinem, satis su-
perque fructuosum esset carere interim tot monstris, quorum vi-
tam, mores, avaritiam denique atque ignaviam audire miserrimum
puto, nedum perpeti. Si ita res se habet, decrevi omnia devorare,
dum aut pax non dubia aut certa arma alicubi effulserint; neque
enim ita multi facio, verum potius, dum alterutrum sequatur, am-
biguitas ista et rerum omnium incertitudo me necat, quamvis ego,
ut dicam quod sentio, iam pridem existimem non modo tranquil-
litati huius miserrimae Italiae, sed saluti et vitae conclamatum.

4   Vale interim, mi anime, et me, ut soles, ama. Romae, III nonas
Iulias <1488>.

less, in some strange way this request and repeated entreaty of yours gives me pleasure, for you would not request it if you did not approve of me. That alone is true praise, as the poet said, to be praised by one who is praised.[2] But since I am perfectly aware of the deep admiration I have for your abilities, I have always considered it was more honorable to say nothing of you than to say too little, as Sallust did of Carthage.[3] Therefore, I put the matter off for some other time, and not without good cause. I did the same in the case of Giovanni di Pierfrancesco, my debt to whom is no secret.

Concerning that Tuscan retreat about which you write, my dear 3 Pico, would that the times were such that I could withdraw with you and be at leisure! For, not to mention the exquisite pleasure of your company, it would be immensely beneficial to be free for a while of so many monstrous individuals whose lives, morals, greed and cowardice I find it impossible to hear about, much less to tolerate. If that is the way things are, I have resolved to conceal all emotions, provided that either a conclusive peace or an unambiguous armed conflict arises somewhere. I am not very much concerned, as long as one or the other supervenes, but this general uncertainty is killing me, although, to express my true feelings, I have long been of the opinion that there is no hope, not only for peace in this forlorn Italy, but also for its well-being and survival.

Farewell for the meantime, my beloved, and love me, as you do. 4 Rome, 5 July <1488>.

: II :

Michael Marullus Paulo Cortesio s.

1   Affecit me maximo dolore acerbissumus obitus Alexandri fratris tui, in quo alii quidem multum litterarum, multum virtutis amiserunt, ego vero multum etiam benivolentiae; sed multo magis me exulceravit tuus moeror immoderatus, quo te audio quottidie confici. Ille enim quanquam et doctus et probus et, quod maxime miserandum videtur, in ipso aetatis flore, tamen homo mortalis naturae concessit, cui paulo post nihilominus fuerat concedendum; tu autem, ab ineunte aetate litteris atque institutis doctorum hominum enutritus, si fratrem ademptum doles, si memoriam eius lacrimis etiam interdiu prosequeris, facis quidem, etsi fortasse parum fortiter, humane tamen et pietati tuae convenienter. Caeterum, nisi ut in rebus fere omnibus sic in hac quoque parte medium rationemque retinueris, vide ne parum dignitati tuae, parum opinioni de te omnium satisfeceris.

2   Nam, per deos immortales, quae dementia maior, quae insignior esse potest, quam, quem scias moriturum tam pertinaciter mortuum flere deque eius interitu tam misere queri, cui in hoc ipsum nato paulo ante studiosissime gratulabaris? Quasi vero aut maius aliquod aut praestabilius a natura donum feramus quam mortem, quam qui accusant, ignorare mihi videntur hominum vitae conditionem hoc uno non miserrimae, quod, cum libet, possumus mori et tanquam ex turbulentissima procella in tutissimum nos portum recipere. Sed nos omnia ex libidine magis quam ex vero metimur. . . .

: II :

Michael Marullus to Paolo Cortesi,[4] *greetings.*

The untimely passing of your brother, Alessandro, caused me 1
great sorrow. At his death many felt a great literary loss, many oth-
ers lost a paragon of virtue, and I am deprived of great kindness,
but what intensified my sorrow was your uncontrolled grief, with
which I am told you are consumed every day. Although he was a
learned and upright man, and what is most to be pitied, in the
prime of life, nevertheless, as a mortal man, he yielded to nature,
to which he would have to yield shortly afterward just the same. In
your case, however, reared from your early years on literature and
the teachings of learned men, if you grieve the loss of your brother,
if you honor his memory with tears all through the day, you be-
have in a human way and with fitting respect, albeit perhaps not
very courageously. But if, as in nearly all human affairs, you do not
observe some measure and good sense in this situation as well,
take care not to detract from your personal dignity and from peo-
ple's opinion of you.

For, by the immortal gods, what greater and more manifest 2
madness is there than when you weep so unremittingly over the
death of one who you know was destined to die, and so pitifully
bemoan the death of one whom just a little while ago you were
fervently congratulating on being born for this very purpose? As if
we received any greater or more excellent gift from nature than
death, and those who condemn it seem to me to be unaware that
the condition of man's life is not entirely desperate for this one
reason, that whenever we wish, we can die and withdraw our-
selves, as it were, from a turbulent storm into a safe harbor. But
we measure everything more by our own pleasure than by the
truth. . . .

Note on the Text

The Latin text used in this volume is that of Alessandro Perosa, *Michaelis Marulli Carmina* (Zurich, 1951), a paragon of Renaissance Latin critical texts. I have made very few changes: three are cases of correcting what seem certainly to be printing errors, *Epigrammata* 2.11.7 *haec* for *heac*, *Hymni naturales* 1.1.39 *obscoenis* for *obscoaenis*, and *Hymni naturales* 2.4.25 *Jovis* for *Iovi*. At *Epigrammata* 1.47.4, I print 'Nec tam ipse' respondit for 'Nec tam' ipse respondit (I owe this shrewd correction to John Grant), and at *Epigrammata* 2.25.4 *caeli* for *coeli* (a conjecture of James Hankins). Other corrections: at *Epigrammata* 3.24.3 *suspiratibus* for *suspirantibus* (the word occupies the same metrical position as in Ovid, *Metamorphoses* 14.129); at *Epigrammata* 3.39.1 *suppernas* for *supernas* (*metris causa*); *Epigrammata* 4.15.3 *lex Falcidia*. I accept Coppini's conjecture *deam* for *deum* at *Hymni naturales* 4.3.20. In *Institutiones principales* I have corrected only printing errors, changing *pensilibibus* to *pensilibus* (v. 109), *vanaqua* to *vanaque* (v. 303), *concurrerrit* to *concurrerit* (v. 375).

One last change: *Neniae* 3.41, *obortis* to *abortis*. In an article originally appearing in *Rinascimento* 3 (1952): 167–72, Perosa reports his find of a new manuscript containing *Neniae* 3 on the death of Giovanni di Pierfrancesco de' Medici, Monacensis graecus 289 of the Bayerische Staatsbibliothek in Munich. It is obviously independent of other sources of the text, which attests to its importance in the textual tradition. In his edition Perosa printed *obortis* . . . *fletibus*, a reminiscence of the classical expression *obortis lacrimis*, found in Vergil and Ovid, but in view of this new find reverted to the variant, *abortis*, with the same meaning, found in medieval manuscripts and early printed editions. I have wanted to respect this *pentimento* of Perosa.

I have maintained Perosa's orthography, which reproduced as

far as possible the idiosyncrasies of Marullus's orthography and that of his contemporaries, as indicated by the best manuscripts, but I have made numerous changes in the punctuation in conformity with modern uses, especially in the case of the dash and the colon, the latter used very frequently in the Renaissance. I have retained the colon, however, in the *Epigrams* when it signals the "point" to be made in the succeeding line or lines.

In the Appendix, containing two prose letters of Marullus illustrative of his literary connections, I filled in the lacuna left in the last paragraph of the second letter. Some words had escaped Perosa's eye and they were supplied by Carlo Dionisotti in his review of the edition: 'tam pertinaciter mortuum flere,' *Giornale storico della letteratura italiana* 130 (1953): 89. I have omitted several *carmina varia*, which Perosa included just before the Appendix. One of the *carmina* is a tetrastich in praise of Innocent VIII of little artistic value, found only in one Cortona manuscript. Another is a *strambotto* in Italian of uncertain origin, which Perosa considered insignificant. The third is a *sonetto caudato* directed against Poliziano. The language is a very racy type of Tuscan vernacular used in the exchange of burlesque sonnets between Luigi Pulci and Matteo Franco. It is most unlikely that Marullus could master or would want to experiment in such a style.*

For the *Institutiones principales* I consulted two manuscripts that were unknown to Perosa: Vatican City, Biblioteca Apostolica Vaticana, Barb. lat. 2163, and Vat. lat. 5225, via microfilm copies in the Manuscripta Pius XII Memorial Library, Saint Louis University. The first ends at verse 538 and the second omits verses 507–55. They offer nothing of importance.

---

* Massimo Danzi argues for its authenticity in "Novità su Michele Marullo e Pietro Bembo," *Rinascimento*, ser. 2, 30 (1990): 205–33, but even he has to admit that Marullus must have been "sorretto e aiutato nella gestione dell'attacco da un fiorentino amico, che gli perfezionasse quello stile pulciano," 217.

Notes to the Translation

࿊࿊࿊

Book I

1. The Muses, named for Aonia, the part of Boeotia where Mt. Helicon was situated.

2. Lorenzo, son of Pierfrancesco de' Medici (1463–1503), nicknamed Il Popolano. Marullus stayed with him during his years in Florence from 1489–94 and dedicated the collection of his *Epigrams* to him.

3. Maximilian I; see note 11.

4. Paul Tarchaniotes, uncle of the poet, was a leading member of the court of the Byzantine emperor, Constantine XI.

5. Antonello Sanseverino (1458–99), grand admiral of the fleet of the kingdom of Naples, was the head of the Barons' Revolt against King Ferrante I in 1485. In 1487 he went to France to join the forces of Charles VIII. Marullus followed him there in 1494 and took part in the invasion of Italy. He dedicated the 1497 edition of the *Hymns to Nature* to him.

6. Homer was said to have been born in Maeonia in the eastern part of Lydia in Asia Minor.

7. Achilles, son of Peleus.

8. Again Achilles, who was born in Phthia in Thessaly.

9. Theodore Gaza (1398–1475) was born in Thessalonica and fled to Italy when the city was captured by the Turks in 1430. He became professor of Greek in the newly founded University of Ferrara in 1447 and later went to Rome at the invitation of Pope Nicholas V. He translated many works of Aristotle into Latin. Poliziano wrote four epitaphs for him in Latin and two in Greek.

10. Francesco Scales (d. before 1497) was sent by the king of Naples to the Holy See in 1480 to solicit aid to fend off the Turks. It seems also that at the beginning of the following year he was sent to Otranto, where

he met Marullus, who had gone there with the Aragonese armada to liberate the city from the Turks.

11. Maximilian I (1459–1519), formally made king of the Romans in 1486; Holy Roman Emperor from 1493 until his death. Marullus always addresses him as Caesar.

12. Original Phoenician name for Dido of Carthage.

13. Aeneas.

14. Her husband, Sychaeus, was treacherously murdered by her brother Pygmalion, King of Tyre.

15. The Carthaginian tyrant must be Iarbas, king of bordering Mauretania. In some versions of the story Dido burned herself alive on the pyre to escape his demands of marriage.

16. C. Julius Caesar Germanicus, nephew and adoptive son of the emperor Tiberius, was a victorious general in Germany and Asia. It was rumored that he was poisoned by his rival, Gnaeus Calpurnius Piso. He was buried in Rome with great mourning, as described by Tacitus, *Annals* 3.1–6.

17. The future emperor Caligula, famous for his depravity.

18. Manilius Rhallus (d. after 1521), a Spartan by birth, immigrated to Italy. He was a poet of some standing, a good friend of Marullus. A collection of his poems, *Iuveniles ingenii lusus*, was published in Naples in 1520.

19. It was believed that she had a daughter named Cleis.

20. Francesco Sforza (1401–66), mercenary soldier, became duke of Milan in 1450, engineered the Peace of Lodi (1454), a multilateral peace treaty between all the major states of Italy, and developed one of the best standing armies in Europe.

21. Many such poems about a gift of flowers exist in the *Garland of Meleager* that forms the basis of the *Greek Anthology*. Poems 83 and 87 of the *Canzoniere* of Lorenzo de' Medici also concern flowers as gifts.

22. This poem is obviously modeled on Catullus 101 in honor of his brother.

23. A people of Thrace.

24. These were once considered mythical mountains, but for Marullus they were real, a mountain range in Scythia.

25. Patron of Marullus, who stayed with him from 1489 to 1494.

26. I.e., Pluto.

27. The famous Neapolitan poet Iacopo Sannazaro (1456–1530), who took the name Actius Sincerus in the Pontano Academy. He was a good friend of Marullus and wrote many epigrams in praise of him. He also wrote two fierce invectives against Marullus's rival, Poliziano. Five anonymous sonnets directed against Poliziano formerly ascribed to Marullus have been identified by Carlo Vecce as being from the pen of Sannazaro (see Introduction).

28. He was killed by the Turks in 1460.

29. Pope Sixtus IV, born Francesco della Rovere (1414–84), was pope from 1471 to 1484. The Treaty of Bagnolo of August 7, 1484 put an end to the so-called War of Ferrara between the Venetians and the Duke of Ferrara against a league of other Italian cities formed by Sixtus IV, who was not pleased at all with the terms of peace and died five days later.

30. Nepos, *Thrasybulus* 2.6

31. Petrucci, a learned man of letters, a member of the Pontano Academy, was the secretary of Ferrante I, ruler of Naples, from 1458 until his death in 1487. He participated in the Revolt of the Barons in 1484 and was treacherously imprisoned and executed by Ferrante three years later.

32. Giovanni Pontano (1429–1503) was a famous humanist and poet at the Aragonese court in Naples, where he established the Accademia Pontaniana. He was a mentor and friend of Marullus.

33. Lived from 1448 to 1490. It is possible that Marullus lived with him for a time in San Gimignano.

34. Unknown friend of the poet.

35. Simonetta Vespucci (1453–76) was the Genoese wife of Marco Vespucci, cousin of Amerigo, the navigator. She was regarded as one of the most beautiful women of her time.

36. A personage who figures often in Martial.

37. Perosa conjectures that her name may correspond to the Voconti, an ancient tribe that lived near Vaucluse, which may therefore be the birthplace of Marzia. For the Voconti see Sannazaro, *Elegies* 3.2.75.

38. Diana.

39. This poem owes much to Pontano, *Tumuli* 2.55: *Tumulus Thermionillae meretriculae.*

40. *Virgineos focos* is an ironic designation of the convent.

41. An order of nuns founded by Saint Clare (Santa Chiara), a follower of Saint Francis of Assisi, in 1212.

42. Archways in the forum were known as haunts for moneylenders and prostitutes.

43. Cilicia was a country in southeast Asia Minor.

44. Giulio Antonio Acquaviva (1425–81), Duke of Atri, condottiere, father of Andrea. He fought against the Turks at Otranto in 1481, fell into an ambush, and was killed. His decapitated head was brought back on the saddlebow of his horse.

45. Lord of Piombino, a tributary state of the kingdom of Naples, which controlled the channel between the mainland and the island of Elba and exacted tribute from those who passed through it. It seems that Marullus fought together with Appiano under the Neapolitan commander Giulio Antonio Acquaviva in the Tuscan War of 1478–80.

46. Marullus does not use the word *lacerna* (cloak). It seems to be understood from an epigram of Martial, 14.131.1. "Quartus" is Appiano.

47. Andrea Matteo Acquaviva (1455–1529), Marquis of Bitonto, Duke of Atri. Both soldier and scholar, he took part in the war against the Turks in Otranto and sided with the rebellious barons against Ferrante I. He was skilled in both Latin and Greek and translated Plutarch's treatise *On Moral Virtue.*

48. Giulio Antonio Acquaviva; see note 47 above.

49. Kedük Achmed Pasha, admiral of the Turkish fleet, besieged and captured Otranto on August 12, 1481.

50. The Pelasgians were an ancient pre-Greek people who inhabited the northern Aegean region but were often associated with the Greeks of the time of the Trojan War, as Marullus does consistently.

51. When the corpse of Thrasybulus was brought back on his shield, his father Tynichus laid the body on the pyre and said, "Let cowards weep. I will bury you without tears. You belong both to me and to Sparta." *Greek Anthology* 7.229.

52. A similar statement is spoken by a Spartan woman in Plutarch, *Sayings of Spartan Women*, in his *Moralia* 241A.

53. Referring to the Parthians, known for their skill in archery.

54. The first Greek to fall before the walls of Troy. He was the husband of Laodamia.

55. Marullus's mother.

56. Lorenzo Bonincontri (1410–91) of San Miniato, astronomer and poet, exiled from Florence in 1431, served as a mercenary under Francesco Sforza, came to Naples in 1450 and won the favor of Alfonso the Magnanimous. He wrote a poem in hexameters on astrology, *Rerum naturalium liber* (1469–72), dedicated to Lorenzo de' Medici, and another poem on the Trinity and the stars, a blend of paganism and Christianity.

57. A nickname, meaning "godfather" (compare in modern Italian, an affectionate term for a close friend of the family). The person signified is Pietro Golino (ca. 1431–1501), a friend of Marullus and Pontano, member of the Pontano Academy.

58. Gabriele Altilio (1440–1501), bishop of Policastro, teacher of Ferrante I, member of Pontano's academy. He wrote a famous epithalamium for the wedding of Isabel of Aragon and Gian Galeazzo Sforza.

59. Luigi Gallucci (1430–1502). He was called Elisio Calenzio in the academy.

60. Francesco Elia Marchese (ca. 1440–1517), Neapolitan nobleman and writer.

61. Spanish priest, physicist, and scholar of the academy.

62. Lucio Lucido or Fosforo (d. 1503), humanist, painter, made bishop of Segni by Sixtus IV in 1482. He was praised for his learning by Poliziano, Domizio Calderini, Ermolao Barbaro, and others.

63. See note 18 above.

64. Zanobi Acciaiuoli (1461–1519), was a political exile in Naples from 1466 to 1478, at which time he was allowed to return to Florence. He was Marullus's first host in Florence in 1489. He was a disciple of Ficino and later a follower of Savonarola.

65. Sannazaro; see note 27 above.

66. Pontano; see note 32 above.

67. Son of Iphicrates and a Thracian mother.

68. A famous Athenian general, renowned for commanding light-armed infantry (named peltasts for their light shield) against Sparta in the Corinthian War (395–387). Later he went to Thrace, where he married the sister of the Thracian king, Cotys; thus the paradox of Mnesteus's response. The anecdote is told in Cornelius Nepos, *Iphicrates* 3.

69. Lucio Crasso (ca. 1430–90), professor of grammar at the University of Naples, friend and teacher of Sannazaro.

70. He was changed to stone after seeing the Gorgon's head of the Medusa; see Ovid, *Metamorphoses* 5.200.

71. A mountain in Phrygia where Niobe was turned to stone; see Ovid, *Metamorphoses* 6.311–12.

72. Probably silk.

73. A nomadic people from the region of the Don.

74. Domitius Marsus, a Roman poet of the Augustan age whom Martial often acknowledges as one of his models. Among his fragments is an epigram on the death of Tibullus.

75. A beautiful courtesan defended by the orator Hyperion.

76. Wife of Protesilaus, who committed suicide when he was killed before the walls of Troy.

77. Fiery river of the underworld.

78. A similar line occurs in Ovid, *Amores* 3.9.26: *Vatum Pieriis ora rigantur aquis.*

BOOK II

1. Daughter of Helios, given in marriage to Minos, king of Crete. Because of some offense done to him, Poseidon cursed her with a mad love for a white bull that he had sent. With the help of Daedalus, who fashioned a wooden cow for her, she mated with the bull. The resulting offspring was the Minotaur. There is an anonymous poem in the *Greek Anthology*, 9.456, on the same theme, although the *pointe* is more clever. Pasiphaë there asks Love to teach her to low so that she can call her beloved.

2. The daughters of Proteus, king of the Argives, were turned into cows. Ovid, *Metamorphoses* 5.238.

3. The same word, *suaviolum*, is used at the beginning and the end of the poem, an example of the rhetorical figure of anadiplosis. It is found also in Pontano, Landino, and Poliziano.

4. Maximilian was formally made King of the Romans at the Diet of Frankfurt-am-Main in 1486.

5. A people who live in what is now West Flanders who rebelled against Maximilian.

6. A river that flows from northern France to the Lowlands and into the North Sea. It passes through the city of Ghent, where Maximilian put down an uprising in May 1488. The emperor promised reconciliation but actually engaged in a punitive campaign against the perpetrators in the succeeding months.

7. The treaty of Arras of 1482 between King Charles XI of France and Maximilian, then archduke of Austria.

8. Imitation of poems in the *Greek Anthology* 9.61 and 3.97. Poliziano wrote a Greek epigram on the same subject.

9. See *Epigrams* 1.12, note 16.

10. Manius Curius Dentatus, famous Roman general, known for his modesty and incorruptibility. In 275 BCE he was victorious over Pyrrhus.

11. King of Pylos, wise counselor of the Greeks during the Trojan War.

12. Favorite of Hercules.

13. Father of Antonello Sanseverino, a great condottiere; died 1474.

14. Queen of the underworld.

15. Caecubus means an inhabitant of the region of Caecubum in Latium. Perosa conjectures that the poet may have been thinking of Caeculus, son of Vulcan and founder of Praeneste, mentioned in *Aeneid* 7.681 and 7.544.

16. Francisco Nino (1438–1503), doctor to several poets, professor of medicine at Pisa. He was the grandson of the famous papal physician Giovanni Nino.

17. Son of Telamon, half-brother of Ajax. When he returned home from the war in Troy without Ajax, his father banished him to Cyprus, where he founded the city of Salamis. Horace speaks of his exile in *Odes* 1.7.21.

18. This speech is a variation of the famous exhortation of Aeneas to his men in *Aeneid* 1.198–209.

19. The story recounted here is told in Velleius Paterculus 2.19 (a text only discovered by Beatus Rhenanus in 1515). After holding six consulships Marius became implicated in a revolt against Sulla and had to flee Rome. He was found in a marsh near Lake Marica and imprisoned in Minturnae. The slave sent to put him to death by the sword, a German who had been taken prisoner by Marius in the war against the Cimbri, recognized Marius and refused to execute his orders. The citizens gave him food and money and he went to Africa with his son and lived in a hut in Carthage.

20. In antiquity, a famous wine from Campania, much praised by Horace.

21. Michael Marullus, paternal grandfather of Marullus, who together with his son and twenty thousand Greeks perished in a last stand against the Turks in the Peloponnese in the year 1463.

22. Thomas Palaeologus, despot of Achaia, brother of the last Byzantine emperor, Constantine XI.

23. Daughter of the Phoenician king Agenor, whom Jupiter in the guise of a bull carried off to Crete.

24. See *Epigrams* 1.47, note 45.

25. Marcus Porcius Cato, consul 195 BCE and censor 184 BCE, noted for his moral rigidity.

26. See *Epigrams* 1.48, note 47.

27. The poet Sannazaro.

28. Marullus may have in mind Dante's *Rime petrose* (*Rime* 3.43–44; 4.1–2).

29. Servius in his commentary on Vergil, *Eclogues* 3.90 says that Bavius and Mevius were terrible poets and critics of both Horace and Vergil.

30. Catullus refers to him disparagingly at 14.18.

31. Antonello Petrucci was the secretary of Ferrante I but became involved in the Barons' Revolt. He was imprisoned in the dungeons of the Castel Nuovo in Naples and decapitated in the courtyard before the populace on May 11, 1487.

32. See *Epigrams* 1.3, note 2.

33. Diana was often identified, as here, with the Cretan goddess Dictynna.

34. Here called the *Thespiades*, i.e., women of Thespia, a town beneath Mt. Helicon.

35. Mountain ranges in northern Thrace associated with the Muses.

36. A stream rising on Mt. Helicon, sacred to the Muses.

37. Two towns sacred to Venus, one situated in the southwestern part of Caria in Asia Minor, the other on the island of Cyprus.

38. Idalium, Golgi, and Amathus are all towns in Cyprus sacred to Venus. Marullus writes *Colchi* following incorrect readings of Catullus 36.14 and 64.96 current at his time. "Amathunta" for "Amathus" is unexampled.

39. Island off the coast of Cape Malea in the Peloponnese.

40. I adopt Perosa's plausible conjecture that Marullus rejected the cor-

rect reading *Urioi* in Catullus 36.12, where all these place-names occur, choosing *Erioi*, reminiscent of the famous sanctuary of Venus on Mt. Eryx in Sicily. Alternately, there was a town on the Apulian coast near Monte Gargano called Urium, associated with the cult of Venus.

41. Latin god of the underworld identified with Pluto.

42. Daughter of Acrisius, king of Argos, imprisoned in a tower by her father, but Jupiter visited her in a shower of gold.

43. The Sabines were an early Italic people who lived northeast of Rome. They were known for their simple, hardy way of life.

44. Paris, son of Priam, seducer of Helen.

45. Helen, the reputed daughter of Tyndareus, king of Sparta.

46. A hard-hearted maiden who rejected the love of her suitor, Iphis. He hanged himself, and as the bier passed through the street, Anaxarete gazed upon his lifeless body and immediately was turned to stone. Ovid, *Metamorphoses* 14.699–764.

47. City in ancient Achaea on the northern coast of the Peloponnese, now called Kaminitsa.

48. Another name for Rhea Silvia, mother of Romulus and Remus.

49. The Inachus is an Argive river, giving a name to its river god, who was often portrayed as the first king of Argos.

50. Cupid.

51. The mother of Venus, often (as here) identified with Venus herself.

52. God of marriage.

53. Marco Barbo (1420–91) was created cardinal in 1467 and patriarch of Aquileia in 1470 and elected Camerlengo of the Sacred College of cardinals as well as bishop of Palestrina in 1478. He served on many diplomatic missions for the pope. He was an erudite patron of humanists.

54. Territory east of the Adriatic.

55. Father of Marullus. This text, together with other epitaphs of the Marullus and Tarchaniota families, once existed in the church of San Domenico in Ancona.

56. The crippled god Vulcan was often betrayed by his beautiful spouse. Venus was the mother of Aeneas by Anchises.

57. Saladin (1138–93), great hero of Islam, Sultan of Egypt and Syria, recaptured Jerusalem from the Crusaders in 1188. He was greatly respected in the West for his chivalric conduct, which merited for him a place among the *spiriti magni* in limbo in Dante's *Inferno* 4.129.

58. After the battle of Pharsalus, Pompey fled to Egypt, where he hoped to be welcomed by the young Ptolemy XII. Instead he was stabbed as he came ashore and then beheaded. His head was brought to the Pharaoh, but his body was left on the beach. One of his freedmen cremated it. The date was September 28, 48 BCE.

59. Federico di Montefeltro (1422–82) was one of the greatest condottieri of the Renaissance: as the epitaph states, he never lost a war. He commissioned the largest library in Italy after the Vatican Library.

60. He shared the consulship with Caesar in 59 BCE but was rendered completely ineffective by Caesar's power.

61. Imitation of a poem in the *Greek Anthology*, 10.84.

62. A giant defeated by Jupiter and buried under Etna.

63. Orpheus was also killed by Jupiter's thunderbolt.

64. The Gaetulians were a people of northwest Africa.

65. A country in central Asia lying between the Hindu Kush and the Oxus River.

BOOK III

1. Through his marriage to Mary of Burgundy in 1477 he acquired the vast territories of Burgundy.

2. This is the first of four poems to Alessandra Scala (1475–1506), daughter of Bartolomeo Scala (1428–97), the Chancellor of Florence and a leading humanist of his time. She attended the lectures of Janos Lascaris and Demetrius Chalcondylas at the Florentine *Studio* and was a skilled poet in Latin and Greek. Poliziano attests to her great learning and talent in several of his Greek epigrams, 29–33, 48, 50. One of her Greek poems to Poliziano is extant.

3. Sappho was considered a tenth Muse.

4. Chalcondylas (1423–1511), a Greek émigré scholar, began his career as a member of the Bessarion circle in Rome and later became a professor in Padua. He taught Greek at the Florentine Studio (or university) between 1475 and 1491. He supervised the preparation of the first printed edition of Homer.

5. This poem is modeled on a series of epigrams in the *Greek Anthology*, 16.295–298.

6. A famous city in the coastal region of Ionia in Asia Minor.

7. Another city of Ionia that claimed to be the birthplace of Homer.

8. A city in the western part of the Peloponnese said to be the birthplace of Nestor.

9. A large island off the coast of Ionia, opposite Smyrna, a strong contender as the birthplace of Homer.

10. An island in the Ionian Sea, home of Ulysses.

11. An important city of the Peloponnese.

12. A city on the east coast of Cyprus.

13. The Colossus of Rhodes.

14. Island in the Sporades, famous as the reputed burial place of Homer.

15. An island lying off Alexandria.

16. Giovanni Pico della Mirandola (1463–94) was a brilliant humanist, philosopher and scholar. His most famous work is the brief *Oration on the Dignity of Man*. To judge by the peevish tone of this epigram, it does not seem that Marullus was on good terms with him, possibly because he was a close friend and ally of Poliziano. Lilio Giraldi in his *Dialogi de poetis sui temporis* (*Modern Poets*, ed. John N. Grant, [Cambridge, MA, 2011], 39–41) mentions that he heard that Marullus was helped by Pico in the composition of the *Hymns to Nature*. See also Appendix I.

17. A reference to Pico's great project to create a universal theology by bringing into concord all of the world's religions and theologies.

18. Pico wrote some amatory verses to Alessandra Scala.

19. See *Epigrams* 1.51.1 and 2.62.12.

20. According to one legend Siena was founded by Senius, the son of Remus. Depictions of the she-wolf and the suckling children are still to be seen throughout the city.

21. The present architectural remains of the fountain go back to 1246. The facade still contains three huge ogival arches and four stone lions. It was the chief source of the water supply of the city in medieval times.

22. The name means "outlaw" in Greek. Marullus uses it here and in several places as a derogatory name for Poliziano.

23. The philological dispute here concerns poem 66 of Catullus on the lock of Berenice that was transferred to the sky. Oarion, an alternate form for Orion found in Callimachus's *Hymn to Diana* 3.265, is the correct reading, for which Poliziano argued in the *Miscellanea* 69.1–7. Marullus supports the reading "Erigone," another constellation, insinuating that Poliziano chose Orion to suit his homosexual proclivities.

24. Daughter of Icarius, who hanged herself in grief at her father's death and was changed into the constellation Virgo.

25. One of the Muses, usually associated with love poetry.

26. Marullus seems to be referring here to Giacomo da Lentini (ca. 1210–ca. 1260), who is believed to have been the inventor of the sonnet form. The last two *terzine* of the sonnet are in the form of Dante's *terza rima*, which is generally acknowledged to have been the invention of Dante himself.

27. Dante was exiled from Florence in 1301 by the party of the Black Guelfs.

28. Perosa explains that Marullus was deceived by the erroneous reading "Cydon" for "Cylon" in Pausanias 6.14.11, later emended by Casaubon. Cylon slew Aristotimus, tyrant of Elis. The Aetolian League dedicated a statue to him.

29. On Bartolomeo Scala see note 2.

30. A young Neapolitan noblewoman according to Benedetto Croce, *Uomini e cose della vecchia Italia* (Bari, 1927), p. 19, note 2.

31. Ferdinand wrested the city from the control of the Muslims on August 18, 1487. His spouse was Isabella I of Spain (1451–1504).

32. The *rudis* was a wooden sword used by a gladiator in sham battles. It also signifies the wooden sword given to the gladiator when he was discharged from the arena, and figuratively to mean retirement from any job or profession.

33. Cosimo Pazzi (1466–1513), son of Guglielmo Pazzi, was married to Lorenzo il Magnifico's sister, Bianca. Although Guglielmo had no part in the Pazzi conspiracy, he was exiled from Florence, and his son with him. Cosimo later was Archbishop of Florence from 1508 until his death.

34. Marcus Junius Brutus, the assassin of Caesar.

35. This is a character in Catullus 98, a poem which Marullus turns into a very scurrilous piece of invective against Poliziano. He is implicitly criticizing Poliziano's acceptance of the reading *crepidas . . . carcopinas* in Catullus 98.4, meaning "thick-soled shoes" (*Miscellanea* 2.2–5), which again is the correct reading. *Cercolipas* is a corrupt form of *cercops, cercopis*, meaning "a long-tailed monkey" with an obscene connotation. Probably Marullus had to change the vowel in the last syllable from long "o" to short "i" for the sake of the meter.

36. This is probably Sannazaro, a friend of Marullus and an enemy of Poliziano, against whom he wrote some injurious epigrams, using the word *Pulcianos*, as here, with a play on words with *pulex, pulicis* (louse).

37. He murdered Giangaleazzo Sforza at midday in Saint Stephen's Church in Milan, December 26, 1476.

38. A district of Macedonia, often used to refer to the battle of Philippi of 42 BCE, in which Brutus and Cassius were killed.

39. Sixtus IV's successor, Innocent VIII (1432–92), had numerous offspring, sixteen illegitimate "nephews" by some accounts. He was one of the first popes to practice nepotism on a large scale.

40. A Greek goddess of war; see Homer, *Iliad* 5.333. Her Roman counterpart was Bellona.

41. Hannibal took his own life with poison in 183 BCE rather than be captured by the Romans. There is a mausoleum to him in Gebze, Turkey

(the ancient Libyssa) on the Sea of Marmara, where he is supposed to have died.

42. Wine from Mt. Massicus in Campania.

43. A mountain in the northwest corner of Sicily, site of a famous temple of Venus.

44. Wife of Hyperion.

45. Dis, god of the underworld.

46. Apollo is given this name from his birthplace, Mt. Cynthus, on Delos.

47. A country in the southern part of Asia Minor.

48. Apollo killed the Python but had to be punished for this act since the Python was the child of Gaia. He was banned from Olympus for nine years to serve as a shepherd to Admetus, king of Pherae in Thessaly.

49. The sad lament of the nightingale, usually associated with Philomela but sometimes with Procne, as in this case. She and her sister lived in Daulis in Phocis, central Greece. Tereus, husband of Procne, raped her sister Philomela and cut out her tongue so that she could not reveal what happened, but she wove a tapestry that told the story. In revenge Procne killed her own son by Tereus and served him up for dinner to Tereus. In early accounts she was turned into a swallow and Philomela into a nightingale, but at other times the metamorphosis was reversed. Gregorio Correr wrote a well-known tragedy on the story, entitled *Procne*, published in *Humanist Tragedies*, ed. Gary R. Grund (Cambridge, MA, 2011).

50. The *Bessi* were a people of Thrace.

51. The person referred to here is usually identified as the Genoese commander, Giovanni Giustiniani Longo, who was charged with the defense of Constantinople. He was wounded during the fighting, removed from his post, and died. He was sometimes blamed for the fall of the city, especially by Venetians.

52. See Catullus 17.19. Another philological squabble between Poliziano and Marullus, with Poliziano the victor, as always. Marullus reads *separate* (solitary), which makes no sense. The unusual word *supernata*, re-

corded in Festus (ed. Lindsay, 396) means "having the leg cut from below," which fits the context of an alder tree cut down and thrown into the ditch. Poliziano tells us at *Miscellanea* 83.3 that this fragment of Festus was given to him by Manilius Rhallus, a friend of Marullus. As for the meter, *supernata* should really be spelled *suppernata*, which would then have the required long syllable for the second half of the Priapean verse. Poliziano saw this difficulty and opted to change the word to *expernata*.

53. Leader of the Messenians, who sometimes challenged Spartan control of Lacedaemon. See Pausanias 4.14.7.

54. The Greek phrase quoted by Marullus cannot be found in modern texts of Homer. Perosa reported in his notes that this was the reading of Marullus's text of the Homeric *Hymn to Hermes* 502.

55. The last word of Persius's *Prologus* in all modern editions is "nectar," as Poliziano held (*Miscellanea* 43.1–6), whereas Marullus defends a more recent reading, *melos*. This is impossible because a long syllable is needed in this position of the choliambic meter. Wrong again!

56. Antonio Squarcialupi (1429–90) was the organist at Santa Maria del Fiore (il Duomo) in Florence and was a member of Lorenzo's court. He was the most famous organist of his time.

57. A mountain in Lydia. The god of the mountain judged a contest in music between Pan and Apollo. See Ovid, *Metamorphoses* 11.157–61.

58. Nickname for Manlius.

59. A king of Lydia in the sixth century BCE famous for his wealth.

60. King of Troy.

61. Versions of this poem exist in the *Greek Anthology* 9.346 and 16.41.

62. Procne, daughter of Pandion, a king of Athens. See note 49 above.

63. Referring to Colchis, a country southwest of the Black Sea, home of Medea.

64. Poliziano was born in Montepulciano in Tuscany, whence his name.

65. An African tribe who were said to be immune from poison. See Lucan, *Pharsalia* 9.891; Pliny, *Natural History* 7.14.

66. Agesilaus (444–360 BCE) was a highly regarded king of Sparta and a courageous general. In one of the numerous sayings attributed to him, he said that he wished no memorial to be erected in his honor at his death.

67. Maximilian was never very popular in Flanders and was frequently at war with Bruges and Ghent. On January 17, 1488, he summoned the Netherlands Estates General to meet in Bruges. Since he had few troops with him, the burghers imprisoned him for three months. His nine-year-old son Philip sought aid from Frederick III, Maximilian's father, who raised an army of twenty thousand men. When the people heard that this army was on the march, they immediately released him.

68. With reference to one of Hercules's labors, the killing of the Nemean lion in a valley of the Argolis.

Book IV

1. Lorenzo di Pierfrancesco de' Medici.

2. Braccio Martelli (b. 1422), member of Lorenzo il Magnifico's circle, though afterward he favored Charles VIII's plans to invade Italy.

3. Perosa identified him with Cristoforo Risorboli, who was often sent on diplomatic missions by Caterina Sforza to Lodovico il Moro in Milan. He went to the defense of Caterina together with Marullus when she was besieged in her castle in Forlì by Cesare Borgia.

4. Daphne fled the advances of Apollo and was turned into a laurel tree; see Ovid, *Metamorphoses* 1.452–567.

5. The Muses, so-called because they frequented the sacred spring of Castalia on Mt. Helicon.

6. Apollo is here called *Patareus* with reference to the oracle of Apollo in Patara, a maritime city in Lycia in Asia Minor.

7. One of the Titans.

8. Pallas Athena.

9. A poetess who rallied the Argive women to resist Cleomenes, king of Sparta ca. 494 BCE; see Plutarch, *Sayings of Spartan Women*, in his *Moralia* 245C–E.

10. Janos Lascaris (1445–1534), a Greek scholar who, after a sojourn in Rome at the Accademia Romana of Pomponio Leto, came to Florence in 1472; in 1491 he was commissioned by Lorenzo de' Medici to search for manuscripts in various parts of Greece. One of his most famous finds was a manuscript of Proclus's commentary on Plato's *Republic*, which he acquired from the monks of Mt. Athos.

11. King of the Lapiths, who attempted to seduce Juno and for this was condemned to be bound to an ever-revolving wheel in the underworld.

12. The Danaids, the fifty daughters of Danaus, were ordered by their father to kill their husbands on their wedding night. All obeyed except one, Hypermnestra. The others were condemned to carry water in leaky vessels for all eternity in the underworld.

13. The punishment of Prometheus, chained to a rock in the Caucasus.

14. Sisyphus.

15. Tantalus.

16. A mountain range in northwest Arcadia.

17. The Greek goddess of retribution.

18. This may be a certain Jacopo Modesti of Prato, of whom little is known, or Publio Francesco Modesti of Rimini (1471–1557), a well-known Neo-Latin poet of the next generation, or Johannes Antonius Modestus, an Umbrian professor of rhetoric.

19. Here Quartus is not Jacopo Appiano, as in *Epigrams* 1.47, but Pope Sixtus IV.

20. Giambattista Fiera (1469–1538), a doctor, philosopher, and poet of some celebrity from Mantua.

21. Of the various women of that name in Florence during that period, Perosa believed her to be the wife of Antonio Pico della Mirandola. She died in 1491.

22. A rustic Roman god, later identified with Pan.

23. River nymphs.

24. A law of 40 BCE which guaranteed a quarter of the estate to the heir or heirs.

25. Bacchus.

26. A pastoral hero, the subject of Vergil's *Fifth Eclogue*.

27. Benedetto Biliotti, a doctor and an associate of Marsilio Ficino and Lorenzo de' Medici.

28. The capital of the Republic of Ragusa, present-day Dubrovnik.

29. Epidauros was an ancient Greek colony dating from the sixth century BCE, situated just nine miles from the modern city of Dubrovnik. It later became the Roman city of Epidaurum.

30. Phaeacia was a mythical land where Ulysses was entertained by King Alcinous. It is often identified as the island of Corfu, which lies off the coast of Epirus. Marullus must be using it here to signify Dalmatia, not far to the north.

31. A mountain outside Dubrovnik, named after Saint Sergius.

32. The Isthmus of Corinth. Dubrovnik itself is situated on an isthmus.

33. Ragusa was under the dominion of the Venetians from 1205 to 1358, save for the brief period from 1232 to 1236, when it was under the rule of Emperor Frederick II. It successfully eluded later attempts of Ladislas of Naples to conquer it.

34. The future Philip IV (1478–1506), now only four years old.

35. Mary, duchess of Burgundy, wife of Maximilian I, who died after a hunting accident in 1482.

36. That is, as long as Maximilian was emperor, there would be no fear of Philip's retaining the title to Burgundy. Actually, Maximilian became emperor in the following year, 1483. (I am most grateful to my colleague, Jonathan Reid, for this explanation.)

37. Braccio Fortebraccio (1368–1424), was a famous condottiere active in various wars in central Italy. He died during the siege of L'Aquila, which had made a pact with Pope Martin V, Fortebraccio's enemy. He was buried in unconsecrated ground by order of the pope since he had been excommunicated, but his mortal remains were brought back to his native city of Perugia through the efforts of his nephew, Niccolò della Stella,

and buried in the church of San Francesco al Prato. Several humanists wrote epitaphs for him, including Leonardo Bruni.

38. Mattyas Hunyadi, called Corvinus, king of Hungary and Bohemia (1443–90), ruled with great skill and energy for thirty-two years. He was a generous patron of the arts and letters and his court was a center of humanist culture. His library was second in size only to the Vatican Library.

39. See note 2 above.

40. A mountain near Florence.

41. A stream near Florence.

42. Venus, worshipped in the town of Cnidus in Caria in Asia Minor.

43. Pope Innocent VIII, born Giovanni Battista Cybo (1432–92), Genoese, pope from 1484 until his death. He was noted for his nepotism and libertine life (he had eight illegitimate sons and eight illegitimate daughters, which earned him the pasquinade title of pater patriae). His papacy was characterized by indolence and lack of initiative, except for his ardent persecution of witches in Germany. See 3.32, above.

44. See following note.

45. Charles VIII (1470–98), best known for his expedition to Italy in 1494, in which Marullus participated to some extent. He took Naples with very little struggle and proceeded to prepare a Crusade to retake the Holy Land, but by March Lodovico il Moro, the duke of Milan, with the help of the pope, had formed a league against him. Charles's army was defeated on July 6, 1495, at Fornovo near Parma. He died from striking his head against a door lintel in the castle of Amboise.

46. Another name for Italy.

47. A Celtic tribe in ancient Gallia Narbonensis, the region between the Rhone River and Lake Geneva, here designating the south of France.

48. Beatrice d'Este (1475–97), wife of Lodovico Sforza. She died giving birth to a stillborn child.

49. Sole survivor with her husband, Deucalion, of the flood sent upon the world by Jupiter; see Ovid, *Metamorphoses* 1.313–415.

50. Giovanni di Pierfrancesco de' Medici (1467–98), a cultivated young man, patron of Marullus. He married Caterina Sforza in 1497, and in the following year a son was born, to whom Caterina gave the name Ludovico; Ludovico later became a famous condottiere known as Giovanni dalle Bande Nere and the father of Cosimo I, Duke of Tuscany.

51. Perosa considers her to be Felicia della Rovere (1483–1536), daughter of Cardinal Giuliano della Rovere, later Pope Julius II. She married the wealthy Gian Giordano Orsini and after his death wielded great power.

52. Venus.

53. Antonello Sanseverino; see *Epigrams* 1.7, note 5.

54. This epithet of Athena derives from Lake Tritonis in Boeotia.

55. A river in the south of Italy in the present-day region of Basilicata.

HYMNS TO NATURE

Book I

1. This dedication to Antonello Sanseverino is a recycling of the dedication of the third book of the *Hymns to Nature*, in an earlier version, which read *Ad Petrum Medicen Laurentii filium*, i.e., Piero, son of Lorenzo il Magnifico. The only change in the text is from *heroum* to *regum* in line 4. The reference to the sun made more sense in the earlier version since the dedication was placed immediately before the hymn to the sun. An earlier redaction of the *Hymns* contained dedications of Book 1 to Lorenzo di Pierfrancesco de' Medici, and of Book 2 to Giovanni di Pierfrancesco (Perosa, xv).

2. The opening line of Aratus, *Phainomena*; Vergil, *Eclogues* 3.60.

3. A name for the Muses taken from the district of Pieria northeast of Mt. Olympus, from which they originated.

4. A Muse from Mt. Pimpla in Pieria.

5. A region in Northern Greece made sacred by the oracle at Delphi, Mt. Helicon, and the Castalian spring.

6. Platonic image; see *Phaedo* 62B.

7. Homer, *Odyssey* 10.233–43.

8. At *Odyssey* 10.305 Mercury offers the mythical herb moly, a plant with white flowers and black root, to Ulysses to protect him against Circe's magic.

9. Pallas Athena. This epithet, μουνογενής in Greek, is used of her in *Orphic Hymns* 32.1.

10. According to Hesiod she is equal to her father in power and wisdom; see *Theogony* 896.

11. *Machina mundi* is a phrase taken from Lucretius, *On the Nature of Things* 5.96.

12. Sea god, son of Ocean, here by metonymy referring to the sea in general.

13. Vergil, *Georgics* 2.460.

14. Seven daughters of Atlas and Pleione, now seven stars in the constellation Taurus.

15. Her name derives from the Greek verb πάλλειν, meaning "to hurl," according to one ancient etymological interpretation.

16. Here called Phorcis after her father, the marine god Phorcus. The Medusa's head was depicted on Athena's shield.

17. Coppini suggests Syracuse, since it was long governed by tyrants. An *Athenaion* was built there in the fifth century BCE. Christine Harrauer, interestingly, suggests the reading *Tyrrhenicum*, which would account for the various references to this region, although it is unmetrical; see her *Kosmos und Mythos*.

18. Probably referring to the island of Capri, said to have been occupied by the Teleboae, who were ruled by King Telon. There was a temple to Minerva on the Sorrento promontory, facing Capri.

19. Pallas was often associated with the Egyptian goddess Neith, patron deity of Sais in the Western Nile Delta.

20. A town of Phthiotis in Thessaly with a famous temple of Athena.

21. A river in Argos to which the statue of Athena was brought in solemn procession to be washed in its waters. On the acropolis of Argos there was a temple of Athena ἀκρία.

22. Mt. Hymettus outside Athens was and is famous for its honey.

23. The five planets plus the sun and moon.

24. There are two short Homeric hymns to Athena, one of eighteen verses, the other of five.

25. Daughter of Apollo and mother of Tiresias, who was blinded because he saw Athena bathing.

26. One of the giants who made an assault upon heaven. He was killed by a lightning bolt of Jupiter and buried beneath Mt. Etna.

27. Hades.

28. See Plato, *Timaeus* 24D.

29. A hermaphroditic god in the Orphic religion, son of Aether, father of Night. He is mentioned in the Orphic hymn to Protogonos. Professor Perosa observed that he was sometimes identified with Pan or Bacchus, but never with Pallas Athena.

30. Plato distinguished between two Aphrodites, Aphrodite Ourania and Aphrodite Pandemos (in Latin Venus Caelestis and Venus Naturalis), one corresponding to a more spiritual love and the other to physical love. See Plato, *Symposium* 180D; Plotinus, *Enneads* 3.5.4. Ficino developed the theme further in his *Commentary on the Symposium* (*De Amore*), in a chapter entitled "De duobus Amoris generibus ac de duplici Venere" (2.7); see Ficino's *Opera omnia* (Basel, 1576; repr., Turin, 1962), 1326–27.

31. Phorcus, son of Neptune and Ocean, had one male child and five daughters, among them Medusa.

32. Hesiod, *Theogony* 116–23.

33. Plato, *Symposium* 195B–D.

34. *Magnum per inane* is a phrase taken from Lucretius, 1.1018.

35. Daughters of Jupiter and Eurynome: Euphrosyne, Aglaia, and Thalia.

36. Iuventa is the goddess of youth, identified with the Greek goddess Hebe, cupbearer to the gods.

37. The personified hours or seasons, daughters of Zeus and Themis. Marullus uses a phrase of Ovid, *spatiis . . . aequalibus*; see *Metamorphoses* 2.26.

38. For this poem Marullus uses the wild, exotic galliambic meter, originally designed to accompany the ecstatic ritual of Cybele's votaries. He is the first humanist poet to use it after Catullus in his poem 63.

39. Here called Thespiades from Thespis, an ancient town of Boeotia at the foot of Helicon.

40. A Greek epithet of Bacchus meaning "noisy" or "rumbling."

41. He was brought forth in the fire when Jupiter appeared to Semele in all his glory.

42. The cry of the Bacchantes to greet Bacchus.

43. The Edonians were a tribe of the Thracian-Macedonian border, celebrated for their worship of Bacchus.

44. Ritual dance in triple time.

45. A stalk or spear surmounted with a pinecone or a tuft of ivy, carried by the worshippers of Bacchus.

46. Secret emblems of the rites of Bacchus.

47. This epithet is used of him in *Orphic Hymns* 30.3.

48. After incinerating Semele, Jupiter put the fetus of the child in his thigh.

49. Mother of Bacchus in some accounts, sometimes equated with Semele.

50. An epithet of Bacchus, literally "good son," referring to his intervention in the war of the giants against Zeus.

51. Since his rites were celebrated at night.

52. An ancient Italic divinity of fertility, later identified with Bacchus as a god of wine.

53. The inhabitants of India were vanquished in battle by Bacchus; see Ovid, *Metamorphoses* 4.20–21.

54. Giants who revolted against Zeus.

55. A king of Thebes who opposed the worship of Bacchus in his kingdom.

56. A king of Thrace who also prohibited the cult of Bacchus and ordered the destruction of vines in his kingdom. He was blinded by Zeus for having pursued the nurses of Bacchus.

57. The pirates refused to take Bacchus from the island of Icaria to Naxos, as he desired. In punishment he turned them into sea monsters. The story is told in Ovid, *Metamorphoses* 3.497–692.

58. The daughters of Minyas were punished for refusing to worship Bacchus. They kept working at their spindles, despising the god and profaning his holy day. Their weft turned to clusters of grapes and as night came on, the rooms were set ablaze and ghostly beasts wandered about. They themselves were turned into bats.

59. A king of Argos who rejected the rites of Bacchus; see Ovid, *Metamorphoses* 4.612–14.

60. The large island of Chios opposite the Turkish coast was famous in antiquity for its wine.

61. Mimallones was a Macedonian name for the Bacchantes; see Statius, *Thebaid* 4.660.

62. A high mountain range in Western Thrace.

63. Marullus uses the Greek word *lychnita*, a precious gem of a red color, used as an epithet of Bacchus in the *Orphic Hymns*.

64. Goddess of justice, but also of prophecy, whose temple was located in Boeotia, hence the mention of the Corycian nymphs, who inhabited a cave on the western slopes of Mt. Parnassus.

Book II

1. She is regarded as the principal Muse as well as the goddess of epic poetry.

2. The panic hour.

3. Parthia is a region northeast of the Caspian Sea. In classical literature reference is usually made to the Libyan or Numidian lion.

4. Apollo.

5. A mountain in Arcadia sacred to Pan.

6. See Vergil, *Eclogues* 2.33: *Pan curat ovis oviumque magistros.*

7. The nightingale, from the myth of Procne and Philomela. In Homer's *Hymn to Pan* 19.15, the garrulous bird cannot rival Pan's music.

8. The Sirens.

9. Goddess of the sea, husband of Oceanus.

10. In a myth narrated in the *Phaedrus*, Jupiter traverses the heavens in a winged chariot followed by an entourage of gods and demons; only Vesta (Hestia, in Greek) remains in the house of the gods. See Plato, *Phaedrus* 246D–247A. In Pythagorean terminology Vesta is the central hearth of the universe, placed at the center of the earth, and is not able to move from there.

11. Earth, sea, and sky are considered to be the limbs of Pan in *Orphic Hymns* 11.1–3

12. See *Timaeus* 30A.

13. The adjective *multivola* is found only in Catullus 68.128, where it means "promiscuous." Marullus uses it here in the sense of "centrifugal."

14. An archaic equivalent of Jupiter. By a false etymology of his name from the Greek adjective *pan,* meaning "all," Pan was sometimes identified with Jupiter.

15. So-called in *Orphic Hymns* 4.3.

16. As affirmed in Proclus, *Theologia platonica* 4.21.

17. *Ope sospita* echoes *bona / sospites ope* in Catullus's hymn to Diana, 34.23–24.

18. Most probably the Muse Urania.

19. See Homer, *Odyssey* 19.163; Hesiod, *Theogony* 35.

20. The Parcae or Fates.

21. In antiquity Cyprus supplied timber for the building of ships.

22. See Hesiod, *Theogony* 123.

23. The *Saturnalia*, a festival celebrated on December 17 and continuing for several days, characterized by great merriment and license.

24. Wife of Saturn and mother of Jupiter.

25. A god of Orphic theology. He is called ταυροβόαν in *Orphic Hymns* 6.3.

26. Chaonia was a region in northwestern Epirus sacred to Jupiter. The town of Dodona was the seat of an oracle of Jupiter in a grove of oak trees. Chaonian repasts were acorns, the food of primitive man.

27. This is a hymn to the planet Jupiter. It bears some resemblance to the Homeric Hymn to Zeus but exhibits many more features of Pontano's hymn in his *Urania*.

28. The Dog Star, metonym for the hot days from July 22 to August 22.

29. Marullus uses the name *Atabolus*, found in Horace, *Epistles* 1.10.16, for this sand-laden wind that blows off the Libyan desert into Malta, Sicily, and Italy in the late summer.

30. Armed with a sickle, Saturn castrated his father, Uranus.

31. River of the underworld whose name means "hatred."

32. Referring to the punishment of Ixion, a king of the Lapiths, bound to an ever-revolving wheel in the underworld for his attempted seduction of Juno.

33. Referring to Sisyphus, condemned to roll a rock up a hill forever that would always roll back down again.

34. Legendary king of Athens who in the war against Sparta sacrificed his life for his country.

35. Muse of history.

36. A title of Mars derived from the verb *gradior*, "to advance in battle."

37. A river that once marked the border between Macedonia and Thrace, now called the Struma.

38. See *Hymns to Nature* 1.1.7, above (Latin text).

39. Perosa convincingly identifies this figure as the poet Pindar, citing Pausanias 9.23.3 and Plutarch, *On the Delays of Divine Vengeance*, in his

Moralia 558A. Pausanias says that the Pythian prophetess ordered the people of Delphi to offer to Pindar half of the offerings made to Apollo. Coppini conjectures that he may have been a priest of Doric Apollo at Thebes.

40. Mts. Ossa and Pelion.

41. Mountain ranges in Thrace, where Mars was believed to have originated.

42. A god identified with Apollo in his capacity as healer, but the name came to mean a hymn of victory, usually addressed to Apollo.

43. A Cyclops, son of Neptune and Amphitrite, who worked in the forge of Vulcan on one of the Aeolian Islands north of Sicily.

44. In imitation of the famous lines in Homer, *Iliad* 1.530.

45. A mountain on Delos sacred to Diana.

46. Latona, the mother of Apollo and Diana, would have been jealous because Mars was named first.

47. The Muse of lyric poetry, especially love poetry.

48. The myrtle was sacred to Venus.

49. Venus is here addressed as Cythera, a name deriving from the island of Cythera at the southern tip of the Peloponnese sacred to her.

50. This adjective is taken from Lucretius 1.7.

51. Coppini appropriately cites here a passage from Ovid, who speaks of two arrows of Cupid, one which incites to love, the other which drives it out; see Ovid, *Metamorphoses* 1.468–71.

52. *Alma Venus* is the appellation of Venus in Lucretius, 1.2.

53. A mountain in the northwest corner of Sicily with a famous temple of Venus on its height. In his first version Marullus wrote *Urios*, relying on what is the authentic reading of Catullus 36.12, but then probably influenced by the variant reading *Erioi* found in various manuscripts of Catullus, changed his text to *Erios*. This is Perosa's very plausible emendation.

54. According to myth, Venus was born from the waves near the island of Cyprus. The city of Paphos was the center of her worship.

55. The sea between Crete and Rhodes is named after the island of Carpathos.

56. The west wind, which in Italy begins to blow in February; see Lucretius 1.11: *aura Favoni*.

57. According to Homer, Venus was the offspring of Jupiter and Dione; see *Iliad* 5.370, 381.

58. With reference to the tripods of the Pythian priestess at Delphi and, by metonymy, poetry.

59. Mother of Mercury by Jupiter.

60. It is difficult to know what Marullus means by "Scythian." Kidwell vaguely suggests that it might mean some Slavic language or even Romanian, speculating that Marullus may have fought under King Stephen III of Moldavia, Stefan cel Mare (Stephen the Great). This is very questionable. Others suggest Croatian, which is more reasonable, since Marullus spent some years in Dalmatia. He might be claiming that he learned the language of the natives, as Ovid learned Scythian and the language of the Getae.

61. Mercury accompanied souls to the next world, hence his Greek title as *psychopompos*. Horace speaks of him as "beloved to the gods above and those below" (*Odes* 1.10.19–20).

62. With reference to Amphion, son of Zeus and Antiope, who together with Zethus miraculously rebuilt the walls of Thebes by playing on the lyre, which he had received from Mercury as a gift. See Horace, *Odes* 3.11.1–2.

63. Hermes Trismegistos; see Cicero, *De natura deorum* 3.56.41.

64. There were three archways named for Janus on the eastern side of the forum, where usurers and merchants gathered.

65. Held in Pisa in Elis near Olympia.

66. The fabled hundred-eyed guardian sent by Juno to spy on Io, one of Jupiter's amours. Mercury killed him on Jupiter's command. *Argocida* seems to be a coinage of Marullus, modeled on the Homeric Ἀργειφόντης.

67. The *caduceum*, Mercury's staff, a token of peace.

68. A deep lake near Pozzuoli, the reputed entrance to the underworld.

BOOK III

1. *Aeneid* 2.121. *Furor* is the Platonic *mania*; see *Phaedrus* 244a.

2. Mt. Parnassus, since the scene is imagined to be Delphi.

3. Recalling Plutarch, *On the Obsolescence of Oracles*, in his *Moralia* 409E–438E.

4. The etymology of the word *sol* from *solus* is explained in Cicero, *De natura deorum* 2.68, who says that the sun "alone" is of that magnitude among the stars, and that when it rises, all the other stars are dimmed and it "alone" is visible. This etymology is found also in Isidore, *Origines* 8.11.53, and Varro, *De lingua latina* 5.68.

5. One of the Titans, son of Uranus and Gaia.

6. Wife of Hyperion, mother of the sun; see Hesiod, *Theogony* 371–74. Coppini cites Julian the Apostate's *Oration to the Sun* and Ficino's gloss on the relevant passage as contained in Florence, Biblioteca Riccardiana MS Ricc. 79. The entire gloss together with a commentary of Pico della Mirandola on the same text is reproduced in Eugenio Garin, "Per la storia della cultura filosofica del Rinascimento. I. Letteratura solare," *Rivista critica di storia della filosofia* 12 (1957): 3–21.

7. Largest river in Greece. It flowed between Aetolia and Acarnania.

8. The word *augmen* is found only in Lucretius.

9. *Visilis* is a neologism of Marullus, modeled perhaps on the Lucretian *sensilis*.

10. The ecliptic, the great circle of the celestial sphere that is the apparent path of the sun among the stars.

11. Coppini mentions that Marullus differs in this respect from Julian, who does not admit this commingling. See Julian, *Oration to the Sun* 11.140D.

12. Marullus uses the word *Aigocerota*, literally "goat-horned," to signify Capricorn. It is used also by Lucretius at 5.615. According to the myth,

Jupiter transformed the son of the goat who had nourished him into this constellation. At the summer solstice the sun passes through Cancer, and at the winter solstice it moves through Capricorn.

13. See Plato, *Republic* 508A–D.

14. They opened up the bags that the East wind gave to Ulysses, thus causing a great storm that drove them away from their destination.

15. They ate the sacred cows of the sun.

16. Referring to Hannibal's seeking refuge, first with King Antiochus of Syria, and then having to flee to Prusias, king of Bithynia, who betrayed him to the Romans. Bithynia was a region in northwest Asia Minor. Pontus lay between Bithynia and Armenia.

17. *Corporis auctus* is an expression used by Lucretius at 2.482 and 5.1171.

18. I.e., the Eastern Mediterranean.

19. With reference to Alexander's conquests. The rivers are the Cydnus, the Granicus, the Euphrates, and the Hydaspes (the modern Jhelum, in India).

20. Like the Pylae pass in Cilicia (Curtius Rufus, *The Histories of Alexander the Great* 3.10–13).

21. King of Punjab, whom Alexander defeated at the Hydaspes.

22. The Atlantic, beyond the Pillars of Hercules.

23. Possibly Roberto Sanseverino, son of Antonello.

24. The death of Clarice Orsini, wife of Lorenzo, in 1488.

25. Marullus refers to the widespread (but false) report that there was a partial eclipse on the day Constantinople fell.

26. McGann, "The Medicean Dedications," argues that this is Piero, son of Lorenzo de' Medici.

27. I agree with Coppini in making an important change in Perosa's punctuation here, putting a comma after *caducam* and a period after *renatae*.

28. Lorenzo di Pierfrancesco de' Medici, patron and protector of the poet.

29. A tutelary deity of flocks and herds.

30. Diana, born on the island of Delos.

31. An epithet used of Diana and also of Juno as goddesses of the moon and therefore of childbirth.

32. Proteus, who when questioned turned into different forms; see for example, *Odyssey* 4.384, and Vergil, *Georgics* 4.387.

33. The old Greek name for Messina. It is supposed to have been changed when it was occupied by the Messenians after their country was conquered by Sparta; see Pausanias, 4.23.5–9.

34. Hecate, goddess of crossroads, represented with three faces or bodies.

Book IV

1. Muse of tragedy.

2. Polyhymnia, Muse of sacred poetry and hymns.

3. Wherever the winged horse struck his hoof, a spring burst forth, one of which was Hippocrene on Mt. Helicon. According to tradition Pegasus later dwelt on Mt. Parnassus and frequented the springs of Castalia and Permessus, thus his connection with poetic inspiration.

4. See Ovid, *Metamorphoses* 1.5–31.

5. The epithets ἀστράπαιος and κεραύνιος are used of Jupiter in *Orphic Hymns* 19 and 20. The Latin designation *Fulgerator* is used by pseudo-Apuleius, *De mundo* 37.

6. A mountain in Messenia in the southwestern corner of the Peloponnese named for the nymph who bathed Jupiter after the Curetes saved him from being devoured by his father, Cronus.

7. Mentioned by Pausanias, *Description of Greece* 8.38.2–3.

8. A nymph mentioned in Pausanias 8.38.2.

9. Nurse of Jupiter; see Pausanias 8.38.3–9.

10. Another of Jupiter's nurses; see ibid. All of these nurses are also mentioned in Callimachus, *Hymn to Zeus* 10–41.

11. The Curetes are usually associated with Crete, but Marullus transports them to Arcadia in his version of the birth of Jupiter. Traditionally they are said to have cared for the infant Jupiter and made noise to keep Cronus, who swallowed up all his children at birth, from hearing his infant wailings.

12. The Arcadians claimed that the Crete where Jupiter was reared was this place, not the island of Crete, as the Cretans would have it. Callimachus also says that the Cretans were liars in claiming that the god was born on their island; see his *Hymn to Zeus*, verse 8.

13. Mountain in Arcadia sacred to Jupiter and Pan.

14. The Sithonians were a Thracian tribe.

15. Two of the giants who attacked Olympus. Marullus uses an unusual Latinization, *Purpureus*, for Porphyrion, found in the archaic poet Naevius, probably for the sake of the meter.

16. A rocky promontory in northwestern Epirus.

17. Son of Mars, king of the Lapiths, he set fire to the temple of Apollo at Delphi, since the god had violated his daughter. In some myths he is annihilated by Jupiter; in others Apollo killed him with his arrows. He is punished in the underworld in *Aeneid* 6.618.

18. The temple of Jupiter Capitolinus stood on the Capitoline Hill.

19. Chomarat believes this to be a mountain near Olympia mentioned by Pindar (Κρόνου λόφος). See *Olympian Odes* 1.111, 3.23, 5.17, 8.17.

20. The Muses.

21. Son of Pelasgus, adoptive parent of Juno. He established three sanctuaries for her in Arcadia; see Pausanias 8.22.1.

22. In ancient art, Juno was often depicted with the pomegranate.

23. Mountain in Arcadia; see Pausanias 8.22.1.

24. An ancient town and stream in Arcadia; see Pausanias 8.14.1. Juno's adoptive parents lived there.

25. There was both a Stymphalus river and lake in Arcadia.

26. A name for Stymphalus used in the Argolis; see Pausanias 8.22.3.

27. Apollo, so named as the slayer of the Python, a giant serpent.

28. Goddess of the sea, daughter of Nereus and Doris, wife of Neptune.

29. See Callimachus, *Hymns* 3.4.

30. Europa, daughter of Agenor, king of Phoenicia, carried off to Crete by Jupiter, who had taken the form of a bull.

31. The old Phrygian couple, Philemon and Baucis, gave hospitality to Jupiter and Mercury in disguise, who had come down to earth to verify mankind's practice of religion; see Ovid, *Metamorphoses* 8.630–724.

32. In the Homeric narrative, *Odyssey* 12.101–10, the female monster Charybdis swallows the water in the strait and spews it out again three times a day, thus constituting a formidable threat to navigators passing through those waters.

33. One of the giants who tried to assault heaven.

34. A sea god, father of the Nereids.

35. Aristotle refutes Democritus's theory that the sea would dry up, comparing it to a fable of Aesop, which relates that Charybdis swallowed the sea three times. After the first swallow mountains appeared, after the second islands appeared, and after the last gulp all was left high and dry. See Aristotle, *Meteorology* 356D.

36. At Taenarus, a promontory at the southernmost point of the Peloponnese, there was a cave through which one entered into the underworld.

37. A marine semi-god, half man, half fish, son of Neptune and the nymph Salacia, usually represented as blowing a conch and skimming over the sea in a chariot drawn by blue horses.

38. Leader of the Nereids, wife of Peleus and mother of Achilles.

39. The moon, daughter of Latona and Jupiter.

40. Proteus; see *Hymns to Nature*, Book 3, at note 32.

41. Marullus coins the word *turriferens*. Ovid uses *turrigera* and *turrifera* in this connection.

42. A mountain range separating Sparta from Messenia, mentioned here since there was a temple to Cybele in Sparta.

43. A mountain in Arcadia sacred to Jupiter and Pan.

44. It was believed that bear cubs were licked into shape by their mothers; see, for example, Pliny, *Natural History* 8.126.

45. Lucretius speaks of nature as a stepmother in *On the Nature of Things* 5.195–234.

46. Ibid., 5.222–27.

47. This river was traditionally (but wrongly) thought to have been in Crete. It is mentioned in Vergil, *Eclogues* 1.65. See the note on this Vergilian line in Wendell Clausen, *A Commentary on Virgil Eclogues* (Oxford, 1994), 56, where he identifies it as the Oxus, now the Amu-darya, which flows into the Aral Sea.

48. See note 11 above.

POEMS OF LAMENT

1. The indication *Liber Primus* appears in one MS. Perosa (pp. xviii–xix) supposes that the collection was left unfinished at Marullus's death.

2. Cyrnus is the Greek name for Corsica. The French fleet, under the command of Antonello Sanseverino, was caught there in a sudden tempest at the beginning of January 1495. The story is related in Philippe de Commynes, *Mémoires* 2.171.

3. Charles VIII.

4. Charles VIII encountered hardly any resistance at all in his Italian campaign. He entered Florence in a triumphal procession in November 1494 after the secret capitulation of Piero de' Medici, then proceeded to Rome, where he was welcomed by Pope Alexander VI; he entered Naples in February 1495 without striking a blow.

5. The son of Lorenzo di Pierfrancesco de' Medici, who died at the age of seven in 1495.

6. Semiramide d'Appiano, daughter of Jacopo III d'Appiano, lord of Piombino. The Appiani were a noble Pisan family, but it is a bit exaggerated to speak of "royal blood."

7. The Mesta River (or Nestos, in Greek) flows through Greece and Bulgaria and empties into the Aegean near the island of Thasos.

8. A lake near Lake Maeotis (the Sea of Azov) in the Crimean peninsula.

9. That is, Romanian.

10. A city on the Adriatic coast of modern Montenegro.

11. An island off the Dalmatian coast.

12. One of the Furies.

13. The Normans were in control of most of southern Italy during the eleventh and twelfth centuries, and the Crown of Aragon ruled Naples from 1442 to 1494. Swabian emperors ruled Naples from 1220 to 1266.

14. Giovanni survived his marriage to Caterina Sforza little more than a year. He became ill during a military mission to Pisa and died on September 14, 1498, at the age of thirty.

15. Piero, son of Lorenzo di Pierfrancesco de' Medici, according to Perosa, "Studi sulla formazione delle raccolte di poesie del Marullo," p. 215.

16. Lodovico Sforza, duke of Milan, joined an alliance with Pope Alexander VI, Spain, and Venice against Charles in 1495.

17. Antonio Baldracanno was the secretary of Caterina Sforza in Forlì and wrote a history of the city.

18. Antonio's father, Giorgio Baldracanno, died at the end of the fifteenth century while Marullus was in Forlì.

19. In ancient Rome the Genius was the indwelling personal spirit of a man, especially as related to his personal appetites, as in the phrase, *genium curare*, meaning "to look after oneself."

MISCELLANEOUS EPIGRAMS

1. Marullus's scornful name for Poliziano. See *Epigrams* 3.11, where the same poetic text is discussed.

2. Catullus 66 is a translation of a poem by the learned Hellenistic poet Callimachus. The Greek original, written soon after 247 BCE, is lost. It concerned a lock of hair vowed as an offering by Queen Berenice of Egypt for the safe return of her new husband, Ptolemy III Euergetes, from a campaign against Syria. Upon his return the lock was dedicated in a temple, but promptly disappeared. The court astronomer, Conon, saved the situation by declaring that it had become a new constellation.

3. Arcturus is the brightest star of the constellation Boötes.

4. A star in the constellation Virgo.

5. Callisto was first turned into a she-bear and then was transferred to the heavens as the constellation Ursa Major. Her father, Lycaon, was a king of Arcadia.

6. Catullus 66.65–68.

7. Another name for Aquarius.

8. Marullus misses the whole point of the final lines of the poem, which constitute the rhetorical figure of adynaton, a form of hyperbole that expresses impossibility. Catullus is saying that the other stars have as much a chance of sharing the privileges of Berenice's lock as Orion has to change his celestial position to be next to Arcturus, which is impossible since he is 120 degrees distant from Arcturus.

9. Marcus Cornelius Cethegus, consul in 204 BCE, much admired for his eloquence.

10. So-called by the early Latin poet Ennius; see *The Annales of Quintus Ennius*, ed. Otto Skutsch (Oxford, 1985), frg. 304, p. 96. The line is quoted by Cicero, *De senectute* 50, where Marullus would have found it.

11. Elisabetta Gonzaga (1472–1526) was married to Guidobaldo da Montefeltro, son of Federico, in 1488. They had no children since Guidobaldo was impotent. Elisabetta is an interlocutor in Castiglione's *Il cortigiano*.

12. Diogenes the Cynic (ca. 412–324 BCE) completely rejected the conventions of civilized life and lived a life of voluntary deprivation.

13. Aristippus, a contemporary of Socrates, known for his worldly life and hedonistic philosophy.

14. Marullus uses the name of Hirus, a beggar in Homer (*Odyssey* 18.5), generically.

15. Heraclitus and Democritus are often mentioned together for their contrasting views. Democritus found the human condition vain and ridiculous and laughed at it, while Heraclitus's reaction was to weep over it.

16. He is hanging them up as a votive offering.

17. Poems on this subject are found in the *Greek Anthology* 9.11–13.

18. In the castle of Amboise April 7, 1498.

THE EDUCATION OF A PRINCE

1. Despite the indication "Book I," only this fragment survives.

2. Compare the beginning of *Hymns to Nature* 1.1.

3. A title of Apollo deriving from his shrine at Thymbra, a place in the Troad.

4. Recalling Plutarch's essay *On the Obsolescence of Oracles*, in his *Moralia* 409E–438E.

5. Referring perhaps to the campaigns of Charles VIII, in which Marullus participated.

6. Considered the father of Western medicine. His dates are very uncertain, approximately 460–380 BCE. A group of writings, the *Corpus Hippocraticum*, circulated under his name.

7. Claudius Galenus (ca. 130–ca. 200), physician, anatomist, and philosopher, whose writings have come down to us in Greek, Arabic, Hebrew, Syriac, and Latin. His theories predominated in medieval and Renaissance Europe. He is famous for his theories of the four humors.

8. Alexander the Great, born in Pella, capital of Macedonia.

9. Famous Athenian statesman and general of the fifth century BCE.

10. King of the Laestrigonians, a man-eating monster. The episode is recounted in Homer's *Odyssey* 10.80–132.

11. A mountain in Paphlagonia in Asia Minor between Bithynia and Pontus, famous for its box trees; see Catullus 4.13.

12. This description of the Great Mother goddess appears in Lucretius 2.604 and 640.

13. Originally from Molossis, a district in the interior of Epirus.

14. Referring to Cyrus II, who was raised by the shepherd Mithridates and his wife Spaco; see Herodotus 1.110.

15. Reputed foster mother of Romulus and Remus.

16. Caeta, the nurse of Aeneas, after whom the city of Gaeta is named.

17. Nurse of Jupiter; see Pausanias 4.33.1 and *Hymns to Nature* 4.2.9.

18. Manius Curius Dentatus, a famous Roman general of the early third century BCE, known for his severity.

19. Alexander wept over the tomb of Achilles because the latter had Homer to sing of him; see Plutarch, *Life of Alexander* 15.

20. The fame of Miltiades at the battle of Marathon robbed Themistocles of his sleep; see Plutarch, *Life of Themistocles* 3.

21. The response of the delegation of Athens to the oracle at Delphi was that they should fortify themselves with wooden walls. Themistocles was able to convince the Athenians that the meaning of the oracle was to increase their fleet and abandon the city. See Plutarch, *Life of Themistocles* 10.

22. Marcus Lucullus Geticus, who defeated the Getae, a Thracian tribe on the lower Danube, in the Third Mithridatic War, in 73 BCE.

23. The title *Creticus* was conferred on Quintus Caecilius Metellus, who subjugated Crete in 68–66 BCE.

24. Caecilius Metellus Delmaticus as consul and proconsul defeated the Delmatae, a warlike Illyrian tribe.

25. The emperor Probus received the title *Germanicus Maximus* after driving back the Germanic tribes along the Rhine in 278 CE.

26. The emperors Trajan, Hadrian, and Septimius Severus all received the title *Parthicus*.

27. Hesiod, *Works and Days* 288.

28. The Hydra of Lerna (a marshy district of Argolis) was killed by Hercules.

29. Between southern Italy and Greece, known for its storms.

30. See *Hymns* 4, note 16.

31. The Isthmian games held every two years in honor of Poseidon.

32. Son of Helios, who was allowed to drive his father's chariot across the sky but lost control and plummeted to earth.

33. Another name for Pallene, a town on the westernmost part of the Chalcidice peninsula in Macedonia, where the giants were struck down by Jupiter's lightning bolts.

34. With reference to the speech of Menenius Agrippa in Livy 2.32.8.

35. *Brutia nigra* is a puzzling phrase. Perhaps it is connected with the word *bryton*, a Thracian beer.

36. Perosa identified him as Ferdinand I (or Ferrante), son of Alfonso of Aragon, who ruled Naples from 1458 to 1494. He slaughtered the leaders of the Barons' Revolt on Christmas Day, 1491.

37. This saying is attributed to the Emperor Caligula in Suetonius' *Life of Caligula* 30. It is a quotation from the Roman tragic poet Accius; see *Tragicorum Romanorum fragmenta* 203.

38. Alfonso II of Naples abdicated on January 23, 1495, in favor of his son and went into voluntary exile.

39. Asiatic nomads who descended into Hungary in 565 and then into the Balkans and Italy.

40. A nomadic Germanic tribe mentioned by the historians Ammianus Marcellinus and Jordanes. They sometimes served as mercenaries in Roman armies but were eventually destroyed by the Ostrogoths.

41. An east Germanic tribe which repeatedly attacked the Roman Empire during the fourth century of our era. In the fifth and sixth centuries they divided up into the Ostrogoths and Visigoths.

42. A nomadic pastoral people from the region beyond the Volga that built up a huge kingdom in the third century. They formed a united empire under Attila, who died in 453 CE.

43. A German people from the lower Elbe River that settled in the valley of the Danube. They invaded Italy in 568 CE under the leadership of Alboin and established a Lombard kingdom which lasted until 774, when it was destroyed by Charlemagne.

44. Herodotus speaks of this enmity at 1.1.3.

45. There were two Tarquin kings in ancient Rome, Tarquinius Priscus and Tarquinius Superbus, but Marullus is probably referring to the son of the latter, Sextus Tarquinius, remembered for his infamous rape of Lucretia.

46. Appius Claudius Crassus, a member of the second decemvirate, led a tyrannical regime in Rome from 450–449 BCE. He lusted after Verginia, daughter of the soldier Lucius Verginius, claiming that she was his slave. Rather than surrender his daughter, Verginius killed her. This incident led to the dissolution of the regime of the Decemviri.

47. A country in the southwest corner of the Peloponnese that was conquered early by the Spartans; its population was enslaved as helots. It revolted several times, most dangerously in 464 BCE.

48. This must refer to Demetrius of Phaleron (350–280 BCE), although he was not noted for any military exploits. He was appointed governor of Athens by the Macedonian general Cassander in 317. When the old democracy was restored in 307, he escaped to Thebes and then to Alexandria, where he enjoyed a high reputation as an orator. Numerous writings of his remain.

49. Ariadne, who opposed her father and fled away with Theseus.

50. This refers to the abduction by the Visigothic King Roderic of Cava, daughter of Don Julián, who governed Ceuta in North Africa. In retalia-

tion he assisted the Arabs in crossing the strait and invading Spain in the year 711.

51. The Malatesta family dominated Romagna, in particular the city of Rimini, from 1295 to 1528. At the height of their power their dominion extended to Ancona, Forlì, and Ravenna.

52. Guido da Polenta, lord of Ravenna from 1316 until 1322. To consolidate an alliance with the Malatesta family, he gave his daughter, Francesca, in marriage to Gianciotto Malatesta, crippled son of Malatesta da Verrucchio. When Francesca came to Ravenna, she fell in love with her brother-in-law, Paolo Malatesta, and both were slain, caught *in flagrante* by Gianciotto. The story is told in the fifth canto of the *Inferno* in Dante's *Divine Comedy*.

53. Galeotto Manfredi (1440–88), lord of Faenza, killed May 31, 1488, by his wife, Francesca Bentivoglia.

54. The two Joans are Giovanna I (1327–82), queen of Naples from 1343 to 1381, and Giovanna II (1371–1435), who reigned from 1414 to 1435. The first had her husband, Andreas, son of Charles I, king of Hungary, murdered, and then executed the murderers. Naples was never at peace under her rule. She was killed by her cousin, Carlo of Durazzo. Giovanna II married Jacques II of Bourbon, who eventually had her sequestered in the Castel Nuovo for a time. He was forced to abdicate, and she appointed her lover, Giovanni Caracciolo, as her grand seneschal, but when he became too ambitious, she had him assassinated. She died three years later.

55. Son of Apollo, god of healing.

56. This is usually the name of the Po, but here it signifies a stream that flowed into the Cephisus near Athens.

57. The adjective *Cecropius* refers to Cecrops, the first king and lawgiver of Attica.

58. A river in Arcadia; see *Hymns*, Book 4, note 8.

59. A Spartan general who was sent to Syracuse in 414 BCE during the Peloponnesian War to repulse the Athenians. He broke their siege and in the following year defeated them in a naval battle.

60. Adrastea is another name for the goddess Nemesis. It means "the ineluctable."

61. A river in the underworld.

62. This echoes a phrase of the poet Ennius quoted by Cicero, *De officiis* 1.84: *Non enim rumores ponebat ante salutem.*

APPENDIX

1. A phrase referring to the fall of Adam taken from the chant *Exultet*, sung in the liturgy of Holy Saturday.

2. Naevius, *Hector proficiscens*; see *Remains of Old Latin* 2, ed. Eric Herbert Warmington (Cambridge, MA, 1936), 118.

3. Sallust, *Jugurthine War* 1.9.2.

4. Paolo Cortesi (1465–1510), a well-known Roman humanist and friend of Marullus, whom he often mentions in his *De cardinalatu*. Cortesi's answer, contained in Florence, Biblioteca Riccardiana, MS Ricc. 974, was edited by Carlo Dionisotti in *Giornale storico della letteratura italiana* 115 (1940): 85, note 1.

Bibliography

❧❧❧

TEXTS AND TRANSLATIONS

Michaelis Marulli carmina. Edited by Alessandro Perosa. Zurich: Thesaurus Mundi, 1951.

Kosmos und Mythos: Die Weltgotthymnen und die mythologischen Hymnen des Michael Marullus: Text, Übersetzung und Kommentar. Edited by Christine Harrauer. Vienna: Österreichischen Akademie der Wissenschaften, 1994.

Michel Marulle. *Hymnes naturels.* Edited by Jacques Chomarat. Travaux d'humanisme et Renaissance 296. Geneva: Droz, 1995. Critical edition with French translation.

Michele Marullo Tarcaniota. *Inni naturali: introduzione, traduzione italiana, commento.* Edited by Donatella Coppini. Florence: Le Lettere, 1995.

SECONDARY WORKS

Brown, Alison. *The Return of Lucretius to Renaissance Florence.* I Tatti Studies in Renaissance History. Cambridge, MA: Harvard University Press, 2010.

Haskell, Yasmin. "Religion and Enlightenment in the Neo-Latin Reception of Lucretius." In *The Cambridge Companion to Lucretius,* edited by Stuart Gillespie and Philip Hardie, 185–203. Cambridge: Cambridge University Press, 2007.

Kidwell, Carol. *Marullus: Soldier Poet of the Renaissance.* London: Duckworth, 1989.

Ludwig, Walther. *Antike Götter und christlicher Glaube. Die "Hymni naturales" von Marullo.* In the *Berichte aus den Sitzungen der Joachim Jungius-Gesellschaft der Wissenschaften E. V., Hamburg,* Jahrgang 10, Heft 2. Hamburg: Verlag Vandenhoeck & Ruprecht, 1992.

McGann, Michael. "The Medicean Dedications of Books 1–3 of the *Hymni Naturales* of Michael Marullus." *Res Publica Litterarum* 3 (1980): 79–80.

———. "Reading Horace in the Quattrocento. The Hymn to Mars of Michael Marullus." In *Homage to Horace: A Bimillenary Celebration*, edited by S. J. Harrison, 329–47. Oxford: Oxford University Press, 1995.

Michael Marullus: Ein Grieche als Renaissance Dichter in Italien. Edited by Eckard Lefèvre and Eckart Shäfer. Tübingen: Narr, 2008.

Perosa, Alessandro. "Aggiunte al testo del Marullo." In Alessandro Perosa, *Studi di filologia umanistica*, edited by Paolo Viti, 3:245–51. Rome: Edizioni di storia e letteratura, 2000.

———. "Studi sulla formazione delle raccolte di poesie del Marullo." In Alessandro Perosa, *Studi di filologia umanistica*, edited by Paolo Viti, 3:203–43. Rome: Edizioni di storia e letteratura, 2000.

Tateo, Francesco. "La poesia religiosa di Michele Marullo." In *Tradizione e realtà nell'Umanesimo italiano*, 129–219. Bari: Dedalo libri, 1969.

Index of First Lines

࿆࿆࿆

E = Epigrams, H = Hymns to Nature, L = Poems of Lament,
M = Miscellaneous Epigrams, P = Education of a Prince

Ab Iove principium: Iovis, H 1.1
Ab Iove principium rursus, P
Acci, non ego tela, E 1.25
Acci, quid piperi, E 2.26
Aedificare, canesque et equos,
  M 9
Agedum, canite patrem, H 1.6
Alcinus hic iaceo, E 2.38
Alme coelestum genitor, H 1.3
Amorem ocellis insidentem,
  E 4.34
Amor Tibullo, Mars tibi, E 1.16
Antiqua Codri progenies, H 2.6
At nos senectae praesidium, L 3
Audi, beatum, H 1.4
Audi, felix patria, H 2.2
Aurea Mulciberum nato, E 2.41
Aurea Saturni redierunt, C5.1
Auxerat Aonias Sappho, E 3.4

Baldracane, Aganippidum, L 5
Bentivola hoc tumulo, E 4.12
Braccius hic situs est, E 4.20

Casta, Pieriae, cohors, E 2.31
Censorius, quod ipse, E 2.21
Claudi iuvatus lumine, E 5.12
Colles Etrusci, vosque, H 3.2
Commendo tibi, Cortesi, E 1.35

Creta, Asia, Illyricum, E 2.34
Cuius hic est tumulus, E 3.34
Cum felix regnoque, E 1.34
Cum ferret medios proles, E 3.22
Cum fugeret civem, E 1.31
Cum male formosum sequeretur,
  E 2.3
Cum modo pacatis devicta, E 3.12
Cum Musae tibi debeant, E 3.15
Cum possis, Line, E 2.24
Cum sit Acidaliae facies, E 1.41
Cum tibi non tacto statuas, E 4.7
Cum tot tela die, E 2.19
Cum tot vasa, aurum, E 2.1
Cum tu candida sis, E 2.44
Cum versu referas, E 3.41

Das gemmas aurumque, E 1.12
Deipyle iacet hic, E 1.24
De puero quondam Lauro, E 2.29
Dic aliquem sodes, E 4.15
Dicturus Iovis optimi, H 4.2
Divae, supremi progenies, H 2.1
Dixerat Autolemo flammas,
  E 3.40
Dixerat immitem Venerem,
  E 2.23
Donec liber eram, E 2.12
Dum cavet astrologus, E 4.16

Dum forte Aemathiis Virtus,
    E 3.30
Dum fugit amplexus, E 3.8
Dum neque Gradivum, E 2.37
Dum nuper nitidos, E 3.2
Dum tu fugaces, L 4
Dum ver Hymetium diu, E 3.5
Dum vota supplex, E 2.15
Dura prius cunctis, E 4.9
Dure, quid angusto, E 2.28

Effigiem quaeris, E 1.17
Ergo restabat mihi, H 2.8
Et petra es, mea lux, E 2.25
Et sapiens et amans, E 2.10
Et Venus est uxor, E 2.35
Et vere et belle, E 4.14
Exhausit Xystus bellis, E 3.32
Extrema est dea Terra, H 4.5

Felix elenche, E 3.18
Felix ingenii, E 3.52
Felix sorte patris boni, E 4.4
Flens primum has auras, E 2.36
Foedus es aspectu, E 3.19
Foenerat, et levis Endymion,
    E 1.55
Forte Iovi dum iactat, E 1.38

Graecari quod luctor ais, E 3.25

Haec certe patriae, L 2
Haec mandata tibi mitto, E 2.32
Has lacrimas tibi, E 3.16
Has violas atque haec tibi, E 1.21
Heraclite et Democrite, E 5.10
Hic Albina iacet, E 1.33

Hic choreae cantusque iacent,
    E 1.42
Hic Gazes iacet, E 1.8
Hoc Maria in tumulo, E 4.23
Huc huc, maligna, verte, E 3.50

Iactor, dispereo, crucior, E 1.37
Iam aestas torrida tertium, E 4.11
Iam fessa longa, Pieri, nenia,
    H 4.1
Iam sat huc illuc, Erato, vagata,
    H 2.7
Iane, vatis amor tui, E 4.6
Ignitos quotiens tuos ocellos,
    E 2.2
Inachii spes una soli, E 2.17
Indignos vita putat Eumelo,
    E 3.48
Ingrate falco et crimen, E 1.4
Inter mille neces, E 1.1
Inventa nuper, nervum, E 1.3
Invicte, Magni, rex, Caroli, E 4.32
Invictus potui, E 2.43
Invisus mihi Ianus adest, E 3.24
Ipsa mihi vocem, H 1.5
Iunonem canimus, deae, H 4.3
Iuppiter pie, Iuppiter, H 2.5
Iuravi fore me tuum perenne,
    E 1.58

Lascivum iratus pater, E 2.18
Laure, Compater, Altili, E 1.54
Legibus imperioque aucto, E 4.22
Lingere carbatinas, E 3.27
Littore dum Phario, E 2.42
Loricam, thoracam, ocreas, E
    5.11

Lucebas superis, mea Lucia,
  E 2.13
Lustrabas, dum vita fuit, E 1.57

Malli, nec tepidi, E 3.47
Mater Lacaena conspicata, E 2.6
Mater nobilium nurum, E 3.10
Matrem rogatus faceret, E 1.56
Miraris, Acci, cur tacet, E 1.44
Miraris quid moesta dies, E 2.20
Moerenda Vitulus atque Asella,
  E 1.15
Moesta Venus rapti casum, E 1.43
Moris erat sceptris, E 2.39
Mutatum, visa Phorcinide, E 1.60

Non tot Attica mella, E 1.49
Non vides verno, E 1.63
Nos circum Medio freto, L 1
Nudus Aristippo nudo Canis,
  E 5.7
Nuntia fama patris, E 1.48
Nuntia magnanimi, E 3.51

Oarionem pro Erigone, E 3.11
Occidis aetatis media, E 4.31
Odi te, mihi crede, E 4.30
Odit Leucothoe, E 1.26
O felix nimium dies, E 3.53
Olim cum Maries audisset,
  E 4.19
Olim rogatus quid sibi, E 1.29
Olim superbus Pane devicto,
  E 3.46
Omnia cum facias, E 3.38
Ore prius pleno solitus, E 5.8

Orphea dum miseranda parens,
  E 2.46
O saepe rerum perpetuas vices,
  H 2.3

Parce, hospes, cineresque pios,
  E 1.27
Parce, hospes, tumulo, E 1.14
Parva, sed nimium tabella felix,
  E 3.31
Per Scythiam Bessosque feros,
  E 1.22
Pice, delitiae novem sororum,
  E 3.7
Placatus mitisque suis, E 5.13
Posse negas dici 'melos', E 3.45
Post maria et terras domitas,
  E 5.14
Puella Etrusca, quae meum,
  E 4.28
Puella mure delicatior Scytha,
  E 1.61
Pulchre convenit optimis amicis,
  E 3.21

Quae lux progeniem optatam
  dedit, E 5.6
Quae modo per terras, E 2.27
Quaenam haec, tam semper,
  E 3.42
Quaenam haec pompa? Aurae,
  E 2.7
Quaenam hoc in tumulo, E 1.52
Quaeris qua niteat, E 5.1
Quaerite Maeoniden, Musae,
  E 1.7

Qualiter in medio, E 3.3
Quam bene pro patria, E 2.22
Quartum rogabam, E 1.47
Quartum rogata cur anus, E 4.10
Quartus hic est tibi promissus,
　E 4.1
Quicquid agit, Veneres, E 1.50
Quidam Pelasgos, E 3.29
Qui dedit Aiaci, E 1.51
Quid frustra totiens, E 1.45
Quid involato nectis, E 3.33
Quid iuvat hostiles, E 3.37
Quid me, Paule, E 1.5
Quid mirare unos, E 2.16
Quid separatam, vane, E 3.39
Quid servitutis dexteram, E 3.23
Quid tantum lacrimis, E 3.44
Quid vaga tot terras, E 3.49
Qui fit, Petruti, E 1.32
Quis male Virginea gladium,
　E 5.4
Quis mihi annosum, E 3.17
Quis novus hic animis furor,
　H 3.1
Quis puer hic? Veneris, E 1.59
Quis sacer hic, Erato, E 3.13
Quo, quo, dura, E 3.26
Quod facias nil, Gemma, E 3.9
Quod levis ima pedum verrit,
　E 2.48
Quod nimium castus liber est,
　E 1.62
Quod nomen titulis, E 4.8
Quod nomen taceam tuum, E 5.3
Quod procul Inachiis tegeris,
　E 4.29

Quod regni, quod opum, E 1.46
Quod Sappho Aoniis decima est,
　E 1.19
Quod solus, bone Laure, E 1.23
Quod tam saepe gravi torqueris,
　Paule, E 4.27
Quod tam tota decens for-
　mosaque, E 4.18
Quod tibi tam multus Caesar,
　E 2.45
Quod tua longinquum diffundo,
　E 3.1
Quo me, saeve, rapis, E 3.20
Quo te, profundi rector, H 4.4
Quo te depereo magis, E 2.8

Rex legum iurisque dator, E 2.5
Rhacusa, multis gens Epidauria,
　E 4.17
Rogas quae mea vita sit, E 1.28

Salve, nec lepido, E 2.33
Salve, nequitiae meae, E 1.2
Sancte, qui Memphin, E 3.36
Saturni celebres dies, H 2.4
Scala, delitium tui Marulli,
　E 1.9
Scribis, agis, recitas, E 1.40
Senserat Ausoniam, E 1.30
Senserat exanimum mater, E 2.30
Sero deorum iam tenentem,
　E 3.14
Servatus modo naufragio, E 5.5
Sic istos oculos tuos, E 1.18
Sic me, blanda, tui, E 1.13
Si coelum patria est, E 3.35

Si genus audieris, spernes, E 1.20
Si lacrimis decoranda novis, E 1.36
Si patriam, patria est Argos, E 4.5
Siquis opum largus, E 1.10
Siste, hospes, atque haec verba,
    E 1.39
Si tibi, rex, longinqua dies, E 4.26
Sollicitus siquis visus, E 2.14
Solverat Eridanus, E 4.33
Somne, pax animi quiesque lassi,
    E 4.21
Spreverat Idalium, E 2.47
Spurcicies, gula, E 4.25
Suaviolum invitae rapio dum,
    E 2.4
Sylvae Morelli, E 4.24
Sylvarum nemorumque Faune,
    E 4.13

Tanta tua est probitas, E 2.9
Terrarum ocelle, patria, E 2.49
Te te, suprema maximi, H 1.2
Tota es candida, E 4.2
Tu, quicunque meo fontem,
    E 3.28
Tu, quicunque virum, E 1.6
Tu, qui me casusque meos, E 1.11
Tu ne hic, Roberte, es, E 2.11
Tuta suis monstris, E 4.3

Vaesanos quotiens tibi furores, E
    2.40
Vane, quid affectas patriam, E 3.6
Versus scribere nos putat, E 5.2
Viderat armatas uni dare, E 3.43
Viderat intactam nuper Venus,
    E 1.53

General Index

ॐ༃༃

Accademia Pontaniana, viii,
405n27, 405nn31–32, 407nn57–
58
Accademia Romana, 420n10
Acca Larentia, 363
Acciaiuoli, Zanobi, 43, 408n64
Achaea, 412n47
Achaemenian king. *See* Cyrus II
Achelous, 257, 432n7
Acheron, 393, 445n61
Achilles, 7, 59, 357, 381, 403nn7–8,
436n38; death of, 329; tomb of,
367, 441n19
Achmed (Kedük Achmed Pasha),
35, 406n49
acorn, 429n26. *See also* oak tree
Acquaviva, Andrea Matteo, 35–39,
406n47
Acquaviva, Giulio Antonio, 35–39,
406nn44–45, 406n48; epitaph
of, 69
Acrisius, 217, 427n59
Actius. *See* Sannazaro, Iacopo
Admetus, 131, 417n48
Adonis, 31, 91
Adrastea, 445n60
Adriatic, 141, 165, 253
adultery, 9–11
adynaton, 439n8
Aegle, 61

Aeneas, 9, 63–65, 119–21, 404n13,
413n56, 441n16
Aeolian Islands, 430n43
Aesop, xviii, 436n35
Aether (personification of the ele-
ment ether), xvi, 195, 223, 279–
85, 295, 305, 425n29,
Aethra, 129, 417n44
Aetolian League, 415n28
Africa, 185
age, and beauty, 29–31. *See also* old
age
Agesilaus, 145, 419n66
Aglaia, 425n35
Agno, 285, 435n10
air, as element, xvii
Aisthesis, 379
Ajax, 41
Albina, epitaph of, 23–25
Alcibiades, 357
Alcinous, King, 421n30
Alcinus, epitaph of, 91
Alemannic region, 367
Alexander the Great, 73, 357, 367,
433n19, 440n8, 441n19
Alexander VI (pope), 333, 437n4,
438n16
Alfonso I (king of Naples; the
Magnanimous), 407n56
Alfonso II of Naples, 442n38

453

Allobroges, 183
Altilio, Gabriele, 43, 407n58
Amathus, 77, 411n38
Amboise, 440n18
Ammianus Marcellinus, 442n40
Amphion, 431n62
Amphitrite, 299, 430n43, 436n28
amphora, perforated, 155, 420n12
anadiplosis, 409n3
Anaxarete, 81, 412n46
Anchises, 93, 413n56
Ancona (church of San Domen-
    ico), vii, 412n55
Andreas (son of Charles I; king of
    Hungary), 444n54
anger, 375–77
anguish, 21
anima mundi, xiii
Antiochus (king of Syria), 433n16
Antiope, 431n62
Antiphates, 359, 441n10
anxiety, 21
Aonian goddesses, 3, 403n1. *See
    also* Muses
Aphrodite, dual, 425n30. *See also*
    Cupid; Venus
Aphrodite Ourania/Venus Caeles-
    tis, 425n30
Aphrodite Pandemos/Venus Nat-
    uralis, 425n30
Apollo, xvii, 27, 49, 51, 75, 105, 131,
    139, 151, 219, 239, 255, 297–99,
    371, 417n46, 417n48, 418n57,
    419n4, 428n4, 440n3, 444n55;
    as Colossus of Rhodes, 107;
    and Daphne, 149; Patareus,

419n6; as slayer of Python,
    436n27
Appiano, Jacopo III, 438n6
Appiano, Jacopo IV d' (Quartus),
    33–35, 67–69, 406nn45–46
Appiano, Semiramide d', 438n6
Appius, 387
Apuleius, xvii
Apuleius (pseudo), *On the Uni-
    verse*, 434n5
Apulians, 169
Aquarius, 439n7
Aquila, Stefano d', ix
Arabia, 237
Arabs, 3
Aragon, Crown of, 438n13
Aratus, *Phainomena*, xii, 423n2
Arcadia, 285, 435n11; Jupiter's
    birth in, xvii
Arctic, 207
Arcturus, 341, 439n3
Argos, 107, 153, 255, 414n11,
    431n66
Ariadne, 443n49
Ariosto, x
Aristippus, 345, 440n13
Aristomenes, 137, 418n53
Aristotimus, 415n28
Aristotle, 436n35; *Meteorology*,
    xviii, 436n35; *On the Heavens*,
    xvi
Arno River, 135, 219, 251
arts, in Siena, 111
Asclepius, 391, 444n55
ash tree, 227, 239
Asia Minor, 89, 183, 363, 387

Assuan, 261

Assyrians, 383

astrologer, 165

astrology, 407n56; sun and, xv–xvi

astronomer, 253

Atabolus (wind), 429n29

Athena. *See* Pallas Athena

Athenians, 441n21

athlete, 253, 339

Athos, Mount, 420n10

Atlantic Ocean, 433n22

Atlas, 199, 211, 279, 424n14

Attica, 39, 391

Aulus, 345

Aura, epitaph of, 57

Aurora, 209

Ausonia, 183

Autolemus, 135

avarice, of priests, 343

Avars, 385, 442n39

Avernus, 255, 432n68

Avita, 33

Azov, Sea of, viii

Bacchantes, 215, 217, 255, 426n42, 427n61

Bacchus (Bromius, Euius), xiii, 213–17, 223, 275, 277, 421n25, 425n29, 426n40, 426n43, 426n50, 426n52, 427nn55–56, 427n59

Bactria, 101, 253

Baldracanno, Antonio, 337–39, 438n17

Baldracanno, Giorgio, 438n18

banquet, 65; of the gods, 223, 377–79; of life, 339; of Ulysses, 265

Barabbas, 91

Barbaro, Ermolao, 408n62

Barbo, Marco, ix, 89, 412n53

Barons, Revolt of (1485), viii, 403n5, 405n31, 406n47, 411n31, 442n36

Basilicata, 423n55

battle: of Marathon, 367, 441n20; of Philippi, 416n38

Baucis, 303–5, 436n31

Bavius, 73, 411n29

beauty, 57, 79, 87, 103, 137, 169, 181, 189, 405n35; and age, 29–31

bee, 105

Bellona, 416n40

Bentivoglia, Francesca, 444n53

Bentivoglio, Costanza, epitaph of, 161

Berenice, lock of, 341, 415n23, 437n2, 439n8

Bessi and Bessians (tribe), vii, 15, 133, 417n50

Bibulus, 97

Biliotti, Benedetto, 165, 421n27

Bithynia, 433n16

Bithynians, 265

Black Guelfs, 415n27

Black Sea, 135

blind man, 347–49

Bocontia, Marzia, 29, 119, 406n37. *See also* Voconti

body, human, 195–97, 377–81

Boeotia, 77

Bonincontri, Lorenzo, viii, 43,
407n56
Boötes, 341
Borgia, Cesare, x, 419n3
Bosporus, 321, 335
Botticelli, portrait of Marullus,
xix
box tree, 359, 441n11
Brazza, viii, 325, 438n11
Britons, 183, 253, 325
Bromius, 213. See also Bacchus
Bruges, 419n67
Bruni, Leonardo, 421–22n37
Brutus, Marcus Junius, 121, 125,
416n34, 416n38
Budua, viii, 325, 438n10
bull, 391
Byce, Lake, viii, 325, 438n8
Byzantia, 75
Byzantium, 37, 239

Cadiz, 101, 207, 253
caduceus, 432n67
Caecubus, 63, 410n15
Caeculus, 410n15
Caesius, 73
Caeta, 441n16
Calabrians, 169
Calderini, Domizio, 408n62
Calenzio, Elisio. See Gallucci,
Luigi
calf, epitaph of, 13
Caligula (emperor), 404n17,
442n37
Callimachus, xii, 439n2; Hymns,
xvii, xviii, 415n23, 435n10,
435n12, 436n29

Calliope, 219, 427n1
Callisto, 341, 439n5
Calpurnius Piso, Gnaeus, 404n16
Camenae, 239, 303
Camilla, 181
Campania, 315
Cancer, 261, 432–33n12
Candido, Pietro, viii, x
Capitoline Hill, 293, 435n18
Capri, 424n18
Capricorn, 261, 432–33n12
Caracciolo, Giovanni, 444n54
Caria, 411n37
Carlo of Durazzo, 444n54
Carpathian Sea, 247
Carpathus, old man of, 277. See
also Proteus
Carthage, 65, 397, 410n19
Cassander, 443n48
Cassius, Quintus Longinus, 125
Castalia, sacred spring of, 215,
419n5, 423n5, 434n3
Castalian chorus (the Muses),
149
Castiglione, Baldassare, Il corti-
giano, 439n11
Cato, Marcus Porcius Censorinis,
69, 411n25
Cato, Marcus Porcius Uticensis,
97
Catullus, xi, xiii, 13, 49, 73, 135,
341, 404n22, 411n30, 411n38,
411n40, 415n23, 416n35, 426n38,
428n13, 428n17, 430n53, 439n2,
439n6, 439n8, 441n11
Caucasus, 71, 337
Cava, 443–44n50

Cecina River, x
Cecrops, 444n57
celibacy, 345–47
Censorius, 69
Ceraunia, 291, 373, 435n16
Ceres, 159, 217, 275
Cethegus, Marcus Cornelius, 341, 439n9
Chalcondylas, Demetrius, 105, 413n2, 414n4
Chaonia, 233, 429n26
Chaos, 197, 207, 281
character, sick, 389–91
character development, 373–83
Chariclo, 203, 425n25
chariot: of Earth, 311; of poet, 279–81; of Sun, 257–59, 261, 442n32; of Triton, 436n37
Charlemagne, 183
Charles Roland (son of Charles VIII), x
Charles I (king of Hungary), 444n54
Charles VIII (king of France), ix, xii, xvi, 177–79, 183–85, 315, 333–37, 349, 403n5, 419n2, 422n45, 437n3, 438n16, 440n5; epitaph of, 349; invasion of Italy, ix, 315–21, 437n4
Charles XI (king of France), 409n7
Charybdis, xviii, 305–7, 436n32
child: death of, 91; newborn, 311–13. See also infant; prince, education of
child rearing, 353–65
China, 253

Chinese, 77
Chios, 107, 414n9, 427n60
Chloe, 119
Christians, and Turks, 183–85
cicada, 177
Cicero, Marcus Tullius, 123; On Duties, 445n62; On Old Age, 439n10; On the Nature of the Gods, 431n63, 432n4
Cilicia, 406n43
cinnamon, 31, 125
Circe, 197, 423n8
citizen militias, 105
Clare, Saint, 406n41
Claudian, Gigantomachia, xiv
Cleanthes, xii; hymns, xviii
Cleis, 404n19
Cleomenes, 419n9
Clio, 239, 429n35
Cnidus, 77, 175, 422n42
Codrus, 237, 429n34
Coeus, 151
Colchis, 143, 418n63
Colophon, 107, 414n7
Colossus of Rhodes, 414n13
Cominius, 343–45
common people, 293
Compatre. See Golino, Pietro
complaints, 21
condottieri, 85, 410n13, 413n59, 421n37, 423n50
Conon, 437n2
Constantine XI, 403n4, 410n22
Constantinople, conquest of (1453), vii, ix, xvi, 133–35, 271, 317, 417n51, 433n25. See also Turks

constellations, 199, 245, 263, 271, 341, 424n14, 437n2
convent, 406n40
conversation skills, 381–83
Corfu, 421n30
Corinthian War, 408n68
Corpus Hermeticum, xviii
Corpus Hippocraticum, 440n6
Correr, Gregorio, 417n49
Corsica, ix, 315
Cortesi, Alessandro, 25, 399
Cortesi, Paolo, 399, 445n4
Corvinus, Matthas (Mattyas Hunyadi; king of Hungary), 173, 422n38
Corycian nymphs, 217
Cosimo I (duke of Tuscany), 423n50
Cosmos, 225
Cotys, 408n68
Crasso, Lucio (Lucius Crassus Neapolitanus), 408n69; epitaph of, 45
Crassus, Appius Claudius, 443n46
creation of the world, 197–201, 245; in *Hymns to Nature*, xii–xiii
Crete, xvii, 89, 435nn11–12, 437n47
Cretea, xvii, 287–89
cripple, 347–49
Croatian language, 431n60
Croce, Benedetto, 415n30
Croesus, 141, 418n59
Cronus, 435n11
Cupid, 23, 43, 51, 57, 67, 87, 119, 137, 205–9, 247, 412n50; two arrows of, 430n51. *See also* Love

Curetes, xvii, 287, 313, 435n11
Curius Dentatus, Manius, 59, 365, 409n10, 441n18
Cybele, 281, 309, 361, 441n12
Cyclops, 359
Cydnus, 433n19
Cylon of Elis, 113, 415n28
Cynthus, Mount, 241, 417n46, 430n45
Cyprian goddess. *See* Venus
Cyprus, 83, 129, 247, 411nn37–38, 428n21, 430n54
Cyrnus, 314, 437n2
Cyrus II (Achaemenian king), 363, 441n14
Cythera, 77, 187, 189, 411n39, 430n49. *See also* Venus
Cytorus, Mount, 359, 439n11

Dacia, 325
Daedalus, 409n1
Dalmatia, 421n30
Dalmatians, 367
Danae, 79, 412n42
Danaids, 420n12
dance, 247–49, 287, 385, 426n44
Dante Alighieri, 113, 415n27; *Divine Comedy*, 413n57, 444n52
Danube, 111–13
Daphne, 149, 419n4
Daphnis, 165, 421n26
Daulian mother. *See* Procne
Daulis, 417n49
day, 199, 257
death: in battle, 7; of brother, 399; of child, 319–21, 345; of Dido, 9–11; of father, 35–39, 337–39;

by fire, 135; of girl, 173; good,
35–39; of king, 349; for one's
country, 19–21, 65–67, 69, 75; of
Orpheus, 97; quick, 321. *See also*
epitaph; suicide
Decemviri, 443n46
deer, 311
degeneration, of noble race, 353–55
Deiphyle, epitaph of, 19
Delia, 275, 277, 279. *See also* Diana
della Rovere, Felicia, 187–91,
423n51
della Stella, Niccolò, 421n37
Delmatae, 441n24
Delphi, 77, 131, 251, 351, 441n21;
temple of Apollo, 435n17
Demetrius of Phaleron, 387,
443n48
Democritus, 347, 436n35, 440n15
deportment, 383
destiny, 225–29, 325
Deucalion, 422n49
dialogue (verse), 45–47, 57, 113,
127–29, 137, 163–65, 275–79
Diana (Lucina), xvi, 29, 75, 163,
406n38, 411n33, 434nn30–31
Dictynna, 411n33
Dido of Carthage, 404n12; image
of, 9–11
Diespiter, 223. *See also* Pan
Diet of Frankfurt-am-Main
(1486), 409n4
Diogenes the Cynic, 345, 440n12
Dione, 87, 125, 187, 431n57. *See also*
Venus
Dionysus, 215
Dis, 129, 417n45

divine frenzy, 255
divine power, 195
Dodona, 429n26
Domillus, 347–49
Don River, 81
dress, importance of, 383–85
Dyme, vii, 81, 412n47

Earth, 241, 245, 309–13; creation
of, 199; as Magna Parens, xviii
East wind, 265, 271, 433n14
eclipse, solar, xvi, 271, 433n25
ecliptic, 259, 432n10
Ecnomus, 111, 117, 123, 135, 139,
143–45, 163–65, 341. *See also*
Poliziano
Edonian women, 215, 426n43
Egypt, 95
elements: air, xvii; Aether and,
281–83; fire, xvi–xvii, 135
elephant, 363
Eliot, George, *Romola*, xix
Elissa, 9. *See also* Dido of
Carthage
Elysian Fields, 17
Elysium, 181
Emathia, 125, 416n38
Empedocles, xii, xvi
Enceladus, 97, 203
endurance training, 389
Endymion, 43
Ennius, 438n10, 445n62
Envy, 103
Enyo, 127, 416n40
Epicureanism, ix
Epidaurum (Epidauros), 165,
421n29

epigram, 13, 414n5; philological, xi

epitaph, 403n9; of Albina, 23–25; of Aura, 57; of Beatrice d'Este, 185–87; of Braccio Fortebraccio, 171; of Caesar Germanicus, 11–13; of calf and she-ass, 13; of Charles VIII, 349; of child Alcinus, 91; of Costanza Bentivoglio, 161; of Countess Laura, 115; of Deiphyle, 19; of Euphrosyne Tarchaniota, 41; of Federico, duke of Urbino, 95; of Francesco Sforza, 15; of Giovanni Pico della Mirandola, 181–83; of Giulio Acquaviva, 69; of Hannibal, 127–29; of Innocent VIII, 177; of Lucia Phoebe, 61; of Lucius Crassus Neapolitanus, 45; of Manilius Marullus, 91; of Maria Martelli, 173; of Michael Tarchaniota, 19–21; on new tomb, 157; of Paul Tarchaniota, 181; of Philippus Marullus, 27; of Pholoe, 29–31; of Roberto Sanseverino, 59; of Simonetta Vespucci, 25; of Telesilla, 153; of Theodore Gaza, 7

Erasinus, 297

Erasmus, Desiderius, xix

Erato, xiv, 113, 243, 415n25, 430n47

Eridanus (Attica), 391

Eridanus (Po River), 185. See also Po River

Erigone, 111, 341, 415n23

Erios, 430n53

Erymanthus, Mount, 155

Eryx, Mount, 77, 129, 247, 412n40, 417n43

Este, Beatrice d', 422n48; epitaph of, 185–87

Eternity, xiii, 211–13

ether, xiii, xvii, 66, 107, 197, 201, 203, 205, 206, 211, 225, 231, 253, 273, 287, 299, 321. See also Aether

Ethiopians, 305

Etna, Mount, 81, 113, 413n62, 425n26

Etruscans, 85

Euius, 215. See also Bacchus

eulogy, 139

Eumelo, 141–43

"Euoe!", 213, 215, 426n42

Euphrates, 433n19

Euphrosyne, 425n35

Euphrosynea, 41

Europa (Sidonian maid), 67, 301–3, 411n23, 436n30

Europe, 387

example, power of, 367

exile, 63–65, 113, 119, 131–35, 141, 165, 181, 251–55, 273, 317, 385, 415n27, 416n33

falcon, 5; trained, 361, 391

Falernian wine, 65, 115

Fall of Adam, 445n1

farmer, 71, 277, 325, 329, 375

farming, 227, 233

Farnese, Alessandro, ix

Fates, 227, 231, 257, 263, 271, 273, 428n20

Faunus, 161–63

Favonius (wind), 141, 247, 259

Fear (personified), 89

Federico of Montefeltro (duke of Urbino), 439n11; epitaph of, 95, 413n59

Ferdinand of Aragon (king of Spain), 115–17, 416n31

Ferrante I (king of Naples), 405n31, 411n31, 442n36

Ferrara, University of, 403n9

Ficino, Marsilio, 408n64, 432n6; *Commentary on the Symposium (De amore)*, 425n30; *On Light*, xv; *On the Sun*, xv; *Platonic Theology*, xiii

Fiera, Giambattista, 159–61, 420n20

Fiesole, 119

fire, 135; as element, xvi–xvii

Flanders, 419n67

Florence, ix, x, xi, 113, 273, 319, 403n2, 407n56, 408n64, 413n2, 445n4

flower(s): as gift, 17, 53, 404n21; girl as, 25

Forlì, fortress of, x, 419n3

Fornovo, 422n45

Fortebraccio, Braccio (Braccio da Montone), 421–22n37; epitaph of, 171

Fortune, 43, 53, 63, 81, 85, 103, 125, 331; harshness of, 315–21. *See also* wheel

fountain: made from urn, 123; in Siena, 111

France, ix, x, xi, 337; personified, 185

Francis of Assisi, Saint, 406n41

Frederick II (emperor), 421n33

Frederick III, 419n67

friends, choice of, 381

friendship, 7–9

Frolic (personified), 77

funeral rites, 125

Furies, 161, 438n12

Gaeta, 441n16

Gaetulians, 413n64

Gaia, 432n5

Galen (Claudius Galenus), 357, 440n7

Galeotto, Manfredi, 389

Gallia Narbonensis, 422n47

Gallucci, Luigi (Elisio Calenzio), 43, 407n59

Ganges, 215, 269

Garin, Eugenio, xv

Garland of Meleager, 404n21

Gauls, 325

Gaza, Theodore, 7, 403n9

Gebze (Turkey), 416n41

Gemma, 41, 109

Genesis, book of, xii–xiii

Genius (personified), 147, 339, 438n19

George, Saint, 347

Germanicus, C. Julius Caesar, 404n16; epitaph of, 11–13

Germans, 385

Germany, 89
Geronteion, Mount, 295, 435n23
Getae, vii, 80, 431n60, 441n22
Ghent, 409n6, 419n67
giants, 289–91, 425n26, 435n15, 436n33, 442n33
gift giving, 33–35
gifts of flowers, 17, 53, 404n21
Giovanna I (queen of Naples), 444n54
Giovanna II (queen of Naples), 444n54
Giovanni dalle Bande Nere, 423n50
Giraldi, Lilio, 414n16
gladiator, 416n32
Glycera, 119, 189
Golgi, 77, 83, 411n38
Golino, Pietro (Compatre), viii, 43, 407n57
Gonzaga, Elizabeth (duchess of Urbino), 343, 439n11
Goths, 385, 442–43nn40–41
gout, 179
Graces, 31, 57, 77, 187, 191, 207, 249, 425n35
Gradivus, 239, 243. See also Mars
Granicus, 433n19
Great Mother. See Cybele
Greece, x, 65, 85, 143, 183, 329
Greek Anthology, 404n21, 407n51, 409n1, 409n8, 413n60, 414n5, 418n61, 440n17
Greeks, vii, xi, 5–7, 121, 123, 133, 143, 271–73, 281, 407n50

Guidobaldo da Montefeltro, 439n11
Guido da Polenta, 389, 444n52
Gyges, 289
Gylippus, 391, 444n59

Hades, 425n27
Hadrian (emperor), 442n26
Haemus, Mount, 77, 241, 430n41
Haletes, 109
Hannibal, 391, 416n41, 433n16; epitaph of, 127–29
Hebe, 425n36
Hecate, 434n34
Hector, 59, 141
Helen, 81, 412nn44–45
Helicon, Mount, 403n1, 411n34, 411n36, 419n5, 423n5, 426n39, 434n3
Hera, xvii. See also Juno
Heraclitus, 347, 440n15
Herculean Sea, 269
Hercules, 410n12, 442n28; labors of, 157, 419n68
Hermes Trismegistus, xiii, 431n63
Herodotus, 439n14, 443n44
Herulians, 385, 442n40
Hesiod, xii; Theogony, 424n10, 425n32, 428n19, 428n22, 432n6; Works and Days, 442n27
Hippocrates, 357, 440n6
Hippocrene, spring of, 434n3
Hippolytus, 41
Hirus, 440n14
Homer, xii, 7, 107, 139, 203, 403n6, 414n4, 414n7, 414n14,

418n54, 441n19; *Iliad*, 416n40, 430n44, 431n57; *Odyssey*, 423nn7–8, 428n19, 434n32, 436n32, 440n14, 441n10
Homeric Hymns, xii, xviii, 425n24; *Hymn to Hermes*, 418n54; *Hymn to Pan*, 428n7; *Hymn to Zeus*, 429n27
homosexuality, 111, 415n23
honey, Hymettian, 203, 425n22
Honor (personified), 147, 373
Hope (personified), 89, 137
Horace, 13, 410n20, 411n29; *Epistles*, 429n29; *Odes*, xiv, xv, 410n17, 431nn61–62
Hours (personified), 213, 426n37
Huns, 105, 385, 443n42
hunt, 389
Hunyadi. *See* Corvinus, Matthas
hyacinth, 141
Hydaspes, 433n19
Hydra of Lerna, 442n28
Hydrochous, 341
Hylas, 59, 345–47, 410n12
Hyllus, 229, 273, 275–79
Hymen, 87
Hymettus, Mount, 425n22
Hyperion, xvii, 257, 285, 408n75, 417n44, 432nn5–6
Hypermnestra, 420n12

Iachus, 165. *See also* Bacchus
Iarbas, 404n15
Iberians, 77
Idalium, 77, 411n38
ilex tree, 227

Illyricum, 89
imitation, literary, 409n8, 413n61
Inachus, 85, 201, 412n49, 424n21
India, 117
infant: breastfeeding of, 353–55; Sun and, 267; weaning of, 355–57
Innocent VIII (pope), 127, 402, 416n39, 422n43; epitaph of, 177
Io, 431n66
Ionian Sea, 373
Ios, 107, 414n14
Iphicrates, 43, 408n68
Iphis, 412n46
Isabel of Aragon, 407n58
Isidore, *Origins*, 432n4
Isthmian games, 375, 442n31
Isthmus of Corinth, 167, 421n32
Ithaca, 107, 414n10
Ithome, Mount, 285, 365, 434n6
Itonus, 201, 424n20
Iuventa, 425n36
Ixion, 155, 237, 420n11, 429n32

Jacques II of Bourbon, 444n54
Janus, 253
Jordanes, 442n40
Julian the Apostate: *Hymn to the Sun*, xiii, xv, xviii; *Oration to the Sun*, 432n6, 432n11
Julius Caesar, 97, 329, 413n60
Julius II (pope; Giuliano della Rovere), 423n51
Juno, xvii–xviii, 75, 295–303, 420n11, 429n32, 431n66, 434n31, 435n22

Jupiter (god), xii, 19, 61, 63, 67, 79, 97, 113, 137, 145, 195–201, 209, 213, 225, 227, 229, 231, 241, 249, 279, 283, 313, 351, 377, 412n42, 413n62, 422n49, 426n48, 428n10, 428n14, 431n57, 431n59, 434n5, 435n13, 436n31, 436n39, 441n17; birth of, xvii, 285–89, 365, 435n11; and giants, 289–91, 425n26, 426n50, 426n54, 442n33; as hurler of thunderbolt (Fulgerator), xvi–xvii, 285–93

Jupiter (planet), xiv, 233–37, 267, 429n27

Kárpathos, island of, 431n55
kings, 193, 327; death of, 349; education of, 351–93; misdeeds of, 293. *See also individual monarchs*
Knossos, 55, 287, 387

Laconia, 305
Ladislas of Naples, 421n33
Lampugnani, Andrea, 125
Landino, Cristoforo, 409n3
Laodamia, 49, 109, 407n54, 408n76
L'Aquila, siege of, 421n37
lark, 331–33
Lascaris, Janos, 153–57, 413n2, 420n10
Latin: language, 251; race, 363
Latona, 29, 219, 430n46, 436n39
Laura, Countess, 415n30; epitaph of, 115
laurel tree, 149, 351, 419n4

lawgiver: Jupiter as, 289; Mercury as, 253
League of Venice, ix
Lentini, Giacomo da, 415n26
Leo, 341
Lernean monster (Hydra), 369
Lethe, 271
Leto, Pomponio, 420n10
Leucothoe, 19
Lex Falcidia, 163, 420n24
Liber, 215, 426n52. *See also* Bacchus
libraries, 413n59, 422n38
Libya, 39, 89, 127, 131, 207
Libyans, 391
lily, 15, 53, 65, 141, 203
Linus, 33, 71
lion, 311; of Cybele, 363; Libyan, 427n3; Nemean, 147; Numidian, 427n3; Parthian, 219
lioness, Libyan, 153, 291
literature, study of, 367–69
Livy, 442n34
lock of Berenice, 341, 415n23, 439n2, 439n8
Lodovico il Moro (duke of Milan), 419n3, 422n45
Lombards, 385, 443n43
Longo, Giovanni Giustiniani, 133–35, 417n51
Lorenzi, Giovanni, ix
Love, 3–5, 27, 31, 33, 45–47, 51, 67, 71, 77, 81, 83, 97, 119, 129–31, 137–39, 187, 205–9
Loyalty (personified), 147
Lucan, *Pharsalia*, 418n65
Lucia Phoebe, epitaph of, 61

Lucido, Lucio (Fosforo), 43, 408n62
Lucina, 275. *See also* Diana
Lucretia, 79, 443n45
Lucretius, xii, xv, xvi, 13, 441n12; Marullus's interest in, viii, ix, xviii; *On the Nature of Things*, xviii, 424n11, 425n34, 430n50, 430n52, 432n8, 432–33n12, 433n17, 437n45
Lucullus, Marcus, Geticus, 367, 441n22
Lusius River, 434n7
Lycaeus, Mount, 219, 309, 428n5, 437n43
Lycaon, 341, 437n5
Lycia, 131, 417n47
Lycurgus, 215, 427n56
Lydia, 418n57
Lyons, ix, xvi

machina mundi, 283, 424n11
Macrobius, *Saturnalia*, xii
Maeonian, the, 7, 403n6. *See also* Homer
Maeotis, Lake, 438n8
Maffei, Raffaello, x
Magna Graecia, 85
Magna Parens, xviii
Maia, 75, 251
Málaga, 115–17
Malatesta, Francesca, 444n52
Malatesta, Gianciotto, 444n52
Malatesta, Paolo, 444n52
Malatesta family, 389, 444nn51–52
Mancinus, 13
Manfredi, Galeotto, 389, 444n53

Mantua, 420n20
manuscripts: Florence, Biblioteca Nazionale Centrale MS Magl. VII 1146, xi; Florence, Biblioteca Riccardiana MS Ricc. 76, xv; Florence, Biblioteca Riccardiana MS Ricc. 79, 432n6; Florence, Biblioteca Riccardiana MS Ricc. 971, xi; Florence, Biblioteca Riccardiana MS Ricc. 974, 445n4
Marathon. *See* battle: of Marathon
marble, Parian, 71, 99
Marchese, Francesco Elia, viii, 43, 407n60
Marius, Gaius, 65, 410n19
marjoram, 287
marriage, 9, 105, 345–47; of Juno and Jupiter, 295–303; proposal of, 77–89
Mars (god), xiv, 29, 75, 91, 137, 237–43, 249, 265, 275, 351, 429n36
Mars (planet), 269
Marsus, Domitius, 49, 408n74
Martelli, Braccio, 147, 173, 419n2
Martelli, Maria, epitaph of, 173
Martial, xi, 406n36, 406n46, 408n74
Martin V (pope), 421n37
Marulli, 85, 131–33
Marullus, János (brother), 15–17
Marullus, Manilius (father), vii, xx n1, 41; epitaph of, 91
Marullus, Michael: as *Constantinopolitanus*, vii; and Cosimo Pazzi, 119; death of, x; as exile, vii; in

Marullus, Michael (continued)
Florence, ix, xi, 403n2; and
French invasion of Italy, ix; to
his companions, 43; influence,
xix; letters, 395–99 (appendix);
in Naples, viii; in Rome, ix;
and Second Revolt of Barons,
ix; service to Caterina Sforza,
x; as stratiota (mercenary sol-
dier), vii
Marullus, Michael, works: Educa-
tion of a Prince, x; Epigrams,
x–xi; Hymns to Nature, x, xi–
xviii, 403n5, 414n16; Hymn to
the Sun, xv; Poems of Lament,
ix, x
Marullus, Philippus (paternal
grandfather), epitaph of, 27
Marullus, Thomas, 27
Mary, Blessed Virgin, 343
Mary of Burgundy, 169, 413n1,
421n35
Marzia, 119
Massic wine, 129, 417n42
Maximilian I (emperor; Caesar),
5, 9, 55–57, 91, 103–5, 111–13,
145–47, 403n3, 404n11, 409n4,
409n7, 419n67, 421nn35–36
May Day, 51
Medea, 143, 387
Medici, Averardolo de' (son of
Lorenzo di Pierfrancesco), 319–
21, 437n5
Medici, Bianca de', 416n33
Medici, Cosimo I (duke of Tus-
cany), 423n50

Medici, Giovanni di Pierfrancesco
de', x, 187–91, 329–33, 397,
423n50, 438n14
Medici, Lorenzo de' (Il Magni-
fico), 407n56, 419n2, 420n10,
438n15; Canzoniere, 404n21
Medici, Lorenzo de' (son of
Lorenzo di Pierfrancesco),
147
Medici, Lorenzo di Pierfrancesco
de' (Il Popolano), ix, x–xi, xvi,
3, 17, 53, 75, 101, 145, 273,
403n2, 405n25, 434n28, 437n5
Medici, Pierfranceso (son of
Lorenzo di Pierfrancesco),
423n1
Medici, Piero di Lorenzo de' (son
of Lorenzo Il Magnifico), 331,
433n26, 437n4, 438n15
Medici family, ix, xvi
Medusa, 47, 201, 424n16, 425n31
melos, 139
Melpomene, 279, 434n1
Memphis, 129
Menander (rhetorician), xii
Menenius Agrippa, 442n34
Mercury, xiv–xv, 27, 75, 249–55,
279, 423n8, 431n59, 436n31; as
psychopompus, 431n61
Messene, 387, 443n47
Messina, 277, 434n33
Mesta River, vii, 323, 438n7
Metellus Delmaticus, Caecilius,
441n24
Metellus, Quintus Caecilius (Cre-
ticus), 441n23

meter, poetic, xi, 135; choliambic, 418n55; galliambic, 426n38; hendecasyllable, 13; Priapean verse, 418n52
Mevius, 73, 411n29
Milan, Church of Saint Stephen, 416n37
military training, 391–93. *See also* warfare
Miltiades, 441n20
Mimallones, 216, 427n61
Mimas, 215
Minerva, 29, 75
Minotaur, 409n1
Minyas, daughters of, 427n58
misery, of human life, 347
Mistra, xix
Mithridates, 441n14
Mnestheus, 43
moderation, 385
Modesti, Jacopo, 420n18
Modesti, Publio Francesco, 420n18
Modestus, 157, 420n18
Molossian hound, 363
moly (herb), 197, 423n8
Monillus, 341–43
Montefeltro, Federico di, 413n59
Montepulciano, 123, 143, 418n64
months, 257
moon, 199, 269, 273–79, 425n23, 436n39; full, 275
Morello Mountain, 175
Morini, 55, 409n5
Muses, 3, 7, 13, 51, 75, 77, 113–15, 119, 135, 149–51, 153, 169, 189, 213, 279, 285, 329, 337, 351, 365, 371, 373, 403n1, 411nn35–36, 419n5, 423nn3–4, 435n20; nine, 49, 107, 161, 191; ten, 15, 105, 414n3. *See also individual Muses*
music and musicians, 385, 418n56
Muslims, 416n31
myrrh, 383
myrtle, 243, 430n48

Naevius, 435n15, 445n2
Naiads, 161
Nais, 163
Nape, 15, 33
Naples, viii, 73, 167–69, 327, 438n13, 442n36, 444n54
Naples, University of, 408n69
narcissus, 17
Nature, 13, 213, 225, 229, 311, 437n45; Mother, 263
nature vs. nurture, 359–65
Nazario, San, viii
Neaera, 3–5, 11, 13–15, 21, 33, 39, 43, 45, 47–49, 53–55, 57–61, 67, 91–93, 95, 99, 103, 121–23, 139, 147–49, 181, 187, 191; absence of, 121; Marullus's proposal of marriage to, 77–89
nectar, 139, 418n55
Neda, 285, 391, 438n8, 444n58
Neith (Egyptian goddess), 424n19
Nemean monsters, 147, 419n68
Nemesis, 123, 137, 157, 177, 333, 393, 420n17, 445n60
Nepos, Cornelius, 408n68; *Thrasybulus*, 405n30

nepotism, papal, 416n39, 422n43
Neptune, xviii, 305, 307, 430n43, 436n37
Nereids, 436n34, 436n38
Nereus, 199, 305, 424n12, 436n34
Nestor, 59, 339, 357, 410n11
Nicholas V (pope), 403n9
Night, 199, 229, 289, 425n29
nightingale, 141, 417n49, 428n7
Nile, 201
Nino, Francesco (of Siena), 63–65, 410n16
Nino, Giovanni, 410n16
Niobe, 47
Normans, 327, 438n13
North Wind, 315, 323, 335, 383, 389
nun, 29–31
nurse, child's, 353–65
nymphs, 129; Corycian, 217, 427n64; of Lusius River, 285–87

oak tree, 159, 291
Oarion, 111, 341, 415n23
Oaxes River, 313, 437n47
Ocean, xviii, 303–9, 341
Oceanus, 299, 428n9
Oedipus, 349
old age, 3, 15, 213, 233, 271, 311, 329, 339; respect for, 381
olive tree, 253
Ollus, 121
Olympia, 293
Olympus, 207, 209, 213, 217, 219, 221, 241, 243, 349, 373
One, the, 225

Orcus, 77
organist, 418n56
orgia, 215, 426n46
Orion, 415n23
Orpheus, 203, 239, 413n63; death of, 97
Orphic Hymns, xvi, xviii, 145, 424n9, 425n29, 426n47, 427n63, 428n11, 428n15, 429n25, 434n5
Orphic religion, xiii
Orsini, Clarice, 433n15
Orsini, Gian Giordano, 423n51
Ossa, Mount, 430n40
Ostrogoths, 442n40
Otranto, ix, 403n10, 406n44, 406n47, 406n49
Ovid, vii, xiii, 436n41; Loves, 409n78; Metamorphoses, 408nn70–71, 409n2, 412n46, 418n57, 419n4, 422n49, 426n37, 426n53, 427n57, 427n59, 430n51, 434n4, 436n31
Oxus (Amu-darya), 437n47

Paean, 241, 430n42
Paestum, 47
Palaeologus, Thomas, 410n22
Pales, 275
Pallas Athena, xiii, 41, 75, 151, 201–5, 209–11, 219, 419n8, 424n9; statue of, 424n21
Pallas Tritonia, 189
Pallene, 442n33
Pan, xiii–xiv, 139, 219–23, 418n57, 420n22, 425n29, 428n5, 435n13
Pandion, 143

Paolo, 179
Paphos, 77, 430n54
Pardo, Giovanni, viii, 43
Paris (son of Priam), 81, 412n44
Parmenides, xii
Parnassus, Mount, 77, 195, 427n64, 432n2, 434n3
Paros, 411n28
Parthia, 427n3
Parthians, 89, 329, 367, 407n53
Pasiphaë, 55, 409n1
Patara, oracle of Apollo in, 419n6
path of learning, 367–69
patriotism, 7, 41, 65–67, 113, 325. See also exile
patronage, ix, xvi, 17, 23, 405n25, 412n53
Paula, 157–59
Pausanias, xvii, 415n28, 418n53, 429n39, 430n39, 434n7, 434n33, 435n21, 435n24, 436n26, 441n17
Pazzi, Cosimo, 119, 416n33
Pazzi, Guglielmo, 416n33
Peace of Lodi (1454), 404n20
pearl, 117
Pegasus, 281, 434n3
Pelasgians, 37, 407n50
Peleus, 436n38
Pelides. See Achilles
Pelion, Mount, 430n40
Pella, 357
Peloponnesian War, 444n59
Peloponnesus (Peloponnese), xix, 410n21, 411n39, 412n47, 414n8, 414n11, 430n49, 434n6, 436n36, 443n47

Penelope, 79
Pentheus, 215, 427n55
Pericles, 357, 441n9
Permessus River, 77, 434n3
Persephone, 61
Persia, 363
Persius, Prologue, 418n55
Perugia, 171; church of San Francesco al Prato, 421–22n37
Petrucci, Antonello, viii–ix, 23, 73, 405n31, 411n31
Phaeacia, 421n30
Phaeacians, 165
Phaethon, 377, 442n32
Phanes, 205, 425n29
Pharos, 95, 107, 414n15
Pheneus, 295, 435n24
Philemon, and Baucis, 436n31
Philip IV (duke of Burgundy), 169, 421n34, 421n36
Philippe de Commynes, Mémoires, 437n2
Philippi. See battle: of Philippi
Philomela, 417n49
Phineus, 47
Phlegethon, 49, 408n77
Phlegra, 377
Phlegyas, 291, 435n17
Phocis, 195, 423n5
Phoebe, 307–9, 436n39
Phoebus Apollo, 191, 307. See also Apollo
Phoenicians, 259
Pholoe, epitaph of, 29–31
Phorcis, 424n16
Phorcus, 205, 425n31
Phrygian guest. See Paris

Phrygians, 9, 436n31
Phryne, 49, 408n75
Phthia, 403n8
Phyllis, 71
Pico della Mirandola, Antonio, 420n21
Pico della Mirandola, Giovanni, 107–9, 414n16, 414n18; epitaph of, 181–83; letter to, 395–97
Pierides, cave of, 81, 195
Pietra, 71
Pimpla, Mount, 423n4
Pimpleus (muse), 195, 423n4
Pindar, 429n39; Olympian Odes, 435n19
Pindus, 77
Piombino, 406n45
Pisan Olympiads, 253, 431n65
planets, 233–37, 425n23; in Egyptian order, xiv
Plato: Laws, xv; Phaedo, 423n6; Phaedrus, xiii, 428n10; Republic, xv, 433n13; Symposium, 425n30, 425n33; Timaeus, xiv, xv, xvi, 425n28, 428n12
Pleasure (personified), 249
Pleiades, 199, 424n14
Pleione, 424n14
Pletho, Gemistus, xv, xix
Pliny, Natural History, 418n65, 437n44
Plotinus, Enneads, 425n30
Plutarch: Life of Alexander, 441n19; Life of Themistocles, 441nn20–21; On Moral Virtue, 406n47; On the Delays of Divine Vengeance,

429–30n39; On the Obsolescence of Oracles, 432n3, 440n4; Sayings of Spartan Women, 407n52, 419n9
Pluto, 19, 405n26, 412n41
poets, 229–31, 341, 343; Alessandra Scala as, 413n2; bad, 73, 411n29; Latin, 13; obscene, 369
Poliziano, Angelo Ambrogini (called Ecnomus), xi, xx n5, 403n9, 405n27, 408n62, 409n3, 409n8, 413n2, 414n16, 415n22, 417n52, 418n64, 437n1; Miscellanea, 415n23, 418n52, 418n55. See also Ecnomus
Polyhymnia, 434n2
Pomerance, church of San Giovanni Battista, x
Pompey, 89, 95, 413n58
Pontano, Giovanni, 23, 43, 405n32, 408n66, 409n3; Tumuli, 406n39; Urania, viii, xiv, 429n27. See also Accademia Pontaniana
Pontus, 265, 433n16
Poor Clares, order of, 406n41
Po River, 185, 329, 444n56. See also Eridanus
Porphyrion, 289
portents, 291–93
Porus, 269, 433n21
Poseidon, 409n1
Postumus, 27, 59, 127, 135, 347
Prato, 420n18
Priam, 141, 418n60

pride, 123; and the powerful, 25

priests, avarice of, 343

primitive man, 83–85

prince, education of, 351–93

Probus (emperor), 442n25

Proclus, xii; commentary on Plato's *Republic*, 420n10; hymns, xviii; hymn to the sun, xv; *Platonic Theology*, xiii, 428n16

Procne, 131, 417n49, 418n62

Prometheus, 55, 377–79, 420n13

prostitute, 29–31, 406n42

Protesilaus, 41, 109

Proteus, 55, 61, 277, 307, 409n2, 434n32, 436n40. *See also* Carpathus

Protogonos, 231, 425n29, 429n25

Prusias, 433n16

Psylli, 143, 418n65

Ptolemy III Euergetes, 439n2

Ptolemy XII, 413n58

Pygmalion, 404n14

Pylos, 107, 414n8

Pyrrha, 185

Pythian father. *See* Sun

Python, 417n48

Quartus. *See* Appiano, Jacopo IV; Sixtus IV

Quinterus, 157

Quintilian (friend of the poet), 49–51

Ragusa (Dubrovnik), vii, 421nn28–29, 421nn32–33; praises of, 165–69

Reason (personified), 377

Remus, 109

repast, Chaonian, 233

Revolt of the Barons. *See* Barons, Revolt of

Rhallus, Manilius, 13, 43, 51–53, 141, 404n18, 418n52

Rhea Silvia, 231, 285, 295, 412n48, 429n24

Rhodes, 107, 139

Rhodope, Mount, 217, 241, 427n62

Rhoetus, 215, 243, 305

Rimaggio, 175

Rimini, 444n51

Riphaean Mountains, 15, 81, 405n24

Risorboli, Cristoforo, 147, 419n3

rock: Scythian, 51; of Sisyphus, 237, 429n33; wordplay on, 71

Roderic (king of the Visigoths), 443–44n50

Romagna, 444n51

Rome, ix, 85, 105, 119, 315, 329, 437n4; Capitoline Hill, 293, 435n18; conquest of, 387; temple of Jupiter Capitolinus, 435n18

Romulus and Remus, 441n15

Ronsard, Pierre, xix; *Hymne à l'Éternité*, xiii

rose, 53, 115, 125, 137, 141, 203

rose garden, 189, 249

Rovere. *See* della Rovere, Felicia

rudis (wooden sword), 416n32

Russia, 337

Sabines, 412n43; women, 79; youth, 85

saffron, Cilician, 31

Sais, 424n19

Salacia (nymph), 436n37

Saladin, 95, 413n57

Salamis, 107, 410n17, 414n12

Sallust, 397; *Jugurthine War*, 445n3

Sannazaro, Iacopo (Actius Sincerus), viii, xx n5, 19, 33, 43, 71, 73, 405n27, 408n65, 408n69, 411n27, 416n36

Sanseverino, Antonello, viii–ix, xii, 7, 11, 21, 33, 59, 187, 191, 193, 403n5, 410n13, 423n53, 437n2

Sanseverino, Roberto, epitaph of, 59, 410n13, 433n23

Sappho, x, 15, 149; as tenth Muse, 105, 414n3

satire, writers of, 371

Saturn (god), xiv, xvii, 229–33, 261, 293, 313, 429n30

Saturn (planet), 269

Saturnalia, 229, 429n23

Satyr, epithet of Bacchus, 215

Savonarola, Girolamo, 408n64

Scala, Alessandra (wife), x, 105, 115, 135–37, 149–51, 163, 169, 413n2, 414n18

Scala, Bartolomeo, x, 113–15, 413n2

Scales, Francesco, 7–9, 403n10

Scaliger, Julius Caesar, xix

Scheldt, 55, 409n6

Scylla, 387

Scythia, vii, 15, 81, 133, 293

Scythian language, 251, 431n60

Scythians, 335

Sele River, 189

Semele, 213, 426nn48–49

Senius, 415n20

Septimilla, 189

Septimius Severus (emperor), 442n26

Sergius, Saint, 421n31

Servius Honoratus, Maurus, 411n29

Sextus Tarquinius, 443n45

Sforza, Caterina (countess of Forlì), x, 419n3, 423n50, 438n14, 438n17

Sforza, Francesco, 404n20, 407n56; epitaph of, 15

Sforza, Giangaleazzo, 407n58, 416n37

Sforza, Lodovico, 333, 422n48, 438n16

she-ass, epitaph of, 13

she-wolf, and suckling children, 415n20

ship: bilge, 387; Cyprian, 227; safe in port, 103; storm-tossed, 211

shipwreck, ix, 343–45

Sicily, 417n43

Sidonian maid. *See* Europa

Siena, 63–65, 415n20; Fonte Branda, 111, 415n21; Marullus's praise of, 109–11

Silber, Eucharius, ix, x

Sincerus, Actius. *See* Sannazaro, Iacopo

Sipylus, 47

Sirens, 221, 428n8

Sirius, 235, 429n28

sirocco, 235

Sisyphus, 237, 420n14; rock of, 429n33

Sithonians, 435n14

Sixtus IV (pope; Francesco della Rovere), 21, 127, 405n29, 408n62, 416n39; as Quartus, 159, 420n19

Slavs, 363

Sleep (personified), 171–73

Smyrna, 107, 414n6

Soavus, 25, 405n34

Socrates, 181

sol, etymology of, 432n4

sonnet, 415n26

souls, of the dead, 255

South wind, 97, 175, 261

southwest wind, 47

Spaco, 363, 441n14

Spain, 185, 335, 387, 438n16, 443–44n50

Spanish, 327

Spartan: baths, 359; wedding, 387; women, 39, 57, 407n52

Spartans, 153, 365, 443n47

Squarcialupo, Antonio, 139, 418n56

Srdj, Mount, 165

Stamperia del Drago, xi

Statius, Thebaid, 427n61

statue, 297; of Athena, 424n21; of Brutus, 121; Colossus of Rhodes, 107

statues, in Siena, 111

Stephen III (king of Moldavia), 431n60

Sterope, 241, 430n43

Straits of Messina, 167–69

Strymon, 239, 429n37

Studio, Florentine, 413n2, 414n4

Stymphalus River, 297, 435–36nn25–26

Styx, 129, 237, 311, 429n31

Suetonius, Life of Caligula, 442n37

suicide: of Dido, 9–11; of Hannibal, 416n41

summer solstice, 432–33n12

Sun (Pythian father), xv–xvi, 193, 199, 209, 255–73, 287, 297, 425n23; as father, 263; immateriality of, xv; and infant, 267; and mankind, 263–71; as solus, 432n4

Swabians, 327, 438n13

swallow, 143, 417n49

Sychaeus, 404n14

syncretism, xviii

Syracuse, 167, 424n17

Syria, 183

Tacitus, Annals, 404n16

Taenarus, 436n36

Tantalus, 420n15

Tarchaniotes, Euphrosyne (mother), vii; epitaph of, 41

Tarchaniotes, Michael (maternal grandfather), 67, 410n21; epitaph of, 19–21

Tarchaniotes, Paul (uncle), 5–7, 403n4; epitaph of, 181

Tarquinius Priscus, 443n45

Tarquinius Superbus, 443n45

Tarquins, 387

Tartarus, 205

Taygetus, Mount, 309, 437n42

Teleboae, 424n18
Telesilla, epitaph of, 153
Telon, 424n18
Telonic cliffs, 201
Temenos, 295, 435n21
Terence, 13
Tereus, 417n49
terza rima, 415n26
Tethys, 221, 299, 428n9
Teucer, 63–65, 410n17
Teutons, 325
Thalia, 43, 425n35
Thebes, 431n62
Theia, 257, 432n6
Theisoa, 285, 434n9
Themis, 217, 427n64
Themistocles, 367, 441nn20–21
Thespia, 411n34
Thespiades, 411n34, 426n39
Thespis, 426n39
Thessalonica, 403n9
Thetis, 307, 436n38
Third Mithridatic War, 441n22
Thrace, vii, 83
Thracians, 325, 391
Thrasybulus, 23, 407n51
Thunderer, the. See Jupiter (god)
Thymbra, 440n3
Thyone, 215
thyrsus, 215, 426n45
Tiber, 315
Tibullus, 13
tiger, 297
Tiresias, 425n25
Tisiphone, 325
Titans, 239, 419n7, 432n5
Tmolus, 139, 418n57

Trajan (emperor), 442n26
travel, 273–79
Treaty of Arras (1482), 57, 409n7
Treaty of Bagnolo (1484), 21,
    405n29
tree: ash, 227, 239; box, 359,
    441n11; fruiting, 371; grafted,
    361; ilex, 227; laurel, 149, 351,
    419n4; oak, 159, 291; olive, 253;
    transplanted, 353
tripods, 251, 431n58
tripudium, 215, 426n44
Triton, 305, 436n37
Tritonis, Lake, 305, 423n54
Trojan War, 407n50, 410n11
Trojan women, 141
Truth (personified), 147
Turks, 135, 167, 183–85, 239,
    405n28, 410n21
Tuscan War (1478–80), 406n45
Tuscany, 239, 329
Tynichus, 39, 407n51
Tyrrhenian Sea, 383

Ulysses, 79, 421n30, 423n8,
    433n14
Urania, 428n18
Uranus, 235, 429n30, 432n5
Urium, 412n40
Ursa Major, 437n5

Varchi, Benedetto, xx n5
Varro, On the Latin Language,
    432n4
Velleius Paterculus, 410n19
Venetians, 167, 391, 421n33
Venice, 335, 438n16

Venus, xiii, xiv, 5, 27, 29, 41, 43, 55, 71, 75, 77, 91, 93, 119, 129, 175, 191, 243–49, 269, 299, 343, 387, 411nn37–38, 413n56, 422n42, 423n52, 430nn48–49, 430n54, 431n57; and Vulcan, 31. *See also* Cupid

Vergil, 13, 73; *Aeneid,* 410n15, 410n18, 432n1, 435n17; *Eclogues,* xii, 411n29, 421n26, 423n2, 428n6, 437n47; *Georgics,* 424n13, 434n32

Verginia, 443n46

Verginius, Lucius, 443n46

Vespucci, Marco, 405n35

Vespucci, Simonetta, 405n35; epitaph of, 25

Vesta/Hestia, 221, 428n10

Vettius, 123, 416n35

violets, 15, 17, 65, 125, 129, 287

Virgo, 341, 439n4

Virtue (personified), 113, 211; Roman, 125

Voconti, 406n37. *See also* Bocontia, Marzia

Vulcan, 31, 91, 93, 413n56, 430n43

warfare, 7, 35–39, 103–5, 133, 145–47, 183–85, 227, 237–43, 267–69, 313, 315–21, 333–37, 347, 371, 391–93

War of Ferrara, 405n29

West wind, 431n56

wet nurse, 353–65

wheel: of fortune, 63, 317; of Ixion, 237, 429n32; nine-circled, 209

winds, 245, 301–3, 323–25, 429n29; Atabolus, 429n29; East, 265, 271, 433n14; Favonius, 141, 247, 259; North, 315, 323, 335, 383, 389; sirocco, 235; South, 261; West, 431n56

wine, 229; Chian, 217; Falernian, 65, 115; Massic, 129, 417n42. *See also* Bacchus

winter solstice, 432–33n12

Wisdom (personified), 7

wolf, 297

woman: kidnapped, 387–89; married, 79; pregnant, 353; Spartan, 39, 57, 407n52

women: in domestic sphere, 151; Edonian, 215; given honor and respect, 93; as poets, 153 (*see also* Sappho); Sabine, 79

wooden sword (*rudis*), 119, 416n32

woodsman, 277

world machine, 283, 424n11

writing tablet, 125–27

Year (personified), 213, 257

Youth (personified), 211, 249

Zancle, 277. *See also* Messina

Zethus, 431n62

Zeus, 151, 431n62. *See also* Jupiter (god)

Zoroaster, xiii

Publication of this volume has been made possible by

The Myron and Sheila Gilmore Publication Fund at I Tatti
The Robert Lehman Endowment Fund
The Jean-François Malle Scholarly Programs and Publications Fund
The Andrew W. Mellon Scholarly Publications Fund
The Craig and Barbara Smyth Fund
for Scholarly Programs and Publications
The Lila Wallace–Reader's Digest Endowment Fund
The Malcolm Wiener Fund for Scholarly Programs and Publications